FROM HELL is the hugely successful graphic novel by Alan Moore and Eddie Campbell. It was completed in 1998 and first published in a single volume in 1999. It is currently published by Top Shelf Productions in the USA, Knockabout in the UK, and has editions in many languages. It has won numerous comics industry awards, and in 2001 it was adapted into a major motion picture starring Johnny Depp and Heather Graham, with Robbie Coltrane.

By the Same Authors:
A Disease of Language
published by Knockabout Comics.

By Eddie Campbell
Alec : The Years Have Pants
published by Top Shelf Productions.

THE FROM HELL COMPANION

Eddie Campbell presents Alan Moore's scripts, sketches, notes and other miscellanies as well as contributions, artistic, anecdotal and scholarly, of his own.

With a foreword by Charles Hatfield and Craig Fischer.

I was unnerved and amazed by the amount of confirming "evidence" that turned up to support my "theory," precisely because I knew it wasn't a theory: it was fiction. I really didn't want to put a toe into the inviting pool of "the truth," because Truth is a well-documented pathological liar. Self-proclaimed fiction, on the other hand, is entirely honest—it says "I'm a Liar" right there on the dust jacket. If I read a biography of Tony Blair, at the end of it I still wouldn't know where I stood with him. I do, however, know where I stand with Hannibal Lecter and the Wizard of Oz.

—Alan Moore (interview, in *What DVD*, Oct 2002)

The From Hell Companion ©2013 Alan Moore and Eddie Campbell. Published jointly by Top Shelf Productions, PO Box 1282, Marietta, GA 30061-1282 USA and Knockabout Comics, 42c Lancaster Road, London, W11 1QR, United Kingdom. Top Shelf Productions® and the Top Shelf logo are registered trademarks of Top Shelf Productions, Inc. All Rights Reserved. No part of this publication may be reproduced without permission, except for small excerpts for purposes of review. Visit our online catalogs at www.topshelfcomix.com & www.knockabout.com. First Printing, May 2013. Printed in Canada.

Foreword

From Hell, a project of dizzying complexity and unflinching nerve, brought together two respected yet stubbornly idiosyncratic talents, Alan Moore and Eddie Campbell, and sent them on a ten-year journey of creation, through a mazy process spanning three countries and thousands of miles. It came to epitomize the collaborative Graphic Novel in all its too-rarely-achieved potential. Certainly **From Hell** has a spot on any serious list of the best graphic novels of the past twenty-five years, and indeed stands as a prototype of what the graphic novel can be. It's the proverbial landmark book, and dense in a way that few other comics have achieved.

It's easy enough to say that **From Hell** depicts the infamous Whitechapel slayings of 1888 — the so-called Jack the Ripper murders — as a conspiracy theorist's dream. It's easy to say that the conspiracy in question involves Freemasonry, esoterism, and a purposeful, sinister, occult vision of history. But the novel goes further, implicating the violent misogyny of all of Victorian society, from Queen Victoria on down — and the misogyny of our own time. Moore and Campbell do propose a more humane and feminist view, but only after dragging us, without blinking, through unimaginable horrors.

Beyond these brief gestures toward explanation, **From Hell** is an achievement that defies summary, a book that warrants documentation and commentary. That is precisely what Eddie Campbell offers here, and abundantly: the archive of **From Hell** made public, along with his own ringside commentary as the artist who visualized the novel's grand design.

Besides **From Hell**'s notoriety, the most obvious reason for a companion volume is the novel's daunting complexity. In **From Hell**'s chapter nine, shortly before William Gull's final ritualistic murder, Mary Kelly describes the pervasive sense of predestination she felt immediately before the death of her first husband: *"It was like things had a pattern I couldn't quite see. It's like there was a kind of lace tyin' things together. A kind of lace over everything."* Our job as readers is to search for the hidden strands of lace — the symbols, the motifs, the repetitions — that knot the narrative together, and this companion is an indispensable guide to **From Hell**'s strands of meaning.

Moore and Campbell sew many of these strands into early chapters of the book, so that they can reappear and take on new meanings in new contexts, across the length of **From Hell.** Consider, for instance, the passages in the book that reference supernatural vision. On the second page of the prologue, Robert Lees confesses that he only pretended to have mystical visions ("The attention, that was the thing..."), but his visions "all came true anyway." **From Hell** is full of prophetic visions experienced, hallucinated, and/or faked by many other characters besides Lees, and the truth or falsehood of each is difficult to determine. Gull interprets his first vision, of the hybrid god Jahbulon, as a harbinger of his great service to Queen Victoria, but Jahbulon could also be a mirage produced by the stroke Gull suffers while walking up a steep hill. In chapter eight, after he triumphantly slaughters a prostitute he believes to be the last of the blackmailers he has been ordered to silence, Gull sees a phallic skyscraper — a grandchild of the obelisks

that, in his view, bind London in a circuit of patriarchal power — and momentarily vanishes. Coachman Netley loses track of Gull "for a minute," and panics. Despite all this magical fanfare, however, Gull has actually killed the wrong woman, and so his "grand work" remains incomplete. Are the skyscraper and Gull's disappearance symptoms of a madness shared between Gull and Netley, or are these supernatural signs somehow true? Did Gull make it up? Did it come true anyway?

Chapter fourteen of **From Hell**, the final chapter before the book's epilogue, is one long cascade of weird visions that Gull experiences as his body dies in a Dickensian asylum for the mentally ill (fittingly, Gull has ended up in the same situation he consigned Annie Crook to in chapter two). Gull's visions include blood raining from the sky, ghosts with scales for skin, and assorted vignettes featuring notorious English murderers of the twentieth century, but in his footnotes Moore cites real-life eyewitness accounts of these Fortean events. Gull's ectoplasmic journey concludes with a trip to the clouds, where he meets such mythic beings as Thoth, Apollo and Jesus, who guide Gull's attention to a hill (another hill, a twin to Jahbulon's hill) and a scene that presents the strongest strand of hope in all of **From Hell**. If we write off Gull's visions as the hallucinations of a dying madman, we lose the redemption too.

The visions and prophecies that spin throughout **From Hell** are only a small part of Moore and Campbell's web. In chapter two, the sixteen-year-old Gull cuts open a wild mouse; much later, at a key moment in chapter sixteen, three young girls offer an alternative to Gull's "we murder to dissect" scientism as they speak of catching a frog and then letting it go. Also in chapter two, Campbell draws the arc of Gull's life in panels that never show the man's face; later, numerous scenes hide from us the face of another significant character, "Emma," the logistics of which Campbell discusses here on pages 132-133. **The From Hell Companion** untangles and explicates many subtleties like this: it's an insightful guide to the narrative structures, explicit and hidden, that Moore and Campbell wove into the graphic novel. Campbell calls these connections and repetitions "echoes" (see pages 148-149 here), and, happily, Moore and Campbell have now shared their echoes with the world.

Beyond its value as a formal primer, **The From Hell Companion** also tells a personal story. It chronicles a deep friendship and artistic collaboration between two rather

unalike yet sympathetic minds. Moore, then fresh from his triumphs in the world of mainstream superhero comics, and Campbell, a veteran of Britain's inspiring small-press comics movement, brought their disparate talents and energies (Moore's architectonic sense of narrative structure, Campbell's grasp of visual culture and history) together for what turned out to be a life-changing project for both. This companion is an honest, lived-in, wryly personal, prodigiously entertaining account of that collaboration, which covered so many years and demanded so much effort. A work of autobiography as well as archaeology, **_The From Hell Companion_** roots the graphic novel in the lives of its creators as well as in all-important larger contexts, and the result is a visionary guide to a visionary book: an essential entry in the shelf of must-read books on the history of comics.

Craig Fischer and Charles Hatfield are associate professors of English at Appalachian State University and California State, Northridge, respectively. Both have published widely on comics and are currently collaborating on a book-length study of Eddie Campbell's work.

Introduction

I was having a problem drawing the alligator.

In a moment early in the script for *FROM HELL*, that enormous graphic novel set in the grimy, sooty and grimly realistic East End of Victorian London and celebrated for its realism, Alan Moore, writer extraordinaire, was asking me, Eddie Campbell, illustrator of said work, to draw an alligator waddling in the gutter.

We didn't often have problems that I had to phone Alan about, but this was giving me a sleepless night. I just didn't feel that I could keep up the level of authenticity we had already established in the opening chapters with this American swamp lizard waddling around in the foreground. I'm not saying such a thing was an impossibility. I just didn't feel that I could put it in there convincingly, with authority. It was me that was at fault, no doubt about it, but if he valued that authenticity, would he be okay with me fudging around that detail? Yes, okay, he said, as long as I got the rest in.

So here is the rest. These are the panels as they appeared in the printed book (Chapter 3, Page 5), followed by Alan's script for the scene. Marie Kelly is making her way across town towards Whitechapel.

MARIE NOW CONTINUES DOWN COMMERCIAL STREET TOWARDS SPITALFIELDS MARKET, DOWN AT THE END OF BRUSHFIELD STREET NEAREST TO CHRIST CHURCH. THE CHURCH ITSELF PROBABLY ISN'T VISIBLE HERE. IN THE FOREGROUND WE SEE THE BIZARRE, DIRTY, SPRAWLING POCKET-WORLD THAT IS THE MARKETPLACE. EVERYTHING CONCEIVABLE IS FOR SALE OR DISPLAY; IN THE FOREGROUND, A MAN LEADS A SKINNY ALBINO MALE THROUGH THE STREET, A ROPE ABOUT THE POOR CREATURE'S NECK. THE ALBINO'S HAIR IS LONG AND STRAGGLY, HIS PALE BROWS TURNED UPWARDS IN ABJECT MISERY, AS HE'S LED THROUGH THE FILTHY AND CLAMOROUS STREETS. SOMEWHERE NEARBY, A BOY HOLDS UP A FISTFUL OF YELLOWING HADDOCK, CALLING OUT TO THE PASSING CROWDS. ELSEWHERE A FAT WOMAN WITH A STRAWBERRY MARK PARADES HER

9

TRAY OF WHELKS. FROM THE BACKGROUND, MARIE WALKS NONCHALANTLY TOWARDS THIS PRESS OF BODIES AND VITALITY, THINKING MORE ABOUT THE COLD SPERM TRICKLING DOWN HER LEGS THAN THE VARIOUS WARES UPON DISPLAY.

I confess that, unbeknownst to Alan, and swiftly needing a subject for a public reading, I once narrated this actual text, with the pictures projected as above. At this stage, I paused, looked at the audience, who had been transported into this expansive vision of a surreal street market that goes on forever, and then I said, 'Panel 2.'

NOW MARIE PUSHES THROUGH THE MARKET CROWD, APPROACHING US DOWN BRUSHFIELD STREET. BEHIND HER, DOMINATING THE WHOLE SCENE LIKE A GIANT STANDING OVER WHITECHAPEL, WE SEE THE GHASTLY, SEPULCHRAL MASS OF CHRIST CHURCH; A GOTHIC MONSTROSITY THAT PSYCHOLOGICALLY OVERSHADOWS ITS ENVIRONMENT. AROUND MARIE THE STREET VENDORS ARE MILLING AS SHE WALKS TOWARDS US, IGNORING THE BUSTLE AROUND HER AND FOOLISHLY TURNING HER BACK UPON NICHOLAS HAWKSMOOR'S AWFUL, WATCHFUL CREATION, LOOMING THERE BEHIND HER.

And then to the third panel in this sequence, its dimensions of less than three inches by two inches hopelessly inadequate to the task requested of it:

HAVING TURNED LEFT AT THE BOTTOM OF BRUSHFIELD STREET, MARIE IS NOW WALKING ALONG CRISPIN STREET TOWARDS THE BRITANNICA PUBLIC HOUSE AT THE CORNER OF CRISPIN STREET AND DORSET STREET. WE CAN JUST SEE A LITTLE OF THE PUB OVER TO THE RIGHT OF THE BACKGROUND HERE AS WE LOOK ACROSS THE STREET AT MARIE FROM THE MOUTH OF AN ALLEYWAY. IN THE ALLEY ARE A BOY OF NINE AND A GIRL OF TEN. THE BOY KNEELS AMONGST THE FILTH AND RUBBISH AND ROTTING FRUIT, HIS TROUSERS AROUND HIS KNEES. THE GIRL, POSSIBLY HIS SISTER, SITS AGAINST THE OPPOSITE WALL OF THE ALLEY WITH HER LEGS SPLAYED. ONE OF HER HANDS IS ROOTING BETWEEN HER OWN LEGS WHILE THE OTHER REACHES OUT AND TAKES HOLD, INEXPERTLY, OF THE BOY'S ERECTION. BOTH CHILDREN ARE GRINNING ENTHUSIASTICALLY, AND BOTH ARE VERY DIRTY. NEITHER OF THEM HAVE ANY PUBIC HAIR YET, AND THEIR ACTIVITIES HAVE A SORT OF SQUALID AND YET PURE INNOCENCE ABOUT THEM THAT CAN PERHAPS BE FOUND AMONGST THOSE THAT ARE BORN DAMNED. ACROSS THE STREET WALKING FROM LEFT TO RIGHT FROM THE CORNER OF BRUSHFIELD STREET TOWARDS THE BRITANNIA, MARIE GLANCES ACROSS THE STREET, TOWARDS THE CHILDREN IN THE FOREGROUND, HER EXPRESSION ONE OF BLAND DISINTEREST. THE CHILDREN TAKE NO NOTICE OF MARIE WHATSOEVER.

I never discussed the illustration of any of this with Alan. It was demanding all my mental strength just to hang on in there, like a passenger in a loop-the-looping two-seater biplane with no safety belt. But I was certain he harboured resentment toward me for just leaving out all that rich detail. My whole way of thinking about pictures and about old London couldn't accommodate it. Anyway, two years later, in Chapter 6, he managed to get it all back in there, putting it in the dialogue where I couldn't play fast and loose with any of it: (*The following 6 panels are not all consecutive, with a break after 4*)

Alan Moore's big scripts were already famous late in 1988 when I got the call. *Watchmen* had been a continuous celebration for two years by that time. But Alan had fallen out with the publisher, DC Comics, and was determined to reinvent his career in a way that did not involve corporate manipulations. His first moves consisted of, on the one hand, self-publishing *Big Numbers* with Bill Sienkiewicz as illustrator, and on the other he lined up a second book to be serialized in *Taboo*, the new horror anthology published by fellow discontent Steve Bissette. This was to be a complex retelling of the story of the Whitechapel murders of 1888. Alan and Steve set their minds to choosing an artist for the job. Like Alan, I had already appeared in the first issue of *Taboo* (Nov 1988) with a short story, *The Pyjama Girl*. I had also worked with Alan once before when I illustrated *Globetrotting for Agoraphobics* (in *Knockabout, 1985*). But my work was otherwise about the contemporary and the quotidian. Horror was not my thing and I must have seemed an odd choice to illustrate the doings of the most infamous serial killer in history, Jack the Ripper. The rationale, as Steve explained, was that ***"It was essential that the artist not be seduced by the violence inherent in the tale..."***

And so it was off and running. *FROM HELL* appeared in *Taboo* for six issues of that publication, and then was assembled and completed in ten volumes of its own title between 1991 and August 1996, published by Tundra and then Kitchen Sink Press. An eleventh volume, *The Dance of the Gull Catchers,* being an appendix, was added two years later in September 1998. The complete work was first published all in one book, under my own Eddie Campbell Comics imprint (all of our previous publishers having by then gone out of business), in the last month of the old millennium, December 1999. It has been continuously in print since then in about twenty languages, still increasing as I write this. When I say continuously, I'm ignoring a one-year hiatus after the printer of our US edition went bankrupt. Considering the collapses of publishers, distributors and a printer, one has to marvel that the complete book got published at all.

The scripts, on the other hand, were never meant for publication, but those for the prologue and first three chapters appeared in a limited hardcover in 1994, titled *From Hell: The Compleat Scripts Volume 1.* In "an entertaining arabesque of an introduction" Alan wrote that the scripts *"were written in the main without regard for necessities of literary style, intended only for the eyes of my esteemed collaborator... I still have no idea why anyone would find a mass of long-winded and often repetitious stage directions edifying."* Rich Kreiner, in his lengthy and excellent review in *The Comics Journal,* wrote: *"The From Hell scripts present the intent of one talent untroubled by practicalities and wholly unmediated by a second talent. Moore routinely invokes sensations outside the ability of his medium, let alone of any co-conspirator. It's not simply the red scarf, or the brown tweed of the royal henchman, in a black and white comic. It's not just the case of impossibly expansive panoramas, equally impossible manipulations of lighting, or the crushing burden of enriching details. The sensibility that animates this book, this series of instructions, is an incessant and irrepressible evocation of the full range of human faculties. There's an inextinguishable, headlong precision, an unapologetic pan-sensual pungency utilized to establish mood, action, and motivation."* (TCJ 173, Dec. 1994)

I lived with the *FROM HELL* scripts for ten years between December 1988, when I received the pages for the prologue plus Chapter 1, and 1998, when I drew the final panel in the *Gull Catchers*. These scripts are rich with incident and information that didn't always, or couldn't, find its way onto the printed page, and also with the revealing give-and-take between writer and artist that can be of interest to anyone hoping to get into this lunatic way of making a living. Some very fine writing is buried in these scripts, and nobody has ever read it except me. I have selected what I find to be the most memorable pages, ninety out of a possible five hundred and one, and I present them here in narrative order, with commentary and some related illustrations. My hope is that they will create a different story, or at least a variation on the known one, happening at a subterranean level of the narrative field.

Regarding the use of capital letters throughout the panel descriptions, note that the captions and dialogue in comic books were once exclusively lettered in capitals. Therefore, in a script, the text to be lettered would instantly stand out from the descriptions in sentence case, which were not to be lettered and were exclusively directed to the illustrator. When comics such as our present subject started using sentence case on the printed pages, Alan simply reversed the process and typed all his descriptions in capitals. I have no idea whether he is the only writer who has done so. I have followed his custom in the transcriptions. The word counts at the top of each selection are my own addition, a statistic that is likely to be of some interest. I've given the count for each entire page, even when I don't transcribe all of it. One other thing worth mentioning is that in the ten years we worked on the book, Alan rarely wrote a letter or memo to me that wasn't contained in the text of the script, therefore the extensive quotations from him that I've employed as commentary and opinion are otherwise taken from published interviews.

The script pile is six inches deep but incomplete. Two chapters are no longer in my possession, and are not represented. However, that won't hamper the story

I want to tell; there's plenty of other stuff in these pages, including excerpts from Alan's notebooks (e.g. the charming panel at left), in which we see his initial composition of the work in a visual shorthand. I didn't know these "thumbnail sketches" existed until Gary Spencer Millidge featured examples of them in his recent book, *Alan Moore, Storyteller* (2011 Ilex Press). These tiny layouts were Alan's first stage of organising his material before proceeding to the typescript. Gary used about one sixth of the FROM HELL stuff that he scanned, and he kindly sent it all to me on a disc. I have sketches for four of the chapters and the appendix. I also have a typed synopsis of the second half of FROM HELL, a curious document which I'll explain in its place, which has a few remarkable alternative scenes in it. To complete the package I have included two sections of colour images with some photos, covers and new, specially produced paintings. The material will throw up other novelties and surprises as we go along.

Eddie Campbell, Australia, May 2012.
...seen at right in the inked sketch for the painted cover of a Bacchus *comic shown on page 180.*

13

Part 1
I find that my selections
have tended to fall around
themes, and into eight parts.
In the first, which started with
the introduction and runs to
page 57, the theme is
Stages.
Then and later, sketch, plan,
evolution, revision.

er 1923

Bloody
shambles
this last
six
years

a shamb
inflicted f
without-
foreign inte
hardly inval
Capitals prem

Contents

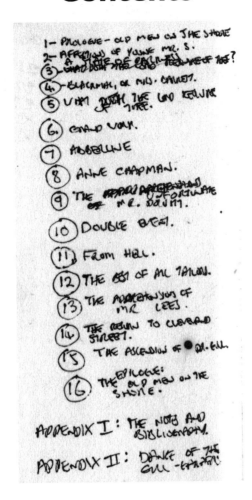

The contents as Alan had them worked out in mid-1992, around the time of Chapter 5, deducing from the neighbouring material in the notebook from which this came. Four chapters (6,7,8,10 above) don't yet have their final titles, but the great debunking that is *The Dance of the Gull Catchers* is already in place. Dramatic accounts of the Ripper story usually manoeuvre the Kelly murder into the climactic moment, as indeed was the case with the movie adaptation of *FROM HELL*. Alan is avoiding that position but later moves even further from the formula. The numbering above is of the 'sixteen installments' as declared on the first page of the prologue, rather than the chapters (i.e. 14 chapters plus prologue and epilogue), but essentially Druitt's story is between the second and third murders but will later be moved to after the final, the fifth, displacing Marie Kelly's demise to earlier, in the third quarter of the book. Overleaf, we see Alan looking back at the shape of the book from five years after the above, with the epilogue done but *The Gull Catchers* still a year away.

Extract from a 1997 interview with Alan Moore,

shortly after the completion of *FROM HELL*, in conversation (by fax) with Dave Sim, from the back pages of *Cerebus #217*

*W*ith FROM HELL, *the seed idea was that of murder, any murder. It had occurred to me that murder is a human event at the absolute extreme of the human experience. It struck me that an in-depth exploration of the dynamics of a murder might therefore yield a more extreme and unprecedented kind of information. All that needed to be decided upon was which murder. Perhaps predictably, I never even considered the Whitechapel murders initially, simply because I figured they were worn out, drained of any real vitality or meaning by the century of investigation and publicity attached to them. I started out by trawling for more obscure and unusual homicides like the case of Dr Buck Ruxton, for example (a kind of 1930s Lord Lucan figure who killed his wife and nanny but never managed to pull off the necessary subsequent disappearance).*

It was only towards the end of 1988, with so much Ripper material surrounding me in the media on account of it being the centenary of the murders, that I began to understand that, firstly, there were still ways to approach the Whitechapel murders that might expose previously unexplored seams of meaning, and secondly that the Ripper story had all the elements that I was looking for. Set during fascinating and explosive times in a city rich with legend, history and association, the case touched peripherally upon so many interesting people and institutions that it provided the precise kind of narrative landscape that I required. You see, to some extent the peripheries of murder... the myth, rumour and folklore attached to a given case... had always seemed more potentially fruitful and rewarding than a redundant study of the hard forensic facts at a murder's hub. This traditional approach to murder might tell us Whodunit (which is admittedly the most immediate of practical considerations), but it does not tell us what happened on any but the most obvious and mechanical level. To find out anything truly significant, we must take the plunge into myth and meaning, and to me a case with the rich mythopoeic backwaters of the Whitechapel murders suddenly seemed like the perfect spot to go fishing.

Having defined the purpose and the territory to my satisfaction, I then undertook my preliminary reading of the ground site. By this, I mean that I visited and explored the territory of the murders personally, and also that I explored the landscape of the murders in terms of the literature surrounding the event. By this, I mean that I made a very broad reading and mapping, as if from a considerable distance from the event itself.

This initial mapping gave me a glimpse of the whole territory in its entirety, if not in detail. I could see what features of the narrative landscape seemed the most significant and promising, even if I couldn't provide a precise soil analysis at that point to say exactly why they seemed promising. The mathematical theories of C. Howard Hinton, son of Gull's friend James Hinton, seemed promising. The Iain Sinclair-inspired reading of London as a mythic and historical constellation seemed promising. The Masonic theories of the late Stephen Knight, whether true or not, seemed to open up fascinating territories of lore and tradition. The Masonic notion of the Universe, of space-time, as a rough and solid block hewn out by the Great Architect, with the job of finishing the work left to the Great Architect's mortal servants, the Dionysiac Artificers and Freemasons, well that seemed to fit in with everything else. Hitler's conception in 1888 seemed highly resonant. The matricentric/ patriarchal notions of myth and history came from the intuitive reading of the "London Pentacle" as described in chapter four, filtered through the intuitions of Robert Graves.

Basically, what I'm saying is that, yes, I did have the broad shape of the whole thing in my head, with many of the details already there, before I started. By chapter two, for example, I already had the Monster-Ripper-Halifax Slasher-Moors Murderers-Peter Sutcliffe arc of murder that we see in the last chapter firmly in my head. I did not, however, find out about Ian Brady's childhood vision of the floating head until later. I knew that I'd later be alluding to Brady when I had Gull ponder aloud the familiarity of the name Brady Street during the first murder, but I was not then aware that Brady's partner Myra Hindley would have her own name commemorated by the sacking manufacturer's premises outside which the third murder occurred. I knew that the last line of the whole book would be Robert Lees's "I think there's going to be another war," but I didn't decide to use the Von Stuck painting of the Wild Hunt, *painted with Adolf Hitler's adult face superimposed upon the god Odin in 1889, the year of Hitler's birth, until about a month before the last issue went to press. I knew that Netley would be dying before the book concluded and that the obelisks were somehow important to the symbology of the book, but I hadn't at this point found all that marvelous shit about Netley's coach colliding with an obelisk and spilling his brains on the cobbles.*

The thing is, if that first high-altitude mapping is perceptive and accurate enough, whatever tiny surface details are unearthed upon closer inspection are bound to fit right into it somewhere. That's how I work, anyway.

As regards my self-deprecating tone during the appendices, it wasn't modesty so much as a gruff attempt at apology for having done such a fucking sloppy and unprofessional job. I mean, "I think I read this in some book somewhere but I can't for the life of me remember which one and I can't be bothered to look for it" is hardly the high standard of investigative reportage that FROM HELL *is often touted as being, is it? And the fact that something hasn't been done in comics before is really no excuse for doing a sloppy job. There's nothing at all wrong with bushels. Sometimes one needs something to hide under. Then again, you're probably right and I'm probably being too hard on myself. At least I didn't forget to draw the main character's head.*

We'll return to the business about the head in its proper place, but for now we go back to the beginning, to page one.

Prologue, page 1

At the beginning of *FROM HELL*, the scripts would arrive a chapter at a time in a formidable bundle; one of them even came bound at the side. A pile of reference materials, including photos and books, would accompany them. This 2000-word opener, mostly describing the intimate details of a rotting seagull, plunged me head first into the horrors of *FROM HELL*. While I can imagine a film opening exactly as Alan describes this scene, complete with an eerie buzzing noise, I found that the vertical frame of our panels was not conducive to it, so I amalgamated the three opening panels into one emblematic banner.

There exist two slightly different versions of the prologue. In one, Robert Lees is without a hat, as he is in the script, but on thinking about it, I convinced myself that an Englishman wouldn't have been out without a hat in September in the 1920s.

PAGE 1. (2073 words) PANEL 1.

OKAY... LET'S GET OUT THERE AND WIN ONE FOR THE RIPPER! (ACTUALLY, THAT'S ROBERT BLOCH'S JOKE, BUT I THOUGHT I'D STICK IT IN ANYWAY.)

THIS FIRST PAGE HAS NINE EVENLY SPACED PANELS, ALL TAKEN FROM A FIXED POINT OF VIEW. YEAR IS 1923, AND WE ARE IN BOURNEMOUTH, DOWN ON THE BEACH QUITE CLOSE TO THE TIDE-LINE. THE MONTH IS SEPTEMBER; A LEADEN AND OVERCAST DAY WITH A BLIND WHITE SKY AND GREY TIDES SULKILY COMING IN TO THE DAMP SAND OF A PALE GREY BEACH. THE TIME IS LATE AFTERNOON OR EARLY EVENING, AND IF WE COULD SEE THE SUN IT WOULD BE GOING DOWN. AS IT IS, THE SUN SINKS UNSEEN AND WITHOUT SPECTACLE BEHIND THE SMOTHERING, FEATURELESS DUVET OF CLOUD. ITS ONLY VISIBLE EFFECT IS THAT THROUGHOUT THIS ENTIRE EIGHT-PAGE EPISODE, THE LIGHT GRADUALLY WORSENS THROUGH DUSK TO THE BEGINNINGS OF DARKNESS. WE ARE LOOKING DOWN THE BEACH, LOOKING ALONG THE EDGE OF THE TIDE FROM A GROUND-LEVEL VIEWPOINT. TO THE RIGHT OF THE PICTURE, STRETCHING AWAY TOWARDS THE DISTANCE, WE SEE THE GREY-BLACK WAVES WASHING SLUGGISHLY IN WITH THEIR SKIRTS OF GRUBBY WHITE FOAM. TO THE LEFT WE HAVE A SMOKY IMPRESSION OF THE GRANITE SEA WALL AND THE BUILDINGS OF THE BOURNEMOUTH SEA FRONT RISING UP STOLIDLY BEHIND IT. THIS TOO STRETCHES AWAY INTO THE DISTANCE, MEETING WITH THE LINE OF THE SEA'S EDGE AT THE VANISHING POINT, WITH A RAGGED RIBBON OF GREY SAND AND OCCASIONAL TUFTS OF MARAM GRASS LYING BETWEEN THE TWO. (I'M GUESSING HERE, EDDIE, SINCE I HAVEN'T YET TRACKED DOWN ANY REFERENCES FOR BOURNEMOUTH DURING THAT PERIOD. WHEN WE FINALLY DO LOCATE REFERENCE WE'LL JUST HAVE

TO ADAPT THESE DESCRIPTIONS AS BEST WE CAN TO FIT THE FACTS. THE BEACH IS DESERTED, AND IF THERE ARE ANY PEOPLE STROLLING ON THE SEA FRONT THEY ARE MUCH TOO FAR AWAY TO SEE AS MORE THAN INDISTINCT DOTS. IN THE VERY FOREGROUND OF THE SHOT HERE, RIGHT UNDER OUR NOSES AS IT WERE, THERE LIES THE INERT BODY OF A DECOMPOSING SEA GULL. IT LIES THERE WITH THE REMAINS OF ONE WING STICKING UP SCRAGGILY: A FEW RIBS ALREADY JUTTING THROUGH THE SOILED WHITE DOWN OF ITS BREAST. ITS CHIPPED BEAK HANGS OPEN STIFFLY, STUPIDLY. ITS STARING EYE IS A TINY WHITE BLOB OF MUCOUS THAT HAS BECOME CLOUDY AND OPAQUE, REFLECTING ONLY BLIND WHITE CLOUDS. A NUMBER OF SAND-FLIES ARE HOPPING AND PICKING OVER THE CORPSE... LITTLE BLACK DOTS WITH LEGS THAT YOU SEE HOPPING AROUND NEAR THE WATER'S EDGE AND AT FIRST MISTAKE FOR SOME OPTICAL DISORDER. SINCE WE HAVE THIS ROTTING BIRD RIGHT UNDER OUR NOSES FOR NINE PANELS, MAKING IT PRETTY LARGE AND RIGHT UP CLOSE IN THE FOREGROUND, MAYBE WE CAN ACTUALLY SHOW THE IDIOSYNCRASIES OF INSECT FEEDING HABITS GOING ON: AN INSIGNIFICANT LITTLE BALLET GOING ON WHILE THE REAL ACTION GRADUALLY ENCROACHES FROM THE BACKGROUND. ALL I MEAN BY THIS IS MAYBE WE HAVE ONE FLY UP ON THE HEAD WHO REMAINS ALMOST MOTIONLESS THROUGHOUT THE ENTIRE SEQUENCE. ANOTHER HOPS ABOUT ALL OVER THE PLACE, LOOKING FOR THE RIGHT DINING AMBIENCE. A THIRD TURNS UP HALFWAY THROUGH AND PRESUMPTUOUSLY STARTS TO TUCK IN RIGHT NEXT TO THE SECOND, WHO TAKES UMBRAGE AND FLIES OFF... JUST BLACK DOTS MOVING AROUND, TO GIVE THE UNPLEASANT IMPRESSION OF TEEMING BUGS AS NATURALISTICALLY AS POSSIBLE, WITHOUT OVERDOING IT. WHILE THIS IS GOING ON IN THE FOREGROUND, WE GRADUALLY BECOME AWARE OF TWO FIGURES APPROACHING ALONG THE BEACH FROM THE BACKGROUND, FOLLOWING THE LINE OF THE TIDE AS THEY WALK SLOWLY TOWARDS US. HERE, THEY ARE TINY LITTLE BLACK DOTS, NO BIGGER THAN THE FLIES THAT WE SEE FEEDING IN THE FOREGROUND. THE TITLE LETTERING, EITHER IN BLACK ON WHITE OR REVERSED, AS APPROPRIATE, IS SUPERIMPOSED SOMEWHERE IN THE CENTRE OF THIS FIRST PANEL AS IF IT WERE THE OPENING TITLE OF A FILM. THE LETTERING IS THAT UPON THE HEADING OF THE NOTE RECEIVED BY THE WHITECHAPEL POLICE IN OCTOBER OF 1888: STARK, SIMPLE AND SCRUFFY; A COUPLE OF TINY SPATTERED INK BLOTS TO THE RIGHT OF THE 'F' AND JUST ABOVE THE 'r' IN 'From'.

OKAY, SO THAT'S THE SET-UP FOR THIS FIRST PAGE. BEFORE WE CARRY ON THOUGH I SHOULD JUST REITERATE WHAT I WAS SAYING OVER THE PHONE ABOUT HOW I WORK; NONE OF THIS RAMBLING JUNK IS SACRED. IF THERE'S STUFF THAT DOESN'T WORK VISUALLY OR THAT YOU THINK WOULD WORK BETTER ANOTHER WAY THEN JUST GO AHEAD AND DO IT. I ONLY PUT ALL THIS LABORIOUS DETAIL IN SO THAT YOU'LL HAVE AN IDEA OF THE EFFECT THAT I'M AFTER. IF YOU HAVE A BETTER WAY OR A MORE PRACTICAL WAY TO ACHIEVE IT, THEN THAT'S FINE BY ME. FOR FUCK'S SAKE DON'T BE INTIMIDATED BY IT, AND PLEASE SLING IN ALL THE IDEAS AND SUGGESTIONS THAT YOU WANT. I WANT YOU TO HAVE AS MUCH FUN ON THIS AS I'M HAVING, SO JUST KICK OFF YOUR SHOES, LOOSEN YOUR BELT AND RELAX. JUST DON'T FALL ASLEEP.

LOGO: From Hell

PANEL 2.
SAME SHOT EXACTLY, EXCEPT THE FLIES HAVE MAYBE MOVED AROUND A BIT AND THE WAVES ARE EITHER CRASHING IN OR RATTLING BACK ACROSS THE SHINGLE... WHICHEVER THEY WEREN'T DOING LAST PANEL, BASICALLY. THE TWO BLACK DOTS OF THE MEN APPROACHING DOWN

THE BEACH ARE LARGER HERE, THOUGH NOT BY VERY MUCH. THE SUB-LOGO AND CREDITS ARE SUPERIMPOSED ACROSS THE MIDDLE OF THE PANEL AGAIN, THIS TIME PROBABLY IN AN ELEGANT AND ANTIQUATED-LOOKING TYPEFACE.

CREDITS: Being a melodrama in sixteen installments
                  by ALAN MOORE AND EDDIE CAMPBELL

PANEL 3.

SAME SHOT, THE TIDES AND THE FLIES HAVING MOVED ACCORDINGLY. THE FIGURES, AGAIN, ARE A LITTLE CLOSER HERE, ALTHOUGH STILL VERY SMALL. ONCE MORE, THE TITLE LETTERING IS SUPERIMPOSED OVER THE PANEL'S CENTRE, PROBABLY IN THE SAME PSEUDO-VICTORIAN TYPEFACE USED LAST PANEL.

TITLE: Prologue: The old men on the shore.

PANEL 4.

SAME SHOT. WE CAN NOW SEE THAT THE FIGURES ARE THOSE OF TWO MEN, BOTH WEARING LONG COATS AND MUFFLED AGAINST THE COLD. ONE OF THEM IS QUITE SLENDER AND DELICATE LOOKING, A MAN OF AROUND FIFTY YEARS OLD. HE WEARS A SCARF, TOPCOAT AND GLOVES, BUT IS BAREHEADED SAVE FOR HIS FULL AND NEATLY GROOMED HEAD OF GREY HAIR, HIS GREYING MOUSTACHE AND BEARD. HE IS THE MORE GENTEEL-LOOKING AND SLIGHTLY THE BETTER DRESSED OF THE TWO MEN, BUT FROM HIS ATTITUDE HE SEEMS TO BE ATTENTIVE AND FUSSING IN REGARD TO THE OLDER MAN WHO WALKS BESIDE HIM, AS IF CONCERNED THAT THE OLD MAN SHOULD OVER-EXERT HIMSELF OR SOMETHING. I JUST MEAN THAT'S THE OVERALL IMPRESSION HE GIVES OFF WHEN WE SEE HIM WITH THE OLDER MAN: RESPECTFUL AND SOLICITOUS, ALBEIT OCCASIONALLY PRONE TO IMPATIENCE WHEN GOADED BY THE OLDER MAN'S CANTANKEROUSNESS. HERE THEY JUST WALK SIDE BY SIDE, HANDS DEEP IN THEIR GREATCOAT POCKETS. THE YOUNGER MAN IS CALLED ROBERT LEES. HIS ASSOCIATE IS FREDERICK ABBERLINE. ABBERLINE IS THE OLDER OF THE TWO MEN, AND THE MORE NOTICEABLY FROM YEOMAN STOCK THAN THE RATHER EFFETE LEES. HE IS PUSHING SEVENTY, ALTHOUGH HE STILL LOOKS A FAIRLY SOLID FIGURE, IF SLIGHTLY INCLINED TO PORTLINESS IN THESE, HIS LATER YEARS. I DON'T HAVE A PHOTO REFERENCE OF FRED ABBERLINE YET, BUT I'M GUESSING THAT HE'S THE FAIRLY STOCKY FIGURE DESCRIBED ABOVE, WITH A MOUSEY MOUSTACHE AND MUTTONCHOP SIDEWHISKERS. HIS HAIR, THOUGH RECEDING, SEEMS TO HAVE KEPT AT LEAST SOME OF ITS COLOUR. AS WE SEE HIM HERE HE IS WEARING A DERBY HAT AND CARRYING A GENTLEMAN'S WALKING CANE. HE MOVES MORE STIFFLY THAN LEES, AND IT IS HIS DIFFICULTY IN WALKING THAT ACCOUNTS FOR THE PAIR'S SNAIL-PACED PROGRESS ALONG THE BEACH TOWARDS US HERE. WHEN ABBERLINE GETS CLOSER, I FANCY THAT WE MIGHT SEE HIS NOSE AS BEING SLIGHTLY RED AND BULBOUS, THOUGH NOT TO EXCESS. BY ALL ACCOUNTS HE DRANK A LOT, AND WALKING ROUND WHITECHAPEL IN THE FOG SWIGGING RAW SPIRITS WOULDN'T DO ANYBODY'S NOSE A LOT OF GOOD, WOULD IT? ANYWAY, WE CAN'T MAKE OUT ANY OF THIS DETAIL YET SINCE THE PAIR ARE STILL TOO FAR AWAY. THE CAPTION GIVING THE PLACE AND DATE ARE SOMEWHERE UP TOWARDS THE TOP LEFT OF THE PANEL. SINCE THERE WON'T BE MANY CAPTIONS AT ALL THROUGHOUT THIS ENTIRE BOOK (JUST PLACE-AND-DATE CAPTIONS, LIKE HERE) THE CAPTIONS CAN EITHER BE LETTERED IN THE VICTORIAN TYPEFACE MENTIONED ABOVE OR IN A MORE NORMAL AND PROSAIC FASHION. I LEAVE IT ENTIRELY UP TO YOU. WHATEVER YOU THINK LOOKS BEST.

CAP: Bournemouth. September, 1923

PANEL 5.

THE TWO FIGURES CONTINUE TO GET CLOSER. THE FLIES CONTINUE TO FEED ON THE DEAD
SEAGULL AND THE WAVES CONTINUE TO LURCH AGAINST THE SHORE. ABBERLINE, WHO IS
PROBABLY THE FIGURE ON THE LEFT OF THE PAIR AS THEY WALK TOWARDS US, APPEARS TO BE
SAYING SOMETHING TO HIS COMPANION HERE: HE SPROUTS A SMALL WORD BALLOON, BUT THERE
ISN'T ANY REAL LETTERING IN IT... JUST A BUNCH OF TINY UNREADABLE SCRATCHES THAT
LOOK LIKE WORDS AND CONVEY THE IMPRESSION OF AN INAUDIBLE CONVERSATION.

ABBERLINE (V SMALL):   `````````````

PANEL 6.

THE FIGURES CONTINUE TO GET CLOSER, MORE AND MORE DETAIL BECOMING EVIDENT AS THEY
DO SO. HERE, THEY BOTH HAVE WORD BALLOONS. THE BALLOONS ARE STILL VERY SMALL, AND
THE WORDS IN THEM ARE LETTERED AS TINY AS POSSIBLE WHILE STILL REMAINING JUST-
ABOUT-LEGIBLE, TO GIVE THE EFFECT OF A CONVERSATION GRADUALLY BECOMING AUDIBLE AS
THE SPEAKERS GET CLOSER TO US.

ABBERLINE (v small):   ...bloody shambles, this last six years.

LEES (V SMALL):   A shambles inflicted from WITHOUT. Foreign interference
                         hardly invalidates Capital's premise.

PANEL 7.

THE FIGURES COME STILL CLOSER. FROM THEIR ATTITUDES NOW WE CAN SEE THAT THEY ARE
DEBATING. LEES LOOKS THE MORE AGITATED OF THE TWO, GESTICULATING AS HE ATTEMPTS TO
MAKE HIS POINT. ABBERLINE CONTINUES TO PLOD SLOWLY AND IMPLACABLY FORWARD, DIGGING
THE END OF HIS CANE INTO THE DAMP SAND AS HE DOES SO. HE NEEDS ALL HIS ENERGY
FOR WALKING AND CAN SPARE NONE OF IT FOR EXTRANEOUS HAND MOVEMENTS. THEIR WORD
BALLOONS HERE ARE BIGGER THAN LAST TIME, ALTHOUGH STILL NOT QUITE AS BIG AS THE
FULL-SIZED NORMAL LETTERING THAT WE WILL SEE IN OUR NEXT PANEL.

ABBERLINE (SMALL):   Oh, DO come on, Mr. Lees! Really! They've had nothing but
                         war, poverty...

LEES (SMALL):   Despite which they have SURVIVED! Surely that confirms rather
                         than contradicts what Mr. Marx has said:

LEES (SMALL):   Socialism is INEVITABLE.

PANEL 8.

THEY ARE VERY CLOSE TO US NOW, FILLING THE WHOLE PANEL. ABBERLINE IS A FEW PACES
AHEAD OF LEES, AND THUS THE CLOSEST TO US HERE, WALKING ALONG SWINGING HIS STICK
AND THEN DIGGING IT DOWN IN THE SAND, SO THAT ITS POINT, WHEN VISIBLE, HAS A
CLINGING SHEATH OF DAMP SAND ADHERING TO THE LAST FEW INCHES OF ITS TIP, A FEW
GRAINS FALLING OFF HERE AND THERE. AS HE WALKS TOWARDS US HE DOESN'T LOOK ROUND AT
LEES. RATHER HE LOOKS DOWN AT THE DEAD GULL IN HIS PATH. A SLIGHT FROWN OF DISTASTE
WRINKLES HIS FEATHERS AS HE STARES AT THE DECAYING BIRD AND THE FLIES FEASTING
UPON IT. LEES, SLIGHTLY BEHIND ABBERLINE AS THE PAIR WALK TOWARDS US, DOES NOT
APPEAR TO HAVE NOTICED THE BIRD AND IS LOOKING AT THE BACK OF ABBERLINE'S TURNED
BACK. LEES' EXPRESSION IS VERY EARNEST, HIS SAD EYES MORE OR LESS BEGGING ABBERLINE
TO SEE REASON AND ACCEPT HIS ARGUMENT. LEES HAS EYES LIKE A SPANIEL, AND LOOKS

SORRY FOR THE WHOLE WORLD, PARTICULARLY HIMSELF.

LEES: Why, I myself am testament to its increasing influence. I am undoubtedly a product of the middle classes, yet none espouse socialism more volubly than I...

PANEL 9.

IN THIS LAST PANEL, ABBERLINE HAS MOVED SO CLOSE THAT WE CAN NO LONGER SEE HIS UPPER BODY AT ALL. WE SEE HIM FROM AROUND ABOUT THE KNEE DOWN HERE. IN ANOTHER STEP HE'LL BE OUT OF THE PANEL ENTIRELY. WITH THE END OF HIS WALKING CANE HE SWATS THE DEAD GULL TO ONE SIDE SO THAT IT FLIES LIMPLY UP INTO THE AIR, SPINNING BEAK OVER TAIL WITH A MINIATURE THUNDERHEAD OF BLACK FLIES BILLOWING UP FROM IT IN SEARCH OF LESS HAZARDOUS PASTURES. LEES, STILL TRAILING A COUPLE OF STEPS BEHIND THE OLDER MAN, IS STILL NOT LOOKING AT THE GULL. INSTEAD, HE DIRECTS HIS GAZE TOWARD THE POINT OFF PANEL ABOVE WHERE ABBERLINE'S HEAD MUST BE. HE LOOKS PUZZLED, IN A TROUBLED SORT OF WAY, AS HE GAZES AT THE BACK OF ABBERLINE'S OFF-PANEL HEAD. ABBERLINE'S BALLOON ISSUES FROM OFF-PANEL ABOVE IN THE F/G.

ABBERLINE (OFF):   My point precisely, Mr. Lees.

ABBERLINE (OFF):   My Point precisely.

The house that Jack bought.

In my Alec: The Years Have Pants, *there's a sequence drawn in 2000, in which my wife and I buy a house from the proceeds of the* FROM HELL *movie. As a parallel, I quoted the closing panels of page 8 of the original prologue. However, I thought it would be interesting to redraw them to see to what extent I might improve on the then 12-year-old original. It came out a little tidier, but I don't think the new version added anything. (old version is shown in the no-hat variant.)*

Chapter 1, page 1.

In which the machinery of our story is sparked into motion. This page is shown in two states. Alan was still thinking cinematically, with large blocked title lettering superimposed on the opening scene (or "shot"). I thought it would be more in keeping with the ambience of the work to do it in the style of the title page of a book, and had my pal Des Roden calligraph a series of chapter-headings for the original appearances. When I collected the work together in 1999, Michael Evans, graphic designer, replaced those with a typeset version. These are in a more funereal white-on-black, with a suggestion of the title cards of old silent movies.

Here I'm earnestly trying to get all the information in. I "zoomed" in for the first panel's label details. Those pasted on xeroxes of period sweets/candy designs helped to establish place and time, giving me enough credit in the bank, I hoped, so that I could concentrate on the people for the rest of the page. Still, in '99 when I looked over the pages before publishing the collected edition, I was unhappy with Eddy's faces, and they are all altered in the second version, with the whole figure in the final panel being replaced. This is a standard problem with the first appearances of characters. Like real people, the artist can't know them fully until they've been around for a while. Later he or she gets comfortable with them and knows exactly how they look and move.

PAGE 1. (1758 words) PANEL 1.
THERE ARE SEVEN PANELS ON THIS FIRST PAGE, PROBABLY WITH A BIG WIDE ONE AT THE TOP OF THE PAGE HERE, SPANNING ITS FULL WIDTH. THE DATE, AS WE SHALL SEE, IS JULY 1884, AND THE PLACE IS CLEVELAND STREET, LONDON, ONE OF THE MORE FASHIONABLE AND UP-MARKET AREAS OF THAT PERIOD, AS FAR AS THE METROPOLIS WENT. WE ARE INSIDE A CONFECTIONERS-CUM-TOBACCONIST SITUATED AT NO. 22 CLEVELAND STREET, AND IN THIS FIRST PANEL WE ARE LOOKING AT A LONG SHELF THAT NEATLY FILLS THE SPACE ALLOWED BY THIS FIRST WIDE, HORIZONTAL PANEL, STRETCHING FROM ONE SIDE OF THE PAGE TO THE

OTHER. UPON THE SHELF THERE ARE OLD-FASHIONED SWEET JARS CONTAINING OLD-FASHIONED SWEETS: ANISEED BALLS, WINTER MIXTURE, MINT IMPERIALS, SUGARED ALMONDS, ACID DROPS, BON BONS AND SO FORTH, ALONG WITH SOME EVIDENCE TO SHOW THAT THE SHOP IS ALSO A TOBACCONIST'S. PERHAPS A BOX OF CIGARS, OR PARTITIONED TRAY OF DIFFERENT TOBACCOS. MAYBE WE CAN SEE A HINT OF THE TOPS OF THE JARS ON THE SHELF BELOW THIS ONE HERE, BUT ONLY IF THERE'S ROOM. OVER ON THE RIGHT OF THE WIDE PANEL, WE CAN SEE THE ARMS OF A TWENTY-FIVE-YEAR-OLD SHOP-GIRL NAMED ANNIE CROOK, A STURDILY BUILT AND TIDILY DRESSED YOUNG WOMAN, AS SHE REACHES UP FROM OFF PANEL BELOW TO TAKE A FEW MORE PIECES OF BARLEY SUGAR FROM A JAR ON THE TOP SHELF. ONE OF HER HANDS MANAGES TO HOLD THE JAR'S LID AND ALSO TO TILT THE OPEN JAR OVER TOWARDS HER. HER OTHER HAND DIPS IN TO RETRIEVE A COUPLE OF SINGLE PIECES OF DEEP ORANGE BARLEY SUGAR. WE CANNOT SEE ANY MORE OF HER THAN HER ARMS, ENTERING THE PICTURE FROM BELOW. THE REST OF THE PANEL IS JUST TOBACCO AND DIFFERENT SORTS OF SWEETS: I WANT THIS TO BE A PANEL THAT YOU CAN ALMOST SMELL, IF YOU KNOW WHAT I MEAN. THE TITLE LETTERING IS SUPERIMPOSED OVER THE LEFT OF THE PANEL SOMEWHERE, DOWN TOWARDS THE BOTTOM.

TITLE: Chapter one.   The Affections of Young Mr. S.

PANEL 2.

NOW WE ARE BEHIND THE COUNTER OF THE SHOP, WITH THE SHOP-GIRL, LOOKING OUT OVER IT. ON THE SHOP'S COUNTER THERE IS AN OLD-FASHIONED WEIGHING SCALE OR BALANCE, INTO ONE OF THE PANS OF WHICH WE SEE ANNIE CROOK DROPPING THE COUPLE OF PIECES OF BARLEY SUGAR THAT SHE'S JUST TAKEN FROM THE JAR, AS IF TO MAKE UP THE WEIGHT. WE CAN STILL SEE NO MORE OF HER THAN HER HANDS AND CUFFS, ENTERING FROM THE LEFT OF THE FOREGROUND HERE. LOOKING OUT ACROSS THE COUNTER AND INTO THE SHADOWY REMAINDER OF THE SHOP WE SEE TWO YOUNG MEN STANDING, WAITING FOR THE WOMAN TO FINISH DELIVERING THE SWEETS THAT THEY ARE PURCHASING. ONE OF THESE, DRESSED IN A MUSTARD COLOUR CHECK SUIT OF SOMEWHAT QUESTIONABLE TASTE AND LOUDNESS, IS YOUNG WALTER SICKERT, AGED 24 YEARS OLD. THE OTHER YOUNG MAN IS MUCH MORE SOMBERLY AND ELEGANTLY DRESSED IN A GENTLEMAN'S BLACK COAT, AND ALTHOUGH HE WILL BE INTRODUCED TO US AS SICKERT'S YOUNG BROTHER ALBERT, HE IS IN FACT THE YOUNG DUKE OF CLARENCE, PRINCE ALBERT VICTOR CHRISTIAN EDWARD... OR PRINCE EDDY FOR SHORT. AT THE TIME OF THIS FIRST SCENE, IN 1884, HE IS ONLY TWENTY YEARS OLD. HE'S QUITE GOOD-LOOKING, BUT THERE'S SOMETHING RATHER BOVINE ABOUT HIS EXPRESSION. HE ISN'T TERRIBLY BRIGHT, KNOWS IT, AND FEELS WRETCHEDLY SELF-CONSCIOUS ABOUT IT. HE'S NAÏVE TO THE POINT OF BEING INFANTILE, AND HAVING LED A RELATIVELY LOVELESS EXISTENCE IS INCLINED TO FALL PASSIONATELY IN LOVE WITH ANYONE HE MEETS. COUPLED WITH THIS, HIS INFANTILE NEEDS FOR GRATIFICATION MANIFEST THEMSELVES IN HIS SEX LIFE TO MAKE HIM FAIRLY PROMISCUOUS... ALTHOUGH THAT'S SOMEWHAT TOO KNOWING A TERM TO CONVEY THE CHILDISHNESS, ALMOST INNOCENCE, OF HIS EMOTIONAL AND SEXUAL EXPERIENCE. HE HAS HAD SYPHILIS SINCE THE AGE OF SIXTEEN, ALTHOUGH THIS WILL NOT MANIFEST ITS WORSE EFFECTS UNTIL LATE IN EDDY'S LIFE. AS HE STANDS WITH SICKERT HERE HE HOLDS A TOP HAT NERVOUSLY AND AWKWARDLY BENEATH HIS ARM, AND IS STARING ALMOST SLACK-JAWED AT THE OFF-PANEL WOMAN BEHIND THE COUNTER, FAR TOO GAUCHE TO CONCEAL HIS WIDE-EYED INTEREST, OR EVEN TO BE AWARE THAT HE IS SHOWING IT. SICKERT, ON THE OTHER HAND,

IS COMPARATIVELY EASY AND RELAXED, A CONFIDENT YOUNG BOHEMIAN ABOUT TOWN. HE HAS A SMART DERBY HAT TUCKED JAUNTILY UNDER HIS ARM, OR IS HOLDING IT IN ONE HAND. HIS GAZE IS DIRECTED AT THE LAST PIECES OF BARLEY SUGAR BEING DROPPED INTO THE SCALE, RATHER THAN AT THE YOUNG WOMAN DOING THE DROPPING, AS IS THE CASE WITH HIS COMPANION. HE SMILES FAINTLY, RELAXEDLY, UTTERLY AT EASE. THE SHOP HAS A LARGE FRONT WINDOW, AND THE BRIGHT SUNSHINE FALLS IN FROM OUTSIDE IN SHAFTS, A SOLID-EDGED RHOMBOID OF WHITE-GOLD LIGHT AGAINST THE MUSTY UMBER DARKNESS OF THE SWEETSHOP, WITH ITS JARS AND TRAYS AND SELECTIONS OF BRIAR PIPES. FALLEN FROM THE OFF-PANEL WOMAN'S FINGERS, THE LAST PIECE OF BARLEY SUGAR HANGS SUSPENDED AND MAGICALLY IN MIDAIR, CAUGHT FROZEN BETWEEN HAND AND WEIGHING SCALE. THE CAPTION CAN BE AT THE TOP OR BOTTOM. UP TO YOU.

CAP: LONDON, JULY 1884.

PANEL 3.

NOW A SIDE-ON SHOT, LOOKING DOWN THE LENGTH OF THE COUNTER TOWARDS THE SHOP'S FRONT WINDOW, SO THAT WE CAN SEE ALL THE THREE PARTICIPANTS CLEARLY. ANNIE STANDS, FULLY VISIBLE FOR THE FIRST TIME, BEHIND THE COUNTER, OVER TO THE LEFT OF PANEL HERE. SHE'S POURING THE BARLEY SUGAR FROM THE PAN OF THE SCALES INTO A LITTLE TRIANGULAR BAG MADE OF WHITE PAPER. THE BARLEY SUGAR LUMPS ARE SOMEWHAT MELTED AND STUCK TOGETHER, ON ACCOUNT OF THE FEROCIOUS AND SWELTERING JULY HEAT. ANNIE IS A LARGE AND STURDILY BUILT WOMAN WITH BROAD FEATURES. SHE ISN'T FAT, YOU UNDERSTAND, JUST BIG; ONLY A LITTLE SHORTER THAN PRINCE EDDY. SHE ISN'T IMMEDIATELY PRETTY OR BEAUTIFUL, BUT HER CHARACTER AND WARMTH ARE EVIDENT, AND DO MUCH TO COMPENSATE FOR THIS BY LENDING HER A UNIQUE AIR OF ANIMATION AND CHARM. SHE SMILES QUIETLY AS SHE POURS THE BARLEY SUGAR INTO THE WHITE PAPER BAG, EYES TWINKLY WITH FRIENDLY AMUSEMENT AS SHE SPEAKS DIRECTLY TO SICKERT. PRINCE EDDY, IN THE BACKGROUND, HOLDS HIS TOP HAT WRETCHEDLY IN BOTH HANDS AND STARES AT THE WOMAN BEHIND THE COUNTER WITH A MOONSTRUCK EXPRESSION THAT BORDERS UPON THE IMBECILIC. SICKERT GRINS AT ANNIE AS HE SPEAKS TO HER. SHE'S MODELED FOR HIM IN THE PAST, AND THE TWO ARE QUITE FRIENDLY AND RELAXED AROUND EACH OTHER. ANNIE COMES FROM SCOTLAND ORIGINALLY, BY THE WAY.

ANNIE: There. Two pennorth on the nail. I'd not want to jew you now, would I?

ANNIE: I'm sorry they're all of a lump. It's this weather.

SICKERT: Nonsense, Annie. They look mouth-watering.

PANEL 4.

SAME SHOT EXACTLY. ALL OF THE SWEETS ARE NOW IN THE BAG, AND ANNIE IS PLACING THE BAG (WITH A TWIST AT THE TOP CORNERS) ONTO THE COUNTER. SICKERT IS IN THE ACT OF TAKING A COUPLE OF COPPER PENNIES FROM HIS COAT POCKET. BOTH ANNIE AND SICKERT SORT OF PAUSE IN MID-MOVEMENT AND TURN THEIR HEADS TO LOOK SLIGHTLY AWAY FROM US TOWARDS EDDY, WHO STANDS FACING US IN THE IMMEDIATE BACKGROUND HERE, IN MORE OR LESS THE SAME POSITION AS LAST PANEL. HE LOOKS DREADFULLY EMBARRASSED, AND, AS IS USUAL AT SUCH TIMES, STARTS TO EVIDENCE A FAINT STAMMER, A MERE ECHO OF HIS FATHER'S FAR MORE SERIOUS SPEECH DIFFICULTY. HE GAZES AT ANNIE WITH CHILDISH, AWESTRUCK ADORATION. YOU CAN SEE HOW PEOPLE MIGHT BE TOUCHED BY THE NAKED SINCERITY OF A YOUNG MAN OF EDDY'S YEARS AND

STATION. SICKERT AND ANNIE LOOK SURPRISED.

EDDY: A-as do you...i-if I may say so.

EDDY: That is, ah...

PANEL 5.

REVERSE ANGLE NOW, SO THAT EDDY FACES SLIGHTLY AWAY FROM US, HEAD AND SHOULDERS IN THE FOREGROUND AS HE GAZES TOWARDS SICKERT AND ANNIE IN THE CENTRE OF THE IMMEDIATE BACKGROUND, STANDING TO EITHER SIDE OF THE SHOP'S COUNTER. EDDY LOOKS WRETCHEDLY AGITATED AND ANXIOUS AND WORRIED IN THE WAKE OF HIS OUTBURST, FEARFUL THAT ANNIE HAS TAKEN OFFENCE. ANNIE, STANDING BEHIND THE COUNTER, TURNS AND GAZES AT EDDY WHILE SHE SPEAKS TO SICKERT. HER EYES ARE WIDE WITH SURPRISE, AND SHE HAS A FAINT SMILE THAT IS SLIGHTLY MOCKING, BUT KINDLY. SICKERT, LAYING HIS TWO PENNIES DOWN ON THE COUNTERTOP, TURNS ALSO TO LOOK AT EDDY, GRINNING BROADLY WITH AMUSEMENT AT THE YOUNG CHAP'S OBVIOUS DISCOMFORT. WITH HIS OTHER HAND HE IS PICKING UP THE SMALL WHITE BAG OF BARLEY SUGAR.

ANNIE: Why, Mr.S. You do entertain the most IMPERTINENT companions.

EDDY: I...please, I apologize. I only meant...

PANEL 6.

NOW BACK TO AN ANGLE SIMILAR TO THAT EMPLOYED IN THE PANELS THREE AND FOUR, WITH THE COUNTER RUNNING AWAY FROM US, ANNIE ON ONE SIDE AND THE TWO GENTLEMEN ON THE OTHER. TOWARDS THE FOREGROUND, ANNIE IS PLACING THE MONEY IN THE DRAWER OF AN OLD-FASHIONED VICTORIAN TILL. IN THE NEAR BACKGROUND, AGAINST THE LIGHT OF THE SHOP WINDOW, SICKERT HAS TAKEN A STEP ACROSS SO THAT HE'S BEHIND EDDY WITH HIS HANDS CLASPED FATHERLY UPON EACH OF EDDY'S SHOULDERS FROM BEHIND AS HE STEERS THE RELUCTANT AND LOVE-STRUCK YOUNG MAN TOWARDS THE COUNTER, IN ORDER TO PROPERLY INTRODUCE HIM TO ANNIE. ANNIE LOOKS AT THE FRIGHTENED AND UNCOMFORTABLE-LOOKING EDDY WITH AMUSEMENT IN HER EYES. SHE THINKS HE'S CUTE. EDDY SHUFFLES FORWARD UNDER SICKERT'S GENTLE PRESSURE FROM BEHIND, HIS TOP HAT IN HIS HANDS.

SICKERT: Oh, come on, old chap. She's just having you on.

SICKERT: Annie, this... this is my younger brother, ALBERT.

SICKERT: Uh, Albert, this is Miss Annie Crook.

PANEL 7.

SIMILAR SHOT NOW. IN THE FOREGROUND, ANNIE SMILES AND REACHES ONE HAND ACROSS THE COUNTERTOP TOWARDS EDDY, AS IF TO SHAKE HANDS. EDDY STARES DOWN STUPIDLY AT THE HAND AS IF NOT SURE WHAT TO DO WITH IT, HIS OWN HAND RISING HESITANTLY TO MEET IT. IN THE NEAR BACKGROUND, SICKERT IS IN THE ACT OF SETTING HIS DERBY ATOP HIS HEAD IN PREPARATION FOR GOING OUTSIDE. PERHAPS HE'S CHECKING HIS REFLECTION IN A GLASS-FRONTED CABINET OR SOMETHING WHILE HE DOES SO. IN ANY EVENT, HE IS NO LONGER LOOKING TOWARDS US, OR TOWARDS EDDY AND ANNIE. ANNIE ALMOST LOOKS AS IF SHE'S GOING TO LAUGH AT THE AWKWARDNESS OF THE HANDSOME YOUNG EDDY AS HE GAWPS AT HER OFFERED HAND.

ANNIE: Oh, a YOUNG Mr. S, eh? I didn't KNOW there was a young Mr. S.

ANNIE: Well...

ANNIE: Pleased to make your acquaintance, I'm sure.

For this page, Alan Moore ruminates on what London should look like in *FROM HELL*. For my part I wanted it to be as matter-of-fact as possible, both the whole of London and the East End, as it would be to the people living in it. It's 40 years since I first went to London. The Houses of Parliament were sooty black. When I visited it again recently, it felt like the same place, ignoring a few new landmarks and everything being a lot cleaner. The Whitechapel murders happened only 80 years before my first visit, so even imagining a double amount of change, I'm certain I could feel a familiarity with the old place. In preparation for drawing Cleveland Street my good friend, Londoner Ed Hillyer, who was working with me on *Bacchus* at the time, shot a reel of film there, including the interior of what used to be the sweetshop (exterior photo on page 100). Looking at the prints I saw a street that could not have been much changed in 100 years.

This shop on the corner of Cleveland Street made a useful fixed point, (panel 9)

The thing I particularly wanted to avoid was drawing an environment that looked stage-designed for mayhem, a problem addressed in *Jack the Ripper — A Legacy in Pictures*, by Clive Bloom. He noted, in reference to Jack the Ripper films in general: ***"The East End is both a geographical location and a location for filmic fantasy. It has to be recreated in filmland as a set, so that it is airless, claustrophobic and without escape... Jack finally strikes and the set constructed around his absence reveals the reason for its construction."*** Tim Burton's Gotham City worked the same way (in the same year I was drawing this — 1989), and something about that bothered me.

PAGE 2. (2084 words) PANEL 1.

A NINE-PANEL PAGE HERE. IN THIS FIRST PANEL WE ARE MORE OR LESS LOOKING THROUGH ANNIE'S EYES, SO THAT ALL WE SEE OF HER IS HER OUTSTRETCHED HAND, ENTERING INTO THE PICTURE FROM OFF PANEL BELOW. WE ARE LOOKING AT EDDY AS HE TAKES HER HAND AND BENDS OVER TO PLANT A GENTLE KISS UPON ITS BACK, HIS EYES UPTURNED TO GAZE AT US

AND AT ANNIE. THERE IS A SADNESS AND VULNERABILITY IN HIS WIDELY SPACED EYES THAT
IS TOUCHING. IN THE BACKGROUND, SICKERT FINISHES ADJUSTING HIS DERBY AND GLANCES
OVER AT THE PAIR WITH A NON-COMMITTAL EXPRESSION, UNLESS YOU WANT TO LEAVE HIM
OUT ALTOGETHER AND JUST CONCENTRATE ON EDDY KISSING ANNIE'S HAND.

EDDY: The...
EDDY: The honour is all mine, dear Lady. I ...
EDDY: I hope we may become better acquainted.

PANEL 2.

BACK TO A SHOT LOOKING DOWN THE COUNTER FROM THE END WITH ANNIE ON ONE SIDE AND EDDY
ON THE OTHER. HE IS STILL HOLDING HER HAND, ALTHOUGH THE HANDS ARE LOWERED NOW AND
HIS IS ABOUT TO RELEASE IT, HAVING STRAIGHTENED UP AFTER STOOPING TO KISS IT. HE
STARES DIRECTLY INTO ANNIE'S EYES. SHE STARES BACK INTO HIS EYES AND SHE IS NO
LONGER MOCKING OR AMUSED. HER EYES HAVE A WONDERING AND ALMOST STARTLED LOOK AS SHE
STARES INTO EDDY'S EYES. SEEMINGLY OBLIVIOUS TO WHAT IS GOING ON IN THE EMPTY SPACE
BETWEEN THEIR EYES, SICKERT CALLS OUT CHEERILY FROM THE NEAR BACKGROUND, GESTURING
WITH HIS THUMB TOWARDS THE FRONT DOOR OF THE SHOP THAT WE CAN SEE IN THE RIGHT OF
THE BACKGROUND BEHIND HIM. IT HAS A GLASS PANEL SET INTO ITS TOP HALF, THOUGH NOT A
TERRIBLY BIG ONE.

SICKERT: Albert, I hate to be a bore, but Netley's waiting outside.
SICKERT: We really must dash, Annie. No doubt we'll call again shortly.
SICKERT: Come along, youngster!

PANEL 3.

SAME SHOT. ANNIE STANDS MOTIONLESS BEHIND THE COUNTER, LOOKING TOWARDS THE DOOR OF
THE SHOP. THE TWO MEN HAVE JUST GONE OUTSIDE. EDDY, CLOSING THE DOOR BEHIND HIM,
LOOKS BACK INTO THE SHOP THROUGH THE GLASS PANE SET INTO THE TOP HALF OF THE DOOR,
HIS LOVESTRUCK GAZE SERIOUS AND MEANINGFUL. ANNIE, UNCONSCIOUSLY, TOUCHES ONE HAND
TO HER BREAST AS SHE GAZES AFTER HIM. THE LITTLE BELL THAT'S RIGGED TO THE SHOP DOOR
TINKLES IN THE OTHERWISE DEAD SILENCE FOLLOWING THE GENTLEMEN'S DEPARTURE.

F.X.   Ti-ting

PANEL 4.

WE ARE NOW OUTSIDE THE SHOP. (FOR THE BASIC LOOK OF THE PLACE, SEE THE ENCLOSED
REFERENCE PHOTOGRAPH. I FIGURE THAT THE SIGN ABOVE THE WINDOW READS "MORGAN'S
TOBACCONIST & QUALITY CONFECTIONER." THE SHOP HAS NEVER BEEN NAMED, TO MY KNOWLEDGE,
BUT THE PROPRIETRESS WAS A MRS. MORGAN, SO THE SIGN OUTSIDE SEEMS FEASIBLE.) THE
SHOP WAS AT NUMBER 22 CLEVELAND STREET, ONLY A LITTLE WAY DOWN FROM ONE OF THE
STREET'S ENDS. CLOSER TO THE END WAS NUMBER 6 CLEVELAND STREET, WHERE ANNIE THE
SHOP-GIRL LIVED IN A BASEMENT FLAT. WALTER SICKERT'S STUDIO WAS DIRECTLY OVER
THE ROAD FROM THE FLAT, AND THE SHOP AND THE FLAT WERE CLOSE ENOUGH TOGETHER FOR
ONE TO SEE BOTH OF THEM FROM THE WINDOW OF SICKERT'S STUDIO. I FIGURE THE HOUSES
WERE SMALLER AND THE STREETS WERE SHORTER THEN... EVERYTHING WAS MORE CRAMPED AND
ECCENTRIC LOOKING. I FIGURE THAT THE COACH THAT IS WAITING FOR SICKERT AND EDDY
OUTSIDE IS NOT ACTUALLY OUTSIDE THE SHOP SO MUCH AS A LITTLE WAY DOWN THE STREET,

TOWARDS THE CORNER, FACING IN THE OPPOSITE DIRECTION FROM THE CORNER TOWARDS THE
OTHER END OF THE STREET. IN THIS PANEL HERE, WE HAVE THE BLINKERED HEAD OF ONE OF THE
COACH HORSES AS IT STANDS STEAMING IN THE SUNSHINE AT THE MERCY OF THE NUMEROUS FLIES
EVIDENT DURING THAT PARTICULARLY HOT SUMMER. WE ARE AT A SLIGHT ANGLE, SO THAT WE'RE
LOOKING UP THE STREET SOMEWHAT TOWARDS THE FRONT OF THE SWEETSHOP. WE SEE SICKERT
STROLLING ALONG THE PAVEMENT TOWARDS US, SMILING INDULGENTLY AS EDDY HURRIES TO CATCH
UP WITH HIM, SETTING HIS TOP HAT ON HIS HEAD AS HE DOES SO. HE IS GRINNING FOOLISHLY
AND EXCITEDLY, BABBLING LIKE A SCHOOLBOY AS HE HURRIES TO CATCH UP WITH SICKERT,
WHO IS WALKING TOWARDS THE COACH THAT IS WAITING OFF PANEL TO THE LEFT OF THE F/G,
BEHIND THE HORSE WHOSE HEAD WE CAN SEE. AS A GENERAL NOTE ABOUT THE STREETS, EVEN
THOUGH CLEVELAND STREET WAS IN ONE OF THE MOST FASHIONABLE AREAS OF TOWN, RUNNING
PARALLEL TO THE TOTTENHAM COURT ROAD, IT WOULD STILL HAVE LOOKED FAIRLY CRUMBLY AND
DIRTY. NOTHING NEAR AS BAD AS WHAT WE'LL LATER SEE IN WHITECHAPEL, OF COURSE, BUT AS
A GENERAL RULE OF THUMB, EVERYTHING WAS DIRTIER THEN; THE STREETS, THE BUILDINGS, THE
PEOPLE AND IN PARTICULAR THE SKIES. THERE WERE TONS OF FACTORIES IN LONDON BELCHING
OUT BLACK SMOKE DAY AND NIGHT, ACCOUNTING FOR THE "LONDON PARTICULAR" FOGS AND AT
LEAST PART OF THE ILL HEALTH SUFFERED BY THE AVERAGE INHABITANT. I'M NOT SURE WHAT
WE WANT EXACTLY HERE, REGARDING THE VISUAL TREATMENT OF LONDON. IT DOESN'T WANT TO
BE QUITE SO STYLISHLY SINISTER AS THE LONDON DAVID LYNCH PORTRAYED IN THE ELEPHANT
MAN, NOR YET SO HEART-TUGGINGLY SORDID AND MELODRAMATIC AS DORÉ'S ENGRAVINGS OF THE
PERIOD, BUT WE DEFINITELY WANT TO GIVE THE WORLD A FEEL THAT IS SUBTLY DIFFERENT TO
THE WORLD OF TODAY. MAYBE THIS IS SOMETHING MORE TO DO WITH PSYCHOLOGICAL AMBIENCE
THAN VISUAL TREATMENT, BUT IF YOU TRY TO CONSCIOUSLY THINK YOUR WAY INTO THE LONDON OF
1888 WHILE YOU'RE DRAWING THIS STUFF I THINK IT'LL HELP. EVERYTHING WOULD HAVE BEEN
MORE PERMANENT THEN, WOULDN'T IT, AND LESS SUSCEPTIBLE TO CHANGE. THE EIGHTIES WERE
AROUND THE TURNING POINT OF THE EMPIRE, AND I FIGURE THINGS WERE ALREADY STARTING TO
LOOK OLD, THEIR TEXTURES ABRADED BY THE RIGORS OF THE URBAN ENVIRONMENT AT ITS MOST
SQUALID. I FIGURE EVERYTHING WAS STARTING TO LOOK A BIT MELANCHOLY AND SAD, LIKE BEER
CANS AND DECORATIONS DO WHEN THE PARTY'S WINDING DOWN, WHEREAS THEY'D LOOKED SOMEHOW
FESTIVE A MOMENT BEFORE. ALBERT'S DEAD AND VICTORIA HAS TAKEN THE WHOLE EMPIRE INTO
HER OBSESSIVE MOURNING WITH HER. SOMEHOW IT SHOWS IN THE DEFEATED LANES, IN THE
LITTER, IN THE DIRTY LIGHT.
ANYWAY... HERE THE HORSE CHOMPS ITS BIT AND TOSSES ITS HEAD TO CLEAR THE FLIES IN THE
FOREGROUND WHILE SICKERT STRIDES TOWARDS US ALONG THE STREET FROM THE BACKGROUND WITH
THE MOONSTRUCK YOUNG PRINCE AT HIS HEELS LIKE A GREAT STUPID OVER-EAGER DOG.

EDDY: I Say, Sickert! Isn't she the most enchanting creature? Have
                   you known her long?
SICKERT: Eddy, you've been too long in captivity and you're
                   mooning after the first shop-girl you meet.
SICKERT: What would your mother say?

PANEL 5.
CHANGE ANGLE. WE ARE NOW BEHIND SICKERT AND EDDY AS THEY PREPARE TO BOARD THE COACH.
THE COACH DOORS AND WINDOWS FILL MUCH OF THE BACKGROUND HERE AS IT STANDS BESIDE THE

CURB, WITH THE HORSES OFF PANEL SOMEWHERE ON THE LEFT. IN THE TOP LEFT CORNER WE CAN SEE THE LOWER HALF OF THE COACHMAN AS HE SITS ATOP THE COACH, HOLDING THE REINS IN HIS HAND. HE WEARS A LONG AND DIRTY COAT THAT HANGS DOWN OVER THE BOX SEAT HERE. EDDY IS OPENING THE COACH DOOR AND PREPARING TO CLIMB INTO ITS INTERIOR. (THE OUTSIDE OF THE COACH IS BLACK, BY THE WAY, BUT THERE IS NO ROYAL CREST ON THE SIDE.) AS HE DOES SO HE PAUSES AND LOOKS WITH ALMOST COMICAL EARNESTNESS AT SICKERT, WHO LAUGHS AND TURNS HIS HEAD TO SPEAK TO THE OFF-PANEL COACH DRIVER, WHOSE NAME IS JOHN NETLEY.

EDDY: She rather RESEMBLES mother, doesn't she?

SICKERT: Oh, Eddy! What are we to do with you?

SICKERT: Netley? Take us to Claridges. I intend to render this young pup incapably drunk before he gets us ALL into trouble.

PANEL 6.

CHANGE ANGLE SO THAT WE'RE UP IN FRONT OF THE COACHMAN, AND HE SITS FACING US HEAD AND SHOULDERS TO THE LEFT OF THE PANEL HERE. LOOKING DOWN BEYOND HIM WE CAN SEE SICKERT LOOKING UP AT NETLEY AND LAUGHING GOOD-NATUREDLY AS HE HIMSELF PREPARES TO CLIMB INTO THE COACH AFTER PRINCE EDDY. NETLEY DOESN'T LOOK ROUND AT SICKERT AS HE SPEAKS TO HIM, BUT CONTINUES TO SURVEY THE OFF-PANEL ROAD AHEAD OF HIM WITH WARY AND WATCHFUL EYES THAT ALWAYS SEEM TO BE LOOKING FOR THE MAIN CHANCE IN A CRAFTY AND CALCULATED WAY. NETLEY IS TWENTY-FOUR YEARS OLD, AND 5´5´´ TALL. HE HAS A FAIR COMPLEXION, DARK HAIR, A SMALL DARK MOUSTACHE... HARDLY MORE THAN A DIRTY GROWTH ON HIS UPPER LIP REALLY, OF NO GREAT IMPORTANCE. IT MAKES HIM LOOK A BIT UNWASHED AND SMELLY, WHICH OF COURSE HE IS. HE HAS A FULL, WIDE FACE WITH A WIDE MOUTH AND QUITE THICK LIPS. HE'S A WOMANIZER AND A BIT OF A JACK-THE-LAD, AND THERE IS SOME-THING CRUEL AND STUPID ABOUT THE GRIN THAT HE CUSTOMARILY WEARS SPREAD ACROSS HIS WIDE MOUTH. HIS SHOULDERS ARE BROAD, AND HE HAS A BUILD LIKE A PIT-BULL. ATOP HIS DIRTY, DARK HAIR HE WEARS A BLACK LEATHER PEAKED CAP. WE DON'T SEE NETLEY AGAIN FOR A COUPLE MORE EPISODES, BUT I WANT TO FIX HIS FACE IN READERS' MINDS SINCE HE PLAYS QUITE A LARGE PART LATER. BEAR IN MIND WHEN GIVING HIM A FACE THAT THIS IS THE MAN WHO WROTE THE 'FROM HELL' LETTER: HE'S A COCKY AND EGOTISTICAL LITTLE SOD WHO'S RUTHLESSLY AMBITIOUS AND WANTS TO GET TO THE TOP BY THE SHORTEST ROUTE POSSIBLE.

NETLEY: Ah, insobriety's no proof against trouble, Mr.Sickert. I got a cousin o' mine in FEARFUL trouble, an' she were as tiddly as I were!

SICKERT: Ha ha ha.

SICKERT: Carry on, Netley.

PANEL 7.

WE ARE NOW STANDING IN THE ROAD ON THE OTHER SIDE OF THE COACH FROM THE PAVEMENT SIDE THAT SICKERT JUST ENTERED BY. NETLEY IS NOW VISIBLE SITTING TO THE TOP RIGHT CORNER ATOP HIS BOX... OR RATHER, HIS LOWER HALF IS VISIBLE. PERHAPS WE CAN SEE THE WHIP IN HIS HAND AS HE GATHERS UP THE REINS. LOOKING THROUGH THE CARRIAGE WINDOW WE CAN SEE PRINCE EDDY LEANING FORWARDS EARNESTLY TO TALK TO SICKERT, WHO SITS OPPOSITE HIM. SICKERT LAUGHS AND SHAKES HIS HEAD IN DISBELIEF AT HIS YOUNG CHARGE'S INFATUATION. BEHIND THE COACH WE SEE THE FAÇADE OF THE HOUSES DOWN TOWARDS THE CORNER OF CLEVELAND

STREET. (THE CORNER ITSELF IS JUST OFF PANEL LEFT IN THE BACKGROUND HERE, IF THAT HELPS YOU GET YOUR BEARINGS.) THE HORSES ARE OFF PANEL RIGHT. NETLEY'S FACE IS NOT VISIBLE HERE BUT HIS BALLOONS ISSUE INTO THE PANEL FROM ABOVE.

NETLEY(off):   GYAP! GYAP, ya bugger! YAA!

EDDY: No, but seriously, Sickert... she DOES look like my mother, doesn't she?

PANEL 8.

SAME SHOT. THE COACH IS NOW PULLING AWAY OUT OF THE RIGHT OF THE PANEL, SO THAT ONLY HALF OF IT IS VISIBLE NOW. PERHAPS WE JUST CATCH A BLURRED GLIMPSE OF EDDY THROUGH THE REAR SIDE WINDOW AS THE COACH PULLS AWAY OVER THE COBBLES, STILL TALKING EARNESTLY TO HIS CHUM. AS THE COACH MOVES AWAY WE CAN OF COURSE SEE MORE OF THE HOUSES BEHIND IT, WHICH WERE PREVIOUSLY OBSCURED BY IT. NETLEY'S BALLOONS TRAIL BACK INTO THE PANEL FROM OFF-PIC RIGHT, WHILE EDDY'S ISSUE FROM THE COACH.

NETLEY (off):   YAA! YAAA!

EDDY (in coach):   She has mother's eyes.

PANEL 9.

SAME SHOT. THE COACH HAS GONE AND WE CAN NOW SEE THE HOUSES THAT WERE BEHIND IT, DOWN ON THE CORNER OF CLEVELAND STREET, STANDING FULLY REVEALED. IF YOU CAN MANAGE IT, GIVEN THE LOGISTICS OF THE SHOT, WE CAN SEE THE CORNER OF CLEVELAND STREET, AT LEAST TO THE POINT WHERE THE STREET SIGN IS VISIBLE BOLTED UP ON THE WALL, EVEN IF WE CAN'T SEE THE ACTUAL CORNER ITSELF. THE SIGN HAS THE WORDS "CLEVELAND STREET" IN STARK BLACK LETTERING. IF IT'S POSSIBLE, WE CAN ALSO SEE THE FRONT DOOR OF NUMBER 6, THREE DOORS DOWN FROM THE CORNER, WITH STEPS LEADING DOWN FROM THE STREET LEVEL TO ITS BASEMENT. IF YOU CAN'T GET BOTH THESE THINGS IN THEN JUST MAKE SURE THAT WE CAN SEE THE "CLEVELAND STREET" SIGN AS THE COACH PULLS AWAY AND FORGET ABOUT THE SHOT OF NUMBER 6 AND ITS BASEMENT. THE STREET SIGN IS THE MAIN THING, STRIKING AND SOMEHOW OMINOUS AS IT HANGS THERE ON THE WALL, GIVING THE NAME OF THE PLACE WHERE ALL THAT FOLLOWED WAS TO HAVE ITS ORIGINS.

No dialogue

Prince Eddy: *I used to feel a twinge of guilt about some of our depictions of people who are not around to defend their reputations. But lately I have come to the conclusion that the sheer daftness of the accumulation of baloney cancels itself out. Quite apart from his connection to the Ripper murders, as posited in 1970 by Thomas Stowell, who half-disguised him as 'Mr. S', Eddy has this in his account: a pair of alternative history novels, written by Peter Dickinson, set in a world where Albert Victor survives and reigns as Victor I. In Gary Lovisi's parallel universe Sherlock Holmes short story, "The Adventure of the Missing Detective", he is a tyrannical king, who rules after the suspicious deaths of both his grandmother and father. The Prince also appears as the murder victim in the first of the Lord Francis Powerscourt crime novels* Goodnight Sweet Prince, *as a vampire in the novel* I, Vampire *by Michael Romkey, and as a murder suspect in the novel* Death at Glamis Castle *by Robin Paige.* (I'm lifting this from his Wikipedia entry.) *In 1964 Philip Magnus called his death a "merciful act of providence", supporting the theory that his death removed an unsuitable heir to the throne, but the real relief in being 120 years dead is that he doesn't have to know about any of this crap. Next up, we picture him with his pants off...*

Chapter 1, page 3.

At the outset Alan had decided there would be no captions in *FROM HELL*. All would be shown and not told. Certainly it would have been easier with captions. A simple matter could be stated in its entirety in one sentence, but in our book we would be taking the labour-intensive path of showing everything. The sex in this scene is forensic "evidence" that Prince Eddy fathered a baby upon Annie Crook, the shop-girl. Exhibit A: the penis. Exhibit B: the vagina. Exhibit A can clearly be seen to enter Exhibit B. Aside from that, it's as funny as real sex. The funniest part, in our house, is that these people, who actually existed in 1888, just happened to have the same names as my wife and me. Some of the dialogue from this page was still being mischievously replayed, by our children at our dinner table, many years after. "Oh Eddy, I think your Mr. Perkins wants to go somewhere."

This was one of the contents that put *Taboo* in disgrace. Issue #2 was printed but several binders (usually a separate specialty operation in the print business) refused to bind it. ***"I have a feeling we became a hot potato,"*** Bissette said, ***"...the word got around about us, because some binders wouldn't even look at the book. We were refused by no less than nine."*** (report, Comics Journal #131 Sept. 1989) *Taboo* #2 was released in Sept. 1989, ten months after the first issue. #3 appeared in March '90, #4 in Feb '91. I took to describing *Taboo* as "a quarterly anthology that comes out once a year," to Steve's eternal annoyance.

PAGE 3. (1,145 words) PANEL 1.
IT IS NOW A MONTH LATER DURING THE SAME YEAR. WE ARE INSIDE THE BASEMENT OF
NUMBER SIX CLEVELAND STREET, IN THE BEDROOM. IT IS LATE AFTERNOON, AND ONLY A FEW
LAST SHAFTS OF SUNLIGHT PENETRATE THE CHINK BETWEEN THE RAILINGS AT STREET LEVEL
OUTSIDE AND THE TOP OF THE BASEMENT WINDOW. THERE ARE JUST LITTLE RANDOM BLOBS OF
SHAFTLESS SUNLIGHT ON THE WALLS AND FLOOR HERE AND THERE, BUT FOR THE MOST PART
THE ROOM IS SLIGHTLY DIMLY LIT. WE CAN'T SEE ANY OF THE ROOM IN THIS FIRST PANEL
HOWEVER, SINCE WE OPEN WITH A TIGHT CLOSE-UP OF THE COUPLE ON THE BED. TO THE LEFT-
HAND SIDE OF THE BED, ANNIE LIES ON HER LEFT SIDE, FACING INWARD. WE CANNOT SEE
HER HEAD AND SHOULDERS HERE. NO MORE OF HER THAN HER TORSO REALLY. LYING ON HIS
BACK ON THE OTHER SIDE OF THE BED, WITH HIS HEAD TURNED TO FACE INWARDS, IS EDDY.
ANNIE LEANS UP ON ONE ELBOW SO AS TO LET HER BREAST TRAIL CLOSE TO EDDY'S FACE.

ONE HAND ENTERS THE PICTURE FROM THE LEFT TO HOLD THE LEFT BREAST SO THAT EDDY CAN GET IT INTO HIS MOUTH. EDDY SUCKS AT THE NIPPLE, WHICH IS WET WITH SALIVA. HIS EYES ARE CLOSED. ONE OF HIS OWN HANDS ENTERS THE PICTURE AND RESTS GENTLY OVER ANNIE'S AS SHE CUPS HER BREAST FOR HIM TO SUCK AT. ANNIE IS NAKED, WHILE EDDIE WEARS ONLY A GENTLEMAN'S WHITE SINGLET WITH NOTHING ON HIS LOWER HALF.
No dialogue

PANEL 2.
NOW WE ARE LOOKING DOWN ON THE BED FROM ROUGHLY ABOVE IT, SO THAT WE CAN SEE BOTH EDDIE AND ANNIE MORE OR LESS FULL FIGURE AS THEY SPRAWL BENEATH US. LEANING UP STILL, ANNIE PULLS BACK SLIGHTLY, WITHDRAWING HER BREAST FROM EDDY'S MOUTH, ALTHOUGH BOTH HIS AND HER HANDS ARE STILL TOUCHING IT. SHE SMILES AS SHE LOOKS DOWN AT HIM. HE GAZES UP AT HER ACROSS HER BREAST AS HE SPEAKS. HIS PENIS IS LOLLING AND HALF-ERECT. HE LOOKS LOVE-STRUCK.

ANNIE:	Do you like my bubbies, Albert? See...they're standing up for you.
EDDY:	They're very beautiful.
EDDY:	YOU'RE very beautiful.

PANEL 3.
NOW WE ARE DOWN TOWARDS THE FOOT OF THE BED, LOOKING ALONG THE LENGTH OF EDDY'S BODY AS ANNIE SITS UP IN BED BESIDE HIM. SHE GAZES SOFTLY DOWN AT HIS HARDENING COCK. EDDY DIRECTS HIS SOFT DOE-EYED GAZE AT HER AS HE REACHES OUT TO LIGHTLY TOUCH HER ELBOW, TAKING HOLD OF IT LIGHTLY IN HIS HAND. BOTH OF THEM HAVE QUIET EXPRESSIONS HERE, AND THERE IS SOMETHING A LITTLE SAD IN EDDY'S DESPITE HIS BURGEONING TUMESCENCE.

ANNIE:	Ah, go on. It's you's the beauty, if you weren't always mopin'. Lookin' after's what you need.
EDDY:	No, that's the TROUBLE. My FAMILY look after EVERYTHING, plan my whole LIFE for me...
EDDY:	Put your hand on my pego.

PANEL 4.
A DIFFERENT ANGLE NOW, AS IF WE WERE ON THE FAR SIDE OF THE BED LOOKING ACROSS ITS LOWER HALF AT ANNIE AS SHE KNEELS UP ON THE BED. ALL WE CAN SEE OF EDDY IS HIS LOWER HALF. HIS SPEECH BALLOON ENTERS THE PANEL FROM OFF-PIC TO THE RIGHT HERE. LEANING UP ON ONE OF HER HANDS, ANNIE TAKES HOLD OF EDDY'S COCK IN THE OTHER AND BEGINS TO MASTURBATE HIM. SHE STARES DOWN AT THE HAND WORKING ON EDDY'S PENIS WITH A KIND OF DISTANT AND DETACHED LOOK... APPARENTLY ABSORBED IN WHAT SHE IS DOING AND YET WITH HER MIND SOMEWHERE ELSE. THE BASEMENT'S FRONT WINDOW IS BEHIND HER SOMEWHERE TO THE RIGHT OF PANEL HERE, WITH THE BED RUNNING PARALLEL TO THE WALL AND WINDOW. IT DOESN'T NEED TO BE VISIBLE HERE, BUT THAT'S WHERE WHAT LITTLE DAPPLING OF SUNLIGHT THERE IS, IS ISSUING FROM.

ANNIE:	Like this, now?
EDDY (OFF):	Oh yes. Yes. Frig me, will you?
ANNIE:	Mm. Your BROTHER doesn't seem much bothered by your family.

PANEL 5.
NOW WE PAN UP THE BED SO THAT WE CAN ONLY SEE EDDY'S TOP HALF AND PERHAPS A LITTLE

OF ANNIE'S BACK AS SHE KNEELS UP HALFWAY DOWN THE BED, HER FACE OFF PANEL HERE AS SHE CONTINUES TO JERK EDDY OFF, ALSO OFF PANEL IN THIS INSTANCE. EDDY TURNS HIS FACE TOWARDS US, EYES CLOSED AND MOUTH OPEN IN A GASP OF PLEASURE. EDDY IS LYING SO THAT LOOKING BEYOND HIM WE CAN SEE THE BASEMENT WINDOW HERE. IT LOOKS OUT ONTO BRICKWORK WITH A LITTLE RIBBON OF RAILINGS AND SKY VISIBLE AT THE TOP.

EDDY: You...you don't understand. It isn't the same for him. He isn't...

EDDY: Oh. Oh, Annie...

PANEL 6.

NOW WE'RE AT THE FOOT OF THE BED AGAIN. TURNING HER BACK TOWARDS US AND THUS FACING EDDY AS HE LIES THERE ON HIS BACK, ANNIE SWINGS ONE LEG OVER EDDY TO KNEEL STRADDLING HIS HIPS. LOWERING HERSELF, SHE REACHES DOWN BETWEEN HER LEGS TO TAKE HOLD OF THE HEAD OF HIS PENIS, GUIDING IT UP BETWEEN THE LIPS OF HER VAGINA. SHE LOOKS DOWN AWAY FROM US IN A BUSINESSLIKE WAY AT WHAT SHE IS DOING, WHILE EDDY GAZES IN SOFT AWE AT HER FACE.

ANNIE: Oh dear. I think your Mr. Perkins has got himself all
                         restless. I think he wants to go somewhere.

ANNIE: Hold still...and never you mind about your rotten family.

PANEL 7.

WE LOOK AT THE BED SIDE-ON NOW. ANNIE LOWERS HERSELF DOWN ONTO EDDY'S COCK, STILL REACHING BEHIND HER WITH ONE HAND TO GUIDE IT INTO HER. EDDY STARTS TO GASP STRAIGHT AWAY, COMING ALMOST AS SOON AS HE'S INSIDE HER. AS HE CLOSES HIS EYES AND GASPS BREATHLESSLY THROUGH GRITTED TEETH, ANNIE'S EXPRESSION REMAINS CALM.

ANNIE: We'll do as we please, and they'll not prevent it.

EDDY: Oh Annie. Annie, my love, I'm going to spend...

PANEL 8.

WE CLOSE IN, PAST THE COUPLE, UPON THE BASEMENT WINDOW. IT LOOKS OUT ONTO SOLID RED BRICK, MOSS GROWING IN THE CHINKS BETWEEN THE BRICKS AND A SLIGHT DEPOSIT OF SOOT AND GRIME ADHERING TO THE BRICKWORK EVERYWHERE. THERE IS SOMETHING CRUEL AND SAD AND SURREAL AND OMINOUS ABOUT A WINDOW THAT LOOKS OUT ONTO SOLID BRICKS. IT LOOKS AS IF THE ONLY WAY OUT IS BLOCKED, BUT MORE CRUELLY THAN IF IT WERE BLOCKED BY A WALL. WINDOWS ARE A SYMBOL OF FREEDOM AND ESCAPE, AND TO HAVE ONE BLOCKED BY DIRTY BRICKWORK HAS A CERTAIN POIGNANCY ABOUT IT. AS WE STUDY THE DULL AND UNINTERESTING BRICKWORK BEYOND THE GLASS, THE CRIES OF THE LOVERS ISSUE INTO THE PANEL FROM OFF PICTURE.

EDDY (OFF):   Uh...uh...oouh...uh.

ANNIE (OFF):   Oh Albert. Oh, my lovely boy.

PANEL 9.

IN THIS FINAL PANEL WE SIMPLY REPRODUCE PART OF A CONTEMPORARY STREET PLAN OF LONDON DURING THAT TIME, SHOWING CLEVELAND STREET AND ITS TRIBUTARIES FROM ABOVE, ALL CLEARLY LABELLED. THE WORDS "CLEVELAND STREET", AS WITH THE LAST PANEL ON PAGE TWO, ARE THE MOST PROMINENT HERE.

No dialogue

Chapter 1, page 4.

The theory that a Masonic cover-up lies behind the Whitechapel murders comes from Stephen Knight's book, *Jack the Ripper: The Final Solution* (1976). The theory sounds convincing at first precisely because so many details fit into its pattern. It's only when you get to pinning down these details, as Alan undertook in writing *FROM HELL*, a process I had to extend in illustrating it, that the theory starts to unravel. One of its foundation stones is the connection between Marie Kelly and Walter Sickert, and the painting by the artist titled *Blackmail or Mrs Barrett*. The painting is usually dated to at least twenty years later than the Ripper murders. While later eruptions from the artist's morbid fascination with the case are documented, it is stretching things to see Kelly in the picture.

One of the details influencing the dating of it, I presumed, is the fashion in women's hats, which became quite large in the later Edwardian period. I tried to diminish the hat's presence here and even more so in subsequent scenes. However, I've just come across this:

> *I knew Marie quite well by sight... She was usually in the company of two or three of her kind, fairly neatly dressed and invariably wearing a clean white apron, but no hat.*

(memoir of Detective Walter Dew (1863-1947) (casebook.org))

In line with my earlier comments on the subject of the commonplace wearing of hats (under prologue, page 1) not wearing one would have attracted attention, so such an observation is likely to carry some weight. This gives us one of the earliest complications in depicting Marie Kelly. While the theory does not fall apart on this specific point, her resemblance to the subject of the painting was something that I felt we shouldn't commit to wholeheartedly.

PAGE 4. (1491 words) PANEL 1.
WE NOW JUMP TO THE JANUARY OF THE FOLLOWING YEAR, 1885, AND ALSO TO THE UPSTAIRS STUDIO OF MR WALTER SICKERT, ON THE OPPOSITE SIDE OF THE STREET FROM ANNIE'S

BASEMENT FLAT AND THE SWEETSHOP EIGHT DOORS DOWN THE STREET FROM IT. BOTH OF THESE
ARE AT LEAST PARTIALLY VISIBLE FROM SICKERT'S WINDOW, AND INDEED, IT IS SICKERT'S
STUDIO WINDOW THAT WE ARE LOOKING OUT THROUGH HERE. UP IN THE FOREGROUND WE CAN
SEE SICKERT'S HANDS ENTERING THE PANEL. HE IS BUSILY SHARPENING A PENCIL OR CRAYON
WITH A SHARP-LOOKING KNIFE IN PREPARATION FOR DOING SOME SKETCHING. PENCIL SHAVINGS
UNPEEL LAZILY AND DROP TO THE FLOOR LIKE THE TURDS OF WOODEN BIRDS. DESPITE THE
FACT THAT HE IS INDOORS, SICKERT IS DRESSED UP VERY WARM. THERE WAS NO CENTRAL
HEATING, AND I IMAGINE IN THE COLDEST WEATHER HE'S PROBABLY HAD TO WORK IN A COAT
AND SCARF IN HIS STUDIO. OUT THROUGH THE WINDOW HERE SNOW IS FALLING UPON CLEVELAND
STREET. LOOKING THROUGH IT WE CAN SEE THE TOBACCONIST-CONFECTIONERS DOWN THE STREET
BELOW GROWING GRADUALLY MORE DICKENSIAN AND PICTURESQUE AS THE SNOW GETS DEEPER.
No dialogue

PANEL 2.

WE NOW PULL BACK SO THAT WE CAN SEE SICKERT MAYBE THREE-QUARTER FIGURE AS HE
STANDS BY HIS EASEL, WHICH HAS ITS BACK TO US, WITH THE WINDOW BEHIND HIM. FRAMED
THUS AGAINST THE FALLING SNOW HE STANDS LOOKING TOWARDS US WITH HIS SHARPENED
PENCIL OR CRAYON IN ONE HAND AND THE KNIFE IN HIS OTHER. HE IS JUST ABSENTMINDEDLY
PLACING THE KNIFE DOWN ON THE WINDOW SILL HERE, HAVING FINISHED WITH IT. SINCE WE
HAVE PULLED BACK SOME WAY ACROSS THE STUDIO, WE CAN NOW SEE IN THE FOREGROUND THE
KNEE OF THE YOUNG WOMAN SITTING POSING FOR SICKERT, HER HANDS RESTING DEMURELY
UPON HER KNEE OR LAP, FOLDED TOGETHER QUITE PASSIVELY. THE WOMAN'S NAME IS MARIE
KELLY, AND ALTHOUGH WE CAN'T SEE HER FACE OR MUCH ELSE OF HER HERE, SHE IS A YOUNG
WOMAN OF IRISH PARENTAGE, AGED ABOUT TWENTY HERE, AND SHE IS PROBABLY THE MOST
CONVENTIONALLY PRETTY OF ALL OUR FEMALE CHARACTERS. AS FAR AS REFERENCE FOR HER
FACE GOES, I'M TRYING TO DIG UP PHOTOGRAPHS, BUT FOR THE MOMENT YOU'LL HAVE TO
RELY UPON THE FACE IN THE SICKERT PAINTING "BLACKMAIL OR MRS BARRETT" ALLEGEDLY
BASED UPON KELLY AND REPUTEDLY BEARING A RESEMBLANCE TO HER. HER VOICE ISSUES
FROM OFF PANEL HERE. AS FAR AS SICKERT'S STUDIO GOES, I'M NOT SURE WHAT THE DÉCOR
WOULD BE LIKE. AT FIRST I THOUGHT OF SOMETHING PICTURESQUELY CLUTTERED WITH THE ODD
PEACOCK FEATHER HERE AND THERE, BUT THAT SEEMS MORE THE STYLE OF A PRE-RAPHAELITE
LIKE HOLMAN HUNT (WHO LIVED JUST UP THE ROAD FROM SICKERT, ALSO IN CLEVELAND
STREET). AS I UNDERSTAND SICKERT, HE WAS RELENTLESSLY AND PASSIONATELY MODERN, AND
DESPISED THE USE OF CLASSICAL THEMES AND TECHNIQUE IN MODERN ART. MAYBE HIS STUDIO
WOULD BE PRETTY AUSTERE AND FUNCTIONAL, WITH SKETCHES AND PAINTINGS ALL OVER THE
PLACE, PINNED TO THE WALLS OR SCATTERED AND PILED ON THE FLOOR IN DRIFTS. ASSUMING
YOU CAN'T FIND ANY REFERENCE TO THE CONTRARY, THEN JUST DO WHAT FEELS RIGHT TO
YOU. HE SMILES FAINTLY HERE AS HE GLANCES AT THE OFF-PANEL MARIE, MUFFLED AGAINST
THE COLD IN HIS STUDIO. HIS BREATH ACTUALLY FOGS SLIGHTLY UPON THE AIR, ESCAPING
HIS SMILING LIPS IN A LITTLE SILK WISP OF VAPOUR.

MARIE:	And there I was thinkin' you'd be wantin' me with not a stitch on.
MARIE:	You'll have me doubtin' me attractions, Mr. Sickert.
SICKERT:	Never, Mary. Perhaps when it's warmer...

PANEL 3.

PULL BACK FURTHER STILL SO THAT MARIE IS NOW HEAD AND SHOULDERS IN THE F/G, IN
PROFILE AS SHE SITS THERE POSING FOR SICKERT. SHE WEARS A BROAD HAT ATOP HER DARK
HAIR (SEE "BLACKMAIL, OR MRS BARRETT") AND AROUND HER PRETTY THROAT SHE WEARS A
NOTICEABLE AND IDENTIFIABLE RED SCARF TIED IN A GAY AND CASUAL KNOT. I DUNNO HOW
YOU'LL MANAGE TO MAKE THE RED SCARF IDENTIFIABLE IN A BLACK AND WHITE COMIC...
MAYBE A PATTERN OF BLACK SPOTS ON IT OR SOMETHING. AS SHE POSES THUS, SEATED IN
PROFILE, SHE HAS A PLEASED SMILE ON HER SMALL LIPS, SATISFIED BY THE COMPLIMENT
THAT SICKERT IS PAYING HER. SHE KNOWS THAT SHE'S PRETTY AND SHE LIKES IT, BUT WHILE
SHE'S A BIT IMMATURE AND PRONE TO PUT ON AIRS, SHE'S NOT AN UNLIKEABLE GIRL. SHE'S
HAD A PRETTY ROUGH AND POVERTY-STRICKEN TIME DURING HER LIFE THUS FAR, AND WAS A
WIDOW AT NINETEEN. AS SHE SMILES CONTENTEDLY AT SICKERT'S WORDS WE LOOK BEYOND HER
TO SEE THE ARTIST HIMSELF, STANDING BY HIS EASEL AND STARTING TO SKETCH. HE LOOKS
DOWN AT THE PICTURE RATHER THAN UP AT MARIE AS HE SPEAKS, AND SHE DOESN'T LOOK AT
HIM AS SHE CAREFULLY HOLDS HER POSE.

SICKERT:	Besides, I want you how I first SAW you, on the convent steps.
SICKERT:	The way the light caught you, in that red scarf... you looked saintly, Mary. Religious.

PANEL 4.

CHANGE ANGLES SO THAT WE ARE NOW LOOKING AT THE SCENE THROUGH SICKERT'S EYES, WITH
HIS EASEL NOW TURNED TOWARDS US IN THE F/G, A PIECE OF DRAWING PAPER TACKED TO IT.
WE SEE SICKERT'S HAND ENTERING FROM OFF PANEL IN THE F/G, LOOSELY SKETCHING THE
SHAPE OF MARIE KELLY'S HEAD. WHAT SICKERT IS DOING HERE IS A PRELIMINARY SKETCH
THAT WILL EVENTUALLY BECOME THE PAINTING, "BLACKMAIL OR MRS. BARRETT", SO MAKE THE
ROUGH SKETCH HERE LOOK LIKE A CONCEIVABLE ROUGH SKETCH FOR THE PAINTING. HIS
SPEECH BALLOON ISSUES FROM OFF PANEL HERE. LOOKING BEYOND WHAT HE IS DRAWING WE SEE
MARIE AS SHE SITS THERE, POSING FOR HIM. SHE LAUGHS, FACE CRINKLING DELIGHTFULLY
AND PECULIARLY IRISH WRINKLES FORMING ON THE BRIDGE OF THE SLIGHTLY UPTURNED NOSE.
SOMEWHERE ON THE WALL BEHIND HER, PINNED UP, IS A CALENDAR, ALTHOUGH WE NEEDN'T
BE ABLE TO SEE IT CLEARLY HERE, SO LONG AS WE ESTABLISH ITS PRESENCE.

MARIE:	SAINTLY! Will you listen to HIM, now! He takes me into his house, feeds me, finds me a job...
SICKERT (OFF):	Oh, yes, the confectioners. How's it going?

PANEL 5.

THIS SHOT IS ALMOST THE SAME AS THAT IN PANEL 2 ON THIS PAGE, WITH ONLY MARIE'S KNEE
AND RESTING HANDS VISIBLE IN THE F/G HERE, WITH HER BALLOON ISSUING FROM OFF PANEL
LEFT. LOOKING BEYOND HER WE SEE SICKERT, NOW SKETCHING FURIOUSLY, WITH A FROWN OF
CONCENTRATION AS HE STARES FIXEDLY AT HIS DRAWING WHILE HE REPLIES TO MARIE.

MARIE (OFF):	Oh, it's very nice... and so's Annie. Lovely couple, her and your brother.
MARIE (OFF):	Doesn't look much like you, for saying, does he?
SICKERT:	No. He, uh, favours his mother more. Do you see much of him?

PANEL 6.

NOW, FROM THE FRONT, WE HAVE A HEAD-AND-SHOULDERS CLOSE-UP OF MARIE, AS SHE TURNS TO STARE AT SICKERT, SMILING KNOWINGLY AND A LITTLE SAUCILY. SICKERT'S BALLOON ENTERS INTO THE PANEL FROM OFF. ON THE WALL BEHIND MARIE WE CAN NOW CLEARLY SEE THE CALENDAR, OPEN AT JANUARY 1885.

EDDY: Not your brother, no... but there's been more to see of Annie
                        lately, if you take my meanin'.

SICKERT: I'm not sure I do. I've not seen her recently. I'm courting
                        myself, you know.

PANEL 7.

PULL BACK FROM MARIE SO THAT IN THE F/G WE SEE THE DRAWING THAT SICKERT IS DOING AND HIS HAND AS HE WORKS UPON IT. LOOKING BEYOND THIS WE SEE MARIE SITTING THERE POSING. SHE LAUGHS AT SICKERT'S WORDS, A LITTLE SCORNFULLY. IN THE FOREGROUND, THE POINT OF SICKERT'S PENCIL SUDDENLY BREAKS AGAINST THE SURFACE OF THE FIGURE HE IS DRAWING. THE FACE ON THE PAPER NOW IS ALMOST EXACTLY A PENCIL SKETCH FOR "BLACKMAIL, OR MRS BARRETT." THE PICTURE IS SET UP SO THAT WE SEE THE PENCIL POINT SNAPPING AFTER WE'VE HEARD MARIE'S WORDS.

MARIE: Ooh, and is it "courtin'" your brother's been doing then?

MARIE: The girl's six months pregnant if she's a day.

PANEL 8.

WE ARE NOW LOOKING AT SICKERT HALF-FIGURE AS HE STANDS THERE FACING US BY HIS EASEL WITH THE WINDOW BEHIND HIM, GREY SNOW FALLING DREAMILY BY. HE STANDS JUST STARING AT US AND THE OFF-PANEL MARIE IN STUNNED DISBELIEF, THE BROKEN PENCIL STILL CLUTCHED USELESSLY IN HIS TRAILING, DANGLING HAND. THE NEWS OF ANNIE'S PREGNANCY HAS OBVIOUSLY COME AS SOMETHING OF A SHOCK TO HIM. ON THE WINDOW SILL BEHIND SICKERT, THE KNIFE IS STILL RESTING WHERE HE PUT IT. MARIE'S BALLOON ENTERS THE PANEL FROM OFF PIC IN THE F/G.

MARIE: Whatever was that? Is that your pencil broken now?
                        You shouldn't be after pressin' so hard, Mr. Sickert.

MARIE: Now you'll have to sharpen it again.

PANEL 9.

FOR THIS FINAL PANEL WE CLOSE IN UPON THE WINDOW, SO THAT WE CAN NO LONGER SEE EITHER SICKERT OR MARIE. WE JUST SEE THE WINDOW, THE SNOW FALLING OUTSIDE AND THE LITTLE SWEETSHOP ACROSS THE STREET. LYING ON THE WINDOW SILL IS A VERY SHARP KNIFE.

No dialogue

Mary Kelly, *or "Marie," as she Frenchified it, perhaps around the time of the holiday trip to France shown in Chapter 1, page 7 of* FROM HELL, *has something of a romantic attraction for men who delve into the story of the Whitechapel murders. They end up wanting to do something for her. In the movie adaptation of the book they unburdened her of the disagreeableness of a sex scene with a paying customer up against a fence (from Chapter 3) by giving it to another woman. One Ripperologist (Morrison) whimsically imagined traveling back in time to try to save her. And I've probably drawn her too pretty in this sketch.*

Chapter 2, page 4.

In which William Gull, our villain, is introduced, as a child, with his dead father laid out in the parlour. It's interesting that Alan, with 20 pages done, is still seeing these scenes in more acute detail than he knows he can get out of me, for instance the dead body not just having a facial mole, but also a "hair growing stoutly from it." A page like this one does not look like it has room for one more mote of airborne dust, but still, I'm sure that in an alternative universe there is a much more detailed *FROM HELL*. Perhaps its artist, a short, blond Eddie Campbell with 20/20 vision, is still working on it. Perhaps three more publishers have gone bankrupt.

PAGE 4. (1,327 words) PANEL 1.

A NINE-PANEL PAGE HERE, WITH ALL THE PANELS SHOT FROM EXACTLY THE SAME ANGLE. WE ARE IN THE FRONT PARLOUR OF THE GULL FAMILY HOUSEHOLD AT THORPE-LE-SOKEN, IN ESSEX. THE FAMILY IS IN MOURNING AND THUS LONG BLACK DRAPES HANG AT THE WINDOW WHICH WE SEE SQUARE ON IN THE BACKGROUND. THE CURTAINS ARE DRAWN BACK HERE, MAKING A RECTANGLE OF DIFFUSED WHITE LIGHT FILTERING FROM THE DAYLIGHT BEYOND THROUGH THE NET CURTAINS HANGING OVER THE LOWER HALF OF THE WINDOWS. IN THE EXTREME F/G WE SEE THE HEAD AND SHOULDERS OF JOHN GULL, WHO IS DEAD. HE LIES UPON HIS BACK WITH HIS EYES CLOSED, FACING TOWARDS THE CEILING OFF PANEL ABOVE. WE SEE THE MOLE UPON HIS NEAREST CHEEK, PERHAPS WITH A HAIR GROWING STOUTLY FROM IT. HE IS DRESSED MORE FORMALLY THAN WHEN WE LAST SAW HIM, IN HIS BEST SUNDAY TOPCOAT AND TIE. HIS HAIR IS NEATLY GROOMED, HIS FACE MADE PALE AND SOMEHOW ODDLY EFFEMINATE BY THE MORTICIAN'S ART. WE ARE LOOKING AT THIS SCENE THROUGH THE EYES OF YOUNG WILLIAM GULL, AGED TEN, EVEN THOUGH WE CANNOT SEE ANY OF HIM IN THIS FIRST PANEL, AS HE STANDS OFF PANEL TO ONE SIDE OF THE BODY AND LOOKING ACROSS IT, WE SEE BEYOND THE CORPSE THE FIGURE OF A DOCTOR WHO IS JUST TURNING AWAY FROM THE BODY AND WALKING BACK ACROSS THE ROOM TOWARDS MRS.GULL, WHO STANDS NEARER TO THE WINDOW. DRESSED IN BLACK MOURNING CLOTHES, MRS.GULL IS A STURDY AND HANDSOME WOMAN OF MEDIUM HEIGHT AND WITH DARK HAIR, HER MANNER STERN AND FORMIDABLE. YOUNGER THAN HER LATE HUSBAND, SHE IS PERHAPS IN HER LATE FORTIES, AND HAS BORNE SIX CHILDREN OF WHOM WILLIAM IS THE YOUNGEST. HER BOSOM IS LIKE THE PROW OF SOME STATELY OCEAN-GOING VESSEL, AND DESPITE HER NO-NONSENSE DEMEANOUR, SHE IS NOT AN UNATTRACTIVE WOMAN FOR HER AGE. AS THE DOCTOR WALKS SOLEMNLY BACK ACROSS THE ROOM TOWARDS MRS.GULL, AS SHE WAITS BY THE WINDOW LOOKING EXPRESSIONLESSLY TOWARDS HIM, HE IS RATHER SELF-CONSCIOUSLY CLEANING HIS SPECTACLES UPON A SMALL PIECE OF MUSLIN, AS IF TO EMPHASISE THAT HE

HAS FINISHED EXAMINING THE CORPSE AND IS CLEANING HIS SPECTACLES PRIOR TO PUTTING THEM AWAY, READY FOR THE NEXT THING HE MIGHT BE CALLED UPON TO LOOK AT.

DOCTOR: Cholera. Just as the London doctors stated.

DOCTOR: Your barges did well to bring the body back to Thorpe-le-Soken so speedily, Mrs.Gull.

PANEL 2.

HAVING REACHED MRS.GULL WHERE SHE STANDS BY THE WINDOW, THE DOCTOR PAUSES AND STANDS TALKING TO HER, BOTH HALF-TURNED AWAY FROM US, GAZING IDLY OUT OF THE WINDOW AS THEY SPEAK TO EACH OTHER. PUTTING AWAY HIS FOLDED SPECTACLES WITHIN AN INNER JACKET POCKET THE DOCTOR CASTS A GLANCE OF SYMPATHETIC WARNING AT MRS.GULL, WHO LARGELY SEEMS TO IGNORE HIM, GAZING OUT OVER HER GARDENS BEYOND THE WINDOW. IN THE FOREGROUND, ENTERING THE PICTURE AT THE VERY BOTTOM, WE SEE ONE OF WILLIAM'S HANDS. IT VERY TENTATIVELY ENTERS THE PANEL AND STARTS TO REACH SURREPTITIOUSLY TOWARDS THE DEAD FACE OF HIS FATHER. NEITHER HIS MOTHER NOR THE DOCTOR HAVE NOTICED THIS AS THEY STAND CHATTING IN THE BACKGROUND. BEING ONLY TEN, WILLIAM'S HAND IS SMALL BUT QUITE MEATY, IN KEEPING WITH HIS GENERAL PROPORTIONS.

MRS.GULL: Ah, Stockport folk may prefer their locomotives, but we'll stick to our barges.

DOCTOR: A widow running a barge-firm should not LIGHTLY dismiss the Public Railway's COMPETITION, Mrs.Gull...

PANEL 3.

NOW MRS.GULL TURNS AROUND TO FACE US, LOOKING DIRECTLY OUT OF THE PANEL AT US HERE. SHE GIVES A SMALL SMILE, FOND OF HER OFF-PANEL SON AS SHE GAZES AT HIM. THE DOCTOR TOO STANDS HALF-TURNED TO LOOK IN THE DIRECTION THAT MRS.GULL IS ADDRESSING, SO THAT HE TOO IS LOOKING AT US HERE. IN THE FOREGROUND, WILLIAM HAS WHIPPED HIS ENQUIRING HAND BACK OUT OF SIGHT AS HIS MOTHER TURNED AROUND. HIS BALLOON ISSUES FROM OFF PANEL, BUT NOTHING ELSE IS VISIBLE OF HIM HERE. IN THE FOREGROUND, JOHN GULL LIES FACING THE CEILING, EYES CLOSED IN ENDLESS SLEEP.

MRS.GULL: Barge people are not WEAK folk, Doctor. We'll hold our own, and see off Mr. Stephenson's contraption.

MRS.GULL: Won't we, William?

WILLIAM (OFF): Yes, mother.

PANEL 4.

THE TWO ADULTS NOW TURN AWAY FROM WILLIAM AGAIN, THEIR BACKS COMPLETELY TOWARDS US AS THEY GAZE OUT OF THE WINDOW AWAY FROM US. THE DOCTOR HAS HIS HANDS CLASPED BEHIND HIS BACK IN A WAY SOMEHOW CHARACTERISTIC OF HIS PROFESSION. NEITHER OF THEM ARE LOOKING TOWARDS WILLIAM. FROM THE FOREGROUND, HIS CHUBBY HAND ENTERS THE PANEL AGAIN, REACHING SLOWLY AND CAREFULLY TOWARDS HIS DEAD FATHER'S CHEEK.

DOCTOR: I'm sure you'll manage your husband's business splendidly.

DOCTOR: Have you considered moving? Thorpe Estate is pleasant; owned by Guy's Hospital...

DOCTOR: ... but perhaps you're attached to Thorpe-le-Soken?

PANEL 5.

STILL FACING AWAY FROM US AND THUS NOT LOOKING AT EITHER US OR WILLIAM, THE TWO

ADULTS CONTINUE TO TALK. MRS.GULL GAZES OUT OF THE WINDOW AS SHE SPEAKS, WITH THE
DOCTOR LOOKING TOWARDS HER IN POLITE ATTENTIVENESS AS HE LISTENS. NEITHER OF THEM
ARE LOOKING AT WILLIAM. IN THE FOREGROUND, HIS FINGERS REACH OUT AND TAKE HOLD OF
THE EYELID OF THE CORPSE, PEELING IT BACK FROM THE GLAZED EYEBALL SO THAT THE EYE
IS OPEN, AND STARING WITH WHAT LOOKS LIKE ALARM AT THE CEILING.

MRS.GULL: Not especially. We only moved here
seven year back, from Colchester.

MRS.GULL: Even so, we'll not be moving again till I'm
certain that the company is steady without John. He...

PANEL 6.

MRS.GULL TURNS ROUND SUDDENLY, WHEELING AROUND TO STARE AT WILLIAM. SHE SEEMS TO
GLARE AT HIM. THE DOCTOR HALF TURNS TO FOLLOW HER GAZE, ALSO LOOKING AT US AND THE
OFF-PANEL WILLIAM WHOSE EYES WE ARE LOOKING THROUGH. WILLIAM HAS AGAIN WHIPPED HIS
HAND BACK OUT OF THE PANEL HERE, BUT HE HAS LEFT THE EYE OF HIS DEAD FATHER OPEN,
STARING AT THE CEILING WITH A LOOK OF FROZEN APPREHENSION. SINCE THE EYE IS ON THE
SIDE OF THE CORPSE THAT MRS.GULL AND THE DOCTOR CANNOT SEE AS THEY STAND ON THE
OTHER SIDE FROM WILLIAM, THEY REMAIN UNAWARE OF WHAT THE BOY HAS DONE.

MRS.GULL: William? Did you laugh?

MRS.GULL: I thought I heard you laugh, boy.

WILLIAM (OFF):   No, mother. I just made a little sound.

PANEL 7.

PLACING A COMFORTING AND PLACATORY HAND UPON MRS.GULL'S SHOULDER THE DOCTOR TURNS
BACK TOWARDS THE WINDOW AND IN DOING SO TURNS MRS.GULL TOO SO THAT SHE IS NO LONGER
LOOKING AT THE BOY. WILLIAM'S HAND IS STILL OFF PANEL IN THE FOREGROUND NOT DARING
TO REACH INTO THE PICTURE UNTIL HIS MOTHER AND THE DOCTOR HAVE TURNED COMPLETELY
AWAY FROM HIM. HIS MOTHER IS LOOKING AT THE DOCTOR HERE.

DOCTOR: The poor child was doubtless attempting to stifle a sob.

DOCTOR: Tell me, have the children taken their father's death badly
to heart?

PANEL 8.

THE ADULTS ARE NOW BOTH FACING FULLY AWAY FROM US AGAIN AS MRS.GULL SPEAKS AND THE
DOCTOR LISTENS. FROM THE FOREGROUND, WILLIAM'S HAND REACHES INTO THE PICTURE FROM
OFF PANEL AND SWIFTLY PULLS THE WAXY EYELID DOWN OVER HIS FATHER'S STARING ORB,
CLOSING THE EYE ONCE MORE.

MRS.GULL: Bargee's lives are cold, flat things, doctor.
We're not reared to make great displays of sentiment.

MRS.GULL: We've private sorrows, private mirth, and strangers think us
cold fish...

PANEL 9.

SAME SHOT. IN THE BACKGROUND, MRS.GULL AND THE DOCTOR ARE STARING AWAY FROM US OUT
OF THE WINDOW INTO THE WAN SUNLIGHT OUTSIDE. IN THE FOREGROUND, WILLIAM HAS WITHDRAWN
HIS HAND. HIS FATHER'S FACE IS BACK HOW IT WAS IN PANEL ONE, THE EYES CLOSED SO THAT
NONE WOULD SUSPECT THAT HIS ETERNAL SLEEP HAD BEEN EVER SO BRIEFLY DISTURBED.

MRS.GULL: Cold fish with no feelings at all.

Chapter 2, page 5.

I remain very fond of this sequence from William Gull's boyhood. It has a Dickensian humour, playing mischief with stiff old-fashioned English politeness. Here Alan continues to have fun at poor old Mrs. Gull's expense. Note also his addressing me as a comics "theorist." I expect I had already bashed his ear *ad nauseam* with my theory that comics are too much "in thrall to the cinematic principle," with which I will further bash the reader's ears elsewhere in this volume. At 2,204 words, this is the largest piece of script for a single page in *FROM HELL*. It uses a type of panel structure that I will discuss later under Chapter 8 page 32. It's one of my theories.

PAGE 5. (2,204 words) PANEL 1.
NOW WE HAVE THE FIRST OF TWO NINE-PANEL PAGES THAT MAKE UP A SEQUENCE FILLING IN THE FORMATIVE YEARS OF WILLIAM GULL AND EXPLAINING HIS MEANS OF INTRODUCTION TO GUY'S HOSPITAL. THE WAY I WANT TO DO THESE TWO PAGES IS BY MEANS OF RHYTHMIC INTERCUTTING BETWEEN TWO DIFFERENT SCENES. I KNOW THIS WILL PROBABLY FEEL A LITTLE FOREIGN TO YOU AS A TECHNIQUE, BUT I THINK IT'LL WORK AND IN THIS INSTANCE I THINK THE USE OF THE TECHNIQUE IS JUSTIFIED: I NEED TO RELATE, BY MEANS OF DIALOGUE, THE MECHANICAL FACTS OF WILLIAM'S LIFE AT THIS TIME. WE NEED TO ESTABLISH THAT MRS.GULL DID MOVE TO THORPE ESTATE, AS SUGGESTED BY THE UNNAMED DOCTOR IN THE LAST SCENE, AND THAT SHE DID THIS WHEN WILLIAM WAS SIXTEEN. WE NEED TO ESTABLISH THAT ONCE THERE SHE MET A RECTOR HARRISON OF BEAUMONT PARISH RECTORY, WHO AGREED TO PRIVATELY TEACH YOUNG WILLIAM EVERY DAY AT THE RECTORY, AS OPPOSED TO THE HUMBLE VILLAGE SCHOOL THAT WAS ALL OF WILLIAM'S EDUCATION PRIOR TO THIS POINT. THE RECTOR'S MOTIVE IN THIS IS THAT HE FANCIED THE HANDSOME WIDOW GULL. HIS IMPORTANCE LIES IN THE FACT THAT HE WAS THE NEPHEW OF BENJAMIN HARRISON, TREASURER OF GUY'S HOSPITAL, THUS FORGING THE IMPORTANT LINK BETWEEN GULL AND GUY'S. OKAY... NOW ALL THE ABOVE INFORMATION IS NECESSARY BUT IT'S PROBABLY A BIT DULL. (I TYPED 'GULL' THERE AND HAD TO GO OVER IT.) NOW, THE OTHER INFORMATION WE HAVE TO GET OVER, NOT NECESSARILY VERBALLY, IS YOUNG WILLIAM'S FASCINATION AND DELIGHT IN EXAMINING THE FLORA AND FAUNA AVAILABLE IN THE GROUNDS OF BEAUMONT RECTORY. THIS ABSORPTION IN THE INTRICACIES AND BEAUTIES OF NATURE IS ONE OF THE THINGS THAT IS THE KEY TO GULL'S ENTIRE LIFE AND PHILOSOPHY. THE THINGS THAT WE SHOW WILLIAM DOING IN THIS

SEQUENCE ARE, ADMITTEDLY, INVENTION. IT'S KNOWN THAT HE TOOK A WILD DELIGHT IN THE FLORA AND FAUNA AVAILABLE AT THE RECTORY, AND IT IS ALSO KNOWN THAT IN LATER LIFE HE BECAME AN ARDENT VIVISECTIONIST. HE ALSO BELIEVED THAT THERE WAS NO GREATER OR MORE LUCID EXPRESSION OF THE MYSTERIES OF GOD'S WORKINGS THAN IN THE FLAWLESS ARCHITECTURE OF THE ORGANIC BODY. GIVEN THE ABOVE, I DON'T THINK IT'S STRETCHING THINGS TO SUGGEST THAT IF THE ADULT WILLIAM, ENSCONCED IN THE RESPONSIBILITIES OF AGE AND POSITION COULD CHEERFULLY CUT UP LIVING ANIMALS, HE MIGHT IN THE HEADY THROES OF ADOLESCENCE HAVE TAKEN IT UPON HIMSELF TO DISSECT A DECEASED RAT OR TWO. TO ME, IT SEEMS A REASONABLY MILD AND CAUTIOUS ASSUMPTION. ANYWAY, GIVEN THAT WE HAVE THESE TWO NECESSARY STRANDS OF INFORMATION TO IMPART (ONE DETAILED, VERBAL AND DULL; THE OTHER SIMPLE, SILENT AND GORILY FASCINATING) I FIGURE IT'S LEGITIMATE FOR US TO INTERTWINE THEM. WHAT I'M TRYING TO EXPLAIN HERE IS THAT I DON'T THINK THE USE OF THIS TECHNIQUE VIOLATES THE AVOWED SIMPLICITY OF OUR STORY STRUCTURE. BOTH STRANDS ARE CLEARLY EXPLAINED IN THE VERY FIRST PANEL, AND BOTH HAPPEN AT THE SAME TIME, ALBEIT IN DIFFERENT PARTS OF THE SAME RECTORY. BECAUSE ONE OF THE STRANDS OF NARRATIVE IS WHOLLY SILENT, AND BECAUSE THE SCENES WITH WILLIAM ARE ALSO ALL SEEN FROM HIS POINT OF VIEW, THEN I THINK THE WHOLE THING WILL ADD UP TO A FAIRLY SIMPLE AND COHERENT READING EXPERIENCE. (SEE HOW NERVOUS I GET WHEN I'M WORKING WITH A RESPECTED COMIC BOOK THEORIST LIKE YOURSELF? ALL THAT WRITHING AND WRIGGLING JUST TO ASSURE YOU I'M NOT GETTING FLASHY).

ANYWAY, IN THIS FIRST PANEL WE ARE SLIGHTLY BEHIND MRS.GULL AS SHE STANDS ON THE FRONT DOORSTEPS OF THE RECTORY OF THE PARISH OF BEAUMONT. IT IS A SUNNY DAY, AND SHE IS DRESSED SOBERLY, ALTHOUGH IN SLIGHTLY MORE SUMMERY ATTIRE THAN USUAL. THE HEAVY OAK FRONT DOOR OF THE RECTORY IS OPEN, AND WE SEE RECTOR HARRISON STANDING IN THE DOORWAY SMILING AS HE USHERS MRS.GULL WITHIN, PERHAPS TAKING HER HAND LIGHTLY AND COURTEOUSLY AS HE DOES SO. SHE RETURNS HIS SMILE. (I HAVE NO PHOTO REFERENCE OF EITHER RECTOR HARRISON OR HIS UNCLE BENJAMIN, WHOM WE MEET IN A COUPLE OF PAGES TIME. THEY AREN'T MAJOR CHARACTERS, AND ONLY APPEAR THIS ONCE, SO DRAW THEM HOW YOU LIKE. I SEE THE RECTOR AS A BESPECTACLED CLERIC IN HIS EARLY FORTIES; A CELIBATE MAN WHO DOES A LOT OF WRITHING IN THE DEAD OF NIGHT AND WHO CLEARLY IS IN THE EARLY STAGES OF AN ABIDING LOVE AND LUST FOR MRS.ELIZABETH GULL, WIDOW OF THIS PARISH). AS WE SEE THE RECTOR IN THIS PANEL HE HAS TAKEN MRS.GULL'S HAND LIGHTLY IN ONE OF HIS OWN, WHILE WITH HIS OTHER HAND HE GESTURES TOWARDS THE INTERIOR OF THE RECTORY, BEYOND THE OPEN DOOR. MRS.GULL SMILES POLITELY AS SHE STEPS FORWARD IN OBEDIENCE OF HIS ENTREATY TO ENTER.

RECTOR HARRISON: My dear Mrs.Gull.

RECTOR HARRISON: Welcome to Beaumont Rectory. I take it young William is
                     already off exploring the grounds?

MRS.GULL: You can be sure he is, Rector Harrison. Never knew a child
                     so keen on nature.

PANEL 2.

NOW WE CUT TO A PANEL SEEN THROUGH THE EYES OF YOUNG SIXTEEN-YEAR-OLD WILLIAM GULL, SO THAT ALL WE CAN SEE OF HIM ARE HIS THICKENING RUDDY FOREARMS AND HIS BROAD,

LONG-FINGERED HANDS. HE IS ON HIS KNEES INSPECTING AN AREA OF THE UNDERGROWTH
SOMEWHERE IN THE GROUNDS OF BEAUMONT RECTORY WHILE HIS MOTHER CHATS WITH RECTOR
HARRISON INDOORS. IT'S A HOT SUMMER DAY, SLIGHTLY AFTER NOON, AND AS WILLIAM KNEELS
THERE IN THE GRASS THAT PRICKS HIS KNEES, HE GLORIES IN THE THICK AND SICKLY GREEN
SCENT OF THE VEGETATION; THE SMELL OF INSECT SEX AND HIS OWN SIXTEEN-YEAR-OLD
SWEAT. THE SUN BURNS RED UPON THE BACK OF HIS THICK NECK, BUT ALL WE CAN SEE HERE
ARE HIS HANDS, WHICH ARE JUST IN THE ACT OF PLUCKING A PARTICULARLY LUSCIOUS AND
RARE-LOOKING ENGLISH WOODLAND FLOWER (I'LL LEAVE IT UP TO YOU WHAT TYPE... IF YOU
HAVE ANY FAVOURITES OR IF THERE'S SOME SPECIES WITH A NAME THAT SEEMS RESONANT
TO MATTERS AT HAND THEN PLEASE STICK IT IN). IMMEDIATELY BEYOND THE FLOWER IS AN
IMPENETRABLE TANGLE OF GREENERY, SUCH AS ONE MIGHT FIND AROUND THE BASE OF A WILD
HEDGEROW, WITH THORN-STUDDED BRAMBLE STEMS LOOPING STIFFLY DOWN INTO THE PICTURE
FROM OFF AND FORMING PART OF THE CLOSE-UP WALL OF GREENERY IMMEDIATELY BEYOND THE
DELICATE FLOWER THAT YOUNG WILLIAM'S HANDS ARE SEEN PICKING HERE.
No dialogue.

PANEL 3.

BACK TO MRS.GULL AND THE RANDY RECTOR. WE ARE NOW INSIDE THE RECTORY, IN ONE OF ITS
SPACIOUS AND BOOK-LINED WITHDRAWING ROOMS, LIGHT FALLING IN THROUGH THE TALL AND
NARROW STATELY WINDOWS OFF TO ONE SIDE. THE RECTOR STILL HAS NOT RELINQUISHED HIS
LIGHT GRIP UPON MRS.GULL'S HAND, AND IS LEADING HER ACROSS THE ROOM TOWARDS ONE OF
THE TWO ELEGANT ARMCHAIRS THAT ARE ARRANGED WITH A LOW TABLE SET BETWEEN THEM. UPON
THIS LOW TABLE RESTS A SILVER TEA SERVICE COMPRISING SUGAR BOWL, MILK JUG, TEA POT,
TWO TEA CUPS WITH SPOONS AND SAUCERS AND A PITCHER OF JUST-BOILED WATER WITH A LID
TO KEEP IN THE HEAT. AS HE LEADS MRS.GULL WITH ONE HAND, HIS OTHER HAND IS ALREADY
REACHING FOR ONE OF THE ARMCHAIRS, PULLING IT UP FOR HER AS SHE STEPS TOWARDS IT.
SHE LISTENS TO THE RECTOR'S WORDS WITH A LOOK OF POLITE INTEREST, WHILE THE RECTOR
AFFECTS WHAT HE HOPES IS AN AUTHORITATIVE AIR. FACIALLY, HE ISN'T A TREMENDOUSLY
ATTRACTIVE MAN. PERHAPS HE HAS A WEAK CHIN, OR A SMILE THAT CANNOT HELP BUT LOOK
INGRATIATING AND CREEPY. A RESPECTED MINOR CHARACTER ACTOR PLAYING A CREEPY VICAR
IN AN EALING FILMS PRESENTATION WOULD SEEM ABOUT THE MARK TO AIM FOR WITH RECTOR
HARRISON, ALTHOUGH NOT OVERDONE TO THE POINT OF FARCE.

RECTOR HARRISON: At sixteen, William is hardly a child. Still, I'm glad he's
                      taken your move to Thorpe Estate so well.
RECTOR HARRISON: At very least it would appear our flora and fauna are of
                      interest to the boy.

PANEL 4.

NOW ANOTHER SHOT THROUGH WILLIAM'S EYES, STILL ON HIS KNEES INSPECTING THE SAME
PATCH OF UNDERGROWTH. WITH THE PLUCKED FLOWER NOW HELD IN ONE HAND, HE IS USING
BOTH HANDS TO GINGERLY SEPARATE THE LOOPING STRANDS OF BRIAR, AS IF TO PEER INTO
THE DARKNESS IMMEDIATELY BEYOND THEM. PERHAPS HE HAS A WHITE LINEN HANDKERCHIEF
WRAPPED AROUND THE BRIAR STEM HE GRASPS MOST FIERCELY, TO PROTECT HIS HAND FROM THE
THORNS. NOT SATISFIED WITH HIS FLOWER AS A PRIZE, HE DIGS DEEPER INTO THE FOLIAGE

TO SEE WHAT OTHER TREASURES MAY BE UNEARTHED.
No dialogue.

PANEL 5.
BACK IN THE RECTORY DRAWING ROOM. IN THE BACKGROUND, WE SEE MRS.GULL SEATED
DAINTILY UPON ONE OF THE ARMCHAIRS. MORE TOWARDS THE FOREGROUND WE SEE RECTOR
HARRISON AS HE COMES TOWARDS US, REACHING OUT TO DRAW UP HIS OWN CHAIR, HIS BACK
TURNED BRIEFLY TO MRS.GULL AS SHE SPEAKS TO HIM. NEVERTHELESS, EVEN THOUGH HE FACES
US HIS EYES SWIVEL SIDEWAYS, AS IF VAINLY ATTEMPTING TO SEE OVER HIS SHOULDER TO
WHERE MRS.GULL SITS BEHIND HIM. THE EFFECT UPON HIS FACE IS SOMEHOW CRAFTY AND
WATCHFUL, BUT SINCE HE IS FACING AWAY FROM HER, MRS.GULL DOES NOT SEE THIS AND
CONTINUES TO CHAT LIGHTLY AND PLEASANTLY.

MRS.GULL: Aa. I just wish he'd put his interest into proper learning.
He talks of nothing but going to sea.

RECTOR HARRISON: What BETTER basis for an education than the appreciation of
Nature in all her terrible glory?

PANEL 6.
WE ARE BACK ON OUR KNEES, LOOKING THROUGH WILLIAM'S EYES. HIS HANDS HAVE DRAWN BACK
THE BRAMBLES LIKE A PAIR OF PAINFUL AND PRICKLY CURTAINS TO REVEAL THE DARK AND
LEAFY ENCLOSURE BEHIND THEM, OPENING IT TO THE LIGHT OF THE EARLY AFTERNOON SUN. IN
THE LITTLE HOLLOW AMONGST THE WEEDS AND BRIARS THERE LIES A DEAD RAT, PERHAPS DEAD
LESS THAN A DAY, ITS GREY BODY ALREADY STIFF AND HARD TO THE TOUCH, LIKE A HARD
STUFFED TOY RATHER THAN A FLESH AND BLOOD ANIMAL. AS WILLIAM'S HANDS DRAW BACK THE
BRIARS TO REVEAL THE DEAD RAT, THE FLOWER DROPS FROM HIS HAND, FORGOTTEN IN THE
THRILL OF THE MOMENT AND THE SUPERIOR CHARMS OF THIS NEW DISCOVERY.
No dialogue.

PANEL 7.
IN THE FOREGROUND NOW, MRS.GULL SITS IN PROFILE TO US, SO THAT WE SEE THE STATELY
BATTLESHIP LINE OF HER BOSOM SWELLING OUT IN A SHAPELESS BUT FORMIDABLE HUMP
AGAINST THE BODICE OF HER HIGH-NECKED DRESS. HER HEAD SHOULD PERHAPS BE OFF
PANEL ABOVE HERE, SO THAT ALL WE SEE IS THE CURVE OF HER BUST AND HER HANDS
FOLDED DEMURELY UPON HER LAP. LOOKING BEYOND THIS WE SEE THE RECTOR AS HE LOWERS
HIMSELF DOWN INTO THE ARMCHAIR JUST ACROSS THE LOW TEA TABLE FROM MRS.GULL. HE
IS STARING FIXEDLY AT MRS.GULL'S BOSOM AS HE SPEAKS. HE LOOKS A LITTLE FLUSHED
AND UNCOMFORTABLE, QUITE OVERCOME BY THIS VISION FROM WHICH HE CANNOT WRENCH HIS
TORMENTED EYES. MRS.GULL'S PHYSICAL PRESENCE OBVIOUSLY QUITE UNSETTLES THE POOR
MAN, THOUGH SHE IS BY NO MEANS A RAVING BEAUTY BY MOST MODERN STANDARDS.

RECTOR HARRISON: Why, the very foundation of science and medicine
lies in a preoccupation with natural forms...

RECTOR HARRISON: Their workings; their shapes...

RECTOR HARRISON: The very marvel in them, that moves men's hearts.

PANEL 8.

BACK ON OUR KNEES IN THE FOLIAGE, LOOKING THROUGH WILLIAM'S EYES. HIS HANDS ARE BOTH RAISED REVERENTLY BEFORE HIM AND CUPPED IN THEM IS THE STIFF CORPSE OF THE DEAD RAT. (IT'S JUST STRUCK ME THAT YOU MIGHT PREFER A BIRD INSTEAD OF A RAT, IN WHICH PLACE PLEASE MAKE THE SUBSTITUTION. ANY SMALL ANIMAL WILL DO, SO ADAPT THIS AS YOU SEE FIT). THE RAT JUST RESTS THERE IN WILLIAM'S POWERFUL YOUNG HANDS, AN OBJECT OF AWE AND REVERENCE WHERE SECONDS BEFORE IT HAD BEEN ONLY THE MEREST CARRION.
No dialogue.

PANEL 9.

BACK INSIDE THE RECTORY, IN THE CENTRE OF THIS PANEL WE HAVE THE TEA TABLE. FROM THE LEFT ENTER THE KNEES OF MRS.GULL, HER HANDS FOLDED PRIMLY UPON THEM. FROM THE RIGHT ENTER THE KNEES AND AT LEAST ONE HAND BELONGING TO RECTOR HARRISON. HE IS CAREFULLY POURING HOT WATER FROM THE JUG INTO THE TEAPOT, WITH STEAM BILLOWING UP INTO THE PANEL. BOTH HIS AND MRS.GULL'S BALLOONS ISSUE FROM OFF PANEL TO THEIR RESPECTIVE SIDES. LOOKING BEYOND THE TEA TABLE TO THE BACKGROUND WE PERHAPS SEE ONE OF THE ROOM'S WINDOWS, THE TREES AND GRASS AND FLOWERS SWAYING IN THE SUMMER BREEZE OUTSIDE. (WHOOPS. JUST NOTICED THAT ONLY MRS.GULL IS SPEAKING HERE, SO SCRATCH THAT BIT ABOVE ABOUT THE RECTOR'S DIALOGUE ISSUING FROM OFF. HE HASN'T GOT ANY. ALL WE SEE OF HIM ARE HIS HANDS AND HIS KNEES AS HE SITS POURING HOT WATER INTO THE TEA POT. MRS.GULL'S HANDS PERHAPS GESTURE AS SHE SPEAKS FROM OFF PANEL. SEE WHAT LOOKS BEST TO YOU).

MRS.GULL (OFF):   Such talk, Rector Harrison. It makes me quite giddy.

MRS.GULL (OFF):   Besides, our William's tutoring at village school is all a widow's income can afford him, providing little opportunity for such fine notions to bear fruit.

The mousie...

Alan invited me above to select a relevant English wildflower. Being far away in Australia, I don't think I gave it as much thought as I should have. I know I made rather a bad job of the rodent the first time out. I originally drew the dead rat in this scene very badly. In one of our various revisions I had a chance to revise it, and I've darkened this so you can see how much whiteout is in the redrawing. (See the panel in place on facing page, dead centre.) I fixed it by grabbing a Beatrix Potter book out of the hands of a nearby child and casting Samuel Whiskers as the poor unfortunate animal. Potter sure knew her mousies.

Chapter 2, page 6.

Continuing with the boy Gull's dissection of the rodent and the Rector's interview with the widow Gull. This is some of Alan's best writing in the FROM HELL scripts. Returning to Rich Kreiner's essay, referred to in my introduction: *"Naturally the **From Hell** scripts slow our pace radically. More leisurely scrutiny is encouraged and greater discovery promoted: it was fresh revelation, dawning only with the scripts, that as the child Gull splits open a dead field mouse, he, in our company, was divining an oracle. We, as he, read the entrails and clearly see the future: there's blood on his hands."* (*TCJ* 173, Dec. 1994)

PAGE 6. (1,269 words) PANEL 1.
ANOTHER NINE PANELS, FOLLOWING THE SAME PATTERN AS ON PAGE FIVE. WE OPEN HERE WITH
A SHOT THROUGH WILLIAM'S EYES AS HE KNEELS. IN THE IMMEDIATE BACKGROUND, THE DEAD
ANIMAL HAS BEEN PLACED CAREFULLY SO AS TO LIE UPON ITS BACK AT THE CENTRE OF WILLIAM'S
OUTSPREAD HANDKERCHIEF. IN THE FOREGROUND, WE SEE WILLIAM'S HANDS. HE IS CAREFULLY
OPENING UP AN OLD-FASHIONED-LOOKING PEN KNIFE. IT LOOKS LIKE IT HAS A GOOD EDGE TO IT.
No dialogue.

PANEL 2.
BACK IN THE RECTORY, WE HAVE THE SEATED FIGURE OF RECTOR HARRISON IN THE F/G
ROUGHLY HEAD AND SHOULDERS TO HALF FIGURE. HE IS MORE OR LESS IN PROFILE TO US
HERE. HE'S FINISHED POURING THE TEA, BUT THE STEAM HAS FOGGED HIS WIRE RIMMED
SPECTACLES, AND HE HAS REMOVED THEM HERE TO WIPE THEM CLEAN WITH HIS HANDKERCHIEF.
AS HE SPEAKS TO MRS.GULL HE DOES NOT MEET HER GAZE BUT RATHER LOOKS DOWN AT THE
GLASSES AS HE WIPES THEM FREE FROM FOG AND CONDENSATION WITH SMALL CIRCULAR
MOVEMENTS OF HIS LINEN-ENSHROUDED FINGERS. ACROSS THE TABLE FROM HIM AND THUS
FACING US FROM THE IMMEDIATE BACKGROUND WE SEE MRS.GULL. HER MOUTH OPENS SLIGHTLY
AND HER EYES WIDEN IN SURPRISE AS THE RECTOR MAKES HIS OFFER. SHE HADN'T EXPECTED
THIS, BUT THEN SHE DOESN'T REALISE THE EXTENT OF THE RECTOR'S CRUSH UPON HER.

RECTOR HARRISON: A shameful waste of one so bright. How would it be if I
should tutor him myself each day, here at the Rectory?

RECTOR HARRISON: Then we shall see what disciplines he turns his hand to
best.

PANEL 3.

BACK IN THE UNDERGROWTH LOOKING THROUGH WILLIAM'S EYES. STEADYING THE STIFF DEAD
RODENT IN ONE HAND, POSITIONED BELLY UP, WILLIAM PUSHES THE KNIFE BLADE INTO THE CENTRE
OF ITS LOWER BELLY AND DRAWS IT UP THROUGH THE TOUGH AND RESISTANT TISSUE, EXPOSING
A WET AND STICKY DARKNESS WITHIN. ALREADY DEAD, THE VAGUELY DISAPPOINTED-LOOKING
MINIMALIST FEATURES OF THE RAT REGISTER NO EXTRA DISTRESS AT THIS FURTHER OUTRAGE OF ITS
CORPOREAL FORM. THE KNIFE SLICES UPWARD, PARTING FUR, PARTING SKIN AND MUSCLE.
No dialogue.

PANEL 4.

IN THE RECTORY WE HAVE A FLOOR-LEVEL SHOT, DOWN BY MRS.GULL'S FEET, WHICH WE SEE
IN THE FOREGROUND HERE. THOUGH SHE SITS WITH HER LEGS CAREFULLY AND PRUDENTLY CROSSED
BENEATH HER VOLUMINOUS SKIRTS, THE HEM OF IT HAS INADVERTENTLY RIDDEN UP TO REVEAL
PERHAPS THREE QUARTERS OF AN INCH OF FLESH IN THE VICINITY OF MRS.GULL'S ANKLE, JUST
ABOVE THE TOP OF HER BLACK LACE-UP BOOTS. AS WE LOOK BEYOND THIS WE SEE THE SEATED
RECTOR HARRISON, FULL FIGURE IN THE BACKGROUND AND LOOKING TOWARDS US. HE IS JUST
RESETTLING THE GLASSES (NOW WIPED CLEAN) UPON THE BRIDGE OF HIS NOSE, AND AS HIS
WORLD SWIMS BACK INTO FOCUS IT SEEMS THAT HIS GAZE IS FIXED UPON THE LIMITED EROTIC
VISTAS OF MRS.GULL'S ANKLE (A SLIGHTLY THICK ONE AT THAT, IT MUST BE ADMITTED). THE
RECTOR, IN DANGER OF BECOMING AN ERECTOR, CROSSES HIS OWN LEGS CONCEALINGLY AND
SHIFTS A LITTLE AGAINST THE HARDNESS OF HIS CHAIR. SOMEWHERE WITHIN THE ROOM, A
CLOCK TICKS AS DUST MOTES TUMBLE IN THE SUNBEAMS. THE LACE OF MRS.GULL'S UNDERSKIRT
RUSTLES INAUDIBLY AGAINST THE CHEAP SILK OF HER STOCKINGS. THE RECTOR SWEATS.

MRS.GULL (OFF):   Oh, I could not impose upon you so. Surely you'd soon grow
                       tired with both of us?
RECTOR HARRISON: With one so charming?
RECTOR HARRISON: Dear Mrs.Gull, I should as soon grow tired with life itself.

PANEL 5.

BACK IN THE UNDERGROWTH, THE OPENING INCISION HAS BEEN MADE AND THE STICKY KNIFE
SET DOWN TO ONE SIDE. THE RAT LIES ON ITS BACK, LEGS SKYWARDS, THERE AT THE CENTRE
OF THE BLOOD-SPECKED HANDKERCHIEF. A SLIGHTLY CYNICAL-LOOKING SIDEWAYS SMILE HAS
BEEN OPENED IN THE FLESH OF ITS STOMACH, AND HERE WE SEE WILLIAM'S BLOOD-BLACKENED
AND STICKY FINGERS PULLING BACK THE LIPS OF THE SMILE TO THRUST INSIDE AFTER THE
TINY, EXPOSED ORGANS. THE SMELL OF BLOOD AND SHIT AND RATS' INNARDS MIXES WITH
THAT OF GRASS AND SWEAT AND SUNSHINE IN WILLIAM'S EXCITED NOSTRILS. THE MOMENT IS
TIMELESS AND GLASSY, GLAZED BY THE BUMBLEBEE-QUIET OF THE SUMMER AFTERNOON.
No dialogue

PANEL 6.

VIRTUALLY A REPLAY OF PANEL TWO UPON THIS PAGE IN TERMS OF CAMERA ANGLE NOW AS WE
CUT BACK TO THE RECTORY. IN THE FOREGROUND, RECTOR HARRISON IS REACHING OUT WITH ONE
HAND TO LIFT THE SILVER TEAPOT. WITH HIS OTHER HAND HE GESTURES TO MRS.GULL, PALM
OUTWARD IN DENIAL OF HER DAZED PROTESTATIONS. EYES CLOSED PIOUSLY AND MOUTH A PRIM
LITTLE BUD IF YOU WANT TO SEE THE RECTOR'S FACE... OTHERWISE HIS FACE COULD BE OFF PANEL

AND JUST HIS HANDS VISIBLE HERE. UP TO YOU. ACROSS THE TABLE, MRS.GULL LOOKS FLUSTERED AND ASTONISHED. ONE HAND RAISES UNCONSCIOUSLY TO LIGHTLY TOUCH THE LINEN SLOPES OF HER UPPER BREAST. HER EYES ARE WIDE AND SURPRISED AS SHE GAZES AT THE RECTOR.

MRS.GULL: Wh-why Rector Harrison, I...

RECTOR HARRISON: Hush. It is settled. Let us hear no more of it.

RECTOR HARRISON: My uncle Benjamin is treasurer at Guy's Hospital. Who
                        knows? In time your son may find his true vocation there...

PANEL 7.

WE ARE LOOKING THROUGH WILLIAM'S EYES AT HIS HANDS, WHICH ARE RAISED BEFORE HIS FACE. IN THE UPPER HAND, BETWEEN FINGER AND THUMB, HE HOLDS THE CARDIAC AND DIGESTIVE SYSTEMS OF THE DEAD RAT, REMOVED FROM ITS OPEN CHEST. THE DELICATE LITTLE RUBBER TUBES AND THE KIDNEY-BEAN-PIP MINIATURE ORGANS GLISTEN WETLY IN THE SUNSHINE, A SMALL AND STICKY BUNCH OF GRAPES FROM WHICH THE STALE BLACK WINE STILL DRIPS. WILLIAM'S OTHER HAND IS DIRECTLY BENEATH THE HAND HOLDING UP THE ORGANS FOR INSPECTION. THE DRIPPINGS FROM THE EVISCERATED INNARDS FALL DOWN TO SPLASH IN A TINY POOL FORMED AT THE CENTRE OF WILLIAM'S BROAD, UPTURNED PALM. EVERYTHING IS STILL. WILLIAM HOLDS HIS BREATH.

No dialogue.

PANEL 8.

BACK IN THE RECTORY, WE ARE LOOKING NOW THROUGH THE EYES OF WILLIAM'S MOTHER, MRS.GULL. PERHAPS ALL WE CAN SEE OF HER ARE HER HANDS CROSSED DEMURELY AND ALMOST PROTECTIVELY UPON THE SLIPPERY FABRIC OF HER KNEE. LOOKING ACROSS THE TABLE, WE SEE THE RECTOR. WITH ONE HAND HOLDING THE LIFTED AND STEAMING TEAPOT AND THE OTHER STEADYING ONE OF THE BONE CHINA CUPS READY TO POUR, HE LOOKS UP BRIGHTLY THROUGH HIS SPECTACLES AT US, LEANING FORWARD ACROSS THE TABLE PERHAPS A LITTLE MORE THAN ONE WOULD REALLY WANT HIM TO IN HIS ATTITUDE OF EAGER ENTREATY. HE SMILES, HIS DESIRE TO IMPRESS HIMSELF ROMANTICALLY UPON MRS.GULL ABSURDLY OBVIOUS BEHIND HIS ATTEMPT AT A RESTRAINED RECTORAL FAÇADE.

RECTOR HARRISON: ...may find a calling deep enough to make him quite
                        forget the ocean's lure.

RECTOR HARRISON: Now, how do you prefer your tea, dear Mrs.Gull...

RECTOR HARRISON: Or might I know you as "Elizabeth"?

PANEL 9.

FINAL SHOT THROUGH WILLIAM'S EYES. WE CLOSE IN UPON THE IMAGE IN PANEL SEVEN, SO THAT ALL WE SEE HERE IS THE LOWER OF WILLIAM'S TWO HANDS, THE PALM UPTURNED TO CATCH THE BLOOD AND THE DEAD JUICES THAT DRIP INTO THE PICTURE FROM OFF PANEL ABOVE. THE POOL IN THE CENTRE OF WILLIAM'S HAND HAS STARTED TO BRIM OVER, THIN BLACK RIVULETS RUNNING DOWN ACROSS THE BLADE-EDGE OF WILLIAM'S HAND TO TRICKLE ROUND, DEFYING GRAVITY, AND GATHER AT HIS KNUCKLES, WHENCE THEY DRIP IN SMALL BEADS TOWARDS THE OFF-PANEL SPEARS OF GRASS BELOW. ALL THE TIME, FRESH DROPLETS CONTINUE TO SPLASH INTO WILLIAM'S PALM FROM ABOVE. IT'S ALL VERY HOLY AND MYSTERIOUS, A PERSONAL GRAIL REVEALED.

No dialogue.

Chapter 2, page 18.

A portrait of Queen Victoria. Alan and I debated Queen Victoria's part in the narrative, with regard to how the chain of command would have worked. To solve the problem of a prominent player not being a Mason as Knight asserted, Alan gave the Queen a more hands-on role in the affair than the Masonic cover-up theory had previously attributed to her. I argued that this would create more problems than it solved, by having the Queen appear to so blatantly command (of William Gull) an assassination (of Annie Crook, the sweetshop girl).

"Well, how else would she command it?" asked Alan.

Never having eavesdropped in the corridors of power, I had no idea, and still haven't got one. Nevertheless, on page 28 of this chapter, Alan ameliorated the Queen's words *"We have promised our grandson that she shall not be killed, but if this scandal is not to rock the throne, she must be SILENCED. We leave it in your hands, Sir William."* to *"We have promised our grandson that she will not feel the fullest extent of our displeasure,"* etc. And the changed lettering on that page, you can see if you look carefully, doesn't quite fit in the space allotted to it.

PAGE 18. (991 words) PANEL 1. (edited to show panel 1 only)
NOW WE HAVE A FOUR-PANEL PAGE, THE FIRST OF TWO IN A SEQUENCE DETAILING AN ENCOUNTER BETWEEN DR. WILLIAM GULL AND HER IMPERIAL MAJESTY, VICTORIA REGINA. THE MAIN POINT TO GET OVER IN THESE TWO PAGES, ASIDE FROM THE OBVIOUS PLOT POINTS LIKE GULL'S APPOINTMENT AS PHYSICIAN IN EXTRAORDINARY AND SO ON, IS THE SHEER BROODING MONUMENTAL PRESENCE OF VICTORIA. SHE WASN'T JUST A FUNNY LITTLE OLD WOMAN WHO SAID, "WE ARE NOT AMUSED" AND REFUSED TO PASS LEGISLATION AGAINST LESBIANS BECAUSE SHE SIMPLY DIDN'T BELIEVE THAT SUCH CREATURES EXISTED. SHE WAS A HOLY TERROR OF A QUEEN, A MONARCH WHO'D PRESIDED OVER THE BUILDING OF BRITAIN'S GREAT EMPIRIC ADVENTURE, A PRESENCE AT THE HEART OF ONE OF THE WORLD'S GREATEST POWER-BLOCS. HER FAMILY AND SERVANTS WERE ALL SHIT-SCARED OF HER, AND FOR HER PART SHE SEEMS TO HAVE HAD LITTLE TIME FOR ANY OF THEM, HOLDING EVEN HER OWN FAMILY IN OBVIOUS CONTEMPT MUCH OF THE TIME. AT THE SAME TIME, SHE WAS THE QUEEN WHO'D GONE INTO A TRULY MONUMENTAL SULK UPON THE DEATH OF HER HUSBAND ALBERT, A SULLENNESS HEWN IN MARBLE AND ENDURING FOR DECADES WHILE THE EMPIRE BEGAN TO ATROPHY AND

ROT ALL AROUND HER. SHE IS A PRESENCE THAT HAS SOMEHOW TRANSCENDED MORTAL LIMITS AND ENTERED HISTORY WITHIN HER OWN LIFETIME, A WOMAN EMOTIONALLY AND POLITICALLY DEAD LONG BEFORE HER ELABORATE FUNERAL. IT IS THIS QUALITY IN VICTORIA, STONE-LIKE, HISTORIC AND MONUMENTAL THAT I WANT TO CONVEY HERE, AND THE WAY THAT I WANT TO DO IT IS BY USING A TENSE AND REPETITIVE SEQUENCE OF STATIC PANELS. YOU'LL SEE WHAT I MEAN AS WE GO ALONG, HOPEFULLY. THIS FIRST PAGE HAS ONE BIG PANEL AT THE TOP THAT TAKES UP TWO THIRDS OR THREE QUARTERS OF THE WHOLE PAGE AREA. BENEATH THIS THERE ARE THREE PANELS THAT GRADUALLY CLOSE IN UPON A DETAIL OF THE OPENING IMAGE. THE FIRST AND BIGGEST PICTURE IS A SHOT OF QUEEN VICTORIA SITTING IN A HUGE AND SHADOWY STONE CHAMBER, ALL ALONE, SOMEWHERE WITHIN BUCKINGHAM PALACE OR THEREABOUTS. THE ROOM IS UNBEARABLY DARK BUT WITH SUGGESTIONS OF HUGE PILLARS AND ARCHES RISING ABOUT THE WALLS OF THE CHAMBER IN THE BACKGROUND, INDISTINCT AND SHADOWY MASSES AGAINST THE MIASMIC DARK OF THE CHAMBER. PERHAPS HUGE DRAPES AND TAPESTRIES EQUALLY DARK, HANG IN A DUST-BOUND SILENCE FROM SOME PARTS OF THE CHAMBER, PERHAPS CONCEALING WINDOWS AND BLOCKING OUT THE LIGHT. THE CHAMBER IS ALMOST BARE, AND IN THE CENTRE OF IT UPON A RAISED STONE SEAT, CUSHIONED WITH SUMPTUOUS FABRICS AND PLUSH BOLSTERS, SITS HER IMPERIAL MAJESTY, SHOWING US THE DISTINCTIVE PROFILE THAT LAUNCHED A THOUSAND POSTAGE STAMPS. THE ONLY SOURCE OF LIGHT IN THE ROOM, A COMPARATIVELY WEAK ONE, SEEMS TO BE ISSUING FROM OFF PANEL LEFT, BEHIND VICTORIA AS SHE SITS FACING TO THE RIGHT. HER FACE IS THEREFORE COMPLETELY OBLITERATED BY A MASK-LIKE BLOT OF SHADOW, WITH ONLY THE BACK OF HER HEAD AND A LITTLE OF THE SIDE OF HER FACE ILLUMINATED HERE. SHE SITS PERFECTLY STILL IN THE SHADOWS, AS IF CARVED OUT OF THE SHADOWS HERSELF. SHE ALREADY LOOKS LIKE ONE OF THE STATUES THAT WILL BE ERECTED AFTER HER DEATH, SO UNEARTHLY IS HER MOTIONLESSNESS. SHE DOESN'T LOOK ROUND AS SHE SPEAKS, AND HER SPEECH BALLOON IS A SMALL THING, HANGING IN THE ECHOING VASTNESS OF HER CHAMBER OF MOURNING. THE QUEEN WEARS MOSTLY BLACK, WHICH TENDS EVEN MORE TO MAKE HER OUTLINE BLEED INTO THE SHADOWS OF THE CHAMBER, HEIGHTENING HER VISUAL AMBIGUITY.

VICTORIA: Dr. Gull.

Drawing paper

With this chapter I introduced a variant art technique. I intended at the time to play around a great deal more with different approaches, but the instances of half-tone wash in Chapter 5 caused some difficulty in reproduction and I played safe after that. In this one I had found a type of paper with a "linen" textured surface. It took ink without bleeding, and I found that I could drag a black crayon over the white paper, and white crayon over black ink also, to obtain an effect I had seen in some early twentieth-century political cartoons. I employed this paper all through Chapter 2 and then brought it back for Chapter 10. It invariably photocopied well, but sometimes it has printed very murkily. However, it looks good in the most recent editions of the book, suggesting that the idea wasn't entirely stupid.

Chapter 3, page 7.

The significant action of Chapter 3 is the coming together of Marie Kelly and her friends. Marie's knowledge of the illegitimate royal baby, which she has just delivered to Sickert in Cleveland Street, leads to the writing of the blackmail letter that starts the terrible wheels of Fate turning. I don't know if it's deliberate but Liz's glass is described as "half full" in panel 1 and in panel 8 it's "half empty."

PAGE 7. (1,476 words) PANEL 1
THIS PAGE HAS NINE PANELS, IN THREE TIERS OF THREE, AND WE CONTINUE WITH OUR BARROOM DIALOGUE BETWEEN THE TWO PROSTITUTES. THE FIRST TIER ON THIS PAGE, THINKING ABOUT IT, WOULD PROBABLY WORK JUST AS WELL AS A WIDE PANEL, OR PERHAPS AS A CONTINUOUS BACKGROUND SHOT THAT SPANS THE WHOLE WIDTH OF THE TIER BUT WHICH IS DIVIDED INTO THREE SMALLER PANELS. OUR BASIC POINT OF VIEW IS THE REVERSE OF THAT MIDDLE TIER ON PAGE SIX, IN THAT WHILE WE STILL SEE LIZ AND MARIE IN PROFILE WE ARE NOW ON THE OTHER SIDE OF THE TABLE, STANDING JUST INSIDE THE WINDOW, SO THAT THE TABLE IS UP IN THE FOREGROUND WITH LIZ SITTING IN PROFILE ON THE LEFT, MARIE IN PROFILE ON THE RIGHT AND THE BAR AND ITS DENIZENS VISIBLE ACROSS THE TABLETOP DIRECTLY BEYOND THEM. IF YOU DO DECIDE TO DO THIS AS A CONTINUOUS BACKGROUND SHOT DIVIDED INTO THREE RATHER THAN AS ONE BIG WIDE PANEL, THEN IN THE FIRST SMALL PANEL WE SEE LIZ STRIDE, SITTING ROUGHLY IN PROFILE AND FACING RIGHT, STILL WEARING THE SAME MOURNFUL LOOK AS IN OUR LAST PANEL ON PAGE 6, AS SHE CONTINUES TO RECOUNT THE STORY OF HER EARLY YEARS. PERHAPS SHE STILL HAS HER CHIN RESTING IN HER HAND. HER GLASS IS HALF FULL ON THE TABLE BEFORE HER AS SHE GAZES DREAMILY ACROSS IN MARIE'S DIRECTION. (MARIE IS NOT VISIBLE HERE, BEING SEATED OVER ON THE FAR RIGHT OF THIS TIER, IN PANEL THREE IF YOU DECIDE TO GO WITH THE CONTINUOUS-BACKGROUND-DIVIDED-INTO-THREE IDEA. BEYOND LIZ, LIFE IN THE STYGIAN AND SMOKE-WREATHED BARROOM GOES ON AS NORMAL.

LIZ: England... so ugly! Once, in Torslanda, I am Elizabeth Gustafsdotter, on my parents beautiful farm, Stora Tumlehe.

LIZ: Now, in England married, I am Elizabeth Stride.

PANEL 2.
PANNING ACROSS WE NOW JUST HAVE A SHOT OF THE TABLE BETWEEN THE TWO WOMEN, WITH THE BEER GLASSES RESTING UPON IT. LOOKING BEYOND THIS, WE SEE MORE OF THE BAR AND THE SHADOWY INDISTINCT FIGURES OF THE COSTERMONGERS LEANING AGAINST IT, VISIBLE THROUGH THE PALL OF TOBACCO SMOKE. LIZ'S BALLOONS ENTER THE PANEL FROM OFF-PIC LEFT HERE.

LIZ: Arrived, we live by canal, Limehouse Cut. I see the ugly

Limehouse church, and I am thinking of Torslanda.

LIZ: It makes me alone, that church.

PANEL 3.

CONTINUING TO PAN ACROSS THIS CONTINUOUS BACKGROUND WE REACH MARIE, SITTING FACING LEFT OVER ON THE RIGHT-HAND SIDE OF THE TABLE OPPOSITE LIZ. SYMPATHIZING STRONGLY WITH LIZ'S OBVIOUS DISENCHANTMENT WITH ENGLAND, MARIE MERELY LOOKS GLOOMILY INTO HER BEER... OR PERHAPS, TO SET UP A BIT OF MINOR BUSINESS FOR THE NEXT PANEL, SHE COULD BE TURNED AWAY FROM US AND FUMBLING AWKWARDLY WITH ONE OF HER BOOTS, STARTING TO TAKE IT OFF SO THAT WE CAN MAYBE SEE HER MASSAGING HER FOOT IN THE NEXT PANEL. IT'S NOT ESSENTIAL, IT'S JUST SOMETHING NATURAL SHE'D BE DOING IF SHE'S JUST SPENT THE LAST HOUR OR SO WALKING BACK TO THE EAST END FROM CLEVELAND STREET. IN EITHER EVENT, IF WE CAN SEE HER EXPRESSION HERE SHE LOOKS SORT OF RESIGNEDLY GLOOMY ABOUT THE CONDITION OF ENGLAND.

MARIE: Ah, they've some ugly buildings, the English. I'm the same
                      about Ireland... or even Wales, where we lived after.

MARIE: Anywhere but bloody London.

PANEL 4.

NOW IF THIS WORKS OUT, THE FIRST TWO PANELS OF THIS TIER ARE ANOTHER CONTINUOUS BACK-GROUND SHOT. IN IT, WE HAVE REVERSED ANGLES SO THAT WE'RE NOW ON THE OTHER SIDE OF THE TABLE, FACING THE WINDOW. WE HAVE ALSO DROPPED DOWN TO FLOOR LEVEL SO THAT IN THIS NEXT PANEL AND THE NEXT ONE WE ARE SEEING ONLY THE LOWER HALVES OF THE TWO WOMEN AS THEY SIT FACING EACH OTHER ACROSS THE TABLE. IN THIS PANEL WE SEE THE LOWER HALF TO THREE QUARTERS OF MARIE KELLY AS SHE SITS FACING TOWARDS THE RIGHT BUT PERHAPS TURNED SLIGHTLY TOWARDS US HERE. IF IT WORKS, AND LOOKS GOOD AS A PIECE OF BUSINESS, WE SEE THAT MARIE HAS TAKEN OFF ONE OF HER SHOES AND IS RUBBING HER SORE FOOT THROUGH THE RIBBED BLACK MATERIAL OF HER STOCKINGS, ATTEMPTING TO SOOTHE THE BLISTERS INCURRED BY HER WALK FROM CLEVELAND STREET. BOTH HER BALLOON AND THE BALLOON OF LIZ STRIDE ENTER INTO THIS PANEL FROM OFF-PIC ABOVE...FROM THE LEFT AND RIGHT-HAND SIDE RESPECTIVELY.

MARIE: It's like you in Limehouse: I lived near that awful George's
                      church, on Ratcliffe Highway.

LIZ: Bad place. Once they hang pirates there, I'm hearing...

PAGE 5.

PANNING ACROSS WE NOW SEE THE LOWER HALF OF LIZ STRIDE, HER HEAD AND SHOULDERS OFF PANEL ABOVE AS SHE SITS FACING TOWARDS THE OFF-PANEL MARIE. IF WE CAN SEE HER HANDS SHE IS JUST RAISING HER GLASS AGAIN HERE TOWARDS HER OFF-PANEL LIPS TO SIP FROM IT. BENEATH THE TABLE, LYING THERE WITH ITS MUZZLE RESTING ON ITS PAWS, WE PERHAPS SEE THE MONGREL DOG THAT I SUGGESTED THAT YOU SHOW TROTTING AROUND THE PUB EARLIER, ITS BELLY RESTING CONTENTEDLY IN THE SAWDUST... MARIE'S BALLOONS ISSUE FROM OFF PANEL LEFT HERE.

MARIE (OFF):   Hangin' and WORSE! Why, they buried the Ratcliffe Highway
                      murderer at a crossroads, stake through his heart an' all.

MARIE (OFF):   Why'd you leave your farm?

PANEL 6.

NOW, UP TO THE RIGHT OF THE FOREGROUND, IN PROFILE AND FACING LEFT, WE HAVE THE FACE

OF LIZ STRIDE. SHE GAZES INTO SPACE WITH HER SAD EYES AND GIVES A SELF-DEPRECATING LITTLE SMILE AT THE THOUGHT OF HER YOUTHFUL FOLLY IN PREFERRING THE BRIGHT LIGHTS OF GOTHENBURG TO THE DREARINESS OF TORSLANDA. LOOKING BEYOND HER AND ACROSS THE TABLE WE SEE MARIE KELLY SIPPING FROM HER HALF PINT OF BEER, STARING KEENLY AT LIZ OVER THE RIM OF THE GLASS AS SHE DOES SO, INTERESTED TO HEAR THIS BIG SWEDISH GIRL'S STORY.

LIZ: Haha. At seventeen, not thinking so much of farms, I go working as servant at Gothenburg. Lars Olofsson. Man with three children.

PANEL 7.

SAME SHOT, BUT IN THE FOREGROUND LIZ'S EXPRESSION HAS LOST ITS LITTLE SMILE, AND SHE JUST LOOKS SAD. THIS ISN'T FUNNY. THIS GUY IN GOTHENBURG AND HIS STILLBORN BABY FUCKED UP LIZ'S ENTIRE LIFE, AND THAT'S WHY SHE'S HERE IN LONDON AT PRECISELY THE WRONG TIME AND THAT'S WHY WITHIN A LITTLE OVER A MONTH SOMEONE WILL SLICE HER THROAT OPEN IN BERNER STREET. HER EYES LOOK MOMENTARILY DEADENED WITH THE SADNESS OF HER LIFE, AND THE SMILE EVAPORATES FROM HER LIPS AS SHE RECOUNTS THE STORY. ACROSS THE TABLE, MARIE KELLY HAS LOWERED THE GLASS FROM HER LIPS AND IS LOOKING AT LIZ WITH A SORT OF WINCE OF SYMPATHY, A SLIGHT SYMPATHETIC GRIMACE CONTORTING ONE CORNER OF THE MOUTH.

LIZ: Four years, every night in my bed he wants me not as his wife, but as servant. When I expect baby, He say "GO".

LIZ: Now I am here. Even born dead, baby changes our life, I think.

PANEL 8.

CHANGE ANGLES. IN THE FOREGROUND ALL WE CAN SEE OF MARIE KELLY IS ONE OF HER HANDS AS SHE RAISES HER HALF-EMPTY GLASS ALOFT INTO THE PANEL, PROPOSING A SOLEMN TOAST TO THE CONTINUING REGULARITY OF THE MENSTRUAL PROCESS. LOOKING BEYOND THE GLASS AND MARIE'S UPRAISED HAND WE CAN SEE LIZ SITTING OPPOSITE US, ONCE MORE CONJURING HER WEAK LITTLE SMILE AS SHE LOOKS UP AT WHAT MARIE IS DOING. HER EYES, HOWEVER, ARE FILLED WITH SADNESS AND LOSS. MARIE'S BALLOON ISSUES FROM OFF-PANEL LEFT.

MARIE: I've got friends as wouldn't argue. Here's to next month's blood, Long Liz. Here's to the curse.

PANEL 9.

IN THIS FINAL PANEL WE CUT AWAY TO A STILL SHOT OF CHRIST CHURCH SPITALFIELDS. IT FILLS THE BACKGROUND HERE, WHILE IN THE FOREGROUND WE SEE AN ANONYMOUS BLACK MAN FROM THE WEST INDIES. HE WEARS A LONG LINEN SMOCK AND HAS A CAREFULLY LETTERED COPPERPLATE SIGN HUNG ROUND HIS NECK, WHICH DECLARES HIM TO HAVE BEEN BATHED IN THE BLOOD OF THE LAMB. AS THE NEGRO STANDS THERE IN THE STREET, A TEPID AND GRIMY RAIN IS JUST STARTING TO FALL FROM THE GREY BLANKET OF CLOUD UP ABOVE. AS THE RAIN DROPLETS TRICKLE OVER HIS BLACK SKIN LEAVING INVISIBLE TRAILS OF SOOT HE TURNS HIS EYES UPWARDS AND STARES MISERABLY INTO THE OVERCAST LONDON SKY. HE DOESN'T KNOW WHAT THE FUCK HE'S DOING HERE. HE ISN'T AT ALL IMPORTANT TO OUR STORY AND WE NEVER SEE HIM AGAIN, BUT I THOUGHT IT WOULD BE NICE TO INCLUDE A SHOT OF HIM AS AN EXAMPLE OF THE UNEXPECTED EXOTICISM OF VICTORIAN LONDON. AS HE STANDS IN THE FOREGROUND HERE, CHRIST CHURCH REARS UP BEHIND HIM, ITS SICKLY WHITE SPIRE THREATENING TO SCAR THE CLOUDS. THE CHURCH IS MORE IMPORTANT THAN THE BLACK GUY HERE. HE'S JUST A BIT OF FOREGROUND BUSINESS THAT WE HAVE TO LOOK BEYOND TO SEE THE PALLID, HUNGRY STONE MONSTER IN THE BACKGROUND, WAITING IN THE RAIN.

No dialogue

Chapter 3: rethink.

The line of dialogue on panel 8 on the facing page, "Here's to next month's blood," reminds me that chapter 3 was once going to be titled *The Harlot's Curse*. That was presumably in the synopsis that Alan gave me over the telephone way back in 1988. I wasn't keen on it at the time, but that was probably because I didn't fully understand its significance.

Re-reading page 7 and some near it (pgs 16,17,18), I'm thinking we must have been having a crisis (as Alan and Bill Sienkiewicz were having on *Big Numbers* around the same time, late 1990). In his review from which I have already quoted, Kreiner also drew attention to "missteps" and "opportunities missed" between the script and the finished art. Alan's descriptions may have veered close to impossible around this time (see my introduction), but my finished pages are also oversimplified. Losing the split-panel technique and all those shifting "camera angles" is perhaps one thing; I like to start with the simplest possible arrangement and then work from there. But I could have made a very nice study of Marie massaging her weary foot at panel 3. I've drawn it now to see how it might have looked.

Panel 9 contains a whole character that I have treated very shabbily. Alan writes: "He isn't important to our story. He doesn't know what the fuck he's doing here." However, Alan describes him so knowingly that I wonder, knowing nothing about "altered states," when you go through the doors of perception: is this guy the "meet and greet" on the other side? As a belated penitential offering, I've drawn a new panel of him too.

Having drawn him, I'm now thinking he looks like he's just about to get involved in the story on the next page. I probably went through all this head-wrenching back and forth the first time around.

Chapter 3, page 15.

Following the previous selection, Marie and Liz were joined by Annie Chapman and Polly Nichols. The four women have now composed their blackmail letter and leave the Ringer's pub, prior to Marie walking all the way back to Cleveland Street to deliver it to Sickert. This page brings together the four Ripper victims who allegedly knew each other; and it relates them to the symbolic Christ Church of Hawksmoor, the significance of which was established by Gull in Chapter 2, and will be elaborated in 4. It also gives us Alan's interesting conceit of "the four whores of the Apocalypse," which sounds to me like one of those fortuitous ideas a writer gets on the wing. It's in the after-the-fact noticing of a pattern you've made that demands not to be ignored. In the script Marie's final balloon comes from off-panel, but I saw a chance to get both the women and the church in one picture so that the church is *"stalking"* them (as Kreiner observed). Fortuitous ideas also occur at the art stage.

PAGE 15. (938 words) PANEL 2. (panel 1 edited out for space)
NOW WE ARE IN BRUSHFIELD STREET WITH THE WOMEN, LOOKING DOWN IT TOWARDS THE FOREGROUND AND PERHAPS CLOSER TO THE RIGHT WE HAVE ANNIE CHAPMAN AND MARIE KELLY AS THEY WALK TOWARDS US. BEHIND AND FURTHER TO THE LEFT WE SEE POLLY NICHOLS IN THE NEAR BACKGROUND AS SHE BUSTLES ROUND THE CORNER FROM CRISPIN STREET LOOKING ANXIOUS AND TRYING TO KEEP UP WITH THE OTHERS. ANNIE CHAPMAN DOESN'T LOOK AT POLLY AS SHE SPEAKS TO HER, BUT IS STARING KEENLY AT MARIE KELLY. MARIE DOESN'T LOOK AT ANNIE BUT JUST LOOKS STRAIGHT AHEAD OF HER, THE WAY SHE'S GOING. SHE SEEMS VERY CALM. UP TO YOU WHETHER WE CAN SEE LIZ STRIDE OR NOT. IF WE CAN SHE IS SOME WAY BEHIND ANNIE AND MARIE BUT NOT AS FAR AWAY AS POLLY, HOBBLING AROUND BEHIND HER. AROUND THE WOMEN THE NIGHT HAS THE DARKNESS OF DIRTY WATER: A SENSE OF DARK SEDIMENT CHURNING.

POLLY:	Wait for ME! I don't like walkin' on me own...
ANNIE:	Oh, shut up and don't be so daft.
ANNIE:	Now, 'ave you got that letter safe, Marie?

PANEL 3.
NOW PERHAPS A PROFILE SHOT OF AS MANY OF THE FOUR WOMEN AS YOU CAN FIT IN COMFORTABLY, WALKING FROM LEFT TO RIGHT ACROSS THE PANEL. POLLY HAS PERHAPS CAUGHT UP HERE, BUSTLING ANXIOUSLY INTO THE PANEL FROM THE LEFT AND LOOKING TOWARDS ANNIE CHAPMAN AS SHE SPEAKS TO HER. IF WE CAN SEE HER, LONG LIZ STRIDE MERELY LOOKS ON AND HOLDS HER PEACE.

REMEMBER THAT LIZ IS CONSIDERABLY TALLER THAN THE OTHER WOMEN, SO YOU SHOULD HAVE A GOOD MIX OF DISTINCTIVE PHYSICAL TYPES TO ARRANGE YOUR PICTURES AROUND.

MARIE: 'COURSE I have. I've not spent all night writin' it to wipe me arse on it now, have I?

POLLY: Shall ye deliver it tonight?

PANEL 4.

WE ARE NOW PROBABLY STANDING AT THE BOTTOM OF THE STEPS OF CHRIST CHURCH, LOOKING ACROSS TOWARDS BRUSHFIELD STREET AS THE FOUR WOMEN COME AROUND THE CORNER AND START TO WALK ACROSS THE STREET TOWARDS US. SINCE CHRIST CHURCH IS DIRECTLY BEHIND US WE CAN SEE NO TRACE OF IT HERE. WE ARE PROBABLY TOO FAR AWAY TO MAKE OUT MUCH ABOUT THE WOMEN HERE, BUT WE CAN PROBABLY TELL WHO THEY ARE FROM THEIR BUILDS AND POSTURES. ANNIE TUBBY, LIZ TALL, POLLY HUDDLED, MARIE DEFIANT. THEY ARE ABOUT TO WALK ACROSS THE TRAM LINES AS WE SEE THEM COMING TOWARDS US HERE.

MARIE: Aa. I could use a walk.

ANNIE: Not me. I'm off lookin' for trade to buy me supper.

ANNIE: I'm starvin'. Only 'ad broken biscuits all day.

PANEL 5.

CHANGE ANGLE NOW. THE WOMEN HAVE CROSSED THE STREET AND ARE NOW WALKING FROM LEFT TO RIGHT ACROSS THE PANEL, ALONG THE PAVEMENT IMMEDIATELY IN FRONT OF CHRIST CHURCH. AS WE SEE THEM HERE, THE STEPS OF CHRIST CHURCH AND PERHAPS THE LOWER REACHES OF THE DORIC PILLARS ARE IMMEDIATELY BEHIND THEM. THE WHORES DO NOT LOOK AT CHRIST CHURCH AS THEY PASS IT BY BUT CONTINUE TO TALK AMONG THEMSELVES.

MARIE: Sure, an I'll take sore feet over a sore fanny any time.

LIZ: Oh, do not speak of it, when I have my ulcers.

PANEL 6.

SAME SHOT, BUT HERE THE WOMEN ARE WALKING OFF THE RIGHT HAND SIDE OF THE PANEL, MARIE LAUGHING AS SHE TALKS TO LIZ STRIDE. IN THE IMMEDIATE BACKGROUND, UNNOTICED BY THE WOMEN, THE STEPS OF CHRIST CHURCH RISE UP AND AWAY FROM US, INVITING US UP UNDER THEIR INHUMANELY BIG PORTICO. MARIE KELLY'S LAUGHTER, BRIGHT AND INFECTIOUS THOUGH IT IS, IS A SMALL THING NEXT TO THE AGE AND POWER AND BRUTAL MASS OF CHRIST CHURCH.

MARIE: Ha ha ha ha

MARIE: Her with her STARVATION, you with yer PLAGUES, an POLLY with her DEATH THREATS...

PANEL 7.

THIS FINAL BIG PANEL IS A SHOT OF CHRIST CHURCH SPITALFIELDS STANDING THERE, AWFUL AND ALONE AGAINST THE MIASMIC NIGHT. I FIGURE WE ARE LOOKING AT THE UPPER REACHES OF THE CHURCH HERE, WITH THE MASSIVE SPIRE RISING UP ABOVE THE GIGANTIC PORTICO: ONE MAN'S STRANGE AND TWISTED EGO IN CORPSEWHITE STONE AND BUILT TO LAST FOR ALL ETERNITY. MARIE'S LITTLE SPEECH BALLOON ISSUES UP FROM OFF PANEL DOWN TOWARDS THE BOTTOM RIGHT OF THE PANEL HERE, HER WORDS DRIFTING BACK ALONG THE STREET TOWARDS US AS SHE WALKS ON, LEAVING US TO GAZE UP AT THE PALLID HELLCHURCH, LOOMING ABOVE US, A TOMB OF DEAD GODS.

MARIE (OFF): We're the four whores of the Apocalypse.

Part 2
The theme is
Alan Moore's London.
This is where his interest
in psychogeography
begins. This part runs
from here to page 93.
See also pages 102-107
in the colour
section.

Chapter 4, page 1.

Alan Moore's concept for this chapter is audacious. It comprises 38 pages of a horror comic in which the protagonist drives around London giving a lecture on architecture. There are two pages in this chapter that make an interesting juxtaposed contrast: page 1, in which Alan makes some very bold decisions, and page 23 (see later), in which he has a crisis of confidence in the plan he sets up here at the beginning.

In comparing script and image, you may think that I'm disregarding the scene as imagined by Alan. But I had the whole chapter in front of me and judged that these flashbacks at the beginning would work well as unframed and imprecise recollections with the coach thrust up front instead of coming from afar, giving a dynamic contrast as an opener. If we were to be concerned that it was going to be a challenge to hold the reader's interest, why not begin with a loud call to attention.

PAGE 1. (1560 words) PANEL 1.
HELLO, EDDIE. SORRY IT'S BEEN SO LONG IN COMING, AND I HOPE IT'S WORTH THE WAIT. BIT OF A FUNNY EPISODE ALL ROUND, THIS: IT'S THE LONGEST TO DATE, AND YET, UNLIKE THE GULL EPISODE, IT ISN'T STAGED IN A RAPID SUCCESSION OF ONE OR TWO-PAGE SCENES THAT HOP ABOUT ALL OVER THE PLACE AND THUS SUSTAIN THE READERS' INTEREST MORE EASILY. WHAT WE HAVE HERE, WITH THE EXCEPTION OF THE FIRST TWO OR THREE PAGES, IS ONE LONG CONTINUOUS SCENE THAT ALL TAKES PLACE OVER THE COURSE OF A SINGLE DAY, AND ALL REVOLVES AROUND A SINGLE CONVERSATION-CUM-LECTURE THAT IS DELIVERED TO JOHN NETLEY BY SIR WILLIAM GULL ON THE OCCASION OF THEIR COACH-JAUNT AROUND THE CITY OF LONDON. IN TERMS OF SUSTAINING A CONVERSATION OVER THIRTY ODD PAGES, I THINK YOU'LL AGREE THAT IT PRESENTS SOME POTENTIALLY SERIOUS STORYTELLING PROBLEMS. IN LIGHT OF THIS, I SPENT A LONG WHILE TRYING TO THINK OF WAYS TO TART THE STRIP UP USING CONTINUOUS BACKGROUND PANELS OR SIMILAR VISUAL DEVICES. I THOUGHT OF LIBERALLY SPRINKLING THE STORY WITH FLASHBACK PANELS TO THE ANCIENT TIMES THAT GULL IS TALKING ABOUT, SO THAT WE COULD LIVEN THINGS UP BY SHOWING BOADICEA IN THE HEAT OF BATTLE, OR HAWKSMOOR CACKLING, RUBBING HIS HANDS TOGETHER AND SACRIFICING CHICKENS AS THEY LAY THE FOUNDATIONS TO CHRIST CHURCH. THINKING ABOUT IT, HOWEVER, I THOUGHT "NAHH". THE

BEST WAY TO DO THIS STORY, I'VE CONCLUDED, IS ABSOLUTELY STRAIGHT AND WITHOUT
EMBELLISHMENT; RATHER LIKE A DRY VOCAL MIX IN A RECORDING STUDIO AS OPPOSED
TO LOTS OF ECHO AND REVERB AND WHATEVER. OF COURSE, THIS WILL ALSO BE THE MOST
DIFFICULT WAY TO DO THE PIECE, BUT I THINK IF WE JUST HAVE CONFIDENCE IN THE
NARRATIVE, WE CAN MANAGE IT.

BROOK STREET, TOWARDS THE GROSVENOR SQUARE END. IT IS AROUND SIX O'CLOCK IN
THE MORNING ON THE FIFTEENTH OF AUGUST, 1888, AND IT IS NOT YET LIGHT. A LOW
BLANKET OF LUKEWARM MIST AND FOG ROLLS THROUGH THE STREETS, LIKE GREY AND GASEOUS
TUMBLEWEEDS, AND EVERYTHING IS STILL. THE HIGH HOUSES TO EITHER SIDE OF THE
STREET ARE SILENT, AND THE ONLY SOUND IS THAT OF DISTANT HOOVES UPON COBBLES,
GROWING SLOWLY CLOSER. AWAY DOWN THE END OF THE STREET WE SEE THE RELATIVELY
SMALL AND INDISTINCT APPARITION THAT IS JOHN NETLEY'S COACH AS IT APPROACHES
THROUGH THE MURK, ITS CARRIAGE LANTERNS BURNING WITH A WEAK AND SULPHUROUS LIGHT.
NETLEY HIMSELF IS ALL BUT INVISIBLE, A BLACK WART PROTRUDING FROM THE BLACK AND
BOX-LIKE SHAPE OF THE CARRIAGE AS IT RATTLES THROUGH THE PRE-DAWN GLOOM TOWARDS
US. THIS EPISODE'S TITLES GO, AS USUAL, IN THE WHITE SPACE TO THE LEFT OF THE
OPENING IMAGE, WITH THE OPENING CAPTION SET IN THE FIRST PANEL ITSELF.

TITLES (IN WHITE SPACE):   Chapter Four

                                     "What doth the Lord require of thee?"

CAPTION (IN FIRST PANEL):   Brook Street, London. August, 1888.

PANEL 2.

THE REMAINING TWO TIERS ON THIS PAGE HAVE THREE PANELS EACH, AND CONSTITUTE THE
FIRST IN OUR SEQUENCE OF THREE FLASHBACKS. THIS FIRST FLASHBACK TAKES PLACE IN A
RECEPTION ROOM, SOMEWHERE WITHIN BUCKINGHAM PALACE, AND WE SHOW THE WRETCHED AND
DISTRAUGHT WALTER SICKERT AS HE SHOWS THE BLACKMAIL LETTER THAT HE HAS RECEIVED
TO ALEXANDRA, THE PRINCESS OF WALES. IN THIS FIRST PANEL, RIGHT UP CLOSE IN THE
FOREGROUND, WE CAN SEE THE SLIM WRIST AND HAND OF THE PRINCESS, ENTERING THE PANEL
FROM OFF TO ONE SIDE AND HOLDING THE BLACKMAIL LETTER THAT WE SAW LAST EPISODE. IT
NEEDN'T BE CLOSE ENOUGH FOR US TO READ IT ALL, BUT WE SHOULD AT LEAST BE ABLE TO
SEE IT CLEARLY ENOUGH FOR THE READERS TO BE AWARE THAT IT IS THE SAME LETTER THAT
THEY SAW AT THE CLOSE OF OUR LAST EPISODE. LOOKING BEYOND THIS, INTO THE SPACIOUS
AND BEAUTIFULLY FURNISHED DEPTHS OF THE ROYAL RECEPTION ROOM, WE SEE WALTER SICKERT
AS HE SITS THERE SLUMPED IN A SUMPTUOUS ARMCHAIR, HIS ELBOWS RESTING ON HIS KNEES
AND HIS HEAD IN HIS HANDS, LONG FINGERS RUNNING DISTRACTEDLY THROUGH HIS SANDY
HAIR. HE DOESN'T LOOK UP AT US OR AT THE OFF-PANEL PRINCESS ALEXANDRA AS HE SPEAKS,
BUT SEEMS LARGELY TO BE CONDUCTING A DIALOGUE OF WRETCHEDNESS WITH HIMSELF. MORNING
SUNLIGHT, PEARLY AND DIFFUSE, FALLS THROUGH THE HIGH WINDOWS INTO THE TICKING-CLOCK
STILLNESS OF THE RECEPTION ROOM, WHILE FROM THE WALLS OLD MASTERS REGARD THE SCENE
DISPASSIONATELY WITH YELLOWED OIL-PAINT EYES.

SICKERT: You're the only person I can turn to, Alix. You're Eddy's
                                  mother...

SICKERT: You see, I just don't have the money. They think I'm rich, but...

PANEL 3.

WE REVERSE ANGLE NOW, SO THAT SICKERT AND HIS CHAIR ARE OVER TO THE RIGHT OF THE
FOREGROUND, WITH PRINCESS ALEXANDRA VISIBLE OVER TOWARDS THE LEFT OF THE BACKGROUND
AS SHE STANDS THERE, HER PROFILE SLIGHTLY TURNED TOWARDS US, READING AND RE-READING
MARY KELLY'S LETTER WITH AN EXPRESSION OF REGRET UPON HER CALM AND QUITE BEAUTIFUL
FEATURES. IN THE FOREGROUND, SICKERT SITS UP A LITTLE, REMOVING HIS HEAD FROM HIS
HANDS SO THAT HE CAN EMPLOY THEM TO MAKE VAGUE, WRETCHED GESTURES IN THE AIR BEFORE
HIM AS HE SITS, PALM UPWARDS AS IF IN EXPLANATION OR SUPPLICATION. THROUGHOUT, HE
KEEPS HIS HAUNTED GAZE FIXED ON THE FLOOR IN FRONT OF HIM, HIS FACE DESPERATE AND
WRETCHED WITH ANXIETY. HE CANNOT LOOK AT ALEXANDRA WHILE HE SPEAKS, AND FOR HER PART
SHE CONTINUES TO READ THE LETTER AND DOES NOT LOOK AT HIM. WE CAN TELL, HOWEVER, THAT
SHE IS LISTENING TO HIS PITIFUL MONOLOGUE WITH AT LEAST HALF AN EAR AS SHE CAREFULLY
RE-READS THE FATEFUL MISSIVE.

| SICKERT: | Well, sometimes I AM, when I've SOLD something, but I don't manage money well, and... |
| SICKERT: | Oh, it's all my fault. You trusted Eddy to me, and I let all this happen: The baby, the wedding... |

PANEL 4.

SAME SHOT, ONLY HERE, IN THE FOREGROUND, SICKERT CLOSES HIS EYES AND LETS HIS HEAD
SINK BACK INTO HIS HANDS IN A GESTURE OF COMPLETE SURRENDER TO DESPAIR AND MISERY.
HIS EYES ARE SCREWED TIGHTLY SHUT AS IF TRYING TO BLOT OUT HIS GUILT AND SELF-
DISGUST, BUT TO NO AVAIL. LOOKING BEYOND HIM, WE SEE ALEXANDRA AS SHE STANDS THERE IN
THE OPALESCENT LIGHT OF THE MORNING ROOM. SHE LOWERS THE LETTER THAT SHE HAS
BEEN READING, BUT DOES NOT PUT IT DOWN. IT HANGS THERE IN HER HAND AS SHE TURNS HER
HEAD TO CALMLY REGARD SICKERT WITH AN EXPRESSION OF DEEP SYMPATHY AND PITY. SHE IS
A KINDLY WOMAN, WHO, FOR THE MOST PART, THINKS AS LITTLE OF THE FAMILY THAT SHE HAS
MARRIED INTO AS THEY DO OF HER. SHE IS THEREFORE NOT UNMOVED BY SICKERT'S PLIGHT,
NOR WITHOUT REGRET IN THE COURSE THAT SHE KNOWS SHE MUST ADOPT. SHE GAZES SADLY AND
STEADILY AT SICKERT'S BOWED HEAD AS HE SITS THERE AND WHIMPERS, PITIFULLY.

| SICKERT: | Oh God, Alix... |
| SICKERT: | What am I going to DO? |

PANEL 5.

WE CHANGE ANGLES NOW, SO THAT AS WE SEE SICKERT HERE HE IS SITTING IN PROFILE TO US,
FACING RIGHT, STILL WITH HIS BROW SUNK IN HIS HANDS. OUR EYE LEVEL IS ROUGHLY THE
SAME AS SICKERT'S IN THIS PANEL, SO ALL WE CAN SEE OF PRINCESS ALIX AS SHE APPROACHES
HIM FROM BEHIND IS A VIEW FROM, SAY, HER SHOULDERS DOWNWARDS, WITH HER HEAD AND
SHOULDERS OFF PANEL UP TOWARDS THE TOP LEFT. SHE REACHES OUT WITH ONE AFFECTIONATE
AND MOTHERLY HAND AND PLACES IT TENDERLY UPON SICKERT'S SHOULDER, A FRAGILE GESTURE
OF CONSOLATION. IN HER OTHER HAND, SHE HOLDS THE LETTER. SICKERT, SUNK DEEP IN THE
WELL OF HIS OWN MISERY, DOES NOT LOOK ROUND AT HER AS SHE SPEAKS FROM BEHIND HIM, OR
RESPOND TO HER LIGHT TOUCH UPON HIS SHOULDER. HE IS INCONSOLABLE. SINCE HER HEAD AND
SHOULDERS ARE OFF PANEL, ALIX'S BALLOONS ISSUE FROM OFF HERE.

```
ALIX (OFF):          Poor Walter.
ALIX (OFF):          Of course, you understand that after the trouble last time,
                     I won't be able to keep this to myself?
ALIX (OFF):          I'm sorry, Walter, but it's Victoria...
```

PANEL 6.

NOW WE HAVE A SHOT AS IF LOOKING UP THROUGH SICKERT'S EYES AS HE LIFTS HIS HEAD
AND LOOKS WEARILY AND UNCOMPREHENDINGLY UP AT THE PRINCESS, WITH SICKERT HIMSELF
NOT VISIBLE HERE. WE LOOK UP INTO ALEXANDRA'S SAD AND PITYING GAZE AS SHE STARES
DOWN AT US WITH A WORLD OF SORROW AND REGRET IN HER EYES. SHE DOESN'T LIKE THE
COURSE OF ACTION THAT SHE MUST TAKE UP, BUT IT IS THE ONLY ONE OPEN TO HER.

```
ALIX:                Victoria will have to be told.
```

PANEL 7.

IN THIS LAST PANEL, WE CHANGE OUR POINT OF VIEW FROM THE LAST SHOT SO THAT WE ARE
NOW LOOKING DOWN, AS IF THROUGH THE EYES OF THE PRINCESS, INTO THE UPTURNED FACE
OF WALTER SICKERT AS HE SITS THERE IN THE PLUSH ARMCHAIR. WE REALLY ONLY SEE HIS
HEAD AND SHOULDERS HERE, LOOKING UP AT US AND THE OFF-PANEL PRINCESS WITH A LOOK
OF DULL, SICK HORROR ON HIS FACE. HAVING SEEN WHAT HAPPENED TO ANNIE CROOK FOR
AN INNOCENT AND UNINTENTIONAL TRANSGRESSION OF THE ROYAL WILL, SICKERT CANNOT
EVEN BEGIN TO DIMLY IMAGINE WHAT MIGHT BE IN STORE FOR THOSE WHO WOULD ATTEMPT
PREMEDITATED BLACKMAIL. HE LOOKS UP AT US, PUPILS DILATED BY SUDDEN COLD DREAD.
HE IS IN HELL ALREADY, WAITING FOR THE REST OF OUR CAST TO JOIN HIM.

No dialogue

Ripperology

Alan rejected Knight's 1976 claim that Sickert was an accomplice in the murders. Jean Overton Fuller in Sickert and The Ripper Crimes (1990) *made him the actual murderer. Patricia Cornwell's* Portrait of a Killer: Jack the Ripper — Case Closed (2002) *took it a step further, going so far as to extract DNA evidence from both a painting and Ripper correspondence in police archives to make it stick.* "Cornwell's book was released to much controversy, especially within the British art world, where Sickert's work is admired, and also among 'Ripperologists,' who dispute her research methods and conclusions. Cornwell has lashed back at these critics, claiming that, if she were a man, or British, her theory would have been accepted." (*Wikipedia*) *But this loony sport came too late to be included in our appendix,* The Dance of The Gull Catchers, *a satirical account of the history of 'Ripperology.'*

Chapter 4, page 4.

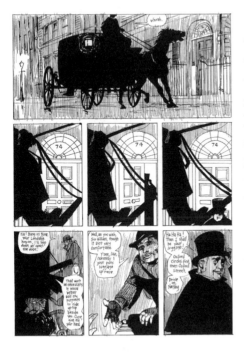

In the descriptions for this page, Alan writes, "I want Gull to be an increasingly unsettling and powerful figure as this book unfolds." In a recent live interview, I found myself improvising some blather about horror story villains that are bought "off the shelf," such as vampires and werewolves. That is, the writer can obtain some ready-made evil that saves him the trouble of having to actually build it himself. I saw a possible landing from my oral flight by bringing the subject around to Alan's fictitious William Gull (by the time we were halfway through, we felt it would be improper to still think of this literary creation as being entirely biographical). When *FROM HELL* first ran in parts, we did not say it was to be about Jack the Ripper, who is of course a "ready-made" in the form that one usually encounters him. Several parts had appeared before most readers made the Ripper connection. By that time, Alan had already constructed his villain, from childhood up, in Chapter 2.

PAGE 4. (1226 words) PANEL 1.
ANOTHER SEVEN-PANEL PAGE HERE, IN WHICH WE BEGIN OUR NARRATIVE PROPER FOR THIS EPISODE, HAVING DISPENSED WITH THE FLASHBACKS. THE LAYOUT IS THE SAME AS ON THE THREE PRECEDING PAGES IN THAT WE HAVE ONE BIG WIDE PANEL TAKING UP THE TOP TIER AND THEN THREE SMALLER PANELS ON EACH OF THE TWO TIERS BENEATH THAT. THE FIRST PANEL ONCE MORE REPEATS THE SAME BASIC IMAGE AS THE FIRST PANEL ON PAGES ONE, TWO AND THREE, BUT HERE NETLEY'S CARRIAGE IS EVEN CLOSER TO US. IT IS SO CLOSE, IN FACT, THAT WE CAN NO LONGER REALLY SEE THE CARRIAGE: ALL WE CAN SEE IS NETLEY AS HIS TRAJECTORY BRINGS HIM UP CLOSE TO US, SO THAT HE IS STARING AT US HEAD AND SHOULDERS FROM THE CENTRE FOREGROUND, HIS EYES STILL HIDDEN BY THE SHADOWS OF HIS DERBY HAT-BRIM. HE HOLDS THE REINS IN ONE HAND AND THE WHIP FOLDED ACROSS HIS CHEST WITH THE OTHER. HIS THIN LIPS OPEN ONLY SLIGHTLY AS HE GIVES THE COMMAND FOR THE OFF-PANEL HORSE TO STOP, AND HIS FACE IS OTHERWISE COLD AND EXPRESSIONLESS. BEHIND HIM, BROOK STREET IS TANGLED IN FOG AND THE GREY WOLF-LIGHT THAT COMES BEFORE DAWN. THE STREETS, OTHER THAN NETLEY AND HIS CARRIAGE, ARE STILL OTHERWISE DESERTED.
NETLEY: Whoah.

PANEL 2.

THE THREE PANELS ON THIS CENTRAL TIER ARE ALL FROM THE SAME SHOT. IN THE FOREGROUND, WHAT WE BASICALLY SEE ARE THE HANDS OF JOHN NETLEY, RESTING THERE ON HIS KNEES AND STILL CLUTCHING THE WHIP AND THE LIMP REINS AS HE PERCHES ATOP HIS BOX. OTHER THAN THIS AND THE VISIBLE BIT OF THE CARRIAGE THAT HE IS SITTING ATOP, WE CANNOT SEE HIM AT ALL. WE CANNOT, FOR EXAMPLE, SEE HIS FACE. LOOKING BEYOND HIS HANDS, THE WHIP, AND THE REINS, WE ARE GAZING AT THE FRONT DOOR OF WILLIAM GULL'S HOUSE, WHICH IS SITUATED AT 74 BROOK STREET. (SEE ATTACHED PHOTO. I'M SURE IT'S BEEN REPAINTED SINCE THEN, BUT THE BASIC STRUCTURE SHOULD BE PRETTY MUCH THE SAME.) WE SEE THE FRONT DOOR AND PERHAPS A LITTLE OF THE IRON RAILINGS THAT FENCE IN THE NARROW DROP DOWN TO THE LEVEL OF THE HOUSE'S BASEMENT. MIST ROILS ACROSS THE PAVEMENT OUTSIDE, AND THERE ARE AS YET NO SIGNS OF LIFE FROM WITHIN. WE ARE JUST LOOKING AT THE CLOSED AND SILENT DOOR WITH THE NUMERAL 74 CLEARLY VISIBLE UPON IT. IN THE FOREGROUND, NETLEY'S HANDS REMAIN CALM AND PATIENT UPON THE SLACK REINS. HE IS WAITING.
No dialogue.

PANEL 3.

SAME SHOT, WITH NETLEY'S HANDS REMAINING STILL IN THE FOREGROUND. LOOKING BEYOND THIS, WE SEE THE FRONT DOOR OF NUMBER 74 BROOK STREET AS IT OPENS AND LETS THE YELLOW GASLIGHT WITHIN TRICKLE OUT INTO THE DARK STREET. ALMOST SILHOUETTED AGAINST THIS AS HE STANDS BRIEFLY FRAMED IN THE OPEN DOOR WE SEE THE FORM OF WILLIAM GULL, STOCKY AND SOLID AND POWERFUL, A THICK CLOAK DRAPED AROUND HIS SHOULDERS AND A BLACK TOP HAT PERCHED UPON HIS ROUND, CANNON-BALL HEAD. BENEATH ONE ARM, ALTHOUGH IT NEEDN'T BE VISIBLE HERE, HE CARRIES A LARGE AND ROLLED UP MAP, AND PERHAPS A DRAUGHTSMAN'S RULER. IN THE OTHER HAND, IF YOU THINK IT MIGHT MAKE A USEFUL PROP FOR LATER ON, HE CARRIES A GENTLEMAN'S WALKING CANE. HE STANDS POISED ON THE ILLUMINATED THRESHOLD OF HIS HOME HERE, ABOUT TO STEP OUT INTO THE DARK STREETS, PULLING THE DOOR CLOSED BEHIND HIM AS HE DOES SO. HIS APPEARANCE AT THE DOOR IS SILENT AND OMINOUS.
No dialogue.

PANEL 4.

SAME SHOT, WITH NETLEY'S HANDS STILL VISIBLE IN THE FOREGROUND. LOOKING BEYOND THIS, WE SEE THAT THE DOOR TO NUMBER 74 IS NOW CLOSED AGAIN, AND THAT SIR WILLIAM'S DARK AND TOP-HATTED FIGURE IS NOW GLIDING ACROSS THE PAVEMENT IN THE DIRECTION OF THE CAB, A DARK AND SHADOWY MASS WHOSE FEATURES ARE NOT VISIBLE HERE. AGAIN, ALL THIS IS CARRIED OUT IN SILENCE.
No dialogue.

PANEL 5.

CHANGE ANGLE. WE ARE NOW SLIGHTLY BEHIND GULL, OUR EYE-LEVEL DOWN AROUND NEAR HIS MIDSECTION, AND LOOKING BEYOND HIM TOWARDS THE CARRIAGE, WHICH WAITS IN THE NEAR BACKGROUND AS GULL APPROACHES IT. WE CAN SEE ONE OF HIS ARMS HANGING DOWN, WITH THE ROLLED UP MAP AND THE LONG RULER TUCKED BENEATH IT, ALTHOUGH AT THIS POINT THEIR PURPOSE IS OBSCURE. OTHER THAN THIS ONE HAND AND A LITTLE OF HIS FLANK, WE CAN'T

SEE MUCH OF SIR WILLIAM IN THIS PANEL. LOOKING PAST HIM AND UP, WE SEE NETLEY AS HE SITS THERE ON HIS BOX, TURNING TOWARDS US AND LOOKING DOWN AT SIR WILLIAM WITH A RATHER OVER-FAMILIAR GRIN OF COMRADELY GREETING. PERHAPS HE REACHES UP AND TOUCHES THE BRIM OF HIS DERBY WITH RESPECT AS HE SPEAKS. FROM HIS GENERAL POSTURE, HE LOOKS AS IF HE MIGHT BE ABOUT TO COME DOWN FROM THE CARRIAGE AND HELP SIR WILLIAM ABOARD. IF THE GESTURE DOESN'T LOOK AWKWARD, WHAT WITH THE MAP AND RULER TUCKED BENEATH HIS ARM, THEN PERHAPS SIR WILLIAM'S VISIBLE HAND, UP TO THE RIGHT OF THE FOREGROUND HAS ITS PALM TURNED OUTWARDS TOWARDS NETLEY AS IF IN MILD PROTEST AT HIS PROPOSAL. NETLEY, ATOP HIS BOX, IS MORE VISIBLE TO THE LEFT OF THE NEAR BACKGROUND HERE.

NETLEY: Ha! Bang on time, your Lordship. 'Ang on, I'll hop down an' open the door...

GULL (OFF):   That won't be necessary. It would better suit my purposes to ride up top, beside you.

GULL:(OFF)   Come, give me your hand.

PANEL 6.

NOW WE ARE SLIGHTLY NEARER THE CARRIAGE, AND LOOKING UP AT IT THROUGH GULL'S EYES. ALL WE CAN SEE OF HIM IS ONE OF HIS HANDS... PROBABLY NOT THE ONE WITH THE MAP AND RULER... REACHING UP INTO THE FOREGROUND FROM OFF PANEL TO ONE SIDE. THE HAND IS REACHING UP TO CLASP THAT OF JOHN NETLEY AS HE LEANS DOWN TO PULL SIR WILLIAM UP ALONGSIDE HIM. AS NETLEY LOOKS DOWN AT US AND THE OFF-PANEL SIR WILLIAM HE LOOKS SOMEWHAT APPREHENSIVE AND ILL AT EASE.

NETLEY: Well, as you wish, Sir William, though it ain't very comfortable.

NETLEY: Y'see, like, normally, I just puts luggage up here ...

PANEL 7.

NOW WE HAVE A SHOT LOOKING THROUGH NETLEY'S EYES AS GULL, NOW ATOP THE CAB, SETTLES HIMSELF ONTO THE BOX BESIDE NETLEY. PERHAPS REACHING UP TO ADJUST HIS TOP HAT SLIGHTLY WITH ONE HAND, GULL SEEMS IN A JOVIAL MOOD AS HE SETTLES HIMSELF INTO HIS SEAT FOR THE RIDE. IT IS A SINISTER JOVIALITY, HOWEVER, THAT ALMOST HAS A MANIC, MOCKING EDGE TO IT. GULL TURNS HIS FACE TOWARDS US AND THE OFF-PANEL NETLEY HERE, THE GASLIGHT DOING STRANGE THINGS TO THE PLANES AND SHADOWS OF HIS FACE. HIS EYES GLITTER AND AS HE SMILES AT NETLEY HIS SMILE IS PREDATORY AND DANGEROUS. I WANT GULL TO BE AN INCREASINGLY UNSETTLING AND POWERFUL FIGURE AS THIS BOOK UNFOLDS, AND IN THIS EPISODE WE FIRST REALLY GET A CLEAR SENSE THAT DR. WILLIAM GULL IS ACTUALLY STARK, STARING MAD; HAS BEEN SINCE HIS STROKE, IN FACT. THE MIST AND SHADOWS SEEM TO SHUDDER AND MOVE BEHIND HIM AS HE SMILES DISARMINGLY AT US, EYES TWINKLING WITH A SECRET FIRE, A SECRET AMUSEMENT.

GULL: Ha ha ha! Then I shall be your luggage!

GULL: Oxford Circus first, then Oxford Street.

GULL: Drive on, Netley.

Chapter 4, page 5.

There is a huge amount going on in this chapter, in terms of information. Since the action takes place in a single day, I saw it as my challenge to capture the environment of London in all the times of day in sequence, with their changes of light and atmosphere, and even weather, since we have a shower of rain in the mid-afternoon. In my youth, I was avidly interested in Impressionism, with its focus on the optical appreciation of the contemporary world, the way light falls upon objects and landscapes and cityscapes, and the way smoke and rain and other atmospheric effects tend to obscure detail. I started in on this chapter with a thrill of anticipation.

Alan mentions Sir Francis Dashwood in the opening paragraph. Along with several other books necessary to draw this chapter, including the London A-Z mentioned in the second paragraph, he threw in a gift of Eric Towers' excellent biography of the 18th century figure. I was at the time planning a comic book about him and his doings. It came to nothing, but Dashwood and some of the ideas went into my four-issue writing stint on a comic titled *Hellblazer* (1994), long out of print.

PAGE 5. (1088 words) PANEL 1.
THERE ARE FIVE PANELS ON THIS PAGE, WITH BIG WIDE PANELS TAKING UP THE TOP AND THE BOTTOM TIER AND THEN THREE SMALLER PANELS OCCUPYING THE CENTRAL TIER. IN THIS FIRST PANEL, WE HAVE A WIDE-ANGLE SHOT LOOKING DOWN BROOK STREET IN THE OPPOSITE DIRECTION TO THAT IN WHICH WE HAVE BEEN LOOKING OVER OUR FIRST FOUR PAGES. AS OPPOSED TO LOOKING DOWN IT TOWARDS THE GROSVENOR SQUARE END WE ARE NOW LOOKING ALONG IT TOWARDS THE HANOVER SQUARE END AS NETLEY STARTS UP THE COACH AGAIN AND SETS IT RATTLING OFF AWAY FROM US ALONG BROOK STREET, HEADING BACK TOWARDS THE CITY. AS THE COACH MOVES SLOWLY AWAY FROM US DOWN THE FOGGY PRE-DAWN STREET WE SEE CLARIDGE'S HOTEL OVER TO OUR RIGHT OF THE STREET, PERHAPS WITH A SOLITARY AND ANONYMOUS DOORMAN STANDING WATCH IN THE EARLY MORNING FOG. THE STREET RUNS AWAY FROM US, CURVING AWAY TOWARDS THE LEFT OF THE BACKGROUND, HEADING TOWARDS HANOVER SQUARE WHERE, ALTHOUGH WE CANNOT SEE IT HERE A GOLDEN BALL IS SET ATOP THE SPIRE OF ST. GEORGE'S CHURCH TO REPRESENT THE ORB OF THE SUN, A FEATURE COPIED BY YOUR PAL SIR FRANCIS DASHWOOD WHEN HE BUILT HIS TEMPLE TO APOLLO AT WEST WYCOMBE PARK.

HERE, THE COACH SHIFTS AND GROANS AS IT TRUNDLES AWAY FROM US, THE BACKS OF THE TWO
FIGURES PERCHED ATOP ITS BOX CLEARLY VISIBLE, SITTING HUNKERED DOWN AGAINST THE FOG
AS THE COACH RECEDES.
No dialogue.

PANEL 2.
HMM... IT STRIKES ME THAT RATHER THAN GIVING GULL A CANE IN ADDITION TO HIS ROLLED
MAP AND RULER BACK ON PAGE FOUR, IT MIGHT HAVE BEEN BETTER TO GIVE HIM A PAPER BAG OF
GRAPES, CLUTCHED PROTECTIVELY TO HIS CHEST AS HE WALKS TOWARDS THE CARRIAGE. SOUNDS
LIKE A MORE USEFUL PROP TO ME, ANYWAY. IF THIS IS INDEED THE CASE, THEN IN THIS
PANEL, AS WE SIT BESIDE GULL AND NETLEY, WE SEE THE BAG OF GRAPES RESTING OPEN IN
GULL'S LAP. AS I SEE THIS PANEL, WE ARE BESIDE GULL, LOOKING PAST HIM AT NETLEY. ALL
WE CAN REALLY SEE OF GULL AS HE SITS IN PROFILE TO THE LEFT OF THE FOREGROUND FACING
RIGHT ARE HIS LAP, HIS HANDS AND A LITTLE OF HIS BODY. ONCE MORE, WE CANNOT SEE HIS
HEAD OR SHOULDERS. HE SITS WITH THE MAP AND RULER RESTING BESIDE HIM, BETWEEN HIM
AND US, AND THE BAG OF GRAPES RESTS IN HIS LAP, HIS OLD, STRONG HANDS FOLDED CALMLY
ABOUT IT. LOOKING BEYOND WHAT LITTLE WE CAN SEE OF GULL WE SEE NETLEY AS HE SITS
HUNCHED FORWARD OVER HIS REINS, TURNING HIS HEAD SLIGHTLY TOWARDS US AS HE SPEAKS TO
SIR WILLIAM WITH A SUITABLY HUMBLE EXPRESSION. THE CARRIAGE HAS BY NOW TURNED LEFT
UP REGENT STREET, AND THUS IT IS REGENT STREET THAT MAKES UP ANY BACKGROUND WHICH WE
MIGHT SEE CRAWLING BY BEYOND NETLEY. I DOUBT WE'LL NEED ANYTHING IDENTIFIABLE HERE,
BUT I'M JUST TELLING YOU WHERE WE ARE SO THAT YOU'LL AT LEAST BE ABLE TO KEEP THE
JOURNEY CLEAR IN YOUR HEAD. IN FACT, I THINK I'LL INCLUDE AN A-Z OF LONDON IN THIS
PACKAGE SO THAT YOU'LL BE ABLE TO FOLLOW THE JOURNEY PROPERLY.

NETLEY: Pardon me for askin', Sir William, but when you sent your
                    message, you said as 'ow you might 'ave some work you could
                    put my way?

PANEL 3.
NOW A LONG SHOT OF THE COACH, LOOKING DOWN OXFORD STREET TOWARDS OXFORD CIRCUS.
FROM THE LEFT OF THE NEAR BACKGROUND, PULLING FROM REGENT STREET AND ACROSS OXFORD
CIRCUS, THE COACH STARTS TO TURN THE CORNER SO AS TO COME TOWARDS US, ALONG OXFORD
STREET. IT IS STILL PRETTY DARK AND MIASMIC, BUT SINCE OXFORD STREET WOULD BE A
MORE WELL-POPULATED AREA THAN BROOK STREET I FIGURE THAT IN THE BACKGROUND HERE WE
CAN MAYBE SEE ONE OR TWO PEOPLE IN THE DISTANCE, GOING ABOUT THEIR EARLY MORNING
BUSINESS. OUR MAIN FOCUS OF ATTENTION HOWEVER IS UPON THE COACH AS IT SWINGS ROUND
THE CORNER TOWARDS US, THE TWO DARK FIGURES OF GULL AND NETLEY PERCHED ATOP ITS BOX.

GULL: Indeed I did, and grand work it shall be.
GULL: TOO grand, I fear, to be encompassed by a coachman's
                   cul-de-sac philosophies...
NETLEY: You TRY me! You just try me, sir! I'm sharper than I look.

PANEL 4.
NOW WE HAVE A REVERSE OF PANEL TWO, IN THAT IT IS NOW AS IF WE ARE SITTING BESIDE
NETLEY AND LOOKING PAST HIM AT GULL. NETLEY AND GULL ARE BOTH IN PROFILE, FACING

LEFT, BUT ALL WE CAN SEE OF NETLEY HERE, ENTERING THE PANEL FROM OFF RIGHT, ARE HIS HANDS AND KNEES AND PERHAPS A LITTLE OF HIS JACKET FRONT. HIS HEAD AND SHOULDERS ARE OFF PANEL SO AS TO FOCUS THE ATTENTION PAST HIM AND ONTO GULL. GULL, SITTING IN PROFILE A LITTLE MORE TO THE LEFT OF THE PANEL HERE DOES NOT LOOK ROUND AT NETLEY AS HE SPEAKS. ONE HAND IS SLIGHTLY RAISED, TRANSPORTING A GRAPE TOWARDS HIS MOUTH FROM THE PAPER BAG THAT HE CRADLES UPON HIS LAP. ALTHOUGH HIS EYES ARE HIDDEN BY THE SHADOWS OF HIS TOP HAT, HIS FACE IS CREASED WITH SINISTER MERRIMENT, LAUGHING AS HE RESPONDS TO NETLEY. ALL THE WHILE HE KEEPS HIS EYES UPON THE ROAD BEFORE THEM, PAYING CAREFUL ATTENTION TO THEIR ROUTE.

GULL: Ha ha ha! Let us HOPE so, Netley. Let us hope so most fervently.

GULL: Very well. I shall attempt an explanation while we ride. Left at Gray's Inn Road incidentally.

GULL: Make for King's Cross.

PANEL 5.

THIS LAST SHOT TAKES UP THE WHOLE BOTTOM TIER. WE ARE LOOKING STRAIGHT DOWN THE LENGTH OF OXFORD STREET, AND THE SQUEAKING, LISTING BULK OF NETLEY'S COACH IS PROPELLING ITSELF TOWARDS US WITH THE TWO SINISTER FIGURES CROUCHED ATOP IT. BEHIND AND ABOUT IT, THE GLOOM IS SLOWLY LIGHTENING AS DAWN APPROACHES, AND THE EARLY MORNING FOG SEEMS SOMEWHAT THINNER. THE SHOPFRONTS FAN OUT TO EITHER SIDE, CLOSED AND SHUTTERED, NOT YET OPEN FOR THE BUSINESS OF THE DAY. THE AIR OF DESERTION IS QUITE STRONG, AS IN MOST CITIES AT THIS TIME OF THE MORNING. SINCE THEY HAVE SO MANY PEOPLE CROWDING THROUGH THEM DURING THE DAY, THEY TEND TO LOOK ALL THE MORE EMPTY WHEN THEY ARE RELATIVELY UNPOPULATED. IF WE CAN SEE GULL CLEARLY ENOUGH FROM THIS DISTANCE, HE IS JUST POPPING A SUCCULENT BLACK GRAPE INTO HIS MOUTH, TEETH TEARING DOWN THROUGH THE BLACK SKIN TO THE SWEET PULP BENEATH.

No dialogue.

An honourable man, *"and an outstanding physician, a giant besmirched by pygmies,"* was the opinion of Ripperologist *Melvin Harris on Knight's theory that Gull was the Whitechapel murderer* (The Ripper File, 1989 - *a useful work that is still on my shelf). "It was just so much clever deception, a deception that has been fully exposed in my book,* Jack the Ripper: The Bloody Truth." *He was scathing about the 1988 movie based on the theory:* "On screen we saw coachman Netley carrying the Duke to the whores *and Gull to the shambles. It was an affront to every viewer who had been waiting for an authentic solution." I saw the end of that film myself recently and it looked so daft I wondered how anybody could get ruffled about it. Michael Caine played Abberline, having replaced previously-cast Barry Foster. Interestingly, Foster had earlier replaced Caine on Hitchcock's* Frenzy *because Caine wouldn't play a killer who mutilates women. (*source Wikipedia*).*

Chapter 4, page 9.

In his first paragraph, Alan addresses the problem of keeping things visually interesting in this episode. I found the whole thing delightful to draw, as I've already said, concerning myself with light and the time of day and imagining how it would be to ride around on a coach all day. I recognise that there are many who wouldn't find it interesting in the least, and I leave them to their video games. However, more than keeping it interesting for the reader, I was concerned with the challenge of keeping it logical. For example, what would be the difference between traveling to Hackney in comparison to traveling back from there? I thought that establishing a sense of east and west might be useful, since the map of London is to play an important part in the story. Thus, as Gull and Netley go from west to east in this page, I have them travelling to the right, conventional map location of the east. There isn't really a return trip and they end up moving mostly eastward, but we do see them turning to face west in places, such as on page 31.

PAGE 9. (1639 words) PANEL 1.
THERE ARE SEVEN PANELS ON THIS PAGE WITH THREE ON THE TOP TIER, ONE BIG ONE TAKING UP THE MIDDLE TIER AND THEN THREE SMALLER ONES ON THE BOTTOM TIER. I SHOULD POINT OUT THAT WITH THIS EPISODE, SINCE IT'S GOING TO BE SUCH A BLOODY DIFFICULT THING FOR YOU TO KEEP IT VISUALLY INTERESTING, I'D BE PERFECTLY HAPPY IF YOU WANT TO RE-JIG THINGS SO THAT THREE SMALL PANELS ARE COMPRESSED INTO ONE TIER-WIDTH PANEL OR WHATEVER. SOME BITS OF THE NARRATIVE REQUIRE SPECIFIC PICTURES TO GO WITH THEM, BUT IN THE STRETCHES WHERE THERE'S ONLY GULL TALKING YOU SHOULD FEEL FREE TO TAKE WHATEVER LIBERTIES YOU LIKE WITH THE PANEL ARRANGEMENTS OR THE VISUALS. MY PANEL NOTES DURING THESE SEQUENCES ARE, AS EVER, ONLY THERE TO GIVE YOU A WORKABLE SEQUENCE OF PICTURES THAT WOULD FIT WITH THE DIALOGUE IF YOU CAN'T COME UP WITH ANYTHING BETTER. OKAY, ASSUMING YOU GO FOR THE SEVEN-PANEL PAGE LAYOUT MENTIONED ABOVE,THEN THIS FIRST TIER HAS THREE PANELS WITH MORE OR LESS THE SAME SHOT. WE ARE SITTING UPON THE BOX ALONGSIDE GULL, WHOM WE CAN JUST SEE ENTERING THE PANEL FROM THE LEFT OF THE FOREGROUND, IN PROFILE AND FACING RIGHT, QUITE CLOSE TO US, PERHAPS HALF-FIGURE AS HE SITS AND THUS NOT VISIBLE BELOW THE KNEES. THE CURLED-UP MAP AND RULER LAY BESIDE GULL ON OUR SIDE, ALTHOUGH IT DOESN'T MATTER IF WE CANNOT SEE THEM

HERE. THE BAG OF GRAPES RESTS IN GULL'S LAP, AND AS WE SEE HIM HERE HE'S REACHING
INTO IT AND TUGGING AT A SINGLE GRAPE HELD IN BETWEEN HIS FOREFINGER AND THUMB,
ABOUT TO PULL IT FREE AND SNAP IT FROM ITS STEM, PLUCKING IT FROM THE CENTRAL
CLUSTER. HE GLANCES SIDEWAYS AT NETLEY AS HE DOES THIS, ADDRESSING HIS QUESTION
TO THE COACH DRIVER, WHO WE CAN SEE IN THE IMMEDIATE BACKGROUND BEYOND GULL AND
JUST A LITTLE FURTHER TO THE RIGHT OF PANEL. NETLEY CROUCHES ON THE BOX, HIS
REINS IN HAND, IN PROFILE TO US HERE, HIS WEASEL EYES SCANNING THE ROAD AHEAD
FOR POTHOLES OR FOR MUD. BEYOND THE COACH, THE BACKGROUND SHOWS THE WALLS OF
BATTLE BRIDGE ROAD CRAWLING PAST, NOW LIGHTENED BY THE RISING SUN, THE MIST THAT
SHROUDS THEM ALL BUT BURNED AWAY. THE SUNLIGHT IS BRIGHT AND COLD: IT DAZZLES,
BUT AS YET IT DOES NOT WARM, AND MAYBE WE CAN SEE THE TRAVELLERS' BREATH HUNG
ON THE CHILLY AIR, THOUGH THIS EFFECT WILL GRADUALLY DIMINISH AS WE MOVE ON WITH
OUR STORY THROUGH THE DAY AHEAD, JUST AS THE SUN WILL MOVE ACROSS THE SKY. HERE,
NETLEY GRIPS THE LEATHER REINS WHILE GULL PICKS AT A GRAPE AND SHOOTS A SIDEWAYS
GLANCE TOWARDS THE COACHMAN THAT IS ALMOST SLY IN ITS INQUIRY. NETLEY DOES NOT
LOOK AT GULL, AND THUS REMAINS OBLIVIOUS TO THIS NUANCE.

GULL: Do you begin to grasp how truly great a work is
                         London? A veritable textbook we may draw upon in
                         formulating great works of our own!

PANEL 2.

SAME SHOT. GULL TURNS HIS GAZE FROM NETLEY AND REGARDS THE ROAD AHEAD, HIS
EYES AS COLD AS MARBLE, FIXED UPON SOME INNER VISION, HIS FACE EXPRESSIONLESS,
YET SOMEHOW FIRED WITH STERN AND SCIENTIFIC ZEAL, A HARD RESOLVE LIKE THAT OF
BATTLE-HARDENED SCHOOLTEACHERS ON THE FIRST DAY OF TERM. ONE HAND RESTS IN HIS
LAP AROUND THE BAG OF GRAPES. THE OTHER LIFTS TOWARDS HIS LIPS A PURPLE
GRAPE BETWEEN THE THUMB AND FOREFINGER. BEYOND HIM, HUNCHED OVER THE REINS,
JOHN NETLEY TURNS HIS FACE SLIGHTLY TOWARDS US, SO THAT WE CAN SEE HIM IN HALF-
PROFILE NOW. A LOOK OF VAGUE UNEASE FLICKERS ACROSS HIS RODENT FEATURES; AN
ANXIETY. BEYOND HIM, KINGS CROSS STATION FLOATS BY THE EARLY MORNING SUNLIGHT
GLINTING FROM ITS GREY-GREEN GLASS.

GULL: We'll penetrate its metaphors, lay bare its structure and
                         thus come at last upon its meaning.

GULL: As befits great work, we'll read it carefully, and with
                         RESPECT.

PANEL 3.

SAME SHOT. PENTONVILLE ROAD MOVES PAST THERE IN THE BACKGROUND BEYOND NETLEY,
THE SUNLIGHT BRIGHTENING THE BACKDROP MORE WITH EACH SUCCESSIVE PANEL. NETLEY,
THOUGH HE OBVIOUSLY STILL SITS IN PROFILE AT THE REINS, NOW TURNS HIS FACE FULLY
TOWARDS SIR WILLIAM, SO WE SEE IT FULL-ON HERE. IT HAS A WRETCHED LOOK OF WORRY
AS HE MAKES HIS HESITANT CONFESSION. HE'S AFRAID THAT HIS ILLITERACY MIGHT COST
HIM BOTH A LUCRATIVE AND MOST PRESTIGIOUS JOB. UP IN THE FOREGROUND, GULL LOWERS
HIS EMPTY FINGERS FROM HIS LIPS AND THOUGHTFULLY REGARDS THE ROAD AHEAD WHILE
GRAVELY CHEWING ON THE GRAPE.

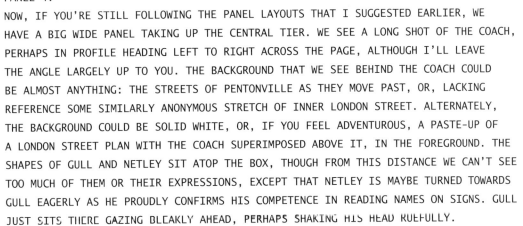

NETLEY: Uh, with respect, sir...
NETLEY: I can't read.

PANEL 4.

NOW, IF YOU'RE STILL FOLLOWING THE PANEL LAYOUTS THAT I SUGGESTED EARLIER, WE
HAVE A BIG WIDE PANEL TAKING UP THE CENTRAL TIER. WE SEE A LONG SHOT OF THE COACH,
PERHAPS IN PROFILE HEADING LEFT TO RIGHT ACROSS THE PAGE, ALTHOUGH I'LL LEAVE
THE ANGLE LARGELY UP TO YOU. THE BACKGROUND THAT WE SEE BEHIND THE COACH COULD
BE ALMOST ANYTHING: THE STREETS OF PENTONVILLE AS THEY MOVE PAST, OR, LACKING
REFERENCE SOME SIMILARLY ANONYMOUS STRETCH OF INNER LONDON STREET. ALTERNATELY,
THE BACKGROUND COULD BE SOLID WHITE, OR, IF YOU FEEL ADVENTUROUS, A PASTE-UP OF
A LONDON STREET PLAN WITH THE COACH SUPERIMPOSED ABOVE IT, IN THE FOREGROUND. THE
SHAPES OF GULL AND NETLEY SIT ATOP THE BOX, THOUGH FROM THIS DISTANCE WE CAN'T SEE
TOO MUCH OF THEM OR THEIR EXPRESSIONS, EXCEPT THAT NETLEY IS MAYBE TURNED TOWARDS
GULL EAGERLY AS HE PROUDLY CONFIRMS HIS COMPETENCE IN READING NAMES ON SIGNS. GULL
JUST SITS THERE GAZING BLEAKLY AHEAD, PERHAPS SHAKING HIS HEAD RUEFULLY.

GULL: Oh, Netley.
GULL: Netley, Netley, Netley, what are we to do with you?
GULL: Proceed by Essex Road to Balls Pond Road, thence to
                    London Fields. I take it street signs aren't beyond your
                    literary grasp?
NETLEY: Oh no, sir! I reads them right enough!

PANEL 5.

NOW ANOTHER THREE SMALL PANELS FROM THE SAME BASIC ANGLE AS THE THREE PANELS ON OUR
TOP TIER, WITH GULL IN THE FOREGROUND FACING RIGHT FROM OVER ON THE LEFT AND NETLEY
VISIBLE BEYOND HIM, ALSO FACING RIGHT AS HE SITS CROUCHED ABOVE HIS REINS. HERE,
IN THE FOREGROUND, GULL PERHAPS REMOVES A GRAPE PIP FROM HIS LIPS WITH ONE HAND AS
HE ADDRESSES NETLEY. HE SMILES, HIS OLD FACE CRINKLING, HIS EYES RECEDING IN THE
SHADOWS CAST ACROSS THEM BY HIS HAT BRIM. WHEN GULL SMILES, HE LOOKS QUITE SATANIC,
KNOWING AND SARDONIC WITH A FIERCE INTELLIGENCE THAT GLITTERS WICKEDLY WITHIN HIS
ANCIENT EYES. I REALLY WANT GULL TO HAVE A PRESENCE THROUGHOUT THIS STORY, UNLIKE
THE KINDLY OLD DOCTOR IN THE MICHAEL CAINE TELEVISION MOVIE. ALTHOUGH MOSTLY GULL'S
COMPOSURE IS AS PERFECT AS COLD MARBLE, FULL OF SILENT DIGNITY AND POWER AND
PRESENCE, SOMETIMES IN HIS EYES WE SHOULD CATCH JUST A GLIMPSE OF SOMETHING MAD AND
ALIEN AND EVIL, LIKE THE GLIMPSES YOU CAN SOMETIMES CATCH WITHIN THE EYES OF THOSE
CARRION BIRDS THAT GULL IS NAMED FOR. IT IS A MIND THAT CAN CONSIDER CENTURIES OF
BLOOD AND WAR AND SLAUGHTER WITH FULL KNOWLEDGE OF THEIR IMPLICATIONS, YET REMAIN
AMUSED. HE SMILES AND TAKES THE GRAPE SEED FROM HIS MOUTH, WHILE NETLEY, IN THE
BACKGROUND, PRUDENTLY RETURNS HIS GAZE TOWARDS THE ROAD AHEAD OF THEM. BEYOND HIM,
ESSEX ROAD MOVES PAST, THE SUNLIT HOUSES GROWING GRADUALLY MORE SLUM-LIKE AND RUN
DOWN AS WE PROGRESS TOWARDS THE FILTHY AND DILAPIDATED SUBURBS THAT ARE ALL THAT'S
LEFT OF PROSPEROUS MERCHANTS' HOMES, THERE IN THE SLUMS OF HACKNEY.

GULL: Splendid! By chance, our lesson for today requires of
                         you no further scholarship.

GULL: The greater part of London's story is not writ in words.

PANEL 6.

SAME SHOT. IN THE FOREGROUND, GULL FLICKS THE GRAPE SEED DOWN INTO THE STREET
DISMISSIVELY, THE SMILE FADING FROM HIS LIPS AS HIS EXPRESSION TAKES UPON ITSELF
A SERIOUSNESS MORE SUITED TO THE GRAVITY OF WHAT HE IS DISCUSSING. ONCE MORE HE
DOES NOT LOOK AT NETLEY BUT INSTEAD GAZES AWAY INTO SOME INNER DISTANCE; SOME POINT
BACK IN LONDON'S DIMMEST HISTORY. BEYOND HIM NETLEY TURNS AND LOOKS AT GULL, STILL
WITH A VAGUE UNEASE IN HIS EXPRESSION. THIS TIME THOUGH, IT'S NOT JUST ANXIETY AT
BEING THOUGHT UNWORTHY FOR HIS JOB: HERE THE UNEASE IS SOMETHING NETLEY FEELS
WITH GULL HIMSELF; THE CURIOUS THINGS HE SAYS; THE ODDLY PURPOSEFUL AND YET
PECULIAR ROUTE THAT HE'S DIRECTING THEM ALONG. NETLEY IS NOT YET AS TERRIFIED
OF GULL AS HE WILL LATER BECOME, BUT FOR THE FIRST TIME IT LOOKS AS IF HE'S
EXPERIENCING A VAGUE SENSE OF DOUBT. BEYOND HIM, BALLS POND ROAD MOVES PAST,
THE SUNLIGHT BRIGHTENING WITH EACH SUCCESSIVE FRAME.

GULL: It is instead a literature of stone, of place-names and
                         associations...

GULL: ...where faint echoes answer back from off the distant,
                         ruined walls of bloody history.

PANEL 7.

SAME SHOT. HERE, IN THE FOREGROUND, GULL LIFTS HIS FINGER AND POINTS TO AN OFF-
PANEL SPOT SOMEWHERE AHEAD OF THE COACH AND OFF PANEL TO THE RIGHT HERE. HIS GAZE
IS ALSO FIXED IN THAT DIRECTION, LOSING A LITTLE OF ITS VISIONARY LOOK AS HE TURNS
HIS ATTENTIONS TO THE PRACTICAL REQUIREMENTS OF DIRECTIONS. HE DOES NOT LOOK AT
NETLEY, WHOM WE SEE THERE BEYOND GULL. NETLEY HAS TURNED HIS HEAD BACK ROUND TO
FACE THE FRONT, SQUINTING BENEATH THE BRIM OF HIS BROWN DERBY HAT TOWARDS THE PLACE
THAT GULL IS POINTING AT. BEYOND, THE GRIM SLUM STREETS OF HACKNEY WANDER BY AS
NETLEY GUIDES THE COACH DOWN GREENWOOD ROAD'S MILD SLOPE TOWARDS THE LONDON FIELDS
THAT WAIT BELOW. THE LIGHT IS THAT OF FULL-FLEDGED MORNING NOW.

GULL: Turn right, down Greenwood Road as far as Albion Drive,
                         then stop.

GULL: "Albion Drive". 'Twould seem auspicious in that we aspire
                         to probe the ventricles of London; England's heart.

Costello to Gull's Abbott

*The Wikipedia entry for John Netley notes that
FROM HELL depicts him as "semi-literate." At
this stage of writing the book, Alan was uncertain
that Netley had been an actual person (I'll come
back to this), but it's the storyteller's craft that keeps
this chapter manageable. part of this is the comedic
relationship that Alan creates between Gull and Netley
in the above page and in the scenes to follow.*

Chapter 4, page 14.

As research for this chapter Alan made a tour around the locations he would need, and in the process satisfied himself that it could be done in one day. He also took a large number of photographs, some of which are shown in our colour section along with the drawings that resulted from them. Alan asked his fellow writer Jamie Delano to be driver for the day: *"I was happy to play Netley to his Sir William Gull; to have the distraction of traffic and navigation to alleviate the dark magic of our treading the paths of obsession... And another church, don't ask me which – derelict, roofless, peopled by a congregation of scrubby trees twisting among its fallen stone. There was a locked wrought-iron gate to climb, a dark crypt with an unhealthy smell to explore. I remember descending into this with Alan, waiting in the half-light at the foot of the steps, watching him set off into the pitch blackness of the interior with a flickering cigarette lighter held futilely over his head to light his way... I fully expected him to plunge at any moment into some unseen abyss and hurtle directly to Hell."* (see bibliography)

There's a line at the end of panel 5's description that is like something out of Raymond Chandler. There are many such lines in the *FROM HELL* scripts. It must have taken an effort to subjugate the words to the image for the 500 pages. In the pedestrian lane, I concentrated on the arrangement of volumes on this page, playing with pictorial space, of which more later.

PAGE 14. (913 words) PANEL 1.
SIX PANELS HERE, IN ANY LAYOUT THAT YOU WISH, ALTHOUGH PERHAPS A LAYOUT OF TWO FRAMES PER TIER WOULD SUIT IT BEST. THIS FIRST SHOT HERE NEED ONLY BE A SMALL ONE, WITH A FRONTAL CLOSE-UP OF SIR WILLIAM GULL AND NETLEY, ROUGHLY HEAD AND SHOULDERS AS THEY COME TOWARDS US, SAT ATOP THEIR BOX. BEHIND THEM DOWN THE ROAD, WE SEE A VIEW OF ST. LUKE'S OLD STREET, OR AT LEAST ITS LOWER PORTIONS, SHADED BY THE GREEN LATE-SUMMER TREES, RECEDING INTO THEM AS WE WITHDRAW FROM IT. JOHN NETLEY, ON THE RIGHT, LOOKS ROUND AT GULL WITH AN EXPRESSION OF REAL INTEREST, THE MENTION OF FREEMASONRY HAVING GAINED HIS ATTENTION. HIS EXPRESSION IS EAGER; ALMOST CHILDLIKE IN ITS NAKEDNESS. GULL, ON THE LEFT JUST SETS HIS HAT MORE FIRMLY ON HIS HEAD, WITH

BOTH HANDS HERE RAISED INTO VIEW. HIS FACE IS NEUTRAL, HIS EXPRESSION SERIOUS. HE DOES NOT LOOK AT NETLEY. OVERHEAD, THE SUN BEGINS ITS CLIMB THROUGH STRATA OF GREY CLOUD TOWARDS MIDDAY.

GULL: Yes, London has its obelisks. So too have Paris, Washington, New York...

GULL: Freemasons in those cities, through this century, have had a hand in situating obelisks at certain points, aware of their significance.

NETLEY: Freemasons, Sir?

PANEL 2.

NOW WE ARE IN NORTHAMPTON SQUARE, LOOKING TOWARDS ITS ENTRANCE FOR WHICH SEE THE REFERENCE PHOTOGRAPHS. THE COACH, WITH GULL AND NETLEY SAT ATOP OF IT, IS TURNING HERE INTO THE SQUARE, COMING TOWARDS US. NOTHING IN THE SQUARE SEEMS THAT REMARKABLE. THE CENTRE OF IT IS A RAILED-OFF AREA OF GREEN, A SMALL PAVILION AT ITS CENTRE. MAYBE HERE WE LOOK TOWARDS THE COACH FROM IN THE RAILED-UP AREA, SO THAT WE HAVE THE IRON RAILS UP IN THE FOREGROUND, JUTTING INTO VIEW, THE COACH APPROACHING FROM BEYOND THEM. ON ITS BOX, NETLEY STILL HAS HIS HEAD TURNED, GAZING HOPEFULLY AT GULL, WHILE GULL STILL GAZES AT THE SQUARE AHEAD OF THEM WITHOUT RETURNING NETLEY'S GAZE. HERE, WITH ONE HAND, GULL INDICATES THE SQUARE, THOUGH THERE SEEMS LITTLE THERE TO INDICATE.

NETLEY: Why, beggin' your pardon Sir William, but I'd 'eard as you yourself was of that order?

GULL: Oh, the world of masonry has many denizens, and many fields of influence.

GULL: Take this Square, for example...

PANEL 3.

WE PULL BACK NOW ACROSS THE SQUARE, RIGHT OVER TO THE OTHER SIDE, SO THAT WE LOOK ACROSS THE CENTRAL RAILED-IN PLOT OF GRASS TOWARDS THE COACH, BEYOND THE RAILINGS ON THE OTHER SIDE. UP IN THE FOREGROUND, ON THE RAILS AND FACING US WE SEE THE SIGN THAT READS NORTHAMPTON SQUARE, FOR WHICH A REFERENCE PICTURE IS ATTACHED. WE GAZE ACROSS THE EMPTY, HAUNTED PARKLAND AT THE COACH, THERE AT ELEVEN O'CLOCK UPON A GREY VICTORIAN MORNING, GULL AND NETLEY TINY FIGURES HERE, THAT SIT ON TOP OF IT.

GULL: Why, with so many London poets uncommemorated, should we name streets after an insignificant marquis?

GULL: Here's why: He was a leading Mason, marquis of Northampton, site of Hawksmoor's Easton Neston Hall, characteristically aligned with local churches...

PANEL 4.

NOW WE HAVE A FAIRLY TIGHT CLOSE-UP OF GULL AND NETLEY, FACING US, BOTH HEAD AND SHOULDERS, WITH GULL ON THE LEFT AND NETLEY ON THE RIGHT. GULL TURNS HIS HEAD JUST SLIGHTLY TO LOOK DOWN AT NETLEY, GIVING HIM A FAINTLY SUPERCILIOUS LOOK, WHILE NETLEY, ON THE RIGHT, LEANS FAR TOO CLOSE TO GULL, HIS FACE WRACKED WITH A WRETCHED, PLEADING SMILE

BEHIND WHICH ALL HIS BURNING NEED FOR SOCIAL ELEVATION IS GROTESQUELY VISIBLE.

NETLEY: Sir ...?

NETLEY: I've 'eard the way a man might best advance 'imself is that he join the Masons.

NETLEY: I-If my work please your Lordship, would you have a word on my behalf, like?

PANEL 5.

STILL IN CLOSE-UP HERE, BUT WITH OUR ANGLE SLIGHTLY CHANGED, WHEREAS IN OUR LAST PANEL WE HAD GULL TOWARDS THE FOREGROUND MORE AND NETLEY JUST BEYOND HIM, HERE, UPON THE RIGHT, WE SEE JOHN NETLEY CLOSEST TO US, WITH GULL TO THE LEFT, AND FURTHER TOWARDS THE BACKGROUND. TURNING TO FACE NETLEY, GULL CLAPS ONE PALE, POWERFUL HAND UPON THE COACHMAN'S SHOULDER, AT WHICH NETLEY SEEMS TO GLANCE DOWN WITH UNEASE AS WE LOOK AT HIM IN THE FOREGROUND HERE. BEYOND HIM, GULL STARES STRAIGHT AT NETLEY, FEATURES WRINKLING INTO THE MOST INSANE AND CHILLING SMILE WE'VE WITNESSED YET. HE LAUGHS, HIS EYES GLITTERING, WHILE NETLEY JUST GLANCES UNCERTAINLY DOWN AT THE HAND ON HIS SHOULDER, AS IF AFRAID THAT IT MIGHT SUDDENLY TRANSFORM INTO A BLANCHED TARANTULA.

GULL: Ha ha! Why, Netley! I can offer more than THAT!

GULL: Promise you'll put your heart and soul into this task and I will guarantee your name shall swiftly pass into Masonic HISTORY.

PANEL 6.

NOW A SHOT OF THE COACH AS IT LEAVES THE SQUARE BY ONE OF THE SQUARE'S OTHER CORNERS, SHOWN HERE IN THE REFERENCE PHOTOGRAPH, AS MARKED. IT HEADS AWAY FROM US, TOWARDS THE SMOKE-HUED BUILDINGS THAT REAR UP BEYOND, WITH NETLEY ON THE LEFT HERE, GULL UPON THE RIGHT. NETLEY IS TURNED TO GULL, GUSHING ENTHUSIASTICALLY IN GRATITUDE, WHILE GULL REMAINS STOCK STILL, SITS STARING AT THE ROAD AHEAD OF HIM AND DOES NOT TURN HIS HEAD TO SPARE EVEN A GLANCE FOR NETLEY.

NETLEY: S-Sir William... this'll change my life! You can't IMAGINE, Sir-

GULL: Oh, but I CAN, dear Netley. Most ASSUREDLY I can.

GULL: Proceed down Clerkenwell to Theobald's Road, then on to Bloomsbury Way.

Netley *"has been in several works based on the Jack the Ripper conspiracy theory. ...He was featured in a TV episode of Sir Arthur Conan Doyle's* The Lost World *called 'The Knife' in which Jack the Ripper was really the collaborated work of Netley, Sir William Gull and a police inspector, Robert Anderson"* (Wikipedia). *It's amusing how all these people pop up in assorted mix-and-match permutations, in their junk culture afterlives.*

Chapter 4, page 17.

Midday and lunch occur at the chapter's mid-point, one a cue to talk of sun-gods, the other to draw dripping meat in counterpoint.

If you're reading this book in order you will have noticed that Alan begins each page by giving the number of panels, and if one or more are joined up he says exactly where. I had asked him to do this to enable my assistant to pencil all the panel outlines using our nine-panel template and then ink-rule them accordingly, without having to search for the information in the body of the script.

FROM HELL's publishing schedule was so exasperating (see pg 32 here), I needed to be doing several other things as well. To keep everything moving and not piling up in a queue, I came up with the idea of employing a casual assistant. First it was a young guy named John Barry, who wasn't an artist, but it was at the beginning of Chapter 2, which involved a lot of straightforward cutting and pasting of flat black paper onto the panels. Right off the bat, John told me all my templates were off-square, so I had him spend time cutting new ones. They're looking very weary now, but I still use them. Money well spent.

PAGE 17. (1031 words) PANEL 1.
THERE ARE FIVE PANELS ON THIS PAGE, WITH ONE BIG WIDE ONE TAKING UP THE TOP TIER AND THEN TWO PANELS ON EACH OF THE TWO TIERS BENEATH THAT. IN THIS FIRST WIDE PANEL I THINK IT'D BE NICE TO HAVE A SHOT OF THE NOON SUN, JUST TO UNDERSCORE ALL THIS TALK OF SOLAR DEITIES WITH A PICTURE OF THE REAL OBJECT ITSELF. MAYBE, IF THE SHOT ISN'T TOO DIFFICULT OR DOESN'T LOOK TOO ARTIFICIAL, WE COULD BE LOOKING STRAIGHT UP AT THE SUN ABOVE US, SO THAT AROUND THE SIDES OF THE PANEL THE TALL VICTORIAN BUILDINGS OF EARL'S COURT LOOM AWAY FROM US IN PERSPECTIVE, POINTING TOWARDS THE BLIND AND STARING SUN THAT HANGS ABOVE THE BUILDINGS. THE SKY MAYBE HAS A FEW DARK STREAKS OF SMOKE RUNNING IN BLACK BANDS ACROSS IT, BUT IS OTHERWISE FAIRLY UNCLOUDED, FOR A CHANGE. THE GLARE OF THE SUN IS BRIGHT AND OPPRESSIVE. IF THIS SHOT DOESN'T WORK FOR YOU, MAYBE A SIMPLE SHOT OF THE SUN IN AN OTHERWISE EMPTY PANEL WOULD BE JUST AS EFFECTIVE... A SIMPLE SKY-SCAPE, WITH GULL'S BALLOONS ISSUING UP INTO IT FROM OFF-PANEL BELOW. IN EITHER EVENT, GULL AND NETLEY ARE OFF-PANEL HERE, AND OUR MAIN FOCUS OF ATTENTION IS THE SUN, A HUGE AND DISTANT THERMONUCLEAR GOD, STARING DOWN UPON LONDON AND ITS INHABITANTS AS A ZOOLOGIST

MIGHT DISPASSIONATELY INSPECT A TERRARIUM.

GULL (OFF):   Crete fell, and the Mycenaeans next occupied the area, employing Crete's artificers, as demonstrated by Cretan designs upon those times' Mycenaean artifacts.

GULL (OFF):   Did the Dionysiacs thus infiltrate Mycenaean culture? Roam the world with them? Help shape that world into their grand and secret edifice?

GULL (OFF):   There are Mycenaean symbols etched upon Stonehenge. Could the Dionysiacs have helped design that ancient Solar shrine, where Druids once made sacrifice?

PANEL 2.

NOW, IF THE LAST SHOT WAS A SHOT LOOKING UP AT THE SUN, MAYBE WE REINFORCE THE EFFECT OF THE SUN STARING HARSHLY DOWN UPON LONDON BY TAKING AN OVERHEAD VIEW FOR THIS PANEL, LOOKING DOWN. WE ARE DIRECTLY ABOVE THE COACH, SOME DISTANCE UP IN THE AIR, SO THAT TO ONE SIDE OF THE PICTURE THE ERODED RED BRICK WALLS OF THE BUILDINGS THAT THE COACH IS PASSING DROP DOWN AWAY FROM US, TOWARDS THE RIBBON OF THE STREET BELOW WHERE THE COACH AND ITS TWO PASSENGERS PROGRESS AT A COMFORTABLE PACE ALONG THE STRIP OF COBBLESTONES THAT IS THE ROAD. IF WE AREN'T TOO HIGH UP TO MAKE OUT ANY SENSE OF POSTURE AT ALL, THEN GULL IS PERHAPS GESTURING EXPANSIVELY WITH BOTH HANDS, IN A SORT OF ALL-INCLUSIVE GESTURE. IF WE'RE TOO HIGH UP TO SEE THIS THEN IT ISN'T IMPORTANT. LIKE A KEPHRA BEETLE HAULING ITS PELLET OF DUNG, THE HORSE AND ITS CARRIAGE CRAWL ALONG THE STREET BENEATH US, WATCHED ONLY BY THE SUN; BATHED IN ITS INDIFFERENT, FAINTLY RADIOACTIVE GAZE.

GULL: Always in the Sun! Whether his name be Lud, Apollo, Helios or Atum.

GULL: Be he Belinos, or Bel, or Baal...

PANEL 3.

NOW WE HAVE A SHOT OF THE COACH COMING TOWARDS US ALONG A CURVING CRESCENT SOMEWHERE IN EARL'S COURT, FOR WHICH SEE THE ENCLOSED REFERENCE PHOTOGRAPHS. I'M AFRAID I DON'T HAVE REFERENCE OF AN ACTUAL PUB IN EARL'S COURT, SO MAYBE YOU COULD SORT OF MAKE ONE UP AND GRAFT IT INTO THE PICTURE SOMEWHERE IN THE FOREGROUND, SO THAT THE COACH IS COMING DOWN THE STREET TOWARDS IT FROM THE BACKGROUND. AS IT COMES CLOSER, WE SEE THAT GULL IS POINTING TOWARDS THE PUB IN THE FOREGROUND WITH A CASUAL GESTURE. ALL ABOUT THEM STAND THE TALL AND VAGUELY STIFF-NECKED BUILDINGS OF EARL'S COURT, FORMAL AND BLAND AND SEDATE. THE COACH, A BLACK SHAPE, MOVES BETWEEN THE WHITE BUILDINGS LIKE A RUMOUR OF PLAGUE.

GULL: Earl's Court, which we approach, was once called Billingswell, after "Belinos' Well", sacred unto the Solar God-King Belinos, son of King Lud.

GULL: Stop at this inn.

PANEL 4.

NOW A SILENT PANEL. IN THE FOREGROUND, WE SEE THE FRONT END OF NETLEY'S HORSE, JUST ITS HEAD AND SHOULDERS PROTRUDING INTO THE PANEL FROM ONE SIDE, A FEED BAG HANGING FROM ITS BRIDLE, WHICH IT MUNCHES WITHIN CONTENTEDLY. THE HORSE IS TETHERED TO

SOME CONVENIENT POST OR RAIL JUST OUTSIDE THE INN, WHICH WE CAN SEE TAKING UP THE IMMEDIATE BACKGROUND. GULL AND NETLEY ARE IN THE MIDDLE GROUND, HEADING AWAY FROM US AND ABOUT TO ENTER THE INN. NETLEY PERHAPS HOLDS THE DOOR OPEN REVERENTLY FOR GULL, ALLOWING HIM TO ENTER FIRST IN A SPLENDID DISPLAY OF FORELOCK-TUGGING CLASS SUBSERVIENCE. GULL DOESN'T GLANCE AT NETLEY AS HE SWEEPS INTO THE RELATIVE DARKNESS OF THE INN, FOR ALL THAT NETLEY'S SOMEHOW DOG-LIKE GAZE IS FIXED HOPEFULLY UPON HIM AS HE GLIDES PAST. IN THE FOREGROUND, THE HORSE MUNCHES AWAY, OBLIVIOUS TO EVERYTHING. No Dialogue.

PANEL 5.

NOW WE ARE INSIDE THE INN, WHICH SEEMS FAIRLY REPUTABLE AND CLEAN. IN THE FOREGROUND, GULL AND NETLEY HAVING DIVESTED THEMSELVES OF THEIR HATS, SIT OPPOSITE EACH OTHER ACROSS A BROAD WOODEN TABLE. A PORTLY INNKEEPER'S WIFE IS JUST SETTING DOWN A TRAY UPON THEIR TABLE UPON WHICH TWO STEAMING PLATES OF KIDNEY PIE WITH POTATOES, CARROTS AND GRAVY ARE RESTING. BEYOND HER, WE CAN JUST MAKE OUT A SUGGESTION OF THE INN'S COMFORTABLE LOOKING INTERIOR. AS SHE SETS THE TRAY DOWN ON THE TABLE AND STARTS TO DISH OUT THE FOOD TO NETLEY AND GULL, GULL LOOKS UP AT HER AND SMILES. IT ISN'T A SINISTER SMILE - IT'S A SMILE OF A GENIAL AND FRIENDLY ELDERLY MAN, COMPLIMENTING A MIDDLE-AGED MATRON UPON THE EXCELLENCE OF HER COOKING. THE INNKEEPER'S WIFE GIVES GULL A SMALL AND GRATEFUL SMILE IN RETURN, PLEASED WITH HERSELF TO BE COMPLIMENTED BY SUCH A GRAND AND WELL-SPOKEN GENTLEMAN. NETLEY MERELY STARES HUNGRILY AT THE FOOD, HIS KNIFE AND FORK ALREADY GRIPPED IN HIS GRUBBY HANDS SO THAT HE CAN DIG IN WITHOUT A SECOND TO SPARE. BENEATH THEIR FLAKING SKIN OF PASTRY THE KIDNEYS STEAM LURIDLY.

GULL:	Ahh! Thank you, my good woman.
GULL:	May I say your kidney pie smells excellent? Most excellent indeed!
INNKEEPER'S WIFE:	Why bless you, sir. Enjoy your meal.

Watercolour

Detail from the signed drop-in plate in the Graphitti Designs 1000-copy limited edition hardcover **FROM HELL** *published in 2000. For a long time that was the only hardcover edition in English. Pleased with the roof of the cab; watercolour is often about the bit where you didn't touch the paper.*

Chapter 4, page 18.

This page has achieved a level of fame out of proportion to its intrinsic artistic value, as it is the one during the writing of which Alan Moore had a life-changing epiphany. It happened after he typed the line, "The one place the gods exist is in our minds, where they are real beyond refute…" That is, the gods exist in the imagination. The important conclusion from this is not that the gods are therefore not real or not important, but rather that the imagination is exquisitely more important than is commonly acknowledged.

From a 2001 interview: *"After writing it I thought, oh shit, that's true. Now I am going to have to rearrange my entire life around this. There is no way to disprove it. I thought I was writing this great piece of Gothic villain dialogue. The gods and monsters inarguably exist and they are real. Because if they don't exist how many people died because of them, or how many history-changing things have been done in the name of these Gods that don't exist? If they don't exist why do they kill so many of us in their name? So at that point, it was just before my 40th birthday. I thought, well I could have a mid-life crisis and just bore everybody to death by going on about, what's it all about, what does it all mean? Or I could sort of just go spectacularly mad, which would at least be more entertaining for those around me."* (Comic Book Resources, Oct 22, 2001)

Alan subsequently declared himself a magician and set his career upon yet another change of direction. Naturally it would be nice to put a date on this page, but all I can offer is that this chapter first appeared in *Taboo* #5 (Nov. 1991.)

PAGE 18. (1,113 words) PANEL 1.
THERE ARE SEVEN PANELS ON THIS PAGE, WITH THREE ON EACH OF THE UPPER TWO TIERS AND THEN ONE BIG WIDE ONE ON THE BOTTOM TIER. THE FIRST THREE PANELS ARE ALL BASICALLY THE SAME SHOT. IT IS AS IF WE ARE SITTING TO GULL'S RIGHT, SO THAT WE SEE A LITTLE OF HIM OVER TO THE LEFT OF THE FOREGROUND, AND THEN WE ARE LOOKING ACROSS THE TABLE AT NETLEY. IF POSSIBLE, I'D LIKE IT IF WE COULD ONLY SEE THE LOWER HALF OF GULL'S FACE, MORE OR LESS IN PROFILE AND FACING ACROSS TOWARDS THE RIGHT OF THE IMMEDIATE BACKGROUND, WHERE NETLEY SITS FACING US OVER HIS PLATE OF KIDNEY PIE AND VEG. WE

CAN'T SEE GULL'S EYES HERE, MAKING NETLEY'S FACE THE FOCUS OF ATTENTION AS HE SITS
ACROSS THE TABLE, GAZING AT US. IN THE FOREGROUND, GULL HAS A LITTLE TRIANGLE OF
PASTRY AND SOME MEAT SPEARS UPON HIS FORK, WHICH HE IS JUST POPPING INTO HIS MOUTH.
ACROSS THE TABLE, NETLEY IS HOLDING A KIDNEY DOWN WITH HIS FORK WHILE HE SAWS AT IT
WITH HIS KNIFE. HE LOOKS UP FROM BENEATH HIS LOW BROWS AT SIR WILLIAM AS HE DOES
THIS, WITH A NEANDERTHAL'S QUESTIONING LOOK OF PUZZLEMENT.

NETLEY: 'Scuse my ignorance, Sir William, but what's all these old
                             Gods got to do with them as 'ave upset 'er Majesty?

PANEL 2.

SAME SHOT. GULL NOW LIFTS HIS NAPKIN TO DAB AT HIS LIPS BEFORE HE REPLIES, HAVING
HASTILY SWALLOWED HIS MOUTHFUL OF PASTRY AND KIDNEY. ACROSS THE TABLE, NETLEY LIFTS
AN IMPALED PORTION OF KIDNEY TOWARDS HIS MOUSTACHE-FRINGED LIPS, NOT TAKING HIS EYES
OFF OF SIR WILLIAM AS HE DOES SO. HIS EXPRESSION IS SERIOUS AND ATTENTIVE, AS IF HE
REALLY IS ANXIOUS TO UNDERSTAND WHATEVER SIR WILLIAM MIGHT BE TELLING HIM, IN CASE
HE HAS TO BE TESTED ON IT BEFORE BEING ALLOWED TO JOIN THE MASONS OR SOMETHING.
WE CAN'T SEE MUCH OF GULL'S EXPRESSION HERE, SINCE HIS MOUTH IS AT LEAST PARTIALLY
CONCEALED BY THE RAISED NAPKIN. WHAT WE CAN SEE IS FAIRLY NEUTRAL, ANYWAY.

GULL: Gmmg. Excuse me...

GULL: Scorn not the Gods. Despite their non-existence in material
                             terms, they're no less potent, no less terrible.

PANEL 3.

SAME SHOT. GULL HAS NOW SET HIS NAPKIN DOWN AND SITS WITH HIS FISTS RESTING ON THE
TABLE, CLUTCHING, RESPECTIVELY, HIS KNIFE AND HIS FORK. HIS EXPRESSION IS ONCE AGAIN
NEUTRAL AS HE GAZES ACROSS THE TABLE DIRECTLY AT NETLEY, AND WE CANNOT SEE HIS EYES.
ACROSS THE TABLE, NETLEY LOWERS THE NOW-EMPTY FORK FROM HIS MOUTH AND CHEWS STUPIDLY
AS HE STARES AT GULL, STILL FROWNING WITH THE EFFORT OF CONCENTRATION AS HE VAINLY
ATTEMPTS TO FOLLOW GULL'S STRAND OF LOGIC, CHEWING A KIDNEY THOUGHTFULLY AS HE DOES SO.

GULL: The one place Gods inarguably exist is in our minds,
                             where they are real beyond refute, in all their grandeur
                             and monstrosity.

PANEL 4.

AS I SEE IT, THE SET-UP FOR THIS SECOND TIER IS PRETTY SIMILAR TO THE SET-UP ON THE
TOP TIER, EXCEPT THAT WE HAVE ZOOMED IN SLIGHTLY CLOSER TO GULL'S PLATE, SO THAT
ALL WE CAN SEE OF GULL AT THIS POINT AT HIS HANDS, HOLDING THE KNIFE AND FORK AS HE
CONTINUES TO EAT HIS MEAL, PILED UP ON THE PLATE WHICH RESTS IN THE IMMEDIATE LOWER
FOREGROUND. LOOKING ACROSS THE TABLE BEYOND THIS WE SEE NETLEY AS HE SITS, STILL
FACING US, TOWARDS THE RIGHT OF THE IMMEDIATE BACKGROUND. IN THIS FIRST PANEL ON THE
LEFT, UP IN THE FOREGROUND, WE CAN SEE GULL'S FORK AS IT PIERCES A WHOLE KIDNEY, THE
TINES PUNCTURING THE SMOOTH OUTER MEMBRANE AND THEN SLIDING THE ORGAN ABOUT ON THE
PLATE IN ORDER THAT IT MIGHT SOAK UP A LITTLE MORE GRAVY. IN HIS OTHER HAND, GULL'S
KNIFE HOVERS POISED, READY TO MAKE THE FIRST INCISION. ACROSS THE TABLE, NETLEY
ABSENT-MINDEDLY SAWS AT ANOTHER PIECE OF KIDNEY AS HE GAZES UP AT THE OFF PANEL
POINT WHERE GULL'S FACE MUST BE. HIS PUZZLED FROWN IS STARTING TO MELT INTO A LOOK

OF HOPELESS MYSTIFICATION.

GULL (OFF):   What's Mars but mankind's violent attributes personified?
Or Aphrodite, save mankind's desires?

GULL (OFF):   The Hemuristic Sages recognized all Gods as aspects of "The
One", yet missed the greater truth.

PANEL 5.

SAME SHOT. HERE, WITH THE KIDNEY FIRMLY TRANSFIXED BY HIS FORK, GULL STARTS TO
SLICE IT IN HALF WITH HIS KNIFE. ACROSS THE TABLE, HIS CONCENTRATION UPON WHAT
GULL IS SAYING STARTING TO MELT AWAY ALONG WITH ANY PRETENCE AT COMPREHENSION.
HE LETS HIS GAZE SINK DOWN TO THE KIDNEY THAT GULL IS SAWING IN HALF, WHICH HE
GAZES AT, ODDLY TRANSFIXED, HIS EXPRESSION DULL AND STARING. HIS OWN KNIFE AND
FORK GRADUALLY GROW STILL UPON HIS PLATE, HIS HANDS COMING TO REST AS HE SINKS
INTO A VAGUE TRANCE OF BOREDOM AND INCOMPREHENSION.

GULL (OFF):   "The One" is US, each with a pantheon of Gods in our Right
Brain, whence inspiration and all instinct springs.

PANEL 6.

SAME SHOT. SPEARED ON THE TINES OF HIS FORK, GULL NOW RAISES A KIDNEY TOWARDS
HIS OFF PANEL MOUTH, A BEAD OF GRAVY DRIPPING VISCOUSLY FROM ITS UNDERSIDE.
ACROSS THE TABLE, NETLEY LOOKS SHARPLY UP AT GULL'S OFF-PANEL FACE ONCE MORE,
AS IF SUDDENLY STARTLED BY GULL'S COMMAND THAT HE SHOULD GET ON AND EAT HIS PIE.
HIS EYES SHOW THIS MILD STARTLEMENT, GAPING AT GULL IN SURPRISE AS HIS HANDS
ONCE MORE START TO RE-BUSY THEMSELVES ABOUT THE TASK OF KIDNEY CUTTING.

GULL (OFF):   Athena gives us automobiles; Mars our Mahdi Uprisings. Is
that not plague and miracle enough to sate the God of Exodus?

GULL (OFF):   Finish your pie. We cannot tarry long.

PANEL 7.

THIS FINAL PANEL TAKES UP THE WHOLE TIER. WE ARE ONCE MORE OUTSIDE THE FRONT OF
THE INN, AND JUTTING INTO THE PANEL FROM ONE SIDE OF THE FOREGROUND WE SEE THE
HEAD AND SHOULDERS OF NETLEY'S HORSE, STILL MUNCHING AT ITS FOOD, ALBEIT WITH
SLIGHTLY LESS INTEREST NOW THAT ITS INITIAL HUNGER HAS BEEN SATISFIED. LOOKING
PAST THIS INTO THE IMMEDIATE BACKGROUND WE SEE THE FRONT DOOR OF THE INN, WHICH
NETLEY IS HOLDING OPEN AS SIR WILLIAM SWEEPS OUT OF THE INN WITH HIS DARK COAT
OR CLOAK DRAPED AROUND HIM, SETTLING HIS TOP HAT BACK UPON HIS HEAD AS HE COMES
TOWARDS US AND THE COACH. ONCE MORE, HE DOESN'T LOOK AT NETLEY AS HE PASSES HIM,
ALTHOUGH NETLEY CONTINUES TO STARE WITH CRINGING AWE AND RESPECT AT SIR WILLIAM.
IT IS A LITTLE LATER NOW, AND THE SHADOWS HAVE STARTED TO
LENGTHEN AGAIN, ALMOST IMPERCEPTIBLY, AS THE SUN MOVES
FURTHER PAST THE ZENITH OF NOON.

No dialogue

Chapter 4, page 19.

And so, it's on into the afternoon, beginning with the weather forecast. And note the description of the stone sphinx in the final panel. You can see Alan's photo of it later in the colour section. On finishing this chapter, I rounded up all the photographs sent by Alan, and photocopies made from books he'd sent, and others accessed by me at the library. The total number of photo-references came to 67 pieces, just for this 38-page chapter. The trick with this sort of thing is to make everything look like it comes from the same artistic eye. An object on a page of comics that attracts too much attention to a photographic origin is likely to rupture the suspension of disbelief rather than support it, which is the reason for using photos in the first place.

PAGE 19. (1216 words) PANEL 1.
THERE ARE SIX PANELS ON THIS PAGE, WITH THREE ON THIS TOP TIER, ONE BIG ONE TAKING UP THE MIDDLE TIER AND THEN TWO PANELS ON THE BOTTOM TIER. IN THIS FIRST PANEL ALL WE SEE IS A LONG SHOT OF THE COACH, WHICH NEEDN'T BE TERRIBLY DISTINCT OR DETAILED. ALL WE NEED TO CONVEY IS THAT THE COACH IS MOVING AGAIN, AND THAT GULL AND NETLEY HAVE THUS PRESUMABLY RESUMED THEIR JOURNEY.
A BACKGROUND ISN'T REALLY NECESSARY, BUT IF YOU SEE ONE YOU LIKE, MAYBE YOU COULD USE ONE OF THE EARL'S COURT BACKGROUND SHOTS THAT YOU HAVEN'T USED ALREADY?   (SEE REFERENCE PHOTOS).

GULL: Myths are the key to your Right Brain; that world of Gods, that,
                         like Atlantis, sank beneath the waters of the Age of Reason.

PANEL 2.
NOW WE MOVE IN FOR A CLOSER SHOT OF THE PAIR, SEEN FROM THE FRONT HERE AS THEY SIT ATOP THE COACH WITH GULL ON THE LEFT AND NETLEY ON THE RIGHT. AS HE SPEAKS, GULL IS STARTING TO UNFURL THE MAP THAT HAS RESTED ON THE SEAT BESIDE HIM THROUGHOUT THIS EPISODE. IT IS A MAP OF LONDON, ALTHOUGH SINCE WE CAN ONLY SEE THE BACK OF THE MAP HERE AS GULL UNROLLS IT, THIS IS NOT YET APPARENT. NETLEY DOES NOT LOOK AT GULL ANY MORE THAN GULL LOOKS AT NETLEY. NETLEY CONTINUES TO PERUSE THE OFF-PANEL ROAD IN FRONT OF HIM WHILE GULL CONCENTRATES UPON UNROLLING HIS MAP. IF WE CAN SEE ANY OF THE SKY, IT IS JUST EVER SO SLIGHTLY CLOUDIER THAN WHEN WE SAW IT BEFORE GULL AND NETLEY WENT IN TO HAVE THEIR LUNCH. IF WE CAN'T SEE THE SKY HERE, THEN DON'T

WORRY. JUST TAKE IT AS A GENERAL STAGE DIRECTION: THE SKY BECOMES GRADUALLY CLOUDIER UNTIL PAGE 22, WHEN IT BEGINS TO RAIN. THIS LASTS ROUGHLY UNTIL PAGE THIRTY-ONE, WHEN THE SUN COMES OUT AGAIN. OKAY ... THAT'S THE END OF THE WEATHER FORECAST. NOW BACK TO THE MAIN NEWS...

GULL: That drowned realm of the mind: those intellects that dive
                            the deepest, salvaging its treasures, we call sorcerers.

GULL: Where next? Let me consult the map...

PANEL 3.

CHANGE ANGLE NOW, SO THAT WE SEE THE TWO MEN IN PROFILE, AS IF WE WERE SITTING TO GULL'S RIGHT AND LOOKING PAST HIM AT NETLEY. THUS, WE SEE A LITTLE OF GULL'S FRONT ENTERING THE PANEL FROM THE LEFT HERE AND FACING RIGHT. WE NEED REALLY ONLY SEE HIS HANDS, UNLESS YOU WANT TO SHOW A LITTLE OF HIS LOWER FACE UP AT THE TOP LEFT CORNER OF THE PANEL. IN HIS HANDS HE HOLDS THE UNFURLED MAP, ALTHOUGH, ONCE AGAIN, SINCE WE SEE IT SIDE ON, WE ARE UNABLE TO MAKE IT OUT PROPERLY. LOOKING PAST THIS WE SEE NETLEY AS HE SITS WITH HIS REINS IN HAND. OVERCOME BY CURIOSITY, HE GLANCES SIDEWAYS TO SEE WHAT GULL IS DOING WITH THE MAP, HIS EYES DARTING BACKWARDS AND FORWARDS BENEATH THE SHADOWS OF HIS DERBY HAT BRIM.

GULL (OFF?):   Ah, yes: Knightsbridge via Cromwell Road, then Grosvenor
                            Place onto Victoria Street...

GULL (OFF?):   I think I'll mark the sites we have already visited...

PANEL 4.

THIS IS A BIG WIDE PANEL, RUNNING RIGHT THE WAY ACROSS THE PAGE. WHAT WE SEE IN IT, BASICALLY, STRETCHED FROM BORDER TO BORDER, IS THE STREET MAP THAT GULL IS LOOKING DOWN AT, FOR WHICH I SUGGEST YOU USE A PASTE UP. I'M CURRENTLY TRYING TO GET A SERIES OF ORDINANCE SURVEY MAPS OF LONDON DURING THE PERIOD, BUT IF I CAN'T THEN ANY OLD MAP OF LONDON COULD BE USED, AS LONG AS IT'S REDUCED ENOUGH TO MAKE THE PLACE NAMES ILLEGIBLE AND THEN PASTED UP ACROSS THIS PANEL. THE ONLY OTHER THINGS WE SEE IN THIS PANEL ARE GULL'S HANDS, ONE OF THEM RESTING ON THE MAP TO STEADY IT WHILE IN THE OTHER HE HOLDS A PENCIL THAT HE HAS PRESUMABLY REMOVED FROM SOME HIDDEN RECESS OF HIS JACKET. HE HAS MARKED WITH CONSPICUOUS CIRCLES OR CROSSES THE SITES ALREADY VISITED, WHICH HE LISTS BELOW. WE DON'T NEED TO SEE ALL THE POINTS THAT HE MENTIONS: WE JUST NEED TO SEE ENOUGH TO GET THE IDEA ACROSS THAT GULL IS MARKING DOWN THE POINTS THAT THEY HAVE VISITED UPON HIS MAP. SEEN HERE, THE POINTS ARE JUST RANDOM MARKS, WITH NO REAL SENSE TO THEM. GULL'S BALLOONS ISSUE FROM OFF PANEL IN THE LOWER FOREGROUND.

GULL (OFF):   There's Battle Bridge, where Matriarchy fell with Boadicea;
                            London Fields where Saxons praised the Moon's assassin;
                            Bunhill Fields, with Blake asleep beneath his obelisk;
                            Old Street, where Hawksmoor raised its twin...

GULL (OFF):   Northampton Square, bought with Masonic gold, and Bloomsbury,
                            St. George, where Hawksmoor raised his pagan mausoleum...

GULL (OFF):   Finally, Earl's Court, where Belinos once had his well. That's
                            all our stops thus far, this random scattering of points...

GULL (OFF):   This earthbound constellation.

PANEL 5.

NOW WE HAVE A SHOT THAT'S PRACTICALLY A REVERSE OF PANEL THREE, IN THAT WE ARE STILL FAIRLY CLOSE TO GULL AND NETLEY AND VIEWING THEM IN PROFILE. THE DIFFERENCE HERE IS THAT WE ARE NOW VIEWING THEM FROM THE OTHER SIDE SO THAT NETLEY IS IN THE FOREGROUND, ENTERING INTO THE PANEL FROM THE RIGHT AND FACING LEFT. THE REINS HELD TIGHT IN HIS HANDS, HE SWIVELS HIS EYES AWAY FROM US TOWARDS GULL, WHOM WE SEE IN THE IMMEDIATE BACKGROUND BEYOND HIM. NETLEY WATCHES GULL, AS GULL ROLLS UP THE MAP AGAIN AFTER USING IT, HAVING NOTED ALL THEIR POINTS OF CALL. AS HE DOES SO, GULL LOOKS TOWARDS NETLEY AND SMILES, FIXING NETLEY WITH HIS UNBLINKING EYES. UP IN THE FOREGROUND, NETLEY LOOKS FAINTLY NERVOUS, ALTHOUGH HE DOES HIS BEST TO CONCEAL IT. SOMETHING ABOUT THE OLD MAN'S PRESENCE IS STARTING TO UNSETTLE NETLEY... SOMETHING BEYOND THE NORMAL UNEASE THAT HE FEELS WHEN TALKING TO MEN WHO ARE MUCH MORE RICH AND POWERFUL THAN HE IS. DIMLY, EVEN THOUGH THE THOUGHT IS TOO BLASPHEMOUS TO FULLY EXPRESS, EVEN TO HIMSELF, IN THE BACK OF HIS MIND NETLEY IS STARTING TO WONDER IF GULL MIGHT POSSIBLY BE INSANE. GULL, ON THE OTHER HAND, HAS NO SUCH ANXIETIES. HE <u>KNOWS</u> THAT HE IS AT LEAST TOUCHED BY INSANITY AND IT DOESN'T BOTHER HIM EVEN SIGHTLY. HE SMILES BENIGNLY AT NETLEY, WHO QUAKES INWARDLY.

GULL: Maps have POTENCY; may yield a wealth of knowledge past imagining if properly divined.

GULL: Encoded in this City's stones are symbols thunderous enough to rouse the sleeping Gods submerged beneath the sea-bed of our dreams...

PANEL 6.

TO THE RIGHT OF THE FOREGROUND HERE, LOOMING INCONGRUOUSLY INTO THE PICTURE, WE SEE A LITTLE OF THE BASE OF CLEOPATRA'S NEEDLE, FLANKED AS IT IS BY SPHINXES, ONE OF WHICH WE CAN PROBABLY SEE HERE. THIS LOOMS STRANGELY IN THE RIGHT OF THE FOREGROUND, WHILE LOOKING BEYOND IT TO THE LEFT OF THE BACKGROUND WE CAN SEE NETLEY'S COACH AS IT APPROACHES THE MONUMENT DOWN THE VICTORIA EMBANKMENT, WITH THE THAMES TO ITS LEFT (OUR RIGHT). IF WE CAN SEE ONE OF THE BLACK SPHINXES THEN IT SMILES FAINTLY AS THE COACH APPROACHES, ALTHOUGH WE CANNOT TELL WHAT IT'S SMILING AT.

GULL (FROM COACH):   ...for better, or for worse.

GULL (FROM COACH):   Stop just ahead.

Variations

This is another panel, in halftone from the original art, from my autobiographical After the Snooter, 2001. *The book has around twenty-five panels of* FROM HELL *variant scenes, created as part of my ruminative narrative. That includes panels shown here on pages 3 and 284. Alec also has a couple of stories about Alan Moore.*

Chapter 4, page 23.

As I wrote above for page 1, having launched into a 38-page chapter consisting entirely of one conversation, or more correctly an occasionally interrupted lecture, without any breaks or diversions apart from the passing scenery, Alan started to worry that he might have bitten off more than we could chew. Remember of course that I received the whole thing in one finished lump so at the time he was writing this page, *FROM HELL* Chapter 4 existed only in Alan Moore's head. This page also has a memorable line of script (end of panel 3's description). Another writer might tell you that "it is raining", but in Alan Moore's script it says that the noise of it is like "like Morse code for some huge, depressing Russian novel."

PAGE 23. (1616 words) PANEL 1.
THERE ARE SEVEN PANELS ON THIS PAGE, WITH THREE EACH ON THE TOP AND BOTTOM TIERS AND THEN ONE BIG WIDE PANEL IN THE MIDDLE. THESE FIRST THREE PANELS ARE BASICALLY THE SAME SHOT, IN THAT WE ARE SITTING BESIDE GULL AND LOOKING PAST HIM TOWARDS NETLEY. THUS, IN THE FOREGROUND TO THE LEFT WE CAN SEE A LITTLE OF GULL, AS HE SITS ROUGHLY IN PROFILE AND FACING RIGHT. AS BEFORE, MAYBE WE SET UP THE PANEL SO THAT WE ONLY SEE HIS FACE FROM THE NOSE DOWN, SO THAT WE CAN JUST SEE HIS MOUTH AND CHIN UP TOWARDS THE TOP LEFT CORNER OF THE PANEL. THE MOST IMPORTANT THING IS THAT WE SEE THE BAG OF GRAPES THAT STILL RESTS IN HIS LAP. AS WE SEE HIM HERE HE HAS TAKEN A GRAPE FROM THE BAG AND IS JUST LIFTING IT TOWARDS HIS LIPS, ABOUT TO PLACE IT IN HIS WAITING MOUTH. LOOKING PAST HIM WE SEE JOHN NETLEY, SITTING HUNCHED OVER HIS REINS AND LOOKING COMPLETELY WRETCHED. HE STARES AHEAD OF HIM INTO THE FALLING RAIN WITH A VAGUELY SICK LOOK. HE IS REALLY STARTING TO WISH THAT HE HADN'T COME.

GULL: Madness is a Dionysian fruit... like grapes.

GULL: Forgive me for not offering you one. Your hands are filthy,
                    and I fear disease.

PANEL 2.
SAME SHOT, ONLY HERE, UP TO THE LEFT OF THE FOREGROUND, GULL HAS PLACED THE GRAPE IN HIS MOUTH AND IS NOW CHEWING IT WITH EVIDENT SATISFACTION, HIS EMPTY HAND LOWERING ITSELF BACK FROM HIS MOUTH TOWARDS HIS LAP AS HE DOES SO. LOOKING BEYOND HIM WE SEE THAT NETLEY HAS TURNED HIS HEAD TO LOOK AT SIR WILLIAM AS HE SPEAKS. WITH HIM FACING US IN THIS MANNER WE CAN SEE HOW ILL AND

WRETCHED HE IS STARTING TO LOOK. HE LOOKS THOROUGHLY MISERABLE AND BLEARY-EYED. THE
RAIN CONTINUES TO FALL AROUND THEM, OBSCURING THE STREETS THAT THEY PASS THROUGH WITH
A VEIL OF COLD LIQUID GREY.

NETLEY: I'm not that 'ungry, sir. I've got bad guts, and feels peculiar, like.

NETLEY: It must 'ave been that pie we 'ad, them kidneys...

PANEL 3.

SAME SHOT. HERE, GULL SITS IN THE FOREGROUND WITH BOTH HANDS RESTING CALMLY ABOUT THE
HALF-EMPTY BAG OF GRAPES. LOOKING BEYOND HIM WE SEE NETLEY, WHO HAS TURNED HIS FACE
AWAY FROM GULL SINCE LAST PANEL SO THAT HE IS NOW VISIBLE TO US IN PROFILE ONCE MORE,
FACING RIGHT. HIS EYES, HOWEVER (OR AT LEAST THE ONE THAT WE CAN SEE) HAVE SWIVELED
TO HIS RIGHT, SO THAT HE REGARDS GULL ANXIOUSLY OUT OF THE CORNER OF HIS EYE AS HE RIDES.
THE RAIN CONTINUES TO FALL LIKE MORSE CODE FOR SOME HUGE, DEPRESSING RUSSIAN NOVEL.

GULL: Possibly... or have these stones and symbols' morbid
                    airs afflicted you?

GULL: Their language speaks direct to our unconscious mind;
                    provokes unease, as well the Dionysiacs knew.

PANEL 4.

NOW WE HAVE A BIG WIDE PANEL TAKING UP THE WHOLE TIER, FOR WHICH I THINK A SIMPLE
LONG SHOT OF THE COACH AS IT MOVES THROUGH THE LONDON RAIN WOULD GO NICELY. JUST
SOMETHING SCRATCHY AND TENTATIVE. A GREY MIST OF HATCHING TO SUGGEST THE DIAGONAL
FALL OF THE RAIN; A SLIGHTLY DARKER PATCH OF HATCHING IN THE CENTRE TO SUGGEST THE
CONTOURS OF THE COACH AS IT CRAWLS ALONG OVER THE SLIPPERY COBBLES, SOMETHING LIKE
THAT? I DUNNO... TO BE FRANK, ED, I'M HAVING A BIT OF A CRISIS OF CONFIDENCE ABOUT
THESE PANEL DESCRIPTIONS AND I'M NOT SURE WHETHER I'M JUST WINGING IT OR WHAT. I
DON'T KNOW IF THIS RELENTLESS AND LIMITED SERIES OF IMAGES (LONG SHOTS OF THE COACH,
FRONT REAR AND PROFILE; CLOSE UP OF GULL AND NETLEY FRONT REAR AND PROFILE) IS ENOUGH
TO HANG THE STRIP ON VISUALLY, AND I SUPPOSE I WON'T KNOW UNTIL YOU'VE HAD A CHANCE
TO READ THE THING AND GET BACK TO ME. BASICALLY, IF THERE IS ANYTHING THAT YOU THINK
MIGHT WORK VISUALLY, THEN TRY IT. IF YOU WANT TO USE INCREASINGLY STRANGE-LOOKING
COLLAGES OF LONDON BUILDINGS FOR BACKGROUND THEN GO AHEAD. IF POINTILLISM LOOKS GOOD
ON THE EARLY MORNING MIST SCENES THEN FEEL FREE TO TRY IT. IF SOME BIG, WIDE, TIER-
WIDTH PANELS WORK BETTER AS THREE SMALLER ONES, THEN DO THEM THAT WAY, AND THE SAME
IF THREE SMALL PANELS COULD SAY AS MUCH IF THEY WERE COMBINED INTO ONE BIG PICTURE.
JUST LET DESPERATION BE THE MOTHER OF INVENTION AND TRY TO LOOK ON IT AS A CHALLENGE
(ALTHOUGH I HAVE A FEELING THAT IN THIS INSTANCE I MIGHT AS WELL SAY "TRY TO LOOK ON
IT AS A CHALLENGE" TO SOMEONE I'VE JUST ASKED TO CATCH A BULLET BETWEEN THEIR TEETH).
ANYWAY, JUST FEEL FREE TO TAKE AS MANY LIBERTIES AS POSSIBLE AND CALL ME IF THERE ARE
REAL PROBLEMS. IN THE MEANTIME, I'LL CONTINUE TO PUT DOWN WHATEVER PANEL DESCRIPTIONS
OCCUR TO ME, BUT YOU SHOULD FEEL FREE TO TAKE ALL OF THEM WITH A PINCH OF SALT, EVEN
MORE SO THAN USUALLY. IN THIS PANEL, UNLESS YOU CAN THINK OF ANYTHING BETTER, THE COACH
CRAWLS SLOWLY FORWARD THROUGH THE RAIN, HEADING TOWARDS CAMBERWELL AND HERNE HILL.

(edited, 4 panels only)

Chapter 4, page 27, (and 28.)

We ran into a problem with this page. Alan has our cheery pair going over Tower Bridge, which was being built at the time and wasn't opened for another six years. This is not something I would have known myself until I sought out the photographic reference. But I wasn't going to let that stand in the way of some collegial mockery. I photocopied the half-built bridge and sent it to Alan with a sketch of the little coach falling off it, and Gull and Netley plunging to their deaths in the river. I attach a copy of it to the end of this page of script.

In the meantime, rather than bother Alan with the problem, I added in an extra page (28 left below), stretched the dialogue out, and sent them the long way round. This way I got to record in our pages a bridge that I find much more interesting. It was built by the great Scottish engineer John Rennie and opened in 1831. In 1968, the bridge was sold to Missouri oil millionaire Robert McCulloch. It was reconstructed and currently stands in Lake Havasu City, Arizona, where it is reckoned to be Arizona's second biggest tourist attraction after the Grand Canyon. Another of Rennie's achievements, Waterloo Bridge, appears on page 21 of this chapter. Although it's still there, it was damaged by German bombs during World War 2 and looks quite altered. "It is frequently asserted that the work force was largely female and it is sometimes referred to as 'The ladies' bridge'" (Wikipedia).

PAGE 27. (666 words) PANEL 1.
THERE ARE FOUR PANELS ON THIS PAGE, WITH TWO ON THE TOP TIER, AND THEN ONE BIG WIDE PANEL ON EACH OF THE TWO TIERS BENEATH THAT. THIS FIRST PANEL IS A SMALL, NORMAL WIDTH PANEL, AND IT JUST SHOWS NETLEY HELPING GULL BACK UP ONTO THE TOP OF

THE COACH. PERHAPS HERE NETLEY HAS CLIMBED ABOARD THE COACH FIRST AND IS PULLING GULL UP BESIDE HIM RATHER THAN PUSHING HIM UP FROM UNDERNEATH. THIS SHOULD BE A SORT OF MIDDLE DISTANCE SHOT, I THINK, SINCE IN THE NEXT PANEL WE SEE THE COACH IN LONG SHOT. GULL CONTINUES HIS HISTORY LESSON IN A GENIAL WAY AS NETLEY, WHO CONTINUES TO LOOK ILL AND WORRIED, HELPS HIM ABOARD THE COACH.

GULL: Druids believed locations were empowered by suffering; soaked up despair and terror which reverberated in the soil and stones for ever more.

PANEL 2.

NOW WE HAVE A DOUBLE-WIDTH PANEL WHICH TAKES UP THE REST OF THE TIER. IT SHOWS A LONG SHOT OF TOWER BRIDGE, WITH THE TOWER ITSELF VISIBLE OVER TO THE RIGHT AND THE COACH APPROACHING IT ACROSS THE BRIDGE FROM THE LEFT. THE RAIN CONTINUES TO EASE UP, AND MAYBE THERE ARE SOME PATCHES OF WHITE AND SILVER STARTING TO SHOW IN THE MISERABLE-LOOKING CLOUDS ABOVE THE RIVER. THE SUN IS NOW DESCENDING SLOWLY FROM MID TO LATE AFTERNOON, ALTHOUGH IT PROBABLY WON'T BE VISIBLE HERE AS ANYTHING EXCEPT A LIGHT AREA IN THE BLANKET OF CLOUD. THE COACH IS QUITE SMALL HERE, WITH GULL'S BALLOONS ISSUING FROM IT AS IT MOVES ACROSS THE BRIDGE, A DARK SHAPE AGAINST THE RAINCLOUDS AND THE RIVER BEYOND.

GULL: This Tower must HUM, a dynamo of Blood and History...

GULL: Built on the "White Mount" named in pagan myths, where Britain's founder Brutus, late of Troy, lies mouldering.

GULL: Guided by Moon Goddess-sent dreams, Brutus seized Britain from its rulers, Gog and Magog, raising New Troy. "Troy-Novantum" ... here, pledged to Diana.

PANEL 3.

WE ARE BEHIND GULL AND NETLEY ATOP THE COACH HERE AS IT RUMBLES ACROSS TOWER BRIDGE. WITH THE BULK OF THE BLOODY TOWER RISING UP IN THE BACKGROUND THEY SIT FACING AWAY FROM US IN THE FOREGROUND, WITH GULL ON THE RIGHT AS THEY GAZE AWAY FROM US HERE. IF IT'S POSSIBLE TO SHOW AMIDST ALL THIS RAIN, A FLOCK OF THE TOWER'S RAVENS ARE MAYBE CIRCLING AGITATEDLY ABOUT SOME POINT OF THE TOWER'S EXTERIOR. I DON'T HAVE REFERENCE PICTURES OF THE TOWER YET, BUT I'LL TRY TO FIND SOME BEFORE I SEND THIS PACKAGE OUT. IF NOT, SHOTS OF THE TOWER SHOULDN'T BE TOO HARD TO FIND OVER THERE.

GULL: Here, Bran's head's buried, Celtic God whose name means "Blessed Raven".

GULL: His birds nest here still. 'Tis said London's destroyed if they depart. Their population is therefore restored occasionally; Ravens imported from elsewhere that seem to stay 'til death.

GULL: The "Sol Tower" of the Sun King Lud stood here, rebuilt by Romans; Normans; Britain's conquerors.

GULL: Here died Jane Grey, Judge Jeffreys, Anne Boleyn, Guy Fawkes, the Little Princes ...infant sacrifices even Druids might admire.

PANEL 4.

NOW IN THIS LAST WIDE PANEL WE ARE ON THE LAWNS IN FRONT OF THE TOWER, WHERE THE RAVENS PICK OVER THE GRASS LIKE A SCATTERING OF CURSES. LOOKING BEYOND THIS WE SEE THE COACH AS IT PASSES THE TOWER AND MOVES AWAY FROM US, OFF THE OTHER SIDE OF TOWER BRIDGE AND HEADING ON TOWARDS BILLINGSGATE. THE RAVENS STARE AT ITS DEPARTURE WITH EYES LIKE LITTLE BLACK WATCH-JEWELS, THEIR FEATHERS SLICK AND SHINY IN THE RAIN.

GULL: Here, 1817, a keeper and his wife perceived a cylinder of viscous azure light, thick as an arm, that hovered briefly, then was gone.

GULL: Another sentry saw a bear-like apparition slide beneath the Jewel-Room door. He fell into a fit, and shortly died.

GULL: Perhaps some places do indeed possess vitality. They dream, and feed, and propagate themselves.

GULL: Take Ratcliffe Highway next, to Billingsgate.

Hollywood's map of London

In Guy Ritchie's Sherlock Holmes *(2009), Robert Downey Jr. and Lord Blackwood (who, like Jack the Ripper, has killed five young women) do battle atop the unfinished bridge in a fictitious 1891. The writer may have seen the joke below, which I showed in print ten years ago, as the film shows no evidence of having consulted anything more serious than comic books. It has been criticized for taking liberties with the layout of London. Blogger Karen, "An American running around London," observed: "One gets the feeling that Guy Ritchie got the idea to look in a history book to see what was happening in London in the late 19th century, found that Tower Bridge was being constructed, and never looked back. At one point in the story, when Holmes realizes he's actually in a Dan Brown novel, he shouts to someone, 'MAP!' If only one person in the production of this movie had done the same."*

Chapter 4, page 29.

Straight after the Tower Bridge problem, we came up against another one. It was important that this page refer to the mythical sun-god, Belinos, (see also page 17 of this chapter) who gave his name to Billingsgate, former site of London's fish market. This just didn't fit the point of the pentagram where it needed to go. Frankly we should be surprised that Alan was able to make anything fit into such a scheme. Due to this insurmountable difficulty, he had to rethink the page from scratch. Therefore in its original form it's a page of script for which there isn't a corresponding page of art. All that's left of the scene, apart from some important lines of dialogue moved to another venue, is the typescript. Shame to have lost the fish.

PAGE 29. (now 30) (800 words) PANEL 1.

THERE ARE THREE WIDE HORIZONTAL PANELS ON THIS PAGE, TAKING UP A TIER EACH. IN THIS FIRST ONE, WE HAVE A WIDE ANGLE SHOT OF BILLINGSGATE FISH MARKET, FOR WHICH I'M AFRAID I COULD GET VERY LITTLE IN THE WAY OF USEFUL REFERENCE. WE SEE THE VARIOUS FISH STALLS SET OUT WITH THE TRADERS AND CUSTOMERS BUSTLING AROUND THEM. THE MAJORITY OF THE BUSTLE SEEMS TO BE GOING ON TOWARDS THE LEFT OF THIS WIDE PANEL, WITH PEOPLE THRONGING ABOUT AMIDST THE BUCKETS OF FISH ENTRAILS, PICKING THEIR WAY OVER COBBLES SHINY WITH PARED-AWAY SCALES AND SLIVERS OF FISH SKIN. OVER TOWARDS THE RIGHT OF THE PANEL, BEYOND THE IMMEDIATE PRECINCT OF THE MARKETPLACE, WE SEE NETLEY'S COACH, WITH HIM AND GULL SITTING ON TOP OF IT, SURVEYING THE SPRAWL OF BILLINGSGATE. ASSAILED BY THE STENCH OF FISH GUTS, NETLEY LOOKS QUEASIER THAN EVER, WHILE GULL SEEMS COMPLETELY RELAXED AMIDST THE STENCH AND CLAMOUR AND CONTINUES TO CONVERSE IN HIS USUAL, GENIAL FASHION. THE RAIN IS DEFINITELY STARTING TO THIN OUT HERE, WITH NO MORE THAN A FEW SPOTS FALLING. ABOVE THE MARKET, THE SUN THREATENS TO PEEK THROUGH ITS RAGGED BANDAGE OF CLOUD, ALTHOUGH IT IS BY NOW VERY LOW ON THE HORIZON, AND NOT FAR AWAY FROM SUNSET. THE BALLOONS BELONGING TO THE MARKET TRADERS ARE ALL FREE-FLOATING AND TAILLESS, AND THEY JUST BOB AROUND ABOVE THE CROWD OVER TO THE LEFT OF THIS WIDE PANEL. GULL'S BALLOONS ARE DISTINGUISHED FROM THEM BY VIRTUE OF THE TAIL THAT POINTS TOWARD GULL.

TAILLESS BALLOON:	YE-O-O! All alive TURBOT!
TAILLESS BALLOON:	Fine grizzlin' SPRATS, large an' no small!
TAILLESS BALLOON:	Had-had-had-had-HADDICK!
TAILLESS BALLOON:	Now or never! Five brill a pound!
TAILLESS BALLOON:	YE-O-O!

GULL :   Sometimes, an act of social magic's NECESSARY: Man's triumph
              over Woman's INSECURE, the dust of history not yet SETTLED.

GULL :   Changing times erase the pattern that constrains society's
              irrational, female side...

PANEL 2.

IN THIS SECOND WIDE PANEL WE CLOSE IN UPON GULL AND NETLEY FACING US ATOP THE BOX OF
THEIR COACH. GULL IS ABSENTLY PLUCKING ONE OF THE REMAINING TWO OR THREE GRAPES, BUT
GAZES STRAIGHT AHEAD AT US WITH HIS PALE GREY EYES. PERHAPS WITH HIS FREE HAND HE
GESTURES TOWARDS THE SQUALOR OF BILLINGSGATE SURROUNDING THEM, THE MURKY OUTLINES OF
WHICH WE CAN SEE RISING UP IN THE BACKGROUND BEYOND THE COACH. NETLEY, SITTING ON THE
RIGHT HERE, LOOKS VERY SICKLY INDEED, AND HAS PERHAPS PULLED OUT A HANDKERCHIEF TO
PROTECT HIS NOSE FROM THE STOMACH-TURNING SCENT OF THE FISH. THE VERY LAST FEW SPOTS
OF RAIN SPLASH DOWN UPON THE REEKING COBBLES, AND THEN THE RAIN IS OVER AND A LATE
AFTERNOON LIGHT ONCE MORE BEGINS TO GRADUALLY PERVADE THE MARKET PLACE.

GULL: Our workers, lately given VOTES, now talk of SOCIALISM, talk
              of RIGHTS, riot in Trafalgar and won't quit 'til they are
              shot, whereon their fury DOUBLES! King Mob's clamour drowns
              out Apollonian debates.

GULL: Reason's BESIEGED: For all our science we are become an age
              of table-rappers, tealeaf readers and Theosophists; where
              Dr. Westcott founds his "Golden Dawn", mistaking hokum for
              the wisdom of Antiquity!

GULL: The Séance-Parlour's murmurings; the gutters' pandemonium...
              these threaten Rationality itself!

PANEL 3.

NOW, FOR THE FINAL SHOT OF THIS PAGE, WE ARE LOOKING ACROSS THE SLAB-TOPPED COUNTER
OF ONE OF THE MARKET STALLS. SPREAD OUT UPON THE SLAB AND RANGING ACROSS THE PANEL ARE A
ROW OF FRESH FISH. THEIR SIGHTLESS EYES ALL STARE COLDLY AT THE LIGHTENING SKY, A CHILL
AND WATERY GLEAM OF LIGHT IS GLISTENING ON THEIR BELLIES. TO ONE SIDE OF THE PANEL, MAYBE
WE SEE THE ARMS OF A FISHWIFE INTRUDE INTO THE PANEL FROM OFF, CAUGHT HERE IN THE ACT OF
SLITTING A FISH'S BELLY OPEN. HELD IN HER STRONG HAND, ITS DEAD EYES STARE AND ITS MOUTH
SAGS IN DISMAY AS THE KNIFE SLICES EFFORTLESSLY UPWARDS THROUGH ITS WHITE FLESH. LOOKING
BEYOND THIS, AND WHATEVER SHADOWY FIGURES ARE GATHERED AROUND THE MARKET STALL WE ARE
LOOKING AT THE REAR OF NETLEY'S COACH AS IT HEADS AWAY FROM US, MAKING ITS WAY BACK ALONG
THE RATCLIFFE HIGHWAY OR THEREABOUTS IN THE DIRECTION OF SPITALFIELDS, ITS PENULTIMATE
STOP. AS THE COACH PULLS AWAY, GULL CONTINUES HIS DISCOURSE WHILE LUCKLESS FISH HAVE
THEIR STOMACHS RIPPED OPEN IN THE FOREGROUND.

GULL: Our Suffragettes demand that women vote, and have equality!
              They'd drag us back to that Primordial nursery, the rule of
              instinct and the Tyranny of mother's milk!

GULL: We can't have that.

GULL: Not though they bawl like all the fisherwives of Billingsgate,
              named for the Sun God Belinos.

GULL: Up Cotton Street, beside East India Docks towards Commercial Road.

GULL: Come, why so SILENT! Is your biliousness worse?

Chapter 4: silent buildings.

The visually repetitive traveling sequences that Alan worried about are strung between a series of large open architectural studies that, if drawn in great detail, I felt would create a pattern to hold the reader's interest through the chapter. They also established the points on the map that would later be joined up to make the London pentacle. These are the ley lines that would be the flight path of Gull's "ascension" in Chapter 14 (not that I knew this at the time). The huge churches were also sombre polarities in later episodes, sucking wrongness into their vicinities.

A young artist named Steve Stamatiadis assisted me on this chapter. I'd letter and lay out these architectural pages and tape the relevant photos to the boards. He would rule up the perspective lines and fill in the laborious detail. Steve's own style was derived from manga and I'm sure he regarded his couple of months with me as drudgery. He didn't want to come back for chapter 5. But he did well, and he worked with me on another book that never got published. Nowadays he runs his own video games company and employs people to do the laborious stuff.

So then I'd take the neatly ruled "technical drawings" and add light source and atmosphere, with particular attention to the time-of-day plan that had been worked out. You can follow the sequence from midday to dusk in the four images shown here.

Alan imagined the chapter's closing image as a double-page spread. Given that the story was to appear in the anthology *Taboo*, each issue a thick squarebound book, I figured that was too complicated and made it just one page (left). Since I had already added a page at the bridge, the count still totaled 38. For this last one I asked Steve to pencil it based on three photocopy references I had lined up, but whose perspectives didn't quite correspond. However, when I came to the final decision on it I found that while it was a great piece of drawing, I couldn't "see" the necessary atmosphere using this approach. I glued the photocopies onto another board and attacked them with ink, adding and subtracting details to pull the parts together. Recently I came across Steve's unused pencil drawing on the back of a contemporaneous page of art from *Doing the Islands with Bacchus*. That's it below.

PAGES 37 & 38 (171 words) (edited)
TO FINISH WE HAVE A DOUBLE PAGE SPREAD THAT SHOWS A WIDE VIEW OF THE ROOFTOPS OF
LONDON. THE CENTRE OF THE NIGHTBOUND CITY IS THE DOME OF ST. PAUL'S, RISING ABOVE
THE STREETS. THE SPIRES OF THE SURROUNDING CHURCHES RADIATE OUT FROM IT IN ODDLY
REGULAR LINES, STRETCHING AWAY TO THE HORIZON. THIS IS LONDON; A FANTASTIC PILE
OF STORIES AND STONES AND LEGENDS AND DEAD MEN, BASKING IN THE LIGHT OF THE LARGE
FULL MOON THAT WE SEE CLIMBING INTO THE DARK NIGHT SKY, SILVERING THE CITY WITH ITS
RAYS. WE CANNOT SEE THE DOCTOR HERE. ALL WE SEE IS THE CITY: OLD AND TERRIBLE.
GULL: ...engraved in stone.

Part 3
Pages 95 to 131.
The theme of this
part is what I call **the
cinematic principle.**
There will be a few
side-glances at the
FROM HELL
movie.

Chapter 5, page 1.

This page of *FROM HELL* first appeared in *Taboo* #6, in July 1992, eight months after the previous chapter. We were 109 pages and some three and a half years in, and we'd only just arrived at the first murder.

This chapter was the one in which Pete Mullins started assisting me in what would amount to an almost full-time capacity for about five years, and on occasion after that. He worked on backgrounds at first and eventually some secondary characters. He had more liberty on my *Bacchus* stories. If you think you can always separate what he did from what I did, then you have a better eye than either of us. Things do tend to look a bit sharper after this, but I was heading in that direction anyway.

The thumbnail sketch is from Alan's notebooks. He sketched each page in miniature entirely for his own benefit as an organising procedure prior to typing the scripts and I believe he worked this way on all his books. His verbal descriptions are so detailed that the sketch is often remarkably similar to the finished design even though I never saw the sketch. Worth noting on this one is that Alan has replaced a provisional title. The scored-out one reads "Grand Work" ("Grand work it shall be," said Gull in Chapter 4, page 5 [p67 here]).

PAGE 1. (1622 words) (edited- panels 1,3,5,8 complete) PANEL 1.
HELLO, EDDIE. WELL, HERE WE ARE: MORE THAN A HUNDRED PAGES INTO THE STORY AND WE FINALLY REACH THE FIRST MURDER. IT STRIKES ME THAT HAVING DONE SUCH A GOOD JOB OF MAKING THE MUNDANE MEANINGFUL AND DRAMATIC FOR THE PAST FIVE INSTALLMENTS, WE MAY HAVE SOMETHING OF A PROBLEM WHEN IT COMES TO THIS FIRST MURDER; THE FIRST CONVENTIONALLY DRAMATIC MOMENT THAT WE'VE BEEN CALLED UPON TO DESCRIBE. I THINK WE NEED TO MAKE IT AS FLAT AND UNEVENTFUL AS WE DID THE SEX SCENE BETWEEN ANNIE AND EDDY BACK IN CHAPTER ONE, ALTHOUGH AT THE SAME TIME WE DO NEED TO CONVEY SOME OF THE HIDEOUS FORCE AND MOMENT THAT HAS GONE INTO THE EVENT. ALSO, WHILE WE MAINTAIN THE AIR OF NORMALITY THAT WE'VE CAREFULLY BUILT UP, WE ALSO HAVE TO MAINTAIN THE ATMOSPHERE OF STRANGENESS THAT WE'VE IMPLIED BEHIND THE EVERYDAY VICTORIAN FAÇADE. A TRICKY ONE, BUT I'M SURE WE'LL HANDLE IT OKAY WHEN WE ACTUALLY GET TO THE SCENE

IN QUESTION.THIS FIRST PAGE IS ONE OF THREE THAT MAKE UP OUR OPENING SEQUENCE, A PUZ-
ZLING AND ANOMALOUS LITTLE VIGNETTE THAT TAKES PLACE IN AUSTRIA. THE FIRST PAGE HAS
THREE TIERS. ON THE UPPERMOST TIER WE HAVE THE BORDERLESS WHITE SPACE TO THE LEFT
WHERE WE TRADITIONALLY SET OUR EPISODE TITLE, AND THEN A DOUBLE WIDTH PANEL TAKING
UP THE REST OF THE TIER. THE LOWER TWO TIERS EACH HAVE THREE PANELS, MAKING THIS AN
EIGHT-PANEL PAGE, INCLUDING THE TITLE PANEL.
TITLES: Chapter V: The Nemesis of Neglect

PANEL 2.
IN THIS FIRST PANEL WE HAVE AN AERIAL SHOT OF A SMALL TWO-STORY BUILDING THAT STANDS
ON THE OUTSKIRTS OF THE UPPER-AUSTRIAN TOWNSHIP OF BRAUNAU. WE ARE LOOKING DOWN AT
THE HOUSE, WHICH STANDS IN A FAIRLY ISOLATED POSITION RELATIVE TO THE REST OF THE
TOWN, THROUGH A FINE VEIL OF POWDERY, FALLING SNOW. WE ARE HIGH ABOVE IT HERE AS WE
LOOK DOWN, AND THE ISOLATED HOUSE IS THE MAIN FOCUS OF OUR VISUAL ATTENTION...
CAPTION: Braunau, Upper Austria. August, 1888.

PANEL 3.
NOW THE FIRST OF THE THREE SMALLER PANELS THAT MAKE UP THIS CENTRAL TIER. SLOWLY, WE
ARE CLOSING IN FROM OUR OPENING IMAGE, ZOOMING SLOWLY DOWN TOWARDS THE HOUSE BENEATH
US. (YOU SEE WHAT A SEMANTIC MUDDLE YOU GET INTO WHEN YOU START USING CINEMATIC
TERMINOLOGY? "ZOOMING SLOWLY".) ALTHOUGH THE SNOWFLAKES STILL BOWL IN A LUMINOUS
FREE-FALL ACROSS THE FOREGROUND OF THE PANEL, WE CAN NOW SEE THE HOUSE IN MUCH
GREATER DETAIL, SINCE WE ARE HOVERING JUST ABOVE THE ROOF AND LOOKING DOWN. WE CAN
CLEARLY SEE THE LIGHT IN THE UPPER-STORY WINDOW, ALTHOUGH THE REST OF THE WINDOWS
ARE DARK. ALTHOUGH IT IS MADE NOWHERE EVIDENT IN THE TEXT THAT FOLLOWS, THE HOUSE IS
THAT BELONGING TO THE CUSTOMS OFFICIAL ALOIS HITLER AND HIS WIFE KLARA. I'M AFRAID
THAT THE BIOGRAPHY OF HITLER THAT I'VE CONSULTED FOR MY REFERENCE HAS NO PICTURE
SECTION, SO YOU'RE ON YOUR OWN AS FAR AS FINDING REFERENCE FOR THIS ONE GOES. IF YOU
CAN'T LOCATE A SPECIFIC IMAGE OF HITLER'S PARENTS' HOUSE THEN JUST DO A PIECE OF
TYPICAL AUSTRIAN ARCHITECTURE FROM THAT PERIOD. AS WE LOOK DOWN ON THE HOUSE HERE,
THE ILLUMINATED WINDOW ON THE UPPER STORY IS BECOMING OUR VISUAL FOCUS OF ATTENTION.

PANEL 5.
NOW WE CLOSE IN SO THAT THE WINDOW FRAME ALSO FILLS THE ENTIRE PANEL, STILL WITH SOME
FLAKES OF SNOW TUMBLING PAST IN THE FOREGROUND. AS WE LOOK DOWN AND THROUGH THE WINDOW
WE CAN SEE INTO THE BEDROOM BEYOND, AND WE CAN SEE THE TOP HALF OF THE DOUBLE BED THAT
IS PRESUMABLY POSITIONED NEAR TO THE WINDOW. THE SCENE INSIDE THE ROOM IS LIT BY AN
OIL LAMP, SOMEWHERE OFF PANEL. SPRAWLED UPON THE BED, ONLY PARTLY VISIBLE TO US HERE,
ARE A MAN AND A WOMAN. THEY ARE HAVING SEX IN THE MISSIONARY POSITION, THE WOMAN'S
LONG NIGHTGOWN PULLED UP IN A CRUMPLED RUCK TO JUST ABOVE THE BREASTS AS SHE LIES FACE
UP BENEATH HER HUSBAND. THIS IS KLARA HITLER, FORMERLY KLARA PÖLZL, AND AS WE SEE HER
HERE SHE IS TWENTY-EIGHT YEARS OLD. THE MAN ON TOP OF HER IS ALOIS HITLER OR HIEDLER,
AND HE IS FIFTY-ONE YEARS OLD. AS WITH THE HOUSE IN WHICH THIS IS HAPPENING, I HAVE NO
VISUAL REFERENCE FOR EITHER OF HITLER'S PARENTS. IF YOU CAN'T FIND ANY EITHER, THEN
JUST GO AHEAD AND MAKE THEM UP. I SEE BOTH OF THEM AS BEING QUITE FLESHY PEOPLE, NOT

ESPECIALLY ATTRACTIVE IN ANY OBVIOUS PHYSICAL SENSE. AS ALOIS GRUNTS AND THRUSTS ON
TOP OF HIS WIFE, HIS OWN NIGHTSHIRT HAVING RIDDEN UP TO HIS WAIST TO REVEAL A DIMPLED
AND CORPULENT BEHIND, BOTH OF THEIR EYES ARE CLOSED. ALOIS CLOSES HIS EYES WITH A
SQUINT OF MIGRAINE-INDUCING EFFORT, WHILE KLARA CLOSES HERS TO ESCAPE TO SOMEWHERE
WITH A MORE PLEASING VIEW. FROM OUR VANTAGE POINT AS WE LOOK DOWN INTO THE ROOM WE CAN
SEE MOST OF THE BED, AND WE CAN PROBABLY SEE THE TWO BODIES MORE OR LESS FULL FIGURE
HERE AS THEY LIE THERE ON TOP OF EACH OTHER. LIT BY THE CREPUSCULAR YELLOW GLOW OF THE
OFF-PANEL OIL LAMP, THE LEANING SHADOWS MAKING SOMETHING STRANGE AND FANTASTIC OF THE
SCENE. IT IS THE LIGHTING OF A CRIMEA SURGICAL TENT, OR THE MURDER ROOM IN A VICTORIAN
MELODRAMA. THE BALLOON, BELONGING TO ALOIS HITLER, IS NEVERTHELESS TAILLESS AND FREE
FLOATING, HANGING THERE IN THE FOREGROUND AMONGST THE TUMBLING SNOW.
TAILLESS BALLOON: ungh

PANEL 8.
IN THIS FINAL PANEL WE CLOSE RIGHT IN FOR A HEAD AND SHOULDERS SHOT OF KLARA AS SHE
FACES UP TOWARDS US FROM UNDER HER HUSBAND, HER EYES TIGHT SHUT AS HER HEAD PITCHES TO
AND FRO WITH THE RHYTHM OF THE COUPLING. THE SWEAT STANDS OUT ON HER BROW, HER FACE
RED AND FILLED WITH BLOOD SO THAT THE SKIN BECOMES TIGHT AND SHINY. IF WE CAN SEE
ANYTHING OF THE BACK OF ALOIS' HEAD IT SHOULD ONLY BE ONE EAR OR A BIT OF ONE SHOULDER,
VISIBLE OVER TO THE EXTREME RIGHT EDGE OF THE PANEL, WITH THE FOCUS OF OUR ATTENTION
BEING FIXED SQUARELY UPON KLARA'S FACE. TO BE MORE EXACT, THE FOCUS OF THE PANEL IS
KLARA'S EYE, SINCE THIS IS THE POINT THAT WE WILL BE ZOOMING IN UPON NEXT PANEL. (I KNOW
THAT YOU HATE MEANINGLESS TIGHT CLOSE UPS OF EYES, BUT THERE IS A VALID STORYTELLING
PURPOSE BEHIND THIS ONE, SO TRUST ME.) THE EXPRESSION OF KLARA'S FACE IS THAT OF SOMEONE
WHO IS TWISTING AND TURNING IN A RESTLESS NIGHTMARE RATHER THAN IN THE THROES OF PASSION.
THE TAILLESS BALLOON HANGS IN SPACE, SOMEWHERE OVER TOWARDS ALOIS' SIDE OF THE PANEL.
TAILLESS BALLOON :   ungh

Alternative sequence. *Early thumbnail version of Chapter 5, pages 4-6. You can see Gull waking in bed at the bottom of far left, and then Polly on the clothesline at bottom in the middle page (more on this after the break). For the rest, they seem to be sharing a horrid dream and then we're back with Hitler's parents in page 6 before this version is abandoned. In the finished book, Mrs. Hitler has a bad dream and then it is forgotten until Mr. Lees describes having had the same one, in 1923 on the last page of the epilogue.*

A pictorial interlude

Steve Bissette gave Alan the inside back covers of *Taboo* for these pastel drawings he made in red, black and white. They appeared in *Taboo* #2-4, Sept. '89, Mar. '90, Feb. '91. They were effectively our first covers for *FROM HELL.*. *Lost Girls* by Moore and Melinda Gebbie started in *Taboo* #5 and supplanted *FROM HELL* in the back cover spot.

Covers from the *FROM HELL* volumes published by Tundra: #1 Apr. '91, #2 July '93. And Kitchen Sink Press: effectively a restart, #3 Dec. '93, #4 Mar. '94; new editions of #1 and #2, June '94.

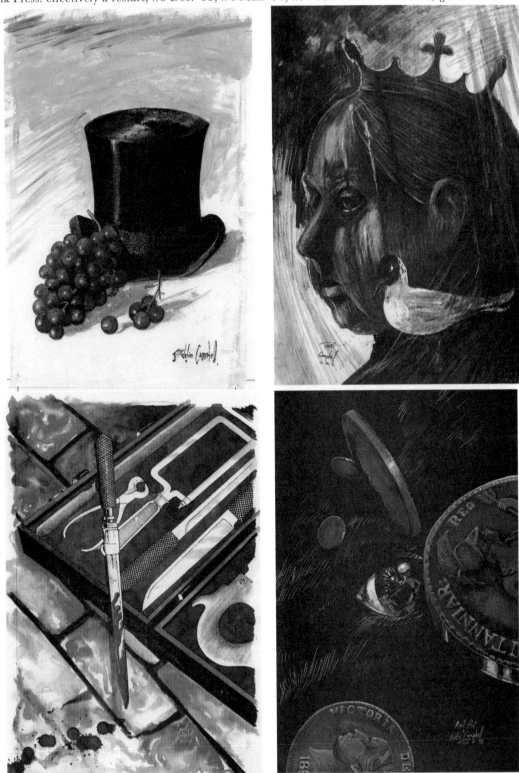

Covers from the *FROM HELL* volumes published by Kitchen Sink Press:
#5 June '94, #6 Dec. '94, #7 Apr. '95, #8 July '95.

For Chapter 4, Alan Moore, with the help of Steve (no relation) Moore and Jamie Delano, made a daylong tour of London, taking copious photographs. (Note that (no relation) has become Steve's middle name in the way that DC heroes used to have middle names, as in Bruce (Batman) Wayne.) Steve is the guy in the blue shirt. On another occasion, Alan photographed Bournemouth. On these pages we're showing some of these along with the black-and-white images I made from them. It was interesting to see the reverse of this situation when the *FROM HELL* movie based some scenes quite clearly on panels from the book, and we present a few of those in later pages.

CHRISTCHURCH, AS SEEN FROM APPROXIMATELY THE TOP OF DORSET STREET

"A SOLEMN + AWEFULL APPEARANCE"

THE PORTICO— SEE ME AND AMBER ON THE LEFT, FOR SCALE

It is a haunt for suicides and ghosts: a naked man is seen, who leaps into the Thames. No splash is ever heard.

They call it Cleopatra's Needle.

He who'd wield it would the BEST of tailors be, to do its work; increase the Sun God's sovereignty...

..For better or for worse. Stop just ahead

22 MORGAN'S TOBACCO AND QUALITY CONFECT

22 MORGAN'S TOBACCO AND QUALITY CONFECT

The drawing below is after a second photo taken on the same occasion (1989).

1986 Brighton *(with Alan's kids)*

1994 Northampton *(with two of mine)*

1998 *(with Melinda Gebbie)*

1999
(with Dave Gibbons)

A page of thumbnails from Alan's notebooks. This is for Chapter 5, pages 10-17. Polly Nichols, Gull, John Merrick. The rethinking of 14-17 is intriguing.

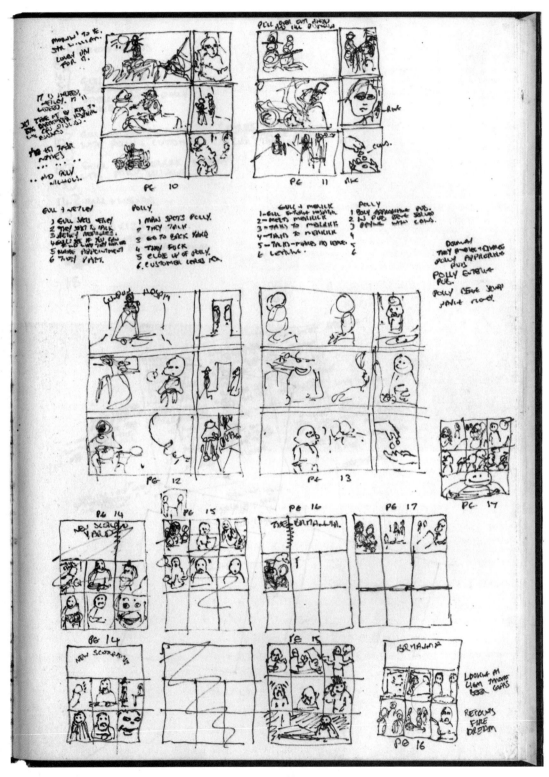

Chapter 5, page 5.

Image from the film From Hell © *20th Century Fox.*

I want to include a couple of scenes here for no other reason than the movie people included them intact in the *FROM HELL* film. It was quite a thrill to see these scenes come out of my head onto the screen. To be truthful, it was in Alan's head first, as you can follow from the thumbnail down through the inked panel to the movie still (©2000 Twentieth Century Fox). The film has the whole female cast sleeping on the "clothesline," not entirely logically since we know at least one of them has a room and a bed, but I presume it was a way of showing a connection among the five women (a theory lately challenged)

PAGE 5. (989 words) PANEL 1.

ONCE AGAIN, THE PAGE IS DIVIDED UP INTO THREE HORIZONTAL PANELS, EACH TAKING UP A FULL TIER. IN THIS FIRST PANEL WE HAVE A CLOSE-UP SHOT OF POLLY NICHOLS, ASLEEP, TO MATCH THE IMAGE OF THE SLEEPING WILLIAM GULL THAT CLOSED OUR LAST PAGE. SINCE THE NEXT SIX PAGES DEPEND TO SOME DEGREE UPON THE RHYTHM OF THE ALTERNATING CROSS-CUTS BETWEEN GULL AND POLLY, MAYBE IT WOULD LOOK GOOD IF YOU FOUND SOME SIMPLE VISUAL WAY TO DIFFERENTIATE BETWEEN THE WORLDS OF THE TWO CHARACTERS. PERHAPS, FOR EXAMPLE, YOU COULD UTILIZE A LOT OF EMPTY WHITE SPACE IN THE IMAGES OF GULL, WHILE WITH THE SHOTS OF POLLY YOU COULD MAYBE USE THAT LITHOGRAPHIC CRAYON OR WHATEVER IT WAS THAT YOU USED IN CHAPTER 2, WHICH WOULD GIVE A FLICKING DARK-LIGHT-DARK-LIGHT-DARK RHYTHM TO THE VISUAL PROGRESSION OF IMAGES. AS EVER, IT'S ONLY A SUGGESTION AND THE END RESULT IS UP TO YOU. HOWEVER YOU DECIDE TO HANDLE IT, THIS PANEL SHOWS A CLOSE UP OF POLLY, ASLEEP. NOW, I CAN'T FIND ANY REFERENCE TO EXACTLY WHERE POLLY STAYED ON THE NIGHT OF THE 29th/30th OF JANUARY, ALTHOUGH IT WOULD SEEM THAT IT MUST HAVE BEEN IN EITHER THE COMMON LODGING HOUSE AT THRAWL STREET, OR IN THE COMMON LODGING HOUSE AT FLOWER AND DEAN STREET. BASICALLY, WE CAN TAKE OUR PICK. WHAT I WOULD LIKE TO SHOW, IF IT

SEEMS RIGHT TO YOU, IS THE PRACTICE OF "SLEEPING ON A CLOTHESLINE" WHICH WAS SEEMINGLY
COMMON IN THE DOSS HOUSES OF THAT PERIOD. THE VAGRANTS UNABLE TO AFFORD EVEN THE
LOWLIEST BED FOR THE NIGHT WOULD PAY A PENNY TO SLEEP SITTING UP IN A ROW AGAINST THE
DOSS HOUSE WALL WITH A LENGTH OF CLOTHESLINE STRETCHED OUT IN FRONT OF THEM TO STOP
THEM FALLING FORWARD COMPLETELY IN THEIR SLEEP. I'D LIKE TO INCLUDE IT BECAUSE OF THE
STRANGENESS OF THE IMAGE, AND ALSO BECAUSE IT WOULD PROVIDE A MORE STRIKING CONTRAST
WITH THE IMAGES OF WILLIAM GULL AWAKENING TO A SUNNY, WELL-FURNISHED BEDROOM IN BROOK
STREET. ON THE OTHER HAND, IF YOU HAVE A BETTER IDEA, OR A DIFFERENT DEPICTION THAT
YOU'RE MORE COMFORTABLE WITH THEN PLEASE STICK IT IN. IF YOU DO DECIDE TO GO FOR THE
CLOTHESLINE IDEA, HOWEVER, THEN WHAT WE SHOW IS AS FOLLOWS: HERE WE SEE A CLOSE-UP OF
POLLY, WHO IS SITTING WITH HER BACK TO THE DAMP AND STAINED DOSS-HOUSE WALL, WHICH
IS OVER TOWARDS THE RIGHT OF THE PANEL. SHE IS ASLEEP, FULLY CLOTHED, AND THE UPPER
HALF OF HER BODY SAGS FORWARD AGAINST THE STOUT ROPE OF THE CLOTHESLINE, HER HEAD
NODDING DOWN ONTO HER NARROW, BIRD-LIKE BREAST. PERHAPS A THIN STRAND OF SOUR DROOL
ESCAPES ONE CORNER OF HER MOUTH AND SETS OUT ACROSS THE BIG ADVENTURE OF HER CHIN.
HER EYES ARE CLOSED AND HER FEATURES SLACK. HER HAIR IS AWRY, WITH THE MOUSEY STRANDS
ESCAPING WISPILY FROM THE BUN OF HER HAIR THAT IS SLOWLY LOOSENING AND UNRAVELING AT
THE BACK OF HER HEAD. SHE IS RIGHT AT THE END OF THE LINE OF SLEEPERS, AND THUS THE
ONLY ONE THAT WE CAN SEE HERE. TO THE LEFT OF THE PANEL, WE CAN SEE WHERE THE END OF
THE CLOTHESLINE IS FASTENED TO EITHER A POST OR A RING IN THE WALL. A PAIR OF MALE
HANDS ARE ENTERING THE PANEL FROM OFF, UNTYING THE KNOT THAT HOLDS THE CLOTHESLINE
WITH DEFT AND PRACTICED FINGERS. THE INTERIOR OF THE DOSS HOUSE ROOM HAS A MIASMIC
AND SOOTY DARKNESS, ALTHOUGH CHINKS OF MORNING SUNLIGHT FALL UPON THE WORN THREADS
OF POLLY'S CLOTHING FROM SOMEWHERE OFF PANEL, WHILE SHE DREAMS ON. UNCONCERNED WITH
POLLY'S DREAM, THE HANDS OVER TO THE LEFT OF THE PANEL CONTINUE TO UNTIE THE ROPE THAT
IS HOLDING UP HER SLEEPING FORM.
No dialogue

PANEL 2. Gull's scene (not in the film and excluded here)

PANEL 3.
WE CUT BACK TO POLLY IN THE DOSS HOUSE. HERE, WE HAVE PULLED BACK A LITTLE FROM
OUR SHOT OF HER AT THE TOP OF THIS PAGE, SO THAT NOW WE CAN SEE HER SITUATION MORE
CLEARLY. WE CAN SEE THE OTHER VAGRANTS SITTING TO POLLY'S LEFT, TOWARDS OUR RIGHT IN
THIS PANEL. THEY ALL SIT FACING US, AND ACROSS TO THE LEFT OF THE PANEL WE CAN SEE
THE LOWER HALF OF THE MAN WHO HAS JUST UNTIED THE CLOTHESLINE, LETTING IT GO SLACK.
AS HE DOES THIS, THE SLEEPING PAUPERS ARE ONCE MORE SUBJECTED TO THE NORMAL COURSE OF
GRAVITY, AND ALL TOPPLE FORWARDS WITH A START, POLLY INCLUDED, HER GUMMY EYES COMING
OPEN AS SHE WAKES TO FIND HER FACE PRESSED AGAINST THE FLOORBOARDS. THE PANEL IS
ARRANGED SO THAT POLLY IS OUR VISUAL FOCUS, WITH MOST OF OUR ATTENTION UPON HER AS SHE
IS RUDELY AWAKENED IN THE CUSTOMARY FASHION. THE EXPRESSION CAUGHT BRIEFLY IN HER
OPENING EYES IS ONE OF A SORT OF DISAPPOINTED BEWILDERMENT.
No dialogue

Chapter 5, page 7.

Image from the film From Hell © *20th Century Fox.*

The second of two scenes that found their way into the movie. Alan asked for a lot of specific refuse around the edges of the street here, but I omitted it, as the noticeable thing I was finding in my research into the poorer areas of big cities in those days is that there was no garbage to be seen, just horseshit and kids with bent legs from rickets and other evidence of deprivation. I presume that whatever there was lying around after market hours would get scavenged pretty quickly.

I never had to make decisions about the colours of women's dresses in *FROM HELL,* but all the gay party frocks on show here strike an odd music hall note. In *Jack the Ripper — A Legacy in Pictures,* Clive Bloom wrote in the caption to a photo: ***"In this publicity shot for* The Hands of the Ripper *(1971), Eric Porter is caressed by actresses dressed in the obligatory boas and feathers which always signify fallen women in such films. The costumes are Victoriana rather than Victorian."*** I used to fret about stuff like that a great deal. William Gaunt, in *The Pre-Raphaelite Tragedy,* observed that the Victorians wore their clothes "an unconscionably long time," and he wasn't talking about the poor folk.

PAGE 7. (647 words) PANEL 1.
BACK TO POLLY FOR THIS FIRST PANEL. SHE IS NOW IN THE EARLY MORNING STREETS OF THE EAST END. THERE ARE CABBAGE LEAVES IN THE GUTTER, AND THE GAUDY TISSUE-WRAPPINGS OF EXPENSIVE TANGERINES. ALONG WITH A COUPLE OF OTHER ANONYMOUS WOMEN, POLLY STANDS NEAR A PUBLIC HORSE TROUGH STRIPPED TO HER PETTICOATS. SHE SITS ON THE SIDE OF THE TROUGH, HOLDING A BROKEN PIECE OF MIRROR IN ONE HAND, COMBING HER FAINTLY GREYING HAIR WITH A BROKEN COMB. SHE GAZES INTO THE MIRROR AS SHE COMBS OUT HER SURPRISINGLY LONG HAIR. SHE HAS HER MOUTH SHUT TO COVER HER MISSING TEETH, AND HER EYES ARE SERIOUS AS SHE STUDIES HER REFLECTION IN THE BROKEN GLASS. SHE REALLY DOES LOOK QUITE PRETTY, IN A FADED WAY, AND A GOOD

FIVE YEARS YOUNGER THAN HER ACTUAL AGE. STARING INTO THE MIRROR, SHE SEEMS TO
LOSE SIGHT OF HER DISMAL SURROUNDINGS FOR A MOMENT, COMPLETELY ABSORBED. NEXT
TO POLLY, STANDING FACING AWAY FROM US, ONE OF THE ANONYMOUS WOMEN WITH WHOM
POLLY SHARES HER ABLUTIONS IS DOURLY LIFTING HER PETTICOATS AND SPLASHING WATER
FROM THE TROUGH UP BETWEEN HER LEGS. IT IS STILL VERY EARLY IN THE MORNING, AND
THE STREET THAT WE SEE STRETCHING AWAY BEHIND THE BATHING WOMEN IS PRACTICALLY
DESERTED SAVE FOR THE OMNIPRESENT RUBBISH. THERE IS A LITTLE LIGHT BETWEEN
THE SQUAT BUILDINGS, AND THE VISUAL TONE OF THE PANEL IS STILL DARK, AS IT IS
THROUGHOUT POLLY'S RUN OF PANELS. POLLY'S BREASTS ARE BARE, AND HER FROCK AND
OTHER CLOTHING ARE DRAPED OVER THE SIDE OF THE HORSE TROUGH, OR ARE LAYING
SOMEWHERE NEARBY, INCLUDING THE BLACK RIBBED STOCKING. POLLY IS ALSO BAREFOOT
HERE. I SEE THE PANEL AS HAVING ALMOST A CLASSICAL COMPOSITION: LIKE SHOTS OF
DIANA AND HER NYMPHS BATHING BESIDE A POOL, BUT GRIMLY TRANSPOSED TO A SQUALID
NINETEENTH CENTURY URBAN SETTING SO THAT THE GODDESS AND HER NYMPHS BECOME
AGEING VAGRANT PROSTITUTES, AND THEIR POOL A WATER TROUGH. BEHIND THEM, BLIGHTED
TERRACES REPLACE THE SYLVAN GLADES. NEVERTHELESS, A SORT OF INNOCENT, CLASSICAL
QUALITY IS RETAINED, IF ONLY IN THE ABSORBED EXPRESSION OF THE SEMI-CLAD WOMEN.
No dialogue.

PANEL 2. (not in the film)
NOW WE CUT BACK TO GULL. HE IS OUT OF THE BATH, AND HAS RETURNED TO THE
ADJOINING CHAMBER TO DRESS. PERHAPS WE COULD SET UP THIS PANEL SO THAT WE ARE
IN THE BATHROOM LOOKING OUT AT GULL, ENABLING US TO SHOW THE NOW-EMPTIED BATH,
THE USED TOWELS CRUMPLED AS THEY HANG OVER ITS SIDE. LOOKING OUT BEYOND THIS
WE SEE GULL AS HE DRESSES, PERHAPS CAUGHT HERE IN THE ACT OF FASTENING HIS
TIE, OR ADJUSTING HIS HIGH, STARCHED COLLAR OR SOMETHING. HIS BLACK COAT IS
DRAPED NEATLY UPON A CONVENIENT HANGER SOMEWHERE NEARBY, PRESSED AND CLEANED
AND READY TO PUT ON. GULL STUDIES HIMSELF IN HIS WARDROBE MIRROR (OR WHATEVER)
WITH SATISFACTION. HIS SHIRT IS A HOLY, PRISTINE WHITE. IT CATCHES THE SUN
BEAUTIFULLY, ALMOST BLINDING TO LOOK AT.
No dialogue

PANEL 3.
CUT BACK TO POLLY. THE PANEL IS ARRANGED SO THAT THE CORNER OF THE HORSE TROUGH
THAT WE SAW LAST PANEL IS NOW IN THE FOREGROUND ON THE LEFT, QUITE LARGE. WE
LOOK ACROSS IT TOWARDS POLLY AS SHE STANDS DRESSING SOME FEW FEET AWAY. HER HAIR
IS NOW DONE UP INTO A FAIRLY NEAT AND PRESENTABLE BUN, AND SHE HAS REPLACED HER
FROCK AND HER STOCKINGS, ONE OF WHICH SHE IS PERHAPS ADJUSTING HERE. SHE LOOKS A
LOT MORE PRESENTABLE THAT SHE DID UPON WAKING, AND HER EXPRESSION IS QUIET AND
SERIOUS AND RESIGNED AS SHE ADJUSTS HER DRESS. BEHIND HER, WE SEE THE TERRACED
DOORSTEPS OF FLOWER AND DEAN STREET, GREY IN THE OVERCAST MORNING LIGHT. PERHAPS
ONLY THE VERY TOPS OF THE HOUSES, IF WE CAN SEE THEM, ARE LIT BY THE RISING SUN,
WITH NO LIGHT FILTERING DOWN INTO THE NARROW STREETS BELOW AS YET.
No dialogue

There's more than one thing going on here, and since Alan wanted to emphasize the darkness, it wasn't easy to draw. Alan extends the comedic roles of Gull and Netley, and to this end I took the liberty of stretching the dialogue over more panels than was requested in the script, for the sake of timing. Thus, the first and last panels now have dialogue. The final panel, which was supposed to take its place in a rhythmic march toward doom (in a five-page sequence with wide silent finishing panels), now has dialogue dished out from the panels above, risking an upset of the balance of the sequence. I never cleared it with Alan. Maybe when we're cranky old geezers, we'll fall out over it.

PAGE 22. (724 words) PANEL 1.
NOW A SEVEN-PANEL PAGE IN WHICH WE RETURN TO GULL AND NETLEY, THE LAUREL AND HARDY OF SERIAL MURDER, AS THEY PROGRESS THROUGH THE EAST END. THE TOP TWO TIERS HAVE THREE PANELS EACH WHILE THE BOTTOM TIER HAS ONE WIDE PANEL. IN THIS FIRST SILENT PANEL WE HAVE A LONG SHOT OF THE DARK BULK OF THE COACH AS IT CREAKS AND RATTLES THROUGH THE MIASMAL BLACKNESS, ONLY JUST DISCERNABLE TO US AS A RECOGNIZABLE HORSE AND CARRIAGE. OTHERWISE, IT IS JUST A VAGUE AND THREATENING MASS TRUNDLING AWAY FROM US THROUGH THE NARROW STREETS. A SINGLE COACH LAMP BURNING DIMLY AND BALEFULLY INSIDE IT.
No dialogue.

PANEL 2.
NOW WE ARE UP ON THE BOX BESIDE GULL, WITH GULL ONLY PARTLY VISIBLE TO ONE SIDE OF THE FOREGROUND. ALL WE CAN REALLY SEE OF HIM ARE HIS LAP AND HIS ARMS AS HE SITS THERE JUST OFF THE PANEL. HE HAS A BAG OF GRAPES IN HIS LAP, AND IN HIS HANDS HE HOLDS THE SMALL BOTTLE OF LAUDANUM, NOW OPENED, AND A SMALL PAINTBRUSH. HE IS JUST DIPPING THE BRUSH INTO THE LAUDANUM HERE, HIS SPEECH BALLOON ISSUING FROM OFF-PANEL. LOOKING BEYOND GULL'S HANDS, THE GRAPES AND THE LAUDANUM WE CAN SEE A HALF-FIGURE SHOT OF JOHN NETLEY AS HE SITS THERE NEXT TO GULL ON THE BOX, HOLDING THE REINS IN ONE HAND AND HIS WHIP IN THE OTHER. HE IS GAZING AHEAD INTO THE DARKNESS AS HE RIDES, RATHER THAN LOOKING TOWARDS US, OR GULL, AND HE WEARS A FAIRLY NEUTRAL EXPRESSION.

GULL (OFF) :   Hark, Netley! It is two o'clock, and still our bag is empty.
GULL (OFF):   You DID locate the woman earlier, according to instructions?

PANEL 3.

SAME SHOT. IN THE FOREGROUND, GULL IS NOW APPLYING THE LAUDANUM-SOAKED PAINTBRUSH
TO THE GRAPES, PAINTING THEM WITH THE STICKY TINCTURE. LOOKING BEYOND GULL'S
HANDS WE CAN SEE NETLEY AS HE TURNS TO FACE US WITH AN ANXIOUS EXPRESSION,
WORRIED THAT SIR WILLIAM MAY BE DISPLEASED WITH HIM, AND ANXIOUS TO GIVE A GOOD
ACCOUNT OF HIMSELF. BEYOND NETLEY THERE IS ONLY DARKNESS AS THE CAB CONTINUES TO
MOVE SLOWLY AND ALMOST SILENTLY THROUGH THE EAST END.

NETLEY: Oh, yes, sir. Three of 'em. Two I'll know again. The third I
                    singled out by givin' 'er a token, like you said.

GULL (OFF):   Excellent! How shall we know her?

PANEL 4.

SAME SHOT. IN THE NEAR BACKGROUND, NETLEY TURNS HIS EYES BACK TO THE ROAD SO
THAT HE IS ONCE MORE IN PROFILE AND NO LONGER FACING TOWARD US OR SIR WILLIAM.
HE ALLOWS HIMSELF A SMUG, SELF-SATISFIED SMIRK, PROUD OF HIS GREAT INITIATIVE AND
CLEVERNESS. IN THE FOREGROUND, GULL'S HAND PAUSES HALFWAY BETWEEN THE GRAPES AND
THE BOTTLE OF LAUDANUM, TOWARDS WHICH IT WAS HEADING TO REFILL THE BRUSH.

NETLEY: I gave 'er a bonnet, sir.

NETLEY: A black bonnet.

PANEL 5.

NOW A LONG SHOT OF THE COACH, SIMILAR TO PANEL ONE. IT IS MOVING AWAY FROM US
INTO THE DARKNESS OF WHITECHAPEL. AN INDISTINCT BLACK SHAPE AGAINST THE EQUAL
BLACKNESS BEYOND. IT IS NOT YET TOO FAR AWAY FROM US HERE, SO THAT WE CAN STILL
JUST MAKE OUT THE HUDDLED FORMS OF GULL AND NETLEY AS THEY SIT ATOP THE COACH.
OTHERWISE, THE PANEL IS ALMOST COMPLETELY BLACK. WHITECHAPEL IS BLACK. THE COACH
IS BLACK. YOU CAN BARELY SEE YOUR HAND IN FRONT OF YOUR FACE.

GULL: A black bonnet. How very helpful.

GULL: Netley, do you know what your foremost distinguishing
                    feature is?

NETLEY: Why, I... I can't think, sir.

PANEL 6.

SAME SHOT, ONLY NOW THE COACH IS FURTHER AWAY, MOVING FURTHER INTO THE IMPENETRABLE
DARKNESS OF THE BACKGROUND, THE SHADOWS SMOTHERING THE IMAGE.

GULL: Precisely.

GULL: Head for Whitechapel Road, and let us hope your eyes are
                    equal to the task your ailing wits have set them.

PANEL 7.

NOW A BIG WIDE PANEL IN WHICH WE SEE A GENERAL VIEW OF THE EAST END AT NIGHT,
DIFFERENT FROM THE SHOT WITH WHICH WE CLOSED PAGE TWENTY-ONE, BUT EVOCATIVE OF THE
SAME THINGS. THERE CAN BE PEOPLE ABOUT, OR NOT, DEPENDING ON HOW YOU FEEL. MAYBE
WE'RE LOOKING ALONG THE DARK LENGTHS OF THE COMMERCIAL ROAD, FOR EXAMPLE, WHERE SMALL
KNOTS OF MEN GATHER IN FOGGY CONVERSATION AROUND THE GLOW OF THEIR CLAY PIPES.

No dialogue

Chapter 5, page 25.

The tension mounts as we arrive at the first of the Whitechapel murders. Alan's script for the final panel on this page was one of the shorter descriptions in the work, but I knew what this low-angle view of the carriage had to clearly say: this is where the horror begins. I also used it to take up the slack for where I'd fudged the details earlier in this dark scene. This more clearly realized coach gets to lend its detail to its more cursory rendition on page 24, the two being adjacent in the book.

PAGE 25. (943 words) (4 panels only) PANEL 1. ANOTHER SEVEN PANEL PAGE, AGAIN WITH THE BIG WIDE PANEL TAKING UP THE BOTTOM TIER AND THREE SMALLER PANELS ON EACH OF THE TIERS ABOVE THAT. IN THIS FIRST SMALL PANEL WE ARE CROUCHING BEHIND POLLY ON THE PAVEMENT, ABOUT WAIST HEIGHT, AND LOOKING UP PAST HER. ALL WE CAN SEE OF HER IS SOME OF HER MIDSECTION OVER TO THE RIGHT OF THE FOREGROUND, HER HANDS CLASPED NERVOUSLY IN FRONT OF HER AS SHE STANDS THERE LOOKING UP AT THE COACH. LOOKING UP PAST HER AT THE COACH, WE CAN SEE GULL AS HE TURNS TOWARDS US AND LOOKS DOWN WITH A FATHERLY SMILE AND A TWINKLE IN HIS EYES. HE TOUCHES THE BRIM OF HIS HAT IN GREETING. BEYOND HIM, NETLEY IS ONLY VISIBLE AS A DARK SHAPE, HUNCHED OVER THE REINS.

GULL: Good morning to you, my child.

GULL: Why, three o'clock's no time for a young lady such as yourself to be out unescorted. Might I offer transport?

PANEL 2.

NOW A SHOT LOOKING DOWN AT POLLY FROM GULL'S POINT OF VIEW, A FORLORN AND ISOLATED FIGURE, LIT ONLY BY THE WEAK GLOW FROM THE CARRIAGE LAMP. IN THE FOREGROUND WE CAN PERHAPS SEE GULL'S HANDS, QUIETLY HOLDING HIS OPEN BAG OF GRAPES. POLLY LOOKS GRATEFUL AND RELIEVED AS SHE GAZES UP AT US, AND OFFERS US A WEAK SMILE BY WAY OF A THANK-YOU. SHE'S STILL WEARING HER BLACK BONNET, FASTENED UNDER HER CHIN IN A BOW, AND I SHOULD ALSO POINT OUT THAT DURING THIS ENTIRE EPISODE, WHENEVER WE SEE POLLY'S HANDS IN CLOSE-UP, WE SHOULD MAKE SURE TO SHOW THE RING THAT WE FIRST SHOWED IN PANEL FOUR OF PAGE ELEVEN. JUST A SMALL CONTINUITY POINT WHICH YOU SHOULD APPLY WHERE APPROPRIATE, IF ANYWHERE. HERE, POLLY LOOKS UP AT US AND GIVES US A WAN SMILE. THE BREEZE RUSTLES THE PAPER BAG IN GULL'S LAP. THE GRAPES HAVE A PALE AND SICKLY GLEAM.

```
POLLY:              Why... why, thank you, sir. You're very kind.

POLLY:              I'd surely feel safer with you than out 'ere in the street.
                    You 'ear so many stories.
```

PANEL 6.

NOW WE ARE LOOKING AT GULL THROUGH POLLY'S EYES AS HE TAKES HIS SEAT BESIDE HER
IN THE CARRIAGE. WE CANNOT SEE HER. ALL WE SEE IS HER VIEW OF HIM AS HE SITS
THERE, THREE QUARTER FIGURE, AND TURNS TOWARDS US. HE SMILES, A SMILE OF ALMOST
BOYISH PLEASURE AND SATISFACTION. HE'S NOT SIR WILLIAM NOW, OR EVEN DOCTOR GULL.
HE'S JUST THE LITTLE BARGE BOY ONCE AGAIN, WHO PLAYED AMONGST THE FLOWERS THERE
AT THE RECTORY; WHO MOVED THROUGH TUNNELS SLOWLY INTO LIGHT.

```
GULL:               William.

GULL:               My name's William.
```

PANEL 7.

IN THIS FINAL WIDE PANEL WE ARE LOOKING AT THE COACH. THE DOORS ARE CLOSED, AND
AS NETLEY SNAPS THE REINS, IT RESUMES MOTION, TRUNDLING SLOWLY OVER THE COBBLES
FROM A DEAD START. A PALE HOSPITAL LIGHT SEEPS FROM THE WINDOWS OF THE COACH,
DIFFUSING INTO DARK. GULL'S BALLOON ISSUES FROM THE NEAREST WINDOW AS THE COACH
TRUNDLES AWAY.

GULL (OFF, FROM WINDOW): Now, tell me, child...

GULL (OFF, FROM WINDOW): Do you like grapes?

The grapes.

Trying to do something in the manner of the clock in Watchmen, *clicking down the minutes till midnight, we had a bunch of grapes appear at the end of each episode of* FROM HELL *when it was in* Taboo, *with one less grape each time around. We swiftly tired of the idea, and I can't recall anything more about it, except that I left it to editor Steve Bissette to deal with, just one of his many uncelebrated contributions to the work in its early days. Alan inserted it into the actual script at the end of Chapter 3, along with an optimistic estimation of how long the whole thing was going to take.*

WE SEE THE UNFINISHED SKETCH OF MARIE KELLY THAT HE WILL LATER DUST OFF
AND TURN INTO "BLACKMAIL OR MRS.BARRETT". THROUGH THE PALL OF GREY SHADOW
THAT FILLS THE ROOM, SCRIBBLED GRAPHITE EYES TWINKLE DARKLY AT US.
AN EXPRESSIVE MOUTH MADE OF LOOSELY KNOTTED PENCIL LINES LIFTS
AT THE CORNERS INTO AN UNREADABLE SMILE. DOWN AT THE
BOTTOM RIGHT-HAND CORNER OF THE PAGE WE SEE THE
BUNCH OF GRAPES, OUR LITTLE SIGNING-OFF MOTIF.
A COUPLE OF THE GRAPES ARE MISSING AS THE
FRUIT BECOMES GRADUALLY WHITTLED DOWN TO
A BARE STEM, PERHAPS SOMETHING OVER
EIGHTEEN MONTHS HENCE.

*(The Taboo grapes are the ones on page 65 here. This bunch
was for the debossed motif on the Graphitti limited edition, 2000.)*

Chapter 5, page 26.

You may notice that my pictures for this page do not follow the framing instructions in Alan Moore's script. In my head, I was trying to get a clearer impression of the action in this scene. The first problem to be addressed is the idea that we're always looking through a camera. In a comic book script it shows itself in ways that we have long stopped being conscious of. For instance, the writer will automatically describe a view as being in long-shot or close-up. We tend to forget that these are movie terms. They have entered into everyday usage. But looking further, if we place a long shot beside a close up, we've introduced another cinematic technique, that of "cutting." And another is "tracking." One of my guiding principles in making comics, long before *FROM HELL* came along, was to eliminate unnecessary cutting and replace it with an observation of body language. In order to record subtle interactions between two bodies, they both need to be seen in each and all of the pictures. My thoughts along these lines developed after reading an interview with artist Bernard Krigstein in which he expressed a feeling that the excessive fragmentation you get in comics goes against pictorial logic and usually works against the drama that the artist is supposed to be expressing. He felt that the Will Eisner way of doing things had led comics down the wrong path. On finding ourselves in the cramped space of this carriage, I reasoned that moving a hypothetical camera around would distract from the action, and also the words, and framed the scene as a repetitive set-up. I can't remember, and have no justification for, why I left Gull's hat on. I'm a hat nut.

PAGE 26. (1,130 words) PANEL 1.
NOW WE HAVE A NINE-PANEL GRID, THE BETTER TO REPRODUCE THE SLIGHTLY CLAUSTROPHOBIC ATMOSPHERE WITHIN THE COACH. IN THIS FIRST PANEL WE ARE LOOKING THROUGH GULL'S EYES, SO THAT ALL WE CAN SEE OF HIM ARE HIS HANDS AS THEY HOLD OUT THE OPEN BAG OF GRAPES TOWARDS POLLY. LOOKING BEYOND GULL'S HANDS AND THE BAG OF GRAPES WE SEE POLLY AS SHE SITS ON THE SEAT BESIDE US, TURNING TOWARDS US AND REACHING OUT ONE HAND TO DIP INTO THE BAG AND TAKE A GRAPE. SHE SMILES WITH DELIGHT, ALMOST DISBELIEVINGLY.
POLLY: Oh, sir, I loves 'em. Never can afford 'em, though.
POLLY: Oh, can I really 'ave one?

PANEL 2.

NOW WE REVERSE ANGLES SO THAT IN THE FOREGROUND WE CAN SEE POLLY IN PROFILE TO US. SHE
HAS HER HEAD TILTED BACK SLIGHTLY AND IS NOT LOOKING AT GULL AS SHE TIPS A COUPLE
OF GRAPES INTO HER MOUTH FROM HER UPLIFTED HAND. SHE LOOKS TO BE IN A STATE OF BLISS
AT BEING ALLOWED SUCH LUXURY. IMMEDIATELY BEYOND HER GULL SITS TURNED SO THAT HE FACES
DIRECTLY AT POLLY AND US. (I SHOULD HAVE MENTIONED, INCIDENTALLY, THAT HE HAS TAKEN OFF
HIS HAT ON ENTERING THE COACH.) HE SMILES QUIETLY AND WARMLY AT POLLY AS HE SPEAKS TO HER.

GULL: Dear Polly, have as many as you wish.

GULL: Now come, child. Tell me all about yourself. Where were you
                         born?

PANEL 3.

NOW A SHOT FROM THE OTHER SIDE OF THE COACH, SO THAT WE ARE LOOKING FACE-ON AT POLLY
AND GULL, BOTH FULL FIGURE, AS THEY SIT THERE SIDE BY SIDE ON THE SEAT OPPOSITE TO
US. WIPING GRAPE JUICE FROM HER LIPS, POLLY LOOKS MOMENTARILY TAKEN ABACK, ALBEIT
IN A PLEASANT WAY. SHE LOOKS AT GULL WITH A SURPRISED AND GRATEFUL SMILE THAT IS
SOMEHOW POIGNANT. GULL RETURNS HER SMILE WITH A QUIET, GENUINELY WARM SMILE OF HIS
OWN, GAZING INTO HER EYES. THE GLADSTONE BAG RESTS BY POLLY'S FEET.

POLLY: Well... nmg... excuse me...

POLLY: Well, sir, I hardly knows where I should start. It's not
                         often anybody shows an interest.

POLLY: I were born in Shoe Lane.

PANEL 4.

HERE WE CLOSE IN, SO THAT WE CAN ONLY SEE POLLY SITTING CLOSE THERE WITH THE WINDOW
BESIDE HER, THE DARKNESS OF WHITECHAPEL CRAWLING BY OUTSIDE. SHE IS LOOKING TOWARDS
GULL, WHOSE HAND ENTERS THE PANEL FROM OFF TO ONE SIDE, HOLDING OUT THE BAG OF
GRAPES. POLLY LOOKS INTO HIS OFF-PANEL EYES AS SHE REACHES OUT AND DIPS INTO THE
BAG FOR ANOTHER GRAPE. AS SHE ROCKS UNSTEADILY FROM SIDE TO SIDE WITH THE MOTION OF
THE COACH, HER BLACK BONNET HAS SLIPPED DOWN SLIGHTLY TO ONE SIDE, SO THAT IT RESTS AT A
SLIGHTLY ODD ANGLE, BUT IT IS STILL FASTENED WITH A BOW BENEATH HER CHIN. AS SHE REACHES
FOR A GRAPE, HER WEDDING RING GLEAMS DULLY UPON HER FINGER.

POLLY: That's off Fleet Street. 1851 it was, 'cause I remember
                         bein' took to see the exhibition.

POLLY: Another grape? Ooh, can I really, sir?

PANEL 5.

NOW POLLY IS IN PROFILE IN THE FOREGROUND AS SHE PUTS THE GRAPES INTO HER STARVING
MOUTH, NOT LOOKING AT GULL AS SHE DOES SO. POLLY IS ROUGHLY HEAD AND SHOULDERS TO
HALF FIGURE AS WE SEE HER HERE. LOOKING BEYOND HER WE SEE GULL AS HE SITS BESIDE HER,
TURNED ROUND SO AS TO GAZE AT BOTH POLLY AND US. HIS FACE LOOKS GENUINELY PAINED AND
SYMPATHETIC AS HE GAZES AT HER, HIS GRAPES STILL HELD IN ONE HAND. AS SHE RECOUNTS
HER TALE, POLLY'S FACE IS MORE OR LESS EXPRESSIONLESS. SHE DOES NOT SEEM TO SEE IT AS
AN OCCASION FOR SELF PITY.

POLLY: Anyway... mmp... me dad, 'e were a blacksmith. 'ad me married off by '64.

GULL: When you were... let me see... Good Lord! When you were but thirteen?

PANEL 6.

NOW WE REVERSE ANGLES SO THAT WE ARE LOOKING AT POLLY THROUGH GULL'S EYES, AND ALL
WE CAN SEE OF GULL HIMSELF ARE HIS HANDS, HOLDING THE BAG OF GRAPES. MOSTLY, WE ARE
LOOKING JUST PAST THIS TO FOCUS ON POLLY AS SHE SITS THERE IN PROFILE TO US, NOT
LOOKING AT US AS SHE SPEAKS. SHE STARES INTO SPACE, TOYING ABSENTMINDEDLY WITH HER
WEDDING RING AS SHE DOES SO, SEEMINGLY UNAWARE OF THE GESTURE. IF WE CAN SEE THEM,
HER PUPILS ARE VERY TINY, AND HER GENERAL MANNER IS ONE OF ENTRANCEMENT. THE LAUDANUM
IS STARTING TO TAKE EFFECT. POLLY SWAYS SLIGHTLY, A CHILDLIKE EXPRESSION SUFFUSING
HER FACE AS SHE REMEMBERS THE SNOW FALLING SLOWLY DURING HER WEDDING AT THE PRINTERS'
CHAPEL. SHE SPEAKS SOFTLY, AS IF IN A DREAM.

POLLY: Aye. To a printer, Billy Nicholls. We was married in the
                    printers' church, St. Bride's...

POLLY: ...an it were winter. Snowin'. Little flakes, caught in me 'air.

PANEL 7.

NOW WE HAVE A SIMILAR SHOT TO THAT IN PANEL THREE, IN THAT WE ARE LOOKING ACROSS THE
CARRIAGE AT GULL AND POLLY AS THEY SIT SIDE BY SIDE ON THE OPPOSITE SEAT, BOTH SEEN
THREE-QUARTER TO FULL FIGURE HERE. POLLY IS NOT LOOKING AT GULL, BUT JUST GAZING
DAZEDLY INTO SPACE, LOOKING IN OUR GENERAL DIRECTION, BUT CLEARLY NOT FOCUSED ON
ANYTHING. BESIDE HER, GULL IS STILL SITTING HALF TURNED TO FACE TOWARDS HER. HE HOLDS
OUT HIS BAG OF GRAPES TOWARDS HER WITH AN EXPRESSION OF DEEP AND HEARTFELT SYMPATHY
THAT SEEMS TO BE SINCERE.

POLLY: We went to live in Stamford Street. Two children. Second
                    one, my Billy, 'e runs off like, with the midwife.

POLLY: Just runs off.

GULL: Poor child. Do have another grape.

PANEL 8.

NOW WE ARE LOOKING THROUGH GULL'S EYES AT THE DAZED-LOOKING POLLY AS SHE TURNS TOWARDS US
AND TAKES ANOTHER DRUGGED GRAPE FROM THE BAG. HER EYELIDS ARE STARTING TO LOOK HEAVIER
OVER HER PIN-PRICK PUPILS, AND HER EXPRESSION IS SORT OF SLACK AS SHE REACHES OUT AND
TAKES ANOTHER GRAPE FROM THE BAG. ALL WE CAN SEE OF GULL IS ONE HAND, HOLDING OUT THE BAG
TOWARDS POLLY. BEHIND HER, THROUGH THE WINDOW, THE WHITECHAPEL DARKNESS CRAWLS BY.

POLLY: Why... why, thank you, sir. You're...

POLLY: You're very kind.

GULL: Think nothing of it, child. Come now, continue
                    with your narrative. Your husband left you...

PANEL 9.

NOW A SHOT OF THE CLOSED GLADSTONE BAG AS IT RESTS THERE BETWEEN POLLY'S FEET
AND THE CARRIAGE DOOR. BOTH POLLY AND GULL'S BALLOONS ISSUE FROM OFF PANEL IN
THE APPROPRIATE DIRECTIONS. THE BLACK LEATHER BAG HAS A DULL GLEAM IN THE
SICKLY LIGHT OF THE CARRIAGE.

POLLY (OFF):   Yes, Yes, 'e did. I went to Lambeth Workhouse...

GULL (OFF):   Lambeth, indeed? A famous poet lived there once, you know...

Chapter 5, page 28.

I always thought of this one as being set up like a scene in a theatrical play, with Gull and Polly on one side of the stage, and John Merrick on the other. The hand gestures are clearly in view, and you can imagine the words echoing around the auditorium. Note Merrick's little hand against his huge head, contrasted with Gull's large hands around his victim's throat.

In the movie, instead of the Elephant Man, Polly is looking out the coach window at Cleopatra's Needle, which is about three miles away. See earlier, page 89, for Hollywood's map of London.

Image from the film From Hell *© 20th Century Fox.*

PAGE 28. (1,198 words) PANEL 1.
A NINE-PANEL PAGE NOW. IN THIS FIRST PANEL WE ARE INSIDE THE CARRIAGE. IN THE FOREGROUND WE CAN SEE GULL'S HANDS AS HE SITS THERE WITH THE GRAPES UPON HIS LAP. LOOKING PAST THIS, WE CAN SEE POLLY ROUGHLY HALF FIGURE. SHE'S NOT LOOKING TOWARDS US, BUT IS SITTING IN PROFILE. ONCE MORE, SHE CLOSES HER EYES AS SHE SPEAKS AND RAISES HER HAND TO HER BROW AS IF DIZZY OR FAINT. BEYOND HER, THROUGH THE CARRIAGE WINDOW, WE CAN ONLY SEE DARKNESS.

POLLY: W-where are we, Sir? I've been all over tonight...
POLLY: I remember... I came out of The Frying Pan, into...
GULL (OFF):   Hush, child. We're by the London Hospital.

PANEL 2.
NOW WE ARE JUST OUTSIDE THE CARRIAGE WINDOW ON POLLY'S SIDE, WHICH IS THE SIDE FACING THE HOSPITAL. FROM THE SOFTLY LIT INTERIOR OF THE CARRIAGE, POLLY IS TURNED TO GAZE OUT OF THE WINDOW AT US, PEERING INTO THE NIGHT. GULL IS VISIBLE SITTING JUST BEYOND

HER, ALSO TURNED TO LOOK IN THE DIRECTION IN WHICH HE IS DIRECTING HER TO TRAIN HER EYES. HE RESTS ONE HAND ON HER SHOULDER IN A FATHERLY WAY, WHILE WITH THE OTHER HE POINTS PAST HER, OUT THROUGH THE CARRIAGE WINDOW TOWARDS US AND OUT INTO THE DARKNESS. HE SMILES, A CALM, DARK SMILE OF TOTAL SELF ASSURANCE. POLLY PEERS UNCERTAINLY OUT INTO THE DARK AT US, NOT QUITE SURE WHAT SHE'S SUPPOSED TO BE LOOKING AT.

GULL: I wish to show you someone. Someone who requires an offering at the commencement of each journey or important venture.

GULL: Look there... between the railings.

PANEL 3.

NOW WE CLOSE IN FROM OUR LAST PANEL, CLOSING IN THROUGH THE WINDOW UPON POLLY'S FACE SO THAT IT ALMOST FILLS THE ENTIRETY OF THE PANEL, OVER TO THE LEFT. SHE SQUINTS OUT INTO THE DARKNESS, TRYING TO SEE WHAT GULL IS ATTEMPTING TO POINT OUT TO HER. IMMEDIATELY BEHIND HER, ON THE RIGHT OF THE PANEL, THE REST OF THE IMAGE SPACE IS TAKEN UP BY GULL AS HE LOOMS OVER HER SHOULDER. HE HAS PLACED BOTH HIS HANDS UPON HER SHOULDERS NOW, WITH ONE ON EACH, AS IF HE IS STEERING HER TO LOOK IN THE RIGHT DIRECTION. IT ISN'T A THREATENING GESTURE, AND IS CONDUCTED VERY GENTLY, WITH A FATHERLY TOUCH.

GULL: Do you see him, Polly?

GULL: Do you see?

PANEL 4.

NOW WE HAVE THE FIRST OF THE THREE SILENT PANELS THAT TAKE UP THIS CENTRAL TIER. IN THIS FIRST ONE WE ARE LOOKING THROUGH POLLY'S EYES WITH POLLY HERSELF NOT VISIBLE. SHE IS LOOKING OUT THROUGH THE WINDOW OF THE COACH, ALTHOUGH IT'S UP TO YOU WHETHER THE FRAME OF THE WINDOW IS VISIBLE OR NOT. WE ARE LOOKING WITH POLLY ACROSS THE COBBLES OF THE WHITECHAPEL ROAD TOWARDS THE RAILED-OFF GROUNDS OF THE LONDON HOSPITAL BEYOND. THERE DOES SEEM TO BE A VAGUE DARK FIGURE MOVING THROUGH THE SHADOWS BEYOND THE RAILINGS, BUT AT THIS DISTANCE IT IS DIFFICULT TO MAKE OUT.

No dialogue.

PANEL 5.

NOW WE START TO CLOSE IN UPON THIS IMAGE, SO THAT WE APPEAR TO HAVE CROSSED THE ROAD AND ARE PASSING THROUGH THE RAILINGS HERE. WE CAN NOW SEE THE FIGURE MORE CLEARLY, BEING CLOSER TO IT, AS IT WANDERS SLOWLY AND FORLORNLY THROUGH THE GROUNDS OF THE HOSPITAL. AS WE SEE IT HERE IT IS SHAMBLING SLOWLY TOWARDS ONE OF THE SICKLY ROSE-BUSHES PLANTED AROUND THE FRINGE OF THE GROUNDS. IT WEARS A CLOAK, AND A GIGANTIC SAILOR'S PEAKED CAP. OVER ITS GIGANTIC HEAD IT WEARS A WHITE BAG WITH A SINGLE EYEHOLE ROUGHLY CUT INTO IT. IT IS STILL PROBABLY TOO SHADOWY AND INDISTINCT HERE TO MAKE OUT ALL THESE DETAILS, BUT I'M JUST TELLING YOU FOR FUTURE REFERENCE. THE FIGURE IS, OF COURSE, JOHN MERRICK, OUT FOR A NOCTURNAL STROLL AROUND THE HOSPITAL GROUNDS.

No dialogue

PANEL 6.

WE CLOSE IN EVEN FURTHER FOR A HALF-FIGURE SHOT OF MERRICK AS HE PAUSES TO GAZE AT THE SICKLY ROSEBUSH. IN WHATEVER WEAK LIGHT SHINES FROM THE HOSPITAL WE SEE HIM,

A SHADOWY YET UNMISTAKABLE FIGURE. HE STOPS BY THE ROSEBUSH, REACHING SLOWLY OUT TOWARDS ONE OF THE BLOSSOMS.
No dialogue.

PANEL 7.
NOW WE ARE WITHIN THE CARRIAGE ONCE MORE, SITTING BESIDE GULL SO THAT HE IS CLOSEST TO US HERE. HE IS TURNED AWAY FROM US WITH POLLY SITTING JUST BEYOND HIM, ALSO TURNED AWAY AS SHE GAZES OUT THROUGH THE WINDOW INTO THE NIGHT. GULL STILL HAS HIS HANDS RESTING GENTLY UPON POLLY'S SHOULDERS FROM BEHIND, BUT SHE APPEARS NEITHER TO MIND NOR NOTICE AS SHE GAZES OUT THROUGH THE WINDOW. IF WE CAN SEE ANY OF HER EXPRESSION SHE LOOKS VAGUELY SURPRISED AND PLEASED TO HAVE LOCATED THE FIGURE THAT SIR WILLIAM WAS POINTING OUT TO HER.

POLLY: Why... why... yes! I sees 'im, standin' by the rosebush there. That mask. He...he looks so quaint...

GULL: Yes, yes. Now, child, there's something you must SAY for me.

PANEL 8.
REVERSE ANGLES NOW SO THAT WE ARE LOOKING AT POLLY FROM THE FRONT AS SHE GAZES TOWARDS US OUT THROUGH THE WINDOW OF THE COACH, ALTHOUGH THE WINDOW NEEDN'T BE VISIBLE HERE, BEING OFF PANEL IN THE FOREGROUND. SHE GIVES AN OPIATED HALF SMILE AND LOOKS VAGUELY PUZZLED, NOT LOOKING ROUND TOWARDS GULL AS SHE DOES SO BUT CONTINUING TO GAZE DREAMILY OUT INTO THE NIGHT TOWARDS US. BEHIND HER, WE SEE GULL. HIS HANDS STILL REST UPON HER SHOULDERS, AND HE HAS COMMENCED TO GENTLY STROKE EITHER SIDE OF HER FACE WITH HIS THUMBS. SHE DOESN'T SEEM TO NOTICE. GULL'S EYES ARE IN SHADOW AND HIS SMILE IS DARK AS HE WHISPERS INTO HER EAR FROM JUST OVER HER SHOULDER,

POLLY: Say, sir?

GULL: Yes. You must say "salutation to Ganesa". Can you do that?

PANEL 9.
IN THIS LAST PANEL WE CLOSE IN UPON THE IMAGE IN OUR LAST SHOT, SO THAT WE ARE SO CLOSE TO POLLY WE CANNOT EVEN SEE ALL OF HER FACE. ALL THAT WE CAN SEE IS THE LOWER HALF OF HER FACE. AND HER EYES ARE NO LONGER VISIBLE. WE CAN ALSO SEE HER NECK AND HER SHOULDERS CLEARLY. GULL'S HANDS ARE VISIBLE, REACHING INTO THE PICTURE FROM BEHIND TO EITHER SIDE OF HER THROAT. THE WAY HIS FINGERS ARE ARRANGED WILL SEEM A LITTLE UNNATURAL, BUT I THINK IT CAN BE DONE: HIS THUMBS REST ON HER CHEEKBONES, OR THEREABOUTS, HOLDING HER FACE IMMOBILE BETWEEN THEM. HIS INDEX FINGER AND HIS SECOND FINGER ARE SPLAYED OUT SO THAT THEY ARE LOWER DOWN, AND ARE JUST RESTING LIGHTLY AGAINST THE SIDES OF POLLY'S THROAT, WHERE HER CAROTID ARTERY IS LOCATED. THE OTHER TWO FINGERS ON EACH HAND CAN BE WHEREVER THEY LOOK BEST. THE HANDS ARE RELAXED HERE. AND STILL ONLY TOUCHING POLLY VERY GENTLY. THEY ARE LIKE THE CARESS OF AN AFFECTIONATE PARENT, OR PERHAPS A LOVER, AND THEY AROUSE NO SUSPICION. POLLY'S EYES ARE DREAMY AND UNFOCUSED AS SHE GAZES OUT OF THE WINDOW AT US, HER MIND CLOUDED BY DRINK AND LAUDANUM.

POLLY: Ha. I... I think I can, sir.

POLLY: "Sa... sal'tation... to Ga-nee-sha."

Chapter 5, page 31.

The first of the murders has been done, and Gull is about to perform his symbolic ministrations upon the body. The case of surgical knives seems to want more attention than I gave it here, but what was I to do in the grim darkness of the location and with nine tiny pictures to put on the page? The film solved the problem with a case lined with blood red velvet, not an option down here in my black and white world. I did show Gull's cutlery in detailed close-up on the cover, both front and inside, of the third volume from Kitchen Sink Press, in which this chapter first appeared. The painted front is reproduced here on page 99.

PAGE 31. (1437 words) (edited) PANEL 1. ANOTHER NINE-PANEL PAGE HERE. TOWARDS THE FOREGROUND, GULL CROUCHES IN A BUSINESSLIKE MANNER BY THE OPEN GLADSTONE BAG, FROM WHICH HE IS REMOVING THE WOODEN CASE CONTAINING THE AMPUTATION KIT. NETLEY HOVERS IN THE BACKGROUND, NEAR WHERE POLLY NICHOLS' BODY LIES SPRAWLED. HE IS LOOKING TOWARDS GULL NERVOUSLY AS HE SPEAKS, HOLDING UP THE LANTERN SO THAT HE CAN SEE GULL PROPERLY. HE LOOKS AGITATED AND SCARED. GULL, CROUCHING OVER THE GLADSTONE BAG, PAYS HIM NO HEED AND DOES NOT LOOK AT HIM. HE CHUCKLES TO HIMSELF AS HE EXTRACTS THE AMPUTATION KIT FROM THE DEPTHS OF THE GLADSTONE.

NETLEY: Right. We'll be away then, shall we, sir?

GULL: Ha ha! With the job half done? I think not. She must be
                 finished with according to the ritual.

PANEL 2.

NOW WE REVERSE ANGLE SO THAT WE ARE SLIGHTLY BEHIND NETLEY, LOOKING PAST HIM AS HE STANDS FACING AWAY FROM US, ROUGHLY HEAD AND SHOULDERS IN THE FOREGROUND, THE LANTERN HELD UP IN HIS HAND. FROM WHAT LITTLE WE CAN SEE OF HIS EXPRESSION HE JUST LOOKS MISERABLE AND UNEASY. LOOKING BEYOND HIM WE SEE GULL, WHO HAS RISEN TO HIS FEET, LEAVING THE OPEN GLADSTONE BAG THERE ON THE COBBLES BEHIND HIM, AND HAS TURNED AND APPROACHED NETLEY. HE HOLDS THE AMPUTATION KIT BEFORE HIM, AND HE IS OPENING IT AS HE SPEAKS TO NETLEY. HE IS LOOKING DOWN AT THE CASE AS HE DOES THIS, RATHER THAN AT NETLEY. THE LANTERN TREMBLES WITH THE PULSE IN NETLEY'S UPRAISED ARM. THE SHADOWS SHIFT AND THEN REGROUP.

NETLEY: But... but she's dead, sir. There's no need...

GULL: Would you be a Mason, Netley? Three Rivals betrayed Hiram
                   Abiff, Masonry's founder.

GULL: Their throats were cut from left to right.

PANEL 3.

CHANGE ANGLES. ALL WE CAN SEE OF GULL IN THE FOREGROUND ARE HIS HANDS, EMERGING
FROM OFF PANEL. IN FACT, IT'S AS IF WE SEE THIS PANEL THROUGH GULL'S EYES. WITH ONE
HAND, HE HOLDS THE SMALL WOODEN AMPUTATION CASE. WITH THE OTHER, HE HAS EXTRACTED
THE LISTON KNIFE FROM ITS SLIT-LIKE RECESS AND IS HOLDING IT UP INTO THE LANTERN
LIGHT, FOR NETLEY TO SEE. IT HAS A LONG, STRAIGHT, DOUBLE-EDGED BLADE OF ABOUT EIGHT
INCHES. THE METAL HANDLE IS A FURTHER THREE INCHES AND HAS A CRISS-CROSS PATTERN
IN THE METAL TO ENHANCE THE GRIP IN SLIPPERY CONDITIONS. IT IS AN EXCEPTIONALLY
BEAUTIFUL KNIFE. LOOKING BEYOND IT WE SEE NETLEY HOLDING UP THE LANTERN AND LOOKING
TOWARDS US AND THE KNIFE WITH A SLIGHTLY SICK EXPRESSION. HE CAN FEEL STRONG
RIPTIDES SUCKING THE SAND AWAY FROM BENEATH HIS FEET. THE CURRENTS ARE STRONGER
HERE THAN HE EVER IMAGINED, AND HE FEARS THAT THEY WILL TUG HIM OUT INTO AN OCEAN
TOO TERRIBLE TO BE THOUGHT OF.

GULL: Now, this is a Liston knife.

GULL: A Crimean battle-surgeon, Liston had legs on the sawdust in
                   less than a minute with these blades.

GULL: Remarkable.

PANEL 4.

NOW WE ARE LOOKING THROUGH NETLEY'S EYES. ALL WE CAN SEE OF NETLEY IS HIS FREE HAND,
THE ONE NOT HOLDING THE LANTERN. IT ENTERS INTO THE PANEL FROM OFF IN THE FOREGROUND.
IN THE IMMEDIATE BACKGROUND, LIT BY THE LIGHT OF THE OFF-PANEL LANTERN, WE SEE GULL
AS HE STANDS FACING US, ROUGHLY HALF FIGURE. HE HAS TUCKED THE SMALL AMPUTATION CASE
UNDER HIS ARM, LEAVING HIS HANDS FREE. WITH ONE HAND, HE GRASPS NETLEY'S VISIBLE
HAND BY THE WRIST, QUITE GENTLY, AND RAISES IT, PALM UPWARDS, INTO VIEW. WITH HIS
OTHER HAND, HE GENTLY PLACES THE COLD LENGTH OF THE LISTON KNIFE UPON NETLEY'S PALM,
GIVING THE COACHMAN THE BLADE AS IF HE WERE A KINDLY GRANDPARENT DISPENSING TREATS ON
CHRISTMAS MORNING. AS HE DOES THIS, HE STARES INTO OUR EYES AND SMILES BENIGNLY, HIS
EYES TWINKLY WITH AMUSEMENT.

GULL: So, Netley...

GULL: Left to right.

PANEL 8.

SAME SHOT. NETLEY MAKES A WILD SWIPE WITH THE BLADE ACROSS POLLY'S THROAT. AS HE DOES
SO, HE TURNS HIS HEAD AWAY AND CLOSES HIS EYES. THE LANTERN LURCHES WILDLY IN HIS FREE
HAND, AND THE SHADOWS LEAP LIKE AN ASYLUM GYMNASTICS TEAM. THE SLASH ACROSS HER THROAT
KNOCKS POLLY'S FACE TO ONE SIDE A LITTLE HERE, AND A FEW DARK SPECKS OF BLOOD FOLLOW
THE BLADE IN ITS UPWARDS ARC AFTER IT HAS TRAVELLED ACROSS THE THROAT. GULL STANDS
MOTIONLESS IN THE BACKGROUND, LOOKING ON INDULGENTLY AS NETLEY BOTCHES THE FIRST CUT.
No dialogue.

PANEL 9.

A SIMILAR SHOT NOW, IN THAT WE ARE STILL DOWN NEAR THE HEAD OF THE BODY. GULL HAS WALKED ACROSS FROM THE BACKGROUND HERE AND IS KNEELING DOWN TO INSPECT THE WORK THAT NETLEY HAS DONE. HE HOLDS POLLY'S CHIN, LIGHTLY AND FIRMLY BETWEEN THE FINGERS OF ONE HAND, TILTING HER HEAD SLIGHTLY THIS WAY AND THAT AS HE INSPECTS THE WOUND ACROSS HER THROAT. WITH HIS FREE HAND, HE REACHES OUT ABSENTLY BEHIND HIM, PALM UP, NOT LOOKING AT NETLEY AS HE ASKS NETLEY TO GIVE HIM THE KNIFE, BUT KEEPING HIS INTERESTED DOCTOR'S GAZE UPON POLLY'S THROAT WHILE HE SPEAKS. LOOKING UP BEYOND GULL AND POLLY WE SEE NETLEY, STANDING TREMBLING IN THE NEAR BACKGROUND. THE LANTERN STILL HANGS IN ONE HAND AS HE LEANS WEAKLY AGAINST THE WALL, AND PERHAPS HE RAISES THE HAND HOLDING THE LISTON KNIFE TO HIS BROW, WIPING THE SWEAT AWAY. HE LOOKS TOWARDS GULL WITH SICK HORROR AS HE DOES THIS. WITHOUT LOOKING AT THE COACH MAN WHILE HE INSPECTS POLLY NICHOLS' CORPSE, GULL HOLDS OUT HIS HAND AND ASKS FOR THE KNIFE.

GULL: Oh, Netley...

GULL: I fear that you will never be a surgeon. See...the blade's glanced off her collar-bone.

GULL: Ah, well, then. Give it here. Give me the knife.

The knives.

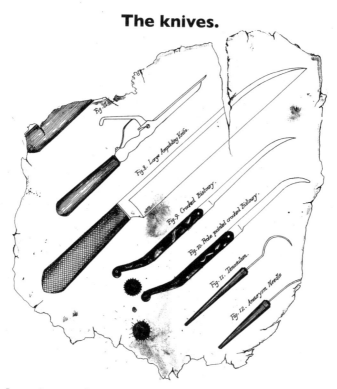

With the next murder I gave the case a foreground spot and lingered on its detail. As I feared, it starts to look like a schematic, like the above diagram that we drew for the inside cover of the Kitchen volume. I say "we" recalling that it was April Post working with me at the time. I also see some of her touches in the backgrounds of the chapter 7 panels on the facing page.

The visions

In our foreword, Hatfield and Fischer wrote at length on the theme of the visions in FROM HELL. With Gull there is an escalation in his "aura phase hallucinations," evolving from the simple but magical light emanating from the innards of Polly Nichols after the first of the murders, through the walk-in fantasia of Gull's Miller's Court vision all the way to his ascension to a kind of godhood in Chapter 14. Just before the second murder, of Annie Chapman in chapter 7 page 24, he looks through a window and sees a twentieth century living room with electric lighting and television. Here Alan was tying the tradition of a local ghost story into the narrative. According to *FROM HELL's* appendix 1, ***"the story is that a Mr Chapman on four separate occasions over a number of years, pulled back his curtains to witness a man and woman disappearing along the passageway of No. 29 Hanbury Street. The man was dressed in a heavy topcoat and tall hat. These apparitions would, it seems, usually occur in the very early hours of morning during Autumn.*** (*FROM HELL*, Appendix 1 p.25) Alan ingeniously incorporated many such sightings into Gull's "ascension" in Chapter 14.

Meanwhile, on the telly in Hanbury Street, I drew that great British funnyman, Eric Morecambe. In twenty years, nobody has ever mentioned noticing this.

Above, chapter 5, page 33; below, chapter 7, page 24

Chapter 5, page 34.

Polly Nichols now lies dead on the cobbles. Alan had the idea that for the next couple of pages she should occupy the same spot exactly in each panel while people come and go around her corpse. To this end, I started the series of repeated panels on the previous page. Altogether there are 28 of them. In retrospect, I think this is a cinematic idea, and the movie makes more of it than I have. Tip of the hat to the Hughes Brothers. On film, the effect is amplified with the characters buzzing around the corpse like flies in some speeded-up sequence of a David Attenborough nature documentary, and all the dialogue is dispensed with (left, below).

PAGE 34. (662 words) PANEL 1.
NOW A SEVEN-PANEL PAGE, WITH ONE WIDE HORIZONTAL PANEL ON THE TOP TIER AND THREE PANELS ON EACH OF THE TIERS UNDER THAT. IN THE FIRST WIDE PANEL ALL WE HAVE IS A STILL LIFE SHOT OF POLLY NICHOLS' BODY AS IT LIES THERE MOTIONLESS UPON THE COBBLES IN THE DARK, THE BONNET BY ITS RIGHT SIDE. I GUESS WHAT THIS PANEL IS SUPPOSED TO BE SAYING IS "SOME TIME PASSES AND POLLY IS STILL DEAD." THIS WIDE PANEL PROBABLY AFFORDS YOU YOUR BEST CHANCE TO DO A STUDY OF THE MURDERED WOMAN'S BODY IN REPOSE, SO MAKE WHAT YOU CAN OF IT.
No dialogue

PANEL 2.
A SIMILAR SHOT HERE TO THE LAST PANEL ON PAGE THIRTY-THREE. POLLY'S BODY LIES IN THE FOREGROUND, AND LOOKING PAST IT WE ARE LOOKING UP THE LENGTH OF BUCK'S ROW TO WHERE IT JOINS BRADY STREET. A SOLITARY FIGURE HAS JUST ENTERED THE STREET AND IS COMING LEISURELY DOWN IT TOWARDS US. ALTHOUGH WE ARE TOO FAR AWAY TO MAKE HIM OUT AS MORE THAN A DARK SHAPE HERE, THE MAN IS IN FACT CHARLES A. CROSS, A CARMAN EMPLOYED BY PICKFORD AND CO. THE TIME IS NOW 3:45 A.M. ON THE MORNING OF THE THIRTY-FIRST OF AUGUST. RELIABLE HISTORY STARTS HERE.

PANEL 3.
SAME SHOT, ONLY NOW CROSS HAS WALKED CLOSER TOWARDS THE FOREGROUND AND HAS DRAWN LEVEL WITH THE BODY. HE STOPS AND LOOKS DOWN AT THE DEAD WOMAN DOUBTFULLY. IT IS TOO

DARK TO SEE THAT HER THROAT IS CUT, OR THAT THERE ARE TERRIBLE WOUNDS IN HER BELLY.

PANEL 4.
SAME SHOT. HERE, ANOTHER DARK FIGURE HAS ENTERED BUCK'S ROW FROM THE TOP ENTRANCE, THERE IN THE BACKGROUND. CROSS, IN THE FOREGROUND, LOOKS ROUND AND NOTICES THIS NEWCOMER AS HE STANDS THERE NEAR THE BODY. RAISING HIS HAND HE CALLS OUT TO THE MAN AS HE ENTERS THE STREET. THE NEW MAN UPON THE SCENE IS ROBERT PAUL, ANOTHER CARMAN, POSSIBLY EMPLOYED BY THE SAME COMPANY. CROSS CALLS OUT TO HIM, EAGER TO ENLIST A SECOND OPINION CONCERNING THE INERT WOMAN LYING AT HIS FEET.

CROSS: OY!
CROSS: OY THERE!

PANEL 5.
SAME SHOT. PAUL HAS APPROACHED A LITTLE CLOSER TO US. BUT HE STILL HANGS BACK WARILY, UNCERTAIN AS TO WHETHER CROSS MEANS TO HARM HIM. CROSS HOLDS OUT ONE PALM TO CALM THE OTHER MAN AND INDICATES THE MOTIONLESS WOMAN LYING AT HIS FEET, WHO DOES NOT MOVE THROUGHOUT THE ENTIRE EXCHANGE.

PAUL: Wha... what are you after?
CROSS: Oh, I'm not about to 'urt yer.
CROSS: Come an' look 'ere. There's a woman. She might be drunk, but...

PANEL 6.
NOW BOTH MEN ARE KNEELING BY THE BODY. CROSS, KNEELING NEAR THE TOP HALF, IS HOLDING UP ONE OF POLLY'S LIMP, DEAD HANDS. PAUL, LOWER DOWN IS SMOOTHING DOWN POLLY'S LIFTED SKIRTS FOR THE SAKE OF DECORUM. HIS OTHER HAND HE PLACES BENEATH POLLY'S BREAST. THE SCENE IS VERY DARK. THERE IS ALMOST NO LIGHT AT ALL.

CROSS: 'Er 'and's cold. Why, I believe she's dead...
PAUL: No... 'er face was warm. I think she's breathin', but it's
                    very little if she is. Let's sit 'er up...

PANEL 7.
SAME SHOT. BOTH MEN HAVE RISEN TO THEIR FEET ONCE MORE AND ARE ABOUT TO DEPART OFF THE RIGHT HAND SIDE OF THE PANEL. CROSS WAVES ONE HAND DISMISSIVELY TO INDICATE THAT HE WANTS NO MORE TO DO WITH THE WOMAN, WHETHER SHE BE DRUNK OR DEAD. HE LOOKS DOWN AT THE BODY WITH DISGUST. PAUL, ON THE OTHER HAND, INDICATES SOME POINT OFF PANEL DOWN THE ROAD WHERE HE HOPES THEY WILL FIND A POLICEMAN. HE LOOKS TOWARDS CROSS FOR APPROVAL. AT THEIR FEET, POLLY LIES MOTIONLESS, COOLING SLOWLY IN THE NIGHT AIR.

CROSS: I'm not goin' to touch 'er. Anyway, I'm late enough for work
                    already...
PAUL: Aa. I am too. We'll try and find a copper down the road, shall we?

Design. *I've got more mileage out of this five minutes work than any other five minutes of my entire life. Mick Evans, designer, ordered me to produce a slash for the title page of the 2000 edition. It's currently on the front of the Knockabout hardcover in blood red against flat solid back, in combination with a second design element, the splatter, which took even less time.*

Chapter 6: *Taboo.*

Taboo was a grand idea, an anthology whose goal was to present the most radical of artistic outrage in the comics medium. It was Steve Bissette's project. Steve and Alan had worked together on the well received *Swamp Thing* horror comic and under the influence of self-publishing guru Dave Sim, both Steve, as Spiderbaby Graphics , and Alan, as Mad Love, had set themselves up as small publishers. Both found the challenge overwhelming and threw in the towel by the middle of the 1990s. The sixth chapter was the last one to make its initial appearance in *Taboo,* in Issue #7, late 1992.

 Taboo was bound up in the conception of *FROM HELL* and publisher/editor Steve Bissette did a great deal to make it work. For example, for Chapter 6 he undertook a load of research into the movements of Buffalo Bill during 1888. We couldn't place him where we needed him so we had to settle for a poster of him and a stand-in named Mexican Joe.

 I didn't think an irregular anthology was the best place to be running an ambitious serial and I pressed to get it out of there.

 We attempted to collect it in self-contained volumes beginning with prologue and chapters 1 and 2 in April 1991 with the publisher Tundra, but this stalled. A new printing plus a second volume with chapters 3 and 4 came out in June 1993, but things didn't pick up until Kitchen Sink Press took over the Tundra operation later that year, with Volume 3 in Dec 1993 reprinting Chapters 5 and 6. (see pages 98-101 for cover gallery). I can no longer recall the precise order of things, but chapter 7 must have been sitting on the shelf a long time before its publication in its own volume in June 1994, as I made a reference to it in my *Dance of Lifey Death* pages in August 1992 (it's in the big Alec book; see here page 174).

FROM HELL was winning awards from its early days in *Taboo*, I think beginning with an Eisner in 1993, and then there was a Harvey the year after that. The one in the background of the photo at left is the SPX Ignatz brick. We got that in 1997, in that halcyon age before 9-11, when it was still possible to take a brick in your cabin carry-on baggage.

Every winner of the Ignatz Award has an anecdote about getting it home.

The beast in the foreground was given to us by the International Horror Critics Guild, for Best Graphic Novel, 1995. It was the second year of the IHG Awards and they were still figuring out how to do it. Nancy Collins, founder of the award, phoned me and asked if the plaster-cast gargoyle statuette had arrived in one piece. I said yes, sure, it arrived fine. In fact it arrived in a multitude of pieces, all broken up and it was quite a challenge gluing it all back together, to the excitement of my kids. If you look closely you can see the various lines on the wing where the parts were re-attached. But I didn't want to cast a shadow over such an impressive endeavour. Nancy was very pleased to hear it as it was the only one of the awards sent out that arrived undamaged, and proved that the idea was a good one after all.

Left,
Alec: The
Years Have
Pants, *from page
543.*
Right, cover
TABOO #2
Sept. 1989,
art by
John Totleben.

131

Fred and "Emma"

Following the first of the murders, Chapter 6 introduces to *FROM HELL* the police and the official investigation, with Fred Abberline unhappily called in to head it. The rest of the chapter is full of autopsy and inquest and introducing key people in positions of authority. Then we go to Fred's extended gripe about Whitechapel, quoted pictorially in my Introduction. At the end of that we left him just about to walk into the Ten Bells Pub. Here he finds himself talking to a woman who calls herself Emma. This

was Alan's invention, "for dramatic purposes." It was a way of enabling a couple of turns in the story, such as Abberline's hatred of prostitutes and Kelly's raising of enough funds to get out of the country, her attempt at blackmail having turned sour. Formally, the device would also weave together two major threads that might otherwise be in danger of being separate stories. In other words, when all the theorizing and sifting of evidence is done, it's the storyteller's art that counts. The quality of this may be gauged by comparison with the movie, which seized upon the device as a way of getting a romance between the attractive leads into the production. If Alan hadn't put it there in his own way, they'd have had to make it up.

So Emma is really Marie Kelly, except of course we can't actually say that since there is no evidence that such a meeting ever occurred, and we've set ourselves the discipline of avoiding any contradiction of recorded facts. Alan wanted to have a scene depicting such a meeting but in which nothing was given as fact, so it was written in a way that "Emma" was only ever seen partially, a hand coming in from off panel,

"EMMA" IS REACHING ONE HAND INTO THE PANEL AND STARTING TO LIFT HER GLASS...

or we're looking from her point of view:

"EMMA" IS STANDING TO THE RIGHT OF THE PANEL AND WE ARE LOOKING DOWN OVER HER SHOULDER...

Given that this was spread over two pages and was a situation that we would be returning to, I thought that might feel inauthentic, not just using filmic technique, but almost the anachronistic technique of the televised

interview, in which the interviewer is known to be off screen but is only heard and half-seen. Or else it was Will Eisner's Octopus, of whom we only ever saw the distinctive gloves, and that was played for comedy. I don't wish to imply that Alan doesn't know what he's doing, but rather that this was a problem best solved at the art stage.

I figured it was within the bounds of authenticity that a person can be seen across a crowded bar, but who never quite turns our way for a clear identification. So I asked Alan to let me just draw Marie Kelly from the back without showing her face. The reader can read that "Fred" is giving himself a false backstory ("a saddlemaker, like me dad"), so it's plausible that "Emma" is doing likewise, and we can trust the reader's intelligence to figure out what we're up to. Alan agreed to give it a try, and I drew it that way. Most readers got it, I presume, but to this day I still occasionally read that Eddie Campbell's women all look the same.

My thinking about the book was that it needed a drawing style that could embrace ambiguity and hypothesis while still presenting a literal narrative happening in front of us. Such and such a person could have been in the room, but we're not saying it definitely. Let's draw that other person just so until a better description turns up. The situation called for a kind of ambiguous drawing that I shall name here "the graphics of theory and guesswork." And I'll come back to it later.

On facing page, Mary Kelly as last seen in Chapter 3, when she walked from Cleveland Street to Whitechapel. On this page left and above, "Emma" (thus named in the script in this and her later appearances) in Chapter 6.)

Part 4
Pages 132 to 170.
The theme is
men and women,
sex and censorship,
with some odd
moments of affection
suspended in the
darkness right at the
centre of the book.

Chapter 8, page 1.

I didn't have a clear grasp of the layout of this room in 1993, but I read now that it was a "single twelve-foot-square room, with a bed, two tables and a chair and a wash-stand." Above the fireplace hung a print of *The Fisherman's Widow*. It's described as cramped, but it sounds better than a couple of places I lived in myself in my early single days. I never had a fireplace, or a fisherman's widow either. The fireplace should be facing the door, and the bed should be on the right as you come in. I think Rick Geary pointed this out at the time. There's too much space in this room, (as there was in contemporary reportage drawings, but that's no excuse). The problem could be solved by cropping everything more tightly (see detail after script).

I couldn't see how light could get from the window all the way across to Mary's sleeping head, as requested in the script, so I let that one go. Believe it or not, even that has been thoroughly documented by the Ripperologists, though I didn't have access to the details. Regarding an examination of the photos later taken in the room: *"...in the middle of the morning of November 9th, 1888, the sun was towards the south (Mary Kelly's windows looked north) and cloud cover was at 100%. Hardly sufficient illumination to create the hot spots of light seen on the items on the table..."* (From *Room 13, Miller's Court*, Simon D. Wood 2005 at casebook.org)

PAGE 1. (858 words) PANEL 1.
THERE ARE EIGHT PANELS ON THIS FIRST PAGE INCLUDING THIS FIRST TITLE PANEL, ARRANGED WITH THREE PANELS ON EACH OF THE TWO LOWER TIERS AND TWO ON THIS FIRST ONE, BEING THE TITLE PANEL AND THEN A DOUBLE SIZED PANEL TAKING UP THE REST OF THE TIER.
TITLES: Chapter Eight: "Love Is Enough"

PANEL 2.

NOW A BIG DOUBLE PANEL TAKING UP THE REST OF THE TIER. WE ARE INSIDE MARIE KELLY'S
SINGLE ROOM IN MILLER'S COURT, LOOKING DOWN UPON THE DILAPIDATED AND RELATIVELY
SMALL DOUBLE BED THAT FORMS THE ROOM'S CENTREPIECE. IT IS SOMETIME AROUND NINE OR
TEN IN THE MORNING, AND PERHAPS A CHINK OF WAN SUNLIGHT FALLS ACROSS THE BED FROM
BETWEEN THE RAGS DRAWN ACROSS THE DIRTY WINDOWS. THE ROOM IS SQUALID, AND YET
FAINTLY COSY, WITH SMALL AND POIGNANT FEMININE TOUCHES HERE AND THERE TO ALLEVIATE
THE WRETCHEDNESS OF THE PLACE. IN THE BED BENEATH US AS WE LOOK DOWN, MARIE KELLY
AND HER COMMON-LAW HUSBAND JOE BARNETT ARE SLEEPING IN A COMFORTABLE CHAOS OF TORN
AND DIRTY SHEETS. THEIR ARMS ARE WRAPPED LIMPLY ABOUT ONE ANOTHER, AND THEY LOOK AS
VULNERABLE AS SLEEPING CHILDREN. PERHAPS THE NEEDLE OF LIGHT FROM THE FILTHY
CURTAINS DRAWS A STRIPE ACROSS MARIE'S CHEEK HERE, INCHING PURPOSEFULLY TOWARDS HER
CLOSED EYELIDS.

CAPTION: Miller's Court, September 22nd, 1888.

PANEL 3.

WE MOVE IN FOR A HEAD-AND-SHOULDERS CLOSE UP OF MARIE AS SHE WAKES UP, BLEARY-EYED
AND SQUINTING, JOE BARNETT'S HEAD RESTING UPON HER SHOULDER AS SHE LIES THERE ON HER
BACK LOOKING UP AT US HALF AWAKE, SHE SCRATCHES AT SOME IRRITATION IN HER HAIR WITH
ONE HAND AND WIPES SALIVA FROM HER CHIN WITH THE OTHER. THERE IS A RAZOR-SLIT OF
SUNLIGHT ACROSS HER EYE.

No dialogue.

PANEL 4.

CHANGE ANGLE FOR A SEMI-LONG SHOT OF THE BED. MARIE HAS SAT UP AND IS SWINGING
HER LEGS OVER THE SIDE OF THE BED, RESTING HER BARE SOLES UPON THE COLD FLOOR.
SHE WEARS A GRUBBY NIGHTGOWN. AS SHE SITS UP ON THE EDGE OF THE BED SHE RAISES
HER HAND TO HER MOUTH TO COVER A YAWN. BEHIND HER, JOE BARNETT SLEEPS ON AMONGST
THE HUMAN MARINADE OF DIRTY SHEETS WHILE THE UNSETTLED DUST DANCES IN THE PILLAR
OF SUNLIGHT, POETRY IN BROWNIAN MOTION. BENEATH THE BED WE SEE A CHAMBER POT.

No dialogue.

PANEL 5.

WE ARE NOW ON THE BED, LOOKING INTO THE DINGY ROOM, SO THAT WE SEE A LITTLE OF
THE BED IN THE BOTTOM FOREGROUND HERE, INCLUDING PERHAPS A PART OF THE SLEEPING
JOE BARNETT AS HE CONTINUES TO SNORE FAINTLY JUST OFF PANEL. LOOKING BEYOND THE
BED AND INTO THE ROOM WE SEE THAT MARIE HAS PULLED THE CHAMBER POT FROM UNDER THE
BED AND IS SITTING UPON IT A COUPLE OF FEET FROM THE BED, FACING AWAY FROM US
WITH HER NIGHTGOWN PULLED UP AROUND THE SMALL OF HER BACK. ABOUT HER IS THE SMALL
AND MISERABLE ROOM THAT SHE HAS ATTEMPTED, POIGNANTLY, TO BRIGHTEN WITH HER FEW
KNICKKNACKS AND PERSONAL TOUCHES. SHE GAZES AT IT, DULLY, STILL ONLY HALF AWAKE AS
SHE RELIEVES HER BLADDER OF THE NIGHT'S PRESSURES.

No dialogue.

PANEL 6.

CHANGE ANGLE AGAIN. THE BED IS IN THE BACKGROUND NOW, WITH JOE BARNETT STILL
ASLEEP ON IT. MARIE STANDS ROUGHLY THREE-QUARTER FIGURE IN THE FOREGROUND, FACING
TOWARDS US AS SHE REACHES OUT EXPRESSIONLESSLY AND PICKS UP A LONG BLACK DRESS
THAT IS HUNG OVER THE BACK OF A WOODEN CHAIR. IN THE BACKGROUND, JOE BARNETT HAS
MOVED SLIGHTLY SO THAT HE NOW RESTS ON HIS BACK RATHER THAN ON HIS SIDE.
No dialogue.

PANEL 7.

CHANGE ANGLE AGAIN. IN THE LEFT FOREGROUND NOW, ANGLED SO AS TO FACE SLIGHTLY AWAY
FROM US INTO THE ROOM, WE HAVE A HEAD-AND-SHOULDER SHOT OF THE RECLINING JOE BARNETT
AS HE HALF OPENS HIS EYES AND GAZES INTO THE ROOM AND TOWARDS MARIE, WHO WE SEE
STANDING DOWN AT THE END OF THE BED, FACING AWAY FROM US AS SHE PULLS THE LONG BLACK
DRESS OVER HER HEAD, OBSCURING HER FACE LIKE ONE OF MAGRITTE'S SHROUDED LOVERS.
BARNETT SMILES WITH A FAINT, HALF-AWAKE PLEASURE AS HE WATCHES MARIE DRESSING.

BARNETT:	Mrm.
BARNETT:	It's a lovely arse you've got on ye, Marie Kelly.
MARIE:	And it's a dirty mouth ye've got on you, Joe Barnett!
	Go back to sleep.

PANEL 8.

CHANGE ANGLE AGAIN SO THAT MARIE IS HALF FIGURE, FACING US IN THE RIGHT OF THE
FOREGROUND WITH HER BACK TO THE REST OF THE ROOM, WHERE WE SEE JOE BARNETT
LOUNGING AGAINST HIS PILLOW IN THE LEFT BACKGROUND AND STILL SMILING FAINTLY AND
PLEASANTLY AS HE TALKS TO MARIE. MARIE IS BUTTONING HER DRESS, OR PUTTING ON HER SHOES
AND STOCKINGS OR WHATEVER LOOKS BEST, GETTING READY TO GO OUT. SHE HAS HER LIPS PURSED
STERNLY AND PRIMLY AS SHE SPEAKS TO JOE WITHOUT LOOKING ROUND AT HIM. BUT THERE IS A
SUGGESTION OF SUPPRESSED AMUSEMENT.

BARNETT:	I can't. I'm off down Billingsgate, lookin' for work.
BARNETT:	God, your hair's a lovely red where the sun catches.
MARIE:	Ha! It's drinking money you're after, is it?

Rethink.

*Although the room is too
spacious, this isn't one to
lose sleep over. But since
I'm about to make a point
(under Chapt. 8, page 8)
about contrasting the cramped
city with the open country, it
would have been nice to get
this right. It could be fixed
as shown in the sample at
right, which I've cropped and
adjusted for perspective.*

Chapter 8, page 4.

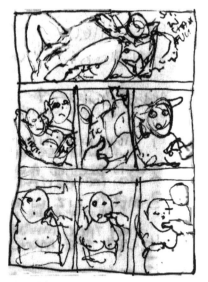

Another lusty sex scene, with something of the spirit of Kurtzman in Alan's thumbnail. In the first paragraph he writes, "If they're going to bust this fucking book, let's give them something to bust us for."

Alan may be referring to a situation that had occurred in South Africa. (I can no longer find the page online; but start looking with the words *CENSORS CAUGHT BETWEEN ROCKETS AND A HARD PLOT:* **"In the light of the Directorate's response to the first four, it is equally likely to ban "From Hell", written by Alan Moore, regarded as poet laureate of ...")***(Weekly Mail, Feb 1, 1992)* Called upon by The TIMES for his view on the matter, Alan could see that he was being manipulated into commenting on the South African political situation. Since the book had also been seized in England, he declined to say anything. **"'How shocking, this brutal regime, those South Africans, what a bunch of bastards.' Which goes without saying, but that wasn't the point."** Later he remarked: **"We showed a lot of women getting chopped up. Nobody minds about that, But occasionally we showed a couple of erect penises. And these are Eddie Campbell penises, which are a squiggle."** When I brought up the subject, with a slight air of mock indignation, he got all mock conciliatory and said, "I meant your drawing, not your actual penis." (ref 1996, interview w/Andy Diggle)

PAGE 4. (772 words) PANEL 1.
A SEVEN-PANEL PAGE HERE WITH ONE PANEL TAKING UP THE TOP TIER AND THEN THREE SMALLER PANELS ON EACH OF THE TIERS BELOW THAT. IN THIS FIRST WIDE-SCREEN PANEL, WE ARE IN THE LODGING ROOM OF JOHN KELLY IN FLOWER AND DEAN STREET, AND IT IS STILL MORNING. WE ARE LOOKING DOWN AT JOHN KELLY AND CATHERINE EDDOWES AS THEY HAVE QUITE STRENUOUS AND SWEATY SEX ON KELLY'S SINGLE BED. MAKE THIS POWERFUL AND ANIMAL, WITH A FERAL QUALITY TO IT. MAYBE EDDOWES BITES AT KELLY'S SHOULDER. IF THEY'RE GOING TO BUST THIS FUCKING BOOK WHATEVER WE DO THEN LET'S AT LEAST GIVE THEM SOMETHING TO BUST US FOR.   No dialogue

PANEL 2.

IT IS AFTERWARDS. WE HAVE A HALF-FIGURE SHOT OF THEM IN BED, THE COVERS UP AROUND THEIR WAISTS IN THE POST COITAL CHILL. THE HEAD OF THE BED IS TOWARDS THE LEFT OF THE PANEL HERE, AND WE SEE HALF OF CATHY AS SHE RESTS ON HER BACK, BLISSFULLY CONTENTED, AGAINST THE STAINED PILLOW. BEYOND HER, LEANING UP IN BED UPON HIS ELBOW AND CRADLING HIS CHEEK AGAINST HIS PALM AS HE GAZES AT CATHY, JOHN KELLY RESTS FACING US. CATHY'S EYES ARE CLOSED, AND SHE SMILES.

KELLY:	God, Kate Eddowes, but you're a marvel.
KELLY:	How old is it y'are now? Your sister said you was forty-three
CATHY:	Ha! That's what she knows!

PANEL 3.

KELLY'S EYE VIEW HERE (KELLY'S EYE?). WE CAN ONLY SEE HIS ARM IN THE FOREGROUND AS HE REACHES OUT TO TRACE THE MARK OF A TATTOO ON THE FOREARM ON THE RECLINING CATHY, WHO RESTS ON HER BACK IN THE BACKGROUND WITH HER HEAD TOWARDS THE RIGHT. AS I SEE HER, SHE HAS ONE ARM RESTING LAZILY ACROSS HER BELLY, BELOW THE BREAST LINE, AND THE OTHER UP BEHIND HER HEAD. DESPITE THE FACT THAT SHE IS BY A SLIGHT MARGIN THE OLDEST OF THE RIPPER'S VICTIMS, SHE WAS ALSO BY ALL ACCOUNTS THE LIVELIEST AND FAR FROM UNATTRACTIVE. SHE SMILES SOFTLY, EYES STILL CLOSED, AS SHE CONTINUES TO CHIDE JOHN KELLY FOR HIS IMPUDENCE. ON HER ARM WE CAN SEE THE LETTERS "T.C." CRUDELY BUT DISTINCTLY TATTOOED, AND IT IS THIS MARK THAT THE LARGELY OFF-PANEL KELLY TRACES WITH HIS FINGERTIP.

CATHY:	Anyway, fancy asking a woman's age when you've just 'ad 'er!
CATHY:	Not that I could tell you. Can't remember. Old enough.
KELLY:	AN' WHAT'S THIS ON YOUR ARM? THIS "T.C."?

PANEL 4.

ANGLE FOR A DOWNSHOT NOW, SO THAT WE ARE LOOKING DOWN ON CATHY AS SHE RESTS THERE WITH ONE HAND UP BEHIND HER HEAD AND THE OTHER RESTING ACROSS HER BELLY. WE SEE HER FROM ABOUT THE WAIST UP, WITH THE EDGE OF THE COVERS VISIBLE DOWN AT THE BOTTOM OF THE PANEL. KELLY IS OFF PANEL TO THE RIGHT, WITH JUST HIS HANDS VISIBLE, ENTERING THE PANEL FROM THE RIGHT. CATHY OPENS HER EYES AND TURNS HER HEAD SLIGHTLY TO LOOK TOWARDS THE OFF-PANEL KELLY WITH A FLICKER OF ANNOYANCE. KELLY'S LEFT HAND, ENTERING THE PANEL FROM THE RIGHT, PLAYS WITH HER LEFT NIPPLE, HAVING MOVED UP FROM THE TATTOO ON HER LEFT ARM, RESTING JUST BENEATH IT. HE TWEAKS IT BETWEEN THUMB AND FOREFINGER. CATHY IGNORES THIS AS SHE REPLIES TO HIM.

CATHY:	You KNOW what it is! I 'ad it done in Wolver'ampton when I left 'ome with old Tommy Conway. I were just nineteen.
KELLY (OFF):	Good ride, was he?

PANEL 5.

SAME SHOT. CATHY LOOKS BACK AWAY FROM KELLY NOW AND GAZES DREAMILY OUT OF THE TOP LEFT OF THE PANEL SOMEWHERE. KELLY'S HAND MOVES UP FROM HER BREAST AND STARTS TO STROKE HER CHEEK AS SHE SPEAKS, NOT LOOKING AT HIM WHILE SHE DOES SO.

CATHY:	Oh, you've no competition. Though he didn't do bad, for a pensioner. Lived off these chapbooks 'e wrote.

CATHY: We 'ad three kids.

PANEL 6.

SAME SHOT, WITH CATHY STILL GAZING DREAMILY OUT OF THE LEFT OF THE PANEL AS SHE SPEAKS.
KELLY'S FINGER HAS MOVED FROM HER CHEEK EVER SO SLIGHTLY AND IS NOW TRACING THE ORBIT
OF HER MOUTH.

CATHY: Not that the little buggers 'ave lifted a finger for me
                      since I left the blind drunk old brute.

CATHY: My Annie, she avoids me now she's married!

PANEL 7.

SAME SHOT. AS KELLY'S FINGERTIP REACHES HER MOUTH, CATHY TURNS HER HEAD, LOWERS HER
EYELIDS AND CLOSES HER LIPS OVER THE TIP OF IT, SUCKING AT IT GENTLY.

KELLY (OFF):   Oh, never you mind her, snotty little madam she is.

KELLY (OFF):   I was thinkin' we might go hop-pickin' you and me. Over in Kent

CATHY: m?

All thumbs

Thumbnails left, chapter 8,
pages 2,3. Marie kisses Joe, goes to
the pub, scene with Liz Stride.

Below, page 5, second page of
Eddowes and John Kelly,
6,7, Liz and Michael Kidney.
Interestingly, on these there is more
repetition than in my finished art.
Liz and Kidney scene discussed on
148-9

Chapter 8, page 8.

Since his last appearance, "Eddy" has become "Eddie," and he's "Eddie" in the comic although he remains Eddy in the notes in the appendix proper to *FROM HELL*. As that was entirely retyped at one point by the wife of my bosom, who knows one Eddie from another, I'm not certain what Alan had there in the first place.

This scene and the following one take place in the British countryside. The two are flanked by scenes in London in which the action takes place in cramped quarters and in close-up. To emphasize the air and space I staged the country scenes at a distance, with full figures. Holding the book at arm's length, the contrast is between the scenes as a whole rather than components within each scene. To get a quick idea of the effect, compare the reduced image at left with the one for Chapter 8, page 12, coming up shortly.

PAGE 8. (965 words) PANEL 1.
THERE ARE SEVEN PANELS ON THIS PAGE, WITH A BIG WIDE ONE TAKING UP THE TOP TIER AND THEN THREE PANELS ON EACH OF THE TWO TIERS BENEATH THAT. IT IS A FEW DAYS LATER, THE TWENTY-SEVENTH OF SEPTEMBER, AND WE HAVE CUT TO THE GROUNDS OR THE MOORLANDS AROUND THE ROYAL RETREAT AT ABERGELDIE IN SCOTLAND (I'M GUESSING HERE, EDDIE, SINCE I HAVE NO IDEA WHAT KIND OF PLACE THE ROYALS HAD AT ABERGELDIE, OR WHAT SORT OF COUNTRYSIDE IT IS. I FIGURED I'D HAVE THE FOLLOWING SCENE TAKE PLACE IN THE GROUNDS TO CUT OUT ANY REFERENCE PROBLEMS THAT WE MIGHT HAVE IN DEPICTING A SPECIFIC BUILDING. IF, HOWEVER, YOU SHOULD STUMBLE ACROSS ANY REFERENCE FOR A BUILDING THEN PLEASE FEEL FREE TO STICK IT IN THE BACKGROUND SOMEWHERE). WE ARE LOOKING AT AN EXPANSE OF ROLLING MOOR WITH PERHAPS A FEW LONELY TREES HERE AND THERE, AND WE CAN SEE PRINCE ALBERT VICTOR CHRISTIAN EDWARD AS HE STANDS WITH A WALKING STICK BENEATH HIS ARM, DRESSED IN OUTDOOR TWEEDS OR SOMETHING SUITABLE TO THE PLACE AND THE CLIMATE. HE IS GAZING OUT MOODILY ACROSS THE MOORLANDS, DEEP IN THOUGHT. HUGE GREY CLOUDS SCUD ACROSS THE SUNLIT SKY BEHIND HIM BUT HE PAYS THEM NO ATTENTION, LOST IN THE WORLD OF HIS OWN.

FROM HIS EXPRESSION, IT DOESN'T LOOK LIKE A TERRIBLY HAPPY WORLD.
No dialogue.

PANEL 2.
NOW WE HAVE PRINCE EDDIE STARING DREAMILY TOWARDS US, HEAD AND SHOULDERS IN THE RIGHT
OF THE FOREGROUND AND GAZING RIGHT OUT OF THE PANEL AT US. HE HAS NOT MOVED SINCE LAST
PANEL, BUT WE HAVE SWUNG ROUND SO THAT WE ARE FACING HIM. LOOKING PAST HIM, ACROSS THE
MOORLANDS OR GROUNDS OR WHATEVER TOWARDS THE BACKGROUND WE CAN SEE THE TALL AND WELL-
BUILT FORM OF A NEW CHARACTER STRIDING TOWARDS US AND THE PRINCE. THIS IS J.K. STEPHEN:
TWENTY-NINE-YEAR-OLD POET, FORMER FELLOW OF KING'S COLLEGE CAMBRIDGE, WHERE HE BECAME
PRINCE EDDIE'S TUTOR AND POSSIBLY LOVER; RELATIVE OF VIRGINIA WOOLF; DIEHARD
MISOGYNIST. STEPHEN, DRESSED FOR OUTDOORS LIKE THE PRINCE BUT PERHAPS WITH MORE OF
A DASH TO HIS CLOTHING, IS STILL SOME WAY OFF HERE, STRIDING THROUGH THE GORSE AND
HEATHER TOWARDS US AND HIS FRIEND. LOST IN HIS THOUGHTS, PRINCE EDDIE DOES NOT HEAR
STEPHEN APPROACH AND CONTINUES TO GAZE MOODILY OUT OF THE PANEL AT US, HIS DARK EYES
SAD, GIRL-LIKE.
No dialogue.

PANEL 3.
SAME SHOT, WITH EDDIE STILL MOONING IN THE FOREGROUND, UNMOVING SAVE FOR SOME STRANDS
OF HIS HAIR THAT ARE FLIPPED THIS WAY AND THAT BY THE HIGHLAND BREEZE DURING THE
COURSE OF THIS THREE-PANEL SEQUENCE. BEHIND HIM, J.K. STEPHEN HAS COME MUCH CLOSER,
WITHIN EARSHOT, AND HE IS RAISING ONE HAND TOWARDS EDDIE'S TURNED BACK IN GREETING
AS HE CALLS OUT TO HIS FRIEND, HIS MOOD SEEMINGLY JOVIAL IN CONTRAST TO EDDIE'S
MOROSENESS. EDDIE DOESN'T RESPOND IN ANY WAY, STILL GAZING THOUGHTFULLY OUT OF THE
PANEL AT US.

STEPHEN: HALLOOO! I say, EDDIE!
STEPHEN: Whatever's the matter old chap? No sooner do we get here to
                 Abergeldie than you're off mooning about on the MOORS!

PANEL 4.
SAME SHOT. EDDIE REMAINS UNMOVED IN THE RIGHT OF THE FOREGROUND, SAVE FOR WHATEVER
STRANDS OF HIS HAIR ARE BLOWING ABOUT, STILL GAZING DISTRACTEDLY OUT OF THE PANEL,
STILL LOOKING SAD AND WORRIED AS HE SPEAKS TO STEPHEN WITHOUT TURNING ROUND AND
LOOKING AT HIM. STEPHEN HAS NOW COME RIGHT UP INTO THE FOREGROUND AND IS STANDING
BEHIND EDDIE OVER EDDIE'S SHOULDER. HE LOOKS AT EDDIE IN PUZZLEMENT.

EDDIE: DEAR JEM.
EDDIE: I was thinking about London. All the terrible things that happen.
EDDIE: These murders...

PANEL 5.
CHANGE ANGLES NOW, SO THAT WE ARE BEHIND STEPHEN, WITH HIM NOW OVER TO THE RIGHT
AND FACING MOSTLY AWAY FROM US TOWARDS EDDIE, WHO STANDS A LITTLE BEYOND HIM AND
MORE TO THE LEFT. EDDIE STILL HASN'T TURNED ROUND, AND IS STILL GAZING OUT OVER
THE MOORS. WE CAN SEE BOTH MEN IN ABOUT A QUARTER PROFILE HERE AS THEY LOOK AWAY
FROM US, AND WE SEE THEM BOTH HEAD AND SHOULDERS TO HALF FIGURE. STEPHEN FROWNS AND

SMILES AT THE SAME TIME AS HE LOOKS AT EDDIE, AS IF AMUSED BUT BEWILDERED BY EDDIE'S PREOCCUPATIONS. EDDIE CONTINUES TO STARE INTO THE DISTANCE AND SAYS NOTHING.

STEPHEN: Eddie, DO buck up! You came to Scotland to get AWAY from London for a bit!

STEPHEN: Whitechapel's MILES away, Eddie. Anyway, what's two whores less?

PANEL 6.

PULL BACK FROM OUR LAST PANEL, SO THAT NOW WE SEE BOTH MEN ROUGHLY THREE QUARTER FIGURE. EDDIE AT LAST TURNS HIS FACE TO GLANCE QUESTIONINGLY AT STEPHEN, STILL WITH THE SAME BIG, SAD REPROACHFUL EYES. STEPHEN RAISES HIS LEFT ARM, PALM UPWARDS IN A REASONING AND EXPLANATORY GESTURE AS HE REPLIES TO EDDIE. HE STARES AT EDDIE WIDE-EYED, MAKING AN ALMOST COMICAL FACE OF INCOMPREHENSION AT EDDIE'S OPINIONS.

EDDIE: Jem... those women. They didn't deserve to die. Not like that. They hadn't DONE anything.

STEPHEN: Oh. Eddie! Come OFF it! They were WOMEN! They must have done SOMETHING!

PANEL 7.

PULL BACK STILL FURTHER, SO THAT NOW WE SEE BOTH MEN FULL FIGURE AS THEY STAND THERE CALF DEEP IN THE HEATHER OR WHATEVER...STILL LOOKING AT THEM FROM BEHIND. THE ARM THAT STEPHEN WAS RAISING LAST PANEL CONTINUES TO RISE AND FINALLY SETTLES AROUND EDDIE'S SHOULDER IN A BROTHERLY HUG. EDDIE HAS TURNED HIS FACE AWAY FROM STEPHEN, SO THAT WE CANNOT SEE IT HERE. STEPHEN LOOKS AT EDDIE WITH A BROTHERLY GRIN OF REASSURANCE, TRYING TO SMOOTH HIS FRIENDS EVIDENTLY HURT FEELINGS.

EDDIE: It isn't funny, Jem.

STEPHEN: EDDIE, I WAS joking. ALRIGHT?

STEPHEN: I just can't see why you're so concerned about wretched hags that you don't even know.

Page 9, second of Eddie and JK. Stephen (under the tree) page 11, second of John Kelly and Cathy Eddowes, at the bottom cut to outside the Ten Bells, kids trying to trap a pigeon, continuing in the scene described on page 150 here.

Chapter 8, page 10.

Alan's sketch for this page, or the top row of it at least, is a work of art in itself, but I'll come to that in a minute. The scene is another in what amounts to a little suite of peculiar, irregular, couples. There was Marie and Joe Barnett, Prince Eddie and JK Stephen, Liz and Michael, Fred and "Emma," Netley and a pornographic print. The title of this chapter, remember, is "Love is Enough," and I think it's my favourite chapter in the book.

This bucolic scene belongs to Cathy Eddowes and John Kelly. Scriptwise it's a long one, coming in at over 1300 words when all its neighbours are under a thousand. Alan draws a page and then describes what he sees on it, what he sees in his mind's eye more than on the paper. The panels he sees must be lifesize, as he sees what everybody's wearing, and he tells me all the colours, even though I don't need to know. He also spent more time than usual on this page's thumbnail, working it in two different inks as though trying to penetrate its tiny mystery, the human fragility in that little sleeping figure. (You can see it in colour in Gary Spencer Millidge's book, referenced elsewhere in here. Even on a whole notebook page surrounded by the thumbnails for the rest of the chapter, it commands attention.)

I wanted to hold onto the spacious open countryside here for as long as possible, so I saved this scene's close-ups for page 11.

Page 10. (1331 words) PANEL 1.
A NINE-PANEL PAGE. IT IS THE SAME DAY, BUT A LOT FURTHER SOUTH, IN THE HOP-FIELDS OF KENT. WE ARE LOOKING STRAIGHT DOWN ON CATHERINE EDDOWES AS SHE LIES SUNBATHING UPON THE GRASS VERGE BENEATH US. HER EYES ARE CLOSED AND SHE HAS A BLACK CLOTH JACKET SPREAD OUT UPON THE GRASS BENEATH HER, WITH IMITATION BLACK FUR AROUND THE

COLLAR AND SLEEVES AND TRIMMINGS AND TWO OUTSIDE POCKETS. (I'M TELLING YOU THIS
FOR FUTURE REFERENCE OBVIOUSLY. WE DON'T NEED TO SEE ALL THIS HERE.) SHE WEARS A
CHINTZ SKIRT WITH THREE FLOUNCES AND A BROWN BUTTON ON THE WAISTBAND AND SHE WEARS
A BROWN LINSEY DRESS BODICE WITH A BLACK VELVET COLLAR AND BROWN METAL BUTTONS DOWN
THE FRONT. HER SKIRT AND THE PETTICOATS BENEATH ARE DRAWN UP ABOVE HER KNEES IN A
VAIN ATTEMPT TO GET SOME SUN TO HER THIN LEGS. SHE WEARS A PAIR OF MEN'S LACE-UP
BOOTS, THE RIGHT BOOT REPAIRED WITH RED THREAD. BESIDE HER ON THE GRASS RESTS A
BLACK STRAW BONNET, TRIMMED WITH GREEN AND BLACK VELVET AND DECORATED WITH BLACK
BEADS, WITH BLACK STRINGS TO FASTEN BENEATH THE CHIN. AS SHE LIES THERE ON HER
BACK, HER BODY, AS IF OBEYING SOME STRANGE PRE-MEMORY, ARRANGES HER LIMBS INTO AN
EXACT DUPLICATE OF THE SPRAWL THAT THEY WILL OCCUPY IN DEATH: HER ARMS BY HER SIDE,
RESTING WITH THE PALMS UPWARDS; HER LEGS STRAIGHT, ONLY SLIGHTLY PARTED; HER HEAD
TURNED SLIGHTLY TO ONE SIDE. CONSIDERING THE UNGAINLINESS OF HER POSTURE AND THE
RAVAGES OF HER AGE AND HER SOCIAL POSITION, SHE IS NOT AN UNATTRACTIVE WOMAN IN
REPOSE. THE TOP HALF OF HER IS IN THE BRIGHT SUNLIGHT, BUT THE FLAT GREY SHADOW OF
A CLOUD IS SLIDING UP OVER HER EXPOSED LOWER LIMBS, WHERE THE GOOSE FLESH STARTS TO
BRISTLE. SHE DOES NOT MOVE. SHE MIGHT BE DEAD.
No dialogue

PANEL 2
SAME SHOT. HERE, THE SHADOW OF THE CLOUD HAS SLID ONWARD SO AS TO COMPLETELY
ENGULF CATHY. SHE IS NO LONGER IN THE SUNLIGHT. SHE OPENS HER EYES AND FROWNS AT
US, PETULANT AND DISAPPOINTED. PERHAPS SHE STARTS TO LIFT HERSELF UP ON HER ELBOWS
SLIGHTLY. SHE HAS THE MANNER OF A BRIGHT AND VIVACIOUS SCHOOLGIRL TRAPPED IN AN
AGING WOMAN'S BODY, AND THERE'S SOMETHING ABOUT THE EFFECT THAT'S QUITE ENDEARING.
CATHY: Tt.

PANEL 3
CHANGE ANGLE NOW SO THAT WE ARE BESIDE CATHY AS SHE SITS UP IN PROFILE, OVER ON
THE LEFT OF THE FOREGROUND AND FACING RIGHT, DRAWING HER KNEES UP AND DRAGGING
THE BLACK JACKET UP AROUND HER SHOULDERS FOR WARMTH, LEAVES AND SPLINTERS AND
DEAD GRASS STILL CLINGING TO IT HERE AND THERE. SHE GAZES OFF THE RIGHT OF THE
FOREGROUND AND SQUINTS HER EYES, FROWNING, PERHAPS WITH HER ARMS LOOPED AROUND
HER DRAWN UP KNEES. LOOKING BEYOND HER, IN THE RIGHT OF THE MIDDLE GROUND WE SEE
HER BOYFRIEND, JOHN KELLY, FACING SLIGHTLY AWAY FROM US AND VISIBLE FULL FIGURE
AS HE STANDS (OR STOOPS) PICKING HOPS, SUITABLY ATTIRED WITH HIS SHIRT SLEEVES
ROLLED UP. BEYOND HIM, TOWARDS THE BACKGROUND AND LESS SIGNIFICANT HERE, WE SEE
AN OLD WOMAN, ALSO PICKING HOPS. KELLY HAS ONE OF CATHY'S SKIRTS, A RAGGED OLD
BLUE ONE WITH A RED FLOUNCE AND A LIGHT TWILL LINING, INTO WHICH HE IS PLACING
THE HOPS THAT HE HAS PICKED. HE DOESN'T LOOK AT US HERE, ABSORBED IN HIS MEAGRE
WORK, AND NEITHER DOES CATHY LOOK TOWARDS HIM AS SHE COMPLAINS TO HIM.
CATHY: The Sun's gone in and I'm cold.
CATHY: We've been here nearly a week now, John, and the work's
                       rubbish. When are we goin' home?

PANEL 4.

SAME SHOT, WITH CATHY SITTING ROUGHLY HALF FIGURE IN THE LEFT OF THE FOREGROUND,
HER KNEES DRAWN UP AND HER JACKET ABOUT HER SHOULDERS. SHE TURNS TO LOOK
TOWARDS JOHN IN THE NEAR BACKGROUND AND LIFTS ONE HAND TO BRUSH HER HAIR BACK
FROM HER FACE. IN THE RIGHT OF THE NEAR MIDDLEGROUND, KELLY HAS TURNED TOWARDS
HER, HOLDING OUT THE SKIRT BETWEEN BOTH HANDS TO SHOW HER THE FAIRLY PITIFUL
NUMBER OF HOPS THAT HE HAS MANAGED TO GATHER IN IT. CATHY FROWNS AT HIM. AWAY IN
THE FAR BACKGROUND, THE OLD WOMAN CARRIES ON PICKING HOPS FOR ALL SHE'S WORTH,
EVIDENTLY DOING BETTER AT IT THAN KELLY HAS.

KELLY: Oh, I don't know about rubbish. Look, I picked all these
                    while you've been asleep

CATHY: I wasn't asleep. Is that my best blue skirt you've got
                    there?

PANEL 5.

SAME SHOT. KELLY HAS NOW WALKED CLOSER TO US SO THAT HE IS DECAPITATED BY THE
UPPER PANEL BORDER AS HE STANDS JUST BEYOND THE SEATED CATHY IN THE IMMEDIATE
BACKGROUND. HE HOLDS OUT THE SKIRT TO SHOW HER THE PITIFUL COLLECTION OF HOPS
THAT NESTLES IN ITS FOLDS. CATHY TURNS HER HEAD AWAY FROM HIM AND THE HOPS AND
GRIMACES WITH CONTEMPT. IN THE BACKGROUND, THE OLD WOMAN IS STILL BENT OVER HER
WORK, GATHERING THE HOPS INTO HER APRON.

KELLY (OFF):   BEST? How long has THIS rag been your best? Anyway, look at
                    what I got...

CATHY: Oh, John, those won't buy us a half of bitter BETWEEN us!

PANEL 6.

CHANGE ANGLE SO THAT NOW WE HAVE THE OLD WOMAN IN THE RIGHT OF THE FOREGROUND,
HALF FIGURE AND FACING TOWARDS US AS SHE CONTINUES TO PICK HOPS AND THEN DROP
THEM INTO HER APRON. KELLY AND THE SEATED CATHY ARE OVER IN THE LEFT OF THE
NEAR BACKGROUND, BOTH OF THEM LOOKING SOMEWHAT SURPRISED AT HER INTRUSION UPON
THEIR PRIVATE DISAGREEMENT. THE OLD WOMAN SPEAKS TO THEM WITHOUT LOOKING ROUND,
CHUCKLING TO HER SELF, FAINTLY SENILE.

WOMAN: Haha! Well, you'll never make good money off 'ops, me duck!

WOMAN: If you want good money you wanna win a CONTEST or a REWARD
                    or summat.

PANEL 7.

SAME SHOT. THE WOMAN CONTINUES TO PICK HOPS HALF FIGURE IN THE RIGHT OF THE
FOREGROUND WITHOUT LOOKING ROUND AT THE PAIR BEHIND HER. IN THE BACKGROUND, KELLY
HAS LOST INTEREST IN THE OLD WOMAN AND IS STARTING TO WANDER OFF DISCONSOLATELY,
LOOKING FOR MORE HOPS TO ADD TO HIS PATHETIC LOAD. CATHY, SEEMING MORE INTERESTED,
IS BRUSHING HERSELF DOWN AS SHE RISES TO HER FEET, KEEPING HER EYES UPON THE OLD
WOMAN WITH A VERY SERIOUS EXPRESSION, LISTENING TO WHAT THE CRONE HAS TO SAY.

WOMAN: Like what they're offering for that Jewish feller who's
                    been doing' them girls over Whitechapel.

WOMAN: That's be worth 'avin'! Hoohoo! What I wouldn't do with that!

PANEL 8.

SAME SHOT, WITH THE WOMAN STILL FACING US IN THE FOREGROUND, BUSILY PICKING, SO THAT WE ONLY SEE HER ELBOW OR SHOULDER OR SOMETHING, WITH HER BALLOON COMING FROM OFF RIGHT. WE ARE MAINLY LOOKING AT CATHY WHO HAS SLOWLY WALKED ACROSS ABOUT HALF OF THE DISTANCE BETWEEN HER AND THE OLD WOMAN SO THAT WE MAYBE SEE HER THREE-QUARTER FIGURE HERE, HER HANDS UP TO RUB HER COLD SHOULDERS AS SHE GAZES AT THE OLD WOMAN, HER FACE SERIOUS AND LOST IN THOUGHT. IN THE FAR BACKGROUND WE SEE JOHN KELLY, FACING AWAY FROM US AS HE SEARCHES FRUITLESSLY FOR HOPS. AS WE LOOK AT CATHY, WE CAN SEE THAT HER INTEREST HAS BEEN AROUSED. SHE HAS REMEMBERED SOMETHING.

WOMAN: Anybody who could tell them anything about what 'appened to Nichols or the other one, Chapman.

WOMAN: More'n two hundred pounds I think they said it was.

PANEL 9.

NOW WE HAVE FLASHBACK PANEL, REPEATING A SCENE FROM LAST EPISODE (CHAPTER SEVEN PAGE EIGHT), ONLY THIS TIME SHOWING IT FROM CATHY'S POINT OF VIEW. WE ARE LOOKING AT WALTER SICKERT AS HE STANDS AT THE BAR OF THE BRITANNIA LOOKING EARNESTLY TOWARDS US, ABOUT HALF FIGURE, HIS BOWLER HAT RESTING ON THE BAR. SINCE WE ARE LOOKING THROUGH CATHY'S EYES HERE WE CANNOT SEE HER.

SICKERT: I'm just looking for a woman. She drinks here sometimes, with her friends. Perhaps you know her?

CATHY (OFF): I know 'er. Always in 'ere with Annie Chapman and Liz Stride

Thumbnails for chapter 8, pages 17-19, including Netley's scene, after which he takes out the coach and horse.

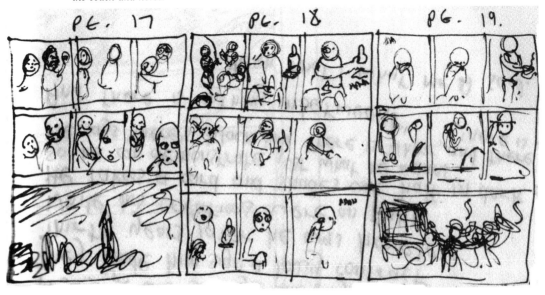

Chapter 8: a thought.

I had the intention of including page 7 from this chapter, but when I reread the script for that page, I was thrown for a loop because it wasn't coming out the way I remembered it. But first, this is how things were tending to work in *FROM HELL*: in Chapter 6, Fred Abberline has Polly Nichols' effects on the floor of his office. In the script is the artistic conceit that the clothes follow the form of the woman after her moment of death:

With regard to Liz Stride, there is also a moment that involves clothes, after Liz has been thrown out in the street by Michael Kidney. In this case it's a pre-echo, but remember that in the Architecture of Time, "pre" and "post" are as arbitrary as reading left to right or right to left. Alan wrote very briefly, in contrast to his usual manner:

PAGE 7, PANEL 5.
SAME SHOT. IN THE NEAR BACKGROUND LIZ TURNS AROUND AS SHE HEARS THE DOOR SLAM
BEHIND HER, LOOKING BACK OVER HER SHOULDER AT US HERE. IN THE FOREGROUND, THE DOOR
OF NUMBER THIRTY-THREE IS CLOSED ONCE MORE, AND LIZ'S BELONGINGS LIE IN AN UNTIDY
SPRAWL ON THE PAVEMENT IN THE FOREGROUND. (No dialogue)
PANEL 6.
SAME SHOT. LIZ HAS TURNED AND IS TRUDGING WRETCHEDLY TOWARDS US, COMING BACK TO
RETRIEVE HER CLOTHING, HER PACE IS LEADEN, WEIGHTED BY MISERY. (No dialogue)

I didn't consult with Alan but presumed that the right thing to do was to make the pile of clothes a pre-echo of Liz's death position.

(left, page 7, below page 33.)

I can no longer recall whether I had the script for page 33 (the death) when I was drawing page 7 (the clothes). This was a chapter that did not come all at once:

EAGER ED— ONLY. FOUR PAGES LEFT AFTER THIS!
BEST— ARRESTED AL

wrote Alan, in mock imitation of Stan Lee's chummy 1960's Marvel manner. But I reasoned that as Mary Kelly got a pre-echo (see script on page 176 herein):

(left Chapter 9 page 17, below Chapter 10 page 30.)

And Catherine Eddowes got one (page 142 herein):

Oh, Lord. Oh, bloody Hell.

(left far, Chapter 8 page 10, left near, page 45.)

...then I should say that Liz Stride is entitled to one, and Alan must have just forgotten to include it. However, if you were to say, "Yeah, but Mary Kelly didn't get one until the next chapter, which you wouldn't have known about yet!" then I would say: "Go back and read what I said above about the Architecture of Time."

Chapter 8, page 12.

Back in the crowded city. The middle panel is not the biggest close-up in the book (that being Gull's eyeball on page 218 herein), but it's pretty big. The page as a whole is somewhat out of style with the previous meetings between Fred and "Emma," because Pete Mullins does much of the inking here. Pete would work with me for four days and on Fridays he'd stay home and do a full-page full-colour cartoon of his own for a sexy Australian magazine. He drew that in what I would unhesitatingly call his own style, but it's difficult to find anything of "Pete's Style" in the *FROM HELL* pages (for example, Pete didn't normally use nibs — see page 187). For that matter, I've never thought that Eddie Campbell's style was in there either.

For *FROM HELL* I worked out a style by studying George du Maurier and Charles Keene, both of London *Punch*, much as Charles Dana Gibson must have done when he was starting out in 1886. When Pete came on board, he worked out his own version of the *FROM HELL* style. It's sharper and more hard-edged than mine. Usually I'd rough the pages up a bit before closing on them, to preserve that ambiguous feeling that's all through the book. But this two-page scene was so striking after Pete had done the finishes that I didn't want to touch anything.

PAGE 12. (878 words)   PANEL 1.
ANOTHER NINE-PANEL PAGE HERE. IN THIS FIRST PANEL WE CAN NOW SEE THE CHILDREN, HEAD AND SHOULDERS, DOWN AT THE BOTTOM OF THE FOREGROUND. FROM THE EXCITED LOOK ON THEIR FACES IT IS CLEAR THAT SOMETHING EXCITING HAS HAPPENED OFF PANEL IN THE BOTTOM FOREGROUND, BUT WE CANNOT SEE WHAT IT IS. LOOKING BEYOND THEM WE CAN SEE FRED ABBERLINE, THREE-QUARTER FIGURE, AS HE PUSHES OPEN THE DOOR OF THE TEN BELLS, ABOUT TO ENTER THE PUB. HE TURNS HIS HEAD TOWARDS US AND GIVES THE CHILDREN A BRIEF AND EXPRESSIONLESS GLANCE AS HE ENTERS. THE CHILDREN IGNORE HIM, THEIR EYES ALIGHT WITH THE PROSPECT OF CRUELTY.
No dialogue.

PANEL 2.
ABBERLINE IS NOW HEAD AND SHOULDERS IN THE LEFT OF THE FOREGROUND, FACING ROUGHLY AWAY FROM US SO THAT WE ONLY SEE HIM IN QUARTER PROFILE HERE AS HE GAZES INTO THE PUB. BEYOND HIM WE SEE THE MODERATELY CROWDED BARROOM OF THE TEN BELLS, WITH THE

USUAL ASSORTMENT OF COSTERMONGERS, WHORES AND GENERAL LOW LIFE. ABBERLINE GAZES OUT
ACROSS THE SMOKY ROOM WITHOUT EXPRESSION, TOWARDS THE BAR. HE OBVIOUSLY HASN'T YET
SEEN WHOEVER HE IS LOOKING FOR.
No dialogue.

PANEL 3.
NOW A FULL FIGURE SHOT OF ABBERLINE AS HE STANDS AT THE BAR, GETTING HIMSELF A DRINK,
IN PROFILE TO US HERE, STANDING ON THE LEFT AND FACING RIGHT. THE LANDLORD FACES
HIM ACROSS THE BAR FROM THE RIGHT, HOLDING OUT ONE HAND TO ACCEPT THE MONEY THAT
ABBERLINE IS DROPPING INTO IT WHILE WITH HIS OTHER HAND HE PUSHES A PINT OF BEER
ACROSS THE TOP OF THE BAR TOWARDS THE PLAINCLOTHES POLICE INSPECTOR.
No dialogue.

PANEL 4.
NOW WE SEE ABBERLINE AS HE PULLS BACK A CHAIR AT AN ISOLATED AND OTHERWISE UNOCCUPIED
TABLE, ABOUT TO SIT DOWN, HIS PINT OF BEER ALREADY RESTING UPON THE TABLE TOP. THERE
IS ANOTHER CHAIR ACROSS THE TABLE FROM HIM, BUT IT IS AS YET UNOCCUPIED. HIS FACE IS
STILL EXPRESSIONLESS.
No dialogue.

PANEL 5.
ABBERLINE IS NOW SEATED, ROUGHLY HALF FIGURE AS WE LOOK AT HIM FROM ACROSS THE OTHER
SIDE OF THE TABLE HERE, AS IF WE WERE SEATED OPPOSITE HIM, SHARING HIS EYE LEVEL.
STILL EXPRESSIONLESS HE LIFTS HIS PINT GLASS TO HIS MOUTH AND SUPS FROM IT, GETTING
A MOUSTACHE OF FOAM SUPERIMPOSED UPON HIS OWN NATURAL GROWTH. FROM THE LEFT OF THE
BACKGROUND, BEHIND ABBERLINE, WE CAN SEE A WOMAN APPROACHING, FULL TO THREE-QUARTER
FIGURE, ALREADY SO CLOSE TO US THAT THE TOP HALF OF HER FACE IS INVISIBLE OFF THE TOP
OF THE PANEL. THIS IS "EMMA", AND UNBEKNOWNST TO THE SUPPING ABBERLINE SHE IS WALKING
PURPOSEFULLY TOWARDS HIS CHAIR FROM THE REAR ACROSS THE CONGESTED PUB.
No dialogue.

PANEL 6.
SAME SHOT AS LAST PANEL. "EMMA" HAS NOW COME RIGHT UP CLOSE INTO THE FOREGROUND AND IS
STANDING IMMEDIATELY BEHIND AND TO OUR LEFT OF ABBERLINE'S CHAIR AS THE INSPECTOR SITS
FACING US ACROSS THE TABLE, JUST LOWERING HIS PINT HERE WITH A LOOK OF SURPRISE IN HIS
EYES AS HE HEARS THE WOMAN'S VOICE BEHIND HIM. SHE IS NOW COMPLETELY DECAPITATED BY
THE UPPER PANEL BORDER, AND WE ONLY SEE HER FROM THE BOSOM DOWN HERE, HER HANDS FOLDED
IN FRONT OF HER AND PERHAPS CLUTCHING A LITTLE CLASP BAG OR SOMETHING.
"EMMA" (OFF):   Hello, Fred.

PANEL 7.
CHANGE ANGLES NOW SO THAT IN THE RIGHT OF THE FOREGROUND, WE SEE "EMMA" HEAD AND
SHOULDERS AS SHE FACES ALMOST DIRECTLY AWAY FROM US TOWARDS ABBERLINE, ONLY THE
MEREST SLIVER OF HER PROFILE VISIBLE TO US HERE. LOOKING BEYOND HER WE SEE A
STARTLED-LOOKING ABBERLINE AS HE SCRABBLES TO HIS FEET AND AWKWARDLY ATTEMPTS TO

PULL OUT THE OTHER CHAIR SO THAT SHE CAN SIT DOWN ON IT, GAPING AT HER LIKE A CROSS BETWEEN A GOLDFISH AND A LOVE STRUCK GOBSMACKED SCHOOLBOY AS HE DOES SO. PERHAPS HE IS EVEN ATTEMPTING TO TAKE OFF HIS HAT TO HER WITH HIS FREE HAND, HIS PINT OF BEER NOW RESTING UPON THE TABLE IN FRONT OF HIM.

ABBERLINE: Oh. Emma. It's you. I was 'opin' I might run into you.

ABBERLINE: I'm just here on me dinner-break, like. Can I get you a drink?

PANEL 8.

NOW A LONG SHOT OF THE TABLE WITH BOTH OF THEM FULL FIGURE, BUT WITH "EMMA" JUST TOO FAR AWAY TO BE RECOGNIZED. SHE IS TAKING THE SEAT THAT ABBERLINE HAS PULLED OUT FOR HER, BUT SHE HOLDS ONE HAND UP, REFUSING HIS OFFER OF A DRINK. STEADYING THE BACK OF HER CHAIR WITH ONE HAND AS SHE SITS, ABBERLINE STARTS TO LOWER HIMSELF BACK INTO HIS OWN SEAT, STARING AT HER ALL THE WHILE.

"EMMA":   No, it's kind of ye but I mustn't stop. I'm only passin'
                     through. There's money needs earning'. Badly.

ABBERLINE: Why, what's up? You're not, y'know in trouble?

PANEL 9.

SAME LONG SHOT, BUT WITH BOTH OF THEM NOW PROPERLY SEATED, FACING EACH OTHER. EMMA LOOKS WEARY AND DISTRAUGHT, AND FRED GAZES TOWARDS HER SYMPATHETICALLY AND LOVINGLY. SHE PUTS ONE HAND TO HER FACE, ALMOST IN EMBARRASSMENT, AND WAVES ASIDE HIS DIAGNOSIS.

"EMMA":   No! No, not like THAT. It...it's just this DEBT I have.

"EMMA":   God, Fred, if I don't find some money somewhere I don't know
                     WHAT'LL become of me!

The weasels. *Pages 25-27, Marie Kelly goes to see the Old Nichol gang. with the two quid Abberline gives her on the page following the above. The way I'd drawn these blokes, Pete thought they looked like the weasels out of an old version of Wind in The Willows (not the '96 film obviously as this was earlier and they were too posh), and spent the rest of the afternoon doing the voices.*

Chapter 8: Netley's horse.

On pages 18-19 of this chapter, Netley sits around feeling miserable and hopeless, has an affair with a pornographic image, and then gets up and we "cut to a shot" of him leading the horse out of its stable. Whose horse? How far away the stable? I did ask these questions at the time, but they got lost in the shuffle.

The way we have depicted Netley, he's certainly not a man of enough substance that could own a horse and carriage. When we first see him in Chapter 1, he's driving Prince Eddy, and he seems to be wearing a uniform of some sort. We see him again in Chapter 2, whereupon it is clarified that it was he who passed word up the line about Eddy and Annie Crook. In that scene he is to be Gull's driver, as though he had been assigned the duty. I gave him a swish-looking limousine of a carriage, with two horses, as requested in the script. Later, when it started to appear unlikely that he was still working under official sanction, that didn't feel right and I tried to make it look less imposing, and with just one horse, without giving enough visual information to imply that it was a different rig altogether.

Was he in the employ of the Royal household, perhaps in a casual capacity? If so, was there a Mason of some rank in charge of the royal stables? Was Netley moonlighting with official property, or does he have a horse on a payment plan? Was somebody somewhere worrying about why their horse was tuckered out when they got up in the morning? We see how everybody else in the book makes a living, but Netley is a mystery.

Hey, I just want the details. I've known some scallywags who could always manage to obtain wheels for a Saturday night, and the details were always interesting, well at least to me. A few years after all this I was working on a western/detective adaptation from a movie script titled *The Black Diamond Detective Agency*. The hero of the piece is on the lam, heading for Chicago. At some point, with the lights of a town up ahead, he cuts his horse loose and slaps it on the rump, the way they do in that kind of story. I ignored that and instead inserted a scene with him coming out of a horse trader's yard, counting the cash he'd just picked up. I figure a hero in a story is thinking about the coins in his pocket as much as I am. And I'm thinking about it all the time.

Chapter 8, page 31.

There's a complicatedness to this scene that would have been beyond my ability when we started the book a few years before. It first appeared in volume #5 June 1994, just a few months before I set myself up as a self-publisher. That isn't relevant to the publishing of *FROM HELL* yet; I mention it purely to underline my growing confidence, where before it might more correctly be described as arrogance.

Netley gives Liz Stride a flower and asks her to meet him later, during which time he brings Gull to the rendezvous. She takes Gull into the back yard of a club's meeting hall inside of which noted Victorian literary man, William Morris, is about to give a reading.

PAGE 31. (999 words) PANEL 1

SORRY, WE'VE GOT ANOTHER NINE-PANEL PAGE HERE. IN THIS FIRST PANEL WE CLOSE IN UPON THE LIGHTED WINDOW ON THE UPPER FLOOR OF THE ADJOINING CLUB THAT WE COULD SEE UP IN THE BACKGROUND OF THE LAST PANEL ON PAGE 30. AS WE CLOSE IN UPON THE WINDOW WE CAN SEE FIGURES INSIDE, INCLUDING PERHAPS A MAN STANDING BEHIND A TABLE AS HE ADDRESSES THE MEETING FROM A PLATFORM, EVEN THOUGH HE NEEDN'T BE DISTINCT AND WE WILL SEE MORE OF HIM IN A PANEL OR SO, WHEN I'LL BE DESCRIBING THE ROOM THAT HE'S IN MORE DETAIL AS WELL. HERE WE SIMPLY CLOSE IN TOWARDS THE LIGHTED UPSTAIRS WINDOW, SO THAT GULL AND LIZ ARE NO LONGER VISIBLE. THE MAN IS CALLED MORRIS EAGLE (also known as Morris Siegal -ec), AND HE IS A RUSSIAN IMMIGRANT WHO TRAVELLED IN JEWELRY AND THUS WOULD PROBABLY BE SMARTLY DRESSED. THERE MAY BE ANOTHER MAN PARTLY VISIBLE STANDING BESIDE THE TABLE FROM BEHIND WHICH EAGLE SPEAKS, IN OUR NEXT PANEL IF NOT THIS ONE. THIS IS MR. WILLIAM MORRIS, NOTED MARXIST, POET AND DESIGNER OF THE PRINT ADORNING THE COVER OF THE HARD-BACKED W.H.SMITH'S NOTEBOOK THAT THE NOTES FOR THIS EPISODE OF "FROM   HELL" ARE SCRIBBLED IN.

Gary Millidge had the foresight to scan the covers of the notebooks. Above is the one by Morris.

EAGLE: If I could have your attention, gentlemen...

PANEL 2.

WE HAVE NOW CLOSED INTO THE ROOM SO THAT WE CAN SEE EAGLE AS HE SITS BEHIND HIS
TABLE, INTRODUCING WILLIAM MORRIS TO THE REMAINING DRINKERS IN THE ROOM, OF WHOM
THERE ARE ABOUT TWENTY OR THIRTY LEFT. EAGLE LOOKS JOVIAL, WHEREAS MORRIS LOOKS A
LITTLE SELF-CONSCIOUSLY LION-LIKE, DOING HIS BEST TO CUT A HEROIC DASH AS HE STANDS
THERE ON THE PLATFORM BESIDE THE SEATED EAGLE, WITH A SLENDER VOLUME OF HIS POEMS IN
HIS HAND. LOOKING OUT OVER THE SMALL CROWD THAT EAGLE IS ADDRESSING, OF WHOM WE CAN
MAYBE SEE A REPRESENTATIVE SAMPLING IN THE BACKGROUND HERE. THE ROOM, ACCORDING TO PAUL
BEGG HAD "PLAIN BENCHES WITHOUT BACKS STRETCHED THROUGH IT CROSSWISE AND ALONG THE
WALLS. ON THE WALLS HUNG A NUMBER OF PORTRAITS: MARX, PROUDHON, LASSALLE OVERTHROWING
THE GOLDEN CALF OF CAPITALISM. AT THE FRONT THE ROOM WAS ENCLOSED BY A SMALL STAGE.
THE ROOM HAD THREE WINDOWS, ALL LOOKING OUT ON THE REAR YARD OF THE BUILDING. MAYBE
ONE OR MORE OF THE PORTRAITS MENTIONED ABOVE COULD BE HANGING ON THE STAGE BEHIND
MORRIS AS HE SPEAKS DURING THE REMAINDER OF THIS SCENE.

EAGLE: I'm returned from walking my lady home, but before those left
                          after tonight's discussion begin more Russian songs, a
                          regular guest has a poem...

EAGLE: Our comrade, Mr. William Morris.

PANEL 3.

START TO CLOSE PAST EAGLE WHO SITS BACK IN HIS CHAIR WITH A LOOK OF SELF-SATISFIED
ANTICIPATION, SO THAT WE ARE ZOOMING IN UPON MORRIS AS HE OPENS HIS BOOK AND
STARTS TO SCAN IT FOR A POEM, EYES DOWNCAST AS HE GLANCES OVER THE PAGES LOOKING
FOR A CROWD-PLEASER.

MORRIS: Thank you, brothers. Next week I'll recite my "Chants for
                          Socialists", but tonight I thought an older work might suffice.

MORRIS: It's entitled "Love is Enough".

PANEL 4.

CHANGE ANGLE FOR A SHOT OF MORRIS FROM THE FRONT, WITH ONE OF THE PORTRAITS
MENTIONED ABOVE HANGING BEHIND HIM... PROBABLY MARX WOULD BE THE MOST ICONIC AND
RECOGNIZABLE. WE SEE HIM ABOUT THREE-QUARTER TO FULL FIGURE AS HE BEGINS TO READ,
WITH EAGLE OFF PANEL SOMEWHERE ON HIS LEFT AND NOT VISIBLE HERE.

MORRIS: "Love is enough:

MORRIS: have no thought for tomorrow
                          If ye lie down this even in rest from your pain.

PANEL 5.

WE ARE BACK IN THE DARK YARD WITH GULL AND LIZ BOTH SEEN MAYBE THREE-QUARTER TO
HALF FIGURE HERE. LIZ LOOKS FRIGHTENED AND IS USING BOTH HANDS TO PUSH GULL AWAY
AS SHE MAKES A BID FOR ESCAPE. SURPRISED, GULL TAKES A STEP BACK. THE YARD IS DARK
AS LIZ STRUGGLES TO GET TOWARDS THE PARTLY OPEN GATES THAT WILL LEAD HER TO THE
STREET BEYOND AND WHICH SHOULD BE VISIBLE IN THE BACKGROUND HERE SO THAT WE KNOW

WHERE LIZ IS HEADED.

No dialogue.

PANEL 6.

CUT BACK TO MORRIS, READING. THE SHOT IS THE SAME AS IN PANEL FOUR, BUT WE HAVE MOVED IN A LITTLE, SO THAT IF HE WAS FULL FIGURE BEFORE HE'S NOW THREE QUARTER FIGURE AS HE STANDS THERE WITH THE PICTURE OF MARX BEHIND HIM, CONTINUING TO READ FROM HIS SLIM BOOK OF POEMS.

MORRIS: "Ye who have paid for our bliss with great sorrow:

For as it was once so it shall be again...

PANEL 7.

NOW WE ARE IN BERNER STREET, JUST OUTSIDE THE GATE ON THE YARD. LIZ COMES FLYING OUT THROUGH THE GATE LOOKING SCARED WITLESS WITH GULL UNSEEN SOMEWHERE IN THE DARK YARD BEHIND HER. NETLEY, KEEPING WATCH, SEES LIZ DOING A RUNNER AND TAKES SOME SWIFT PACES TOWARDS HER TO INTERCEPT HER BEFORE SHE CAN GET FAR, HIS RATTY LITTLE EYES STEELY AND DETERMINED.

No Dialogue.

PANEL 8.

BACK TO MORRIS. SAME SHOT, BUT ONCE AGAIN WE ARE CLOSER TO HIM, SO THAT HE'S MAYBE HALF FIGURE HERE, MARX LOOMING OVER HIS SHOULDER AS HE READS.

MORRIS: "Ye shall cry out for death as you stretch forth in vain."

PANEL 9.

BACK TO BERNER STREET, JUST OUTSIDE THE YARD. ON THE OPPOSITE SIDE OF THE STREET, NEARER TO US AND COMING TOWARDS US SOMEWHERE IN THE FOREGROUND THERE IS A JEWISH-LOOKING PASSER-BY NAMED ISRAEL SCHWARTZ, WHOSE APPEARANCE WAS "SEMITIC AND THESPIAN" WHATEVER THAT MEANS. AS WE SEE HIM HERE, SCHWARTZ IS LOOKING BACK OVER HIS SHOULDER AND ACROSS THE STREET TOWARDS WHERE WE CAN SEE NETLEY AND LIZ OUTSIDE THE GATE OF THE YARD. NETLEY IS GRABBING LIZ BY THE SHOULDERS AND VIOLENTLY SHOVING HER TO THE GROUND. SHE CRIES OUT IN PAIN, AND IT IS THIS THAT ATTRACTS SCHWARTZ'S ATTENTION. GULL, STILL IN THE DARK YARD BEYOND THE GATES, IS NOWHERE TO BE SEEN HERE. NETLEY'S EXPRESSION IS AN ANGRY, DOG-LIKE SNARL.

LIZ: Aaa

Moon dandy

William Morris pops up again in our Snakes and Ladders, *2000, collected in* A Disease of Language, *in which he is cast as a 'moon dandy.'.*

156

Chapter 8, page 32.

This page represents for me one of the most particular attractions of the "nine-panel grid," which is just one of many ways of arranging pictures on a page until you make a feature of it. If two is an accident and three is a pattern, then it follows that 3x3 is the smallest arrangement out of which you can hope to make and find patterns. It's also the basis of the game "noughts and crosses," in which the horizontals, verticals and also the diagonals form independent lines. Looking at this page the reader, whether they think about it or not, simultaneously reads in all directions. For example, follow a line from the bottom left to the top right and it reads as a sequence. Even the wording in this case does not obstruct a backward reading.

PAGE 32. (717 words) PANEL 1.
ANOTHER NINE-PANEL PAGE HERE, KEEPING UP THE SHARP INTERCUTTING BETWEEN MORRIS READING AND THE MURDER HAPPENING. IN THIS FIRST PANEL WE HAVE MORRIS, AGAIN SEEN A LITTLE CLOSER UP THAN WE SAW HIM IN PANEL EIGHT ON THE PREVIOUS PAGE. HE CAN MAKE WHATEVER SMALL GESTURES SEEM APPROPRIATE TO YOU, THROUGHOUT THIS SEQUENCE.

MORRIS: "Feeble hands to the hands that would help but they may not...

PANEL 2.
NOW WE ARE BACK IN BERNER STREET, BUT WE HAVE REVERSED THE ANGLE FROM PANEL NINE ON PAGE 31, SO THAT HERE IN THE FOREGROUND WE HAVE JOHN NETLEY AS HE CROUCHES OVER THE FALLEN LIZ STRIDE, DRAGGING HER ROUGHLY TO HER FEET HERE. AS HE DOES SO, HE GLARES ACROSS THE STREET TOWARDS THE STRONGLY SEMITIC-LOOKING SCHWARTZ, WHO IS GAZING ACROSS THE ROAD AT NETLEY AND LIZ WITH ALARM AND CONSTERNATION, ALTHOUGH HE MAKES NO MOVE TO COME TO LIZ'S AID. THERE MIGHT ALSO BE ANOTHER MAN VISIBLE ON SCHWARTZ'S SIDE OF THE STREET, THIS ONE ENGAGED IN THE ACT OF LIGHTING A PIPE AND ALSO GLANCING ACROSS THE ROAD AND NETLEY AND LIZ WITHOUT ACTUALLY INTERVENING.

NETLEY: What are you looking at?
NETLEY: FUCKING LIPSKI!

PANEL 3.
BACK TO MORRIS, BUT ONCE MORE WE ARE A LITTLE CLOSER AS HE CONTINUES TO READ, THE PICTURE OF MARX IS HUGE BEHIND HIM.

MORRIS: "Cry out to deaf ears that would hear if they could"

PANEL 4.

BACK IN BERNER STREET FOR A SHOT WITH A SIMILAR ANGLE TO THAT USED IN PANEL NINE ON PAGE 31, WITH SCHWARTZ COMING TOWARDS US ON THE RIGHT OF THE FOREGROUND AS HE HURRIES ON HIS WAY, UNNERVED BY WHAT HE HAS SEEN. WE CAN NOW CLEARLY SEE THE SECOND PASSER-BY, HASTILY FOLLOWING SCHWARTZ'S EXAMPLE ON THE SAME SIDE OF THE STREET. ACROSS THE STREET WE SEE NETLEY MANHANDLING LIZ BACK THROUGH THE GATES OF DUTFIELD'S YARD. SCHWARTZ GLANCES BACK AT THIS WITH A LOOK OF DREAD, BUT HURRIES ON ANYWAY.
No dialogue.

PANEL 5.

BACK TO MORRIS AS HE READS, PERHAPS CONTINUING OUR CLOSE IN IF THAT LOOKS GOOD TO YOU. THE PICTURE OF MARX FILLS THE BACKGROUND.
MORRIS: "Til again shall the change come, and words your lips say not..."

PANEL 6.

NOW WE ARE BACK IN THE YARD. GULL IS HALF CROUCHED IN THE RIGHT FOREGROUND, FACING AWAY FROM US TOWARDS THE PARTLY OPEN GATE. HE HAS HIS BAG OPEN BEFORE HIM AND IS REACHING INTO IT AS HE LOOKS TOWARDS THE GATE WHERE NETLEY IS COMING INTO THE YARD, PUSHING THE TERRIFIED LIZ BEFORE HIM, ONE OF HIS HANDS GRABBING HER NECK SCARF BY THE BACK, HIS FACE A MIXTURE OF RAGE AND FEAR. LIZ STARES TOWARDS THE DARK SHAPE OF GULL IN THE RIGHT FOREGROUND. HER EYES SHRUNKEN TO PIN PRICKS WITH FEAR.
No dialogue.

PANEL 7.

BACK TO MORRIS. I FIGURE THAT HERE WE START TO PAN UP OVER MORRIS' HEAD SO THAT HE STARTS TO DROP OFF THE BOTTOM OF THE PANEL WITH PERHAPS ONLY THE TOP OF HIS FACE VISIBLE HERE. WE ARE MOVING IN MORE TOWARDS THE GIANT PORTRAIT OF MARX BEHIND HIM.
MORRIS: "Your hearts make all plain in the best wise they would..."

PANEL 8.

BACK IN THE YARD, IN THE NEAR BACKGROUND LIZ IS FACING TOWARDS US, MAYBE HALF FIGURE. NETLEY IS RIGHT BEHIND HER, HOLDING HER NECK SCARF WITH BOTH HANDS, USING IT TO PULL HER HEAD BACK SO AS TO EXPOSE HER THROAT TO SIR WILLIAM. LIZ HAS ONE HAND UP CLUTCHING AT THE SCARF, HER CHIN PULLED UP AND BACK BY IT SO THAT SHE LOOKS DOWN THE LENGTH OF HER NOSE WITH TERRIFIED EYES TOWARDS THE RIGHT FOREGROUND WHERE WE CAN JUST SEE A LITTLE OF GULL AS HE ADVANCES UPON HER. HIS HEAD IS OFF PANEL. ABOVE IN THE RIGHT FOREGROUND, BUT WE CAN SEE HIS HAND AS HE WITHDRAWS IT FROM THE BAG. IT IS HOLDING THE GLEAMING LENGTH OF THE LISTON KNIFE, AND IT IS UPON THIS THAT LIZ'S EYES ARE FIXED.
No dialogue.

PANEL 9.

BACK TO THE MEETING ROOM FOR A CLOSE-UP SHOT OF THE PORTRAIT OF MARX STARING OUT AT US, WITH MORRIS' BALLOON ISSUING FROM OFF BELOW.
MORRIS(OFF):   "And the world ye thought waning is glorious and good."

The rhythmic interplay climaxed on the previous page. Now the cut, then the applause.

PAGE 33. (1337 words) (edited) PANEL 1. BACK TO THE YARD FOR A FULL TO THREE-QUARTER FIGURE SHOT OF THE THREE OF THEM. NETLEY IS HOLDING LIZ'S HEAD BACK BY MEANS OF THE SCARF, A LOOK OF TERROR IN HIS WHITE EYES AS HE IS CAUGHT IN THE WHITE-HOT MADNESS OF THE INSTANT. HE IS IN THE NEAR BACKGROUND HERE, FACING TOWARDS US OVER LIZ'S SHOULDER AS SHE FACES US FROM JUST IN FRONT OF HIM. HER EYES ARE WIDE OPEN; BLANK, AMAZED AND DISBELIEVING. GULL IS IN THE RIGHT FOREGROUND, FACING AWAY FROM US AT A SLIGHT ANGLE TOWARDS THE LEFT NEAR BACKGROUND. HE IS STARING INTO LIZ'S EYES WITH AN EXPRESSIONLESS YET INTENSE DEGREE OF FIXED ATTENTION. IT IS ALMOST LIKE A KEEN SCIENTIFIC INTEREST. HIS HAND IS CAUGHT HERE AT THE END OF ITS ARC, WITH DROPLETS OF BLOOD HANGING IN SPACE BEHIND THE SCALPEL TO MARK ITS SWIFT PASSAGE THROUGH THE AIR. IT HAS CUT THROUGH LIZ'S LEFT CAROTID ARTERY AND PART OF HER WINDPIPE IN PASSING, AND THERE IS A SPRAY OF ARTERIAL BLOOD, FORCEFUL AND STEAMING IN THE COLD NIGHT AIR AS IT SPATTERS AGAINST THE WALL OF THE YARD TO STRIDE'S LEFT, MOSTLY MISSING SIR WILLIAM. No dialogue

PANEL 2. WE ARE NOW BACK IN THE MEETING ROOMS WHERE MORRIS HAS JUST CONCLUDED HIS READING, POSITIONED SOMEWHERE IN AMONGST THE BENCHES WHERE THE AUDIENCE ARE SEATED, TOWARDS THE BACK SOMEWHERE AND LOOKING THROUGH THE AUDIENCE TOWARDS THE FRONT, WHERE MORRIS STANDS FACING US. HE IS CLOSING HIS BOOK AND BOWING HIS HEAD SLIGHTLY AS HE RECEIVES HIS APPLAUSE. IN THE FOREGROUND, WE ARE IN THE MIDDLE OF A SEA OF APPLAUDING PEOPLE, PEHAPS WITH ONE BIG SET OF CLAPPING HANDS ENTERING THE PANEL FROM THE RIGHT OF THE FOREGROUND. EVERYONE IS CLAPPING. GIVEN THE JUXTAPOSITION WITH THE PREVIOUS PANEL, IT IS ALMOST AS IF THEY ARE UNWITTINGLY APPLAUDING STRIDE'S MURDER. No dialogue

PANEL 4. CHANGE ANGLE NOW SO THAT WE ARE OVER BY THE SLIGHTLY OPEN GATE OF THE YARD, THE BOTTOM OF WHICH WE CAN SEE ENTERING THE FORGROUND OVER ON THE RIGHT. LOOKING BEYOND THIS WE CAN SEE ACROSS THE YARD TO WHERE LIZ LIES DEAD SOME FEW FEET AWAY WITH NETLEY STANDING FULL FIGURE TO OUR LEFT OF THE BODY AT SIR WILLIAM WHO STANDS ON OUR RIGHT OF THE BODY, STILL HOLDING HIS KNIFE. HE IS IGNORING NETLEY, AND STARING

EXPRESSIONLESSLY DOWN TOWARDS THE DEAD WOMAN. HE PERHAPS SQUINTS AND FROWNS SLIGHTLY, AS IF TRYING TO RECALL SOMETHING THROUGH THE LUMINOUS FOGBANKS THAT ROLL THROUGH HIS MND DURING THE MURDERS. NETLEY IS LOOKING SICK AND SCARED, TRAPPED IN AN UNBEARABLE SITUATION WITH NOTHING TO DO BUT GO ALONG WITH IT.

NETLEY: Let's not do any more, sir, ay? Not on this one, ay? I keep thinkin' I 'ear somebody comin'...

GULL: Yes...Yes, I remember now...

PANEL 5.

SAME SHOT, ONLY NOW IN THE RIGHT OF THE FOREGROUND WE CAN SEE THE FEET AND LOWER LEGS OF A POLICE CONSTABLE AS HE ENTERS THE YARD, FACING AWAY FROM US BY HIS STANCE TO GAZE DIRECTLY ACROSS THE YARD AT GULL AND NETLEY. NETLEY, ON THE LEFT OF THE BACKGROUND, TURNS TO LOOK AT THE LARGELY OFF-PANEL NEW ARRIVAL WITH AN EXPRESSION OF JAW-DROPPING DISMAY, WIDE EYED WITH MUTE ALARM. GULL DOES NOT LOOK UP, BUT CONTINIUES TO GAZE DOWN AT THE BODY QUIZZICALLY. HE IS TALKING ALMOST TO HIMSELF, FAR AWAY IN HIS THOUGHTS.

GULL: This is the one that I didn't finish, isn't it?

PANEL 6.

NOW A SHOT THROUGH NETLEY'S EYES, JUST LOOKING SQUARE ON AT THE POLICEMAN FRAMED IN THE GATEWAY OF THE YARD, FACING US ABOUT THREE QUARTER FIGURE. IT IS THE YOUNG POLICEMAN WHOM WE SAW HURRYING AWAY FROM THE POLICE STATION WHERE KATE EDDOWES IS CURRENTLY INCARCERATED. PERHAPS HE IS HOLDING A BULL'S-EYE LANTERN THAT IS TURNED TOWARDS US. HE LOOKS YOUNG, OUT OF HIS DEPTH AND FRIGHTENED TO DEATH, HIS EYES WIDE AND HIS FACE PALE AND SWEATING AS HE STARES AGHAST IN THE BLOOD SPATTERED DARKNESS OF THE YARD.

POLICEMAN: S—Sir William Gull?

PANEL 8.

NOW A SHOT OF ALL THREE MEN, PROBABLY FULL FIGURE, AS THE FRIGHTENED YOUNG POLICEMAN FACES GULL AND THE SHRINKING NETLEY ACROSS THE BODY OF THE MURDERED PROSTITUTE, AT WHICH THE STUNNED-LOOKING YOUNG COPPER IS STARING DOWN FIXEDLY ALL THE WHILE HE IS TALKING. HE CAN'T TAKE HIS EYES OFF THE AWFUL FACT OF IT. GULL JUST STARES AT HIM EXPRESIONLESSLY AND LEVELLY, THE BLOODY KNIFE HANGING FORGOTTEN IN HIS HAND.

POLICEMAN: I...I went to Brook Street. Your wife, Lady Gull, she said you had a patient in Whitechapel. Described your coach.

POLICEMAN: Hours, sir, I've been looking.

PANEL 9.

...GULL IS STANDING CLOSER TO US, ABOUT HALF TO THREE QUARTER FIGURE, SILENTLY AND EXPRESSIONLESSLY GAZING AT THE YOUNG CONSTABLE IN THE FOREGROUND. GULL'S EYE SOCKETS ARE FILLED WITH SHADOW, HIS MONK-LIKE HAIR PLASTERED TO HIS FOREHEAD, MOUTH SET AND JOWLS HEAVY. HIS IS A MASSIVE, STILL AND IMPASSIVE FIGURE AS HE STANDS SILENTLY LISTENING TO THE CONSTABLE BLATHER FROM THE FOREGROUND.

POLICEMAN: I—It's the woman, Sir. Kelly. We've got her at Bishopsgate lock-up, but they throw out the drunks at One.

POLICEMAN: You'll have to hurry.

Chapter 8, page 37, 39.

Gull is interrupted in the killing of Liz Stride and hastens to Mitre Square where a Masonic messenger has informed him he will find Marie Kelly. A mistake has been made, drawing Cathy Eddowes instead into his sights. This is the "double event" numbered as part 10 in the original contents table, a term used by the Ripperologists.

I tend to be suspicious of art that manipulates its audience. If I sense an attempt to manipulate my emotional responses, I always turn off the telly, leave the cinema, close the book. If somebody's in a sad state, just tell me. Don't put me in one too. Thus in *FROM HELL* I occasionally depressed some moments that were meant to be expressive. I levelled them out into statements …He walked up the street… he walked down the street…he effected the following mutilations upon his victim. etc. I avoided the this-is-you "points of view" and other devices intended to put the reader inside the action. That includes images both pathetic (Annie Crook in chapter 3) and repulsive (all over the place). But here, after eight chapters we have an explosion of violence and everything, including me, gets carried along in the rush.

PAGE 37. (1018 words) PANEL 1.
THERE ARE SEVEN PANELS HERE, WITH ONE BIG ONE ON THE MIDDLE TIER AND THREE ON EACH OF THE OTHER TIERS, THE TOP AND THE BOTTOM. IN THIS FIRST PANEL WE HAVE CHANGED ANGLE SO THAT WE ARE IMMEDIATELY BEHIND NETLEY AND CATHY AS THEY WALK AWAY FROM US TOWARDS THE COACH, WHICH WE SEE IN THE BACKGROUND. THE COACH IS PARTLY IN SHADOW, SO THAT ITS WINDOWS ARE DARK AND WE CANNOT SEE ANYONE WITHIN. AROUND THIS, IN THE BACKGROUND, WE CAN PERHAPS SEE A LITTLE OF THE ESTABLISHING DETAILS OF MITRE SQUARE. IN THE FOREGROUND, MAYBE NETLEY IS EVEN LEADING CATHY BY ONE HAND, THE HAND-CLASP LIGHT AND ALMOST REVERENT, AS IF NETLEY WERE GIVING AWAY THE BRIDE, WALKING WITH HER TOWARDS THE ALTAR OF THE COACH. PERHAPS CATHY, ON OUR LEFT HERE, TURNS HER HEAD SLIGHTLY TOWARDS NETLEY AND SPEAKS TO HIM.

CATHY: So, this old chap: Bit of a nob, is 'e? A gentleman, like?
NETLEY: Gentleman? Ho ho! 'e's more than that, gal...

PANEL 2.
SAME SHOT, STILL POSITIONED BEHIND NETLEY AND CATHY AS THEY WALK TOWARDS THE WAITING COACH. NOW HOWEVER, THEY HAVE GOT MUCH CLOSER, SO THAT THE COACH STARTS TO LOOM AND FILL MORE AND MORE OF THE BACKGROUND BEHIND THEM. IT IS STILL DARK INSIDE

THE COACH, BUT WE MAYBE HAVE A MURKY SENSE OF SOMETHING MOVING. THE DOOR OF THE COACH IS STARTING TO OPEN JUST A CRACK, BUT THIS IS PROBABLY IMPERCEPTIBLE HERE. WE ARE PERHAPS EVEN A LITTLE CLOSER UP BEHIND NETLEY AND CATHY, ALMOST AS IF WE WERE ABOUT TO OVERTAKE THEM, ZOOMING IN BETWEEN THEM TO FOCUS ON THE DOOR OF THE COACH.

NETLEY: 'E's one o' the finest.

NETLEY: The finest in the land.

PANEL 3.

WE CLOSE IN UPON THE COACH DOOR. IT IS OPENING OUT TOWARDS US. PERHAPS IN THE CHINK OF THE OPEN DOOR WE CAN EVEN GLIMPSE GULL'S WHITE HAND UPON THE INNER HANDLE, EMERGING FROM THE IMPENETRABLE SHADOWS WITHIN THE COACH. THIS PANEL IS THE SILENT INTRODUCTION TO AN EXPLOSION OF VIOLENCE, THE MOST FRENETIC THUS FAR IN THE STRIP WHICH WILL TAKE US THROUGH THE NEXT TWO OR THREE PAGES IN ONE HEADLONG RUSH, SO GET READY.

No dialogue.

PANEL 4.

BIG PANEL, WITH CATHY AND NETLEY PARTLY VISIBLE IN THE FOREGROUND, PERHAPS HEAD AND SHOULDERS TO EITHER SIDE AS THEY RECOIL AWAY FROM THE DOOR OF THE COACH, WHICH IS BURSTING WIDE OPEN IN THE IMMEDIATE BACKGROUND HERE. HUGE AND DARK, GULL EXPLODES OUT OF THE OPEN DOORWAY TOWARDS US, THE INK-BLOT OF HIS CLOAK SPLASHED OUT BEHIND HIM, MASKING HIS TRUE DIMENSIONS AND MAKING HIS SIZE AMBIGUOUS. HIS WHITE FACE IS STARK MAD AND HIS FIXED STARE IS FEROCIOUS AND INTENSE. HIS HANDS SPREAD, AND IN ONE OF THEM HE CLASPS THE LISTON KNIFE. HE EXPLODES STRAIGHT TOWARDS US OUT OF THE COACH LIKE SOME MONSTROUS AND FRENZIED BIRD BURSTING FREE OF A CAGE FINALLY GROWN TOO SMALL FOR IT. IN THE FOREGROUND, CATHY LOOKS STUNNED WITH SHOCK AND STARTS TO HALF-LIFT HER HANDS AS IF TO COVER HER FACE. NETLEY GASPS AND TAKES A STEP BACK, HIS EYES FIXED ON GULL AND FILLED WITH TERROR. HE KNEW THAT GULL WAS COMPLETELY OFF THE MAP, BUT THIS IS SOMETHING NEW AND TERRIBLE. PERHAPS A STRIPE OF SHADOW FALLS IN A SOLID BAND ACROSS THE TOP OF GULL'S FACE AS HE EMERGES, FROM WHICH HIS WHITE EYES STARE FIXEDLY AT CATHY.

No dialogue.

PANEL 5.

CHANGE ANGLE SO THAT NOW WE HAVE CATHY IN THE FOREGROUND, SEEN IN HALF-FIGURE SHOT HERE AND FACING ROUGHLY TOWARDS THE RIGHT OF THE PANEL SO THAT WE MORE OR LESS SEE HER IN PROFILE, LEAPING OUT OF THE COACH IN A MAD RUSH, GULL IS PASSING CATHY ON HER FURTHER SIDE HEADING TOWARDS THE LEFT OF THE PANEL AND PERHAPS EVEN ABOUT TO VANISH OFF THE SIDE OF IT. HE IS A DARK BLUR AS HE MOVES, THE ONLY MOVING THING IN A LANDSCAPE FROZEN WITH SHOCK. AS HE RUSHES PAST CATHY LIKE A DARK WIND ON HER FAR SIDE HE SNAKES OUT HIS LEFT ARM AND HOOKS IT AROUND CATHY'S NECK, SO THAT HE STARTS TO DRAG HER OVER BACKWARDS WITH HIS MOMENTUM APPLIED TO THIS GRIP UPON HER WINDPIPE. CATHY'S EYES BULGE IN SHOCK, THE PUPILS REDUCED TO PINPOINTS, AND HER HANDS RISE UP IN A FUTILE ATTEMPT TO UNHOOK GULL'S ELBOW FROM AROUND HER THROAT AS SHE IS HELPLESSLY DRAGGED OVER BACKWARDS, WITHOUT EVEN TIME TO SCREAM. GULL ISN'T EVEN LOOKING AT HER AS HE RUSHES PAST, CATCHING HER UP IN HIS WAKE AND BOWLING HER OVER BACKWARDS.

CATHY: wuch...

PANEL 6.
NOW A FULL-FIGURE SHOT FROM ABOUT THE SAME ANGLE BUT PULLED BACK A BIT.
WE SEE CATHY AS SHE FALLS OVER BACKWARDS ONTO THE FLOOR OF THE YARD, THE
BREATH DRIVEN FROM HER AS SHE DOES SO. GULL, WHO HAS BOWLED HER OVER AND FLUNG
HER ON THE FLOOR IS STILL MOVING FORWARDS, ADJUSTING HIS STRIDE NOW AND STEPPING
SO AS HE STRADDLES CATHY'S FALLEN BODY. HE KEEPS HIS EYES FIXED UPON HER FACE
THROUGHOUT, HIS EXPRESSION WHITE HOT AND BURNING IN ITS INTENSITY. HE STILL HAS
THE KNIFE IN HIS RIGHT HAND, PERHAPS STARTING TO DRAW IT BACK JUST A LITTLE HERE.
CATHY: Nnnugh!

PANEL 7.
WE ARE LOOKING UP THROUGH CATHY'S EYES AS GULL STANDS ABOVE HER, HIS LEFT HAND
REACHING DOWN TO CLUTCH THE COLLAR OF HER APRON. HIS RIGHT HAND IS EXTENDING BEHIND
HIM ALMOST STRAIGHT, RUNNING AWAY FROM US IN A PERSPECTIVE THAT ENDS IN THE VANISHING
POINT OF THE LISTON KNIFE'S TIP. PERHAPS IN THE FOREGROUND, ALL WE CAN SEE OF CATHY
IS ONE HAND RAISED UP FEEBLY AS IF ATTEMPTING TO DEFLECT THE BLOW THAT IS ABOUT TO
FALL. GULL STARES DOWN AT HER OFF PANEL FACE, EXPRESSIONLESS SAVE FOR THE INTENSITY
IN HIS EYES, WHICH IS FRIGHTENING. IN THE BACKGROUND WE CAN SEE NETLEY HOVERING,
STILL IN SHOCK AND LOOKING TERRIFIED. PERHAPS THE COACHMAN IS EVEN STARTING TO COVER
HIS EYES, IN ORDER NOT TO SEE WHAT HAPPENS NEXT.
No dialogue.

PAGE 39. (532 words) PANEL 1. (edited- 3 panels only)
CHANGE ANGLE SO THAT WE ARE NOW AT GROUND LEVEL ABOUT A FOOT BEYOND THE TOP OF CATHY'S
HEAD, LOOKING UP AT GULL AS HE CROUCHES ACROSS HER. WE CANNOT SEE CATHY'S FACE HERE.
INSTEAD WE ARE LOOKING UP INTO GULL'S MURDEROUS AND ONLY SEMI-HUMAN FACE AS HE STARTS TO
SLASH PRECISE GROOVES ACROSS CATHY'S FACE, ACROSS HER NOSE AND LIPS.
GULL: Uehh

PANEL 3.
NOW A SHOT THROUGH GULL'S EYES LOOKING DOWN AT THE FUCKING MESS HE'S MADE OF CATHY'S
FACE. BOTH OF THE LOWER EYELID'S ARE CUT THROUGH, ALMOST LIKE THE MAKEUP OF A CLOWN,
WITH OTHER SCRATCHES AND CUTS AROUND THE EYES. THE BRIDGE OF THE NOSE IS SLICED
THROUGH AND THE TIP OF THE NOSE IS ALMOST COMPLETELY SEVERED. THE CHEEKS HAVE BEEN
SLASHED WITH TRIANGULAR FLAPS ABOUT AN INCH AND A HALF LONG PEELING UP AND BACK FROM
THEM. THE UPPER LIP IS SLASHED IN TWO. THE THROAT IS AN OPEN HOLE. HER INTESTINES ARE
OVER HER SHOULDER. SHE IS, AS MIKE HAMMER USED TO SAY, "VERY DEAD'.
No dialogue

PANEL 6.
SAME SHOT. NOW, USING HIS OTHER HAND, GULL PULLS OUT CATHY'S WOMB
SO THAT HE HOLDS HER KIDNEY IN ONE HAND AND HER WOMB (ALONG WITH
THE KNIFE, POSSIBLY) IN THE OTHER. HE BARES HIS TEETH, AND HE IS
PALEOLITHIC, EVEN PRE-HUMAN. NO CIVILIZATION REMAINS.
GULL: mh?

On censorship.

It wasn't usually the mutilation that got us into trouble. Alan: *"I refused to do a strip about serial murder, where it was okay to show someone dissecting a woman but not okay to show two people having consenting loving casual sex. This is the human world, and I'm a grown-up now. I think I should be allowed to write and draw whatever I want. I don't have to go to bed at any special time, and I don't like being condescended to by people who very often I consider to be my intellectual inferiors...*

The Obscene Publications Act relies upon this word "obscene" which is a sort of Victorian, Biblical word. What is obscene? Nobody can come up with a satisfactory definition. The Customs say, "Well, you try importing it, and we'll tell you whether it's obscene." That's what they say. "We're asking you to play Russian Roulette here. We won't tell you what you can or can't import. You try

importing it, and if we don't like it, we'll seize it and burn it. You can appeal against that, but if you do appeal and lose, you might have to spend time in prison." (1996 interview w/Andy Diggle)

By mid-1996, nine of the ten volumes of *FROM HELL* had been published. We had a recurring problem of some volumes being seized by British Customs so that shops couldn't stock the series in its entirety. Tony Bennett's Knockabout was a key distributor of Kitchen Sink Press books in the UK. He had the idea to make a full frontal presentation to HM Customs. He indicated that he *"...would like to start importing this series,"* then showed all the volumes as a pre-emption, pointing out where

164

the offences were, with the aim of getting something in writing to present when problems arise. *"The panels I have found are as follows,"* Tony wrote, *"Chapter 1 page 3, Chapter 5 page 1, Chapter 7 page 10, Chapter 9 page 38."* Two of these I have already looked at here, with a third on this page.

Customs responded: *"Thank you for identifying the pages of the series that you have your doubts over. I notice that some of the pages you mention contain scenes of mutilation. Such scenes in cartoon/comic form no longer fall within the import prohibition, although the sale of violent/horror material is prohibited by the Children and Young Persons Act 1955, for which the police have responsibility for enforcement. I have carefully considered the contents of all the books. Although there are one or two scenes which display minor scenes of ejaculation and intercourse, I would consider these portrayals to be borderline, especially when taken into context with the book itself, and indeed the rest of the series, which tell of the horrors of the ripper murders in Victorian London. If this is taken into consideration a court may conclude that the publications are not obscene. Therefore, in my opinion, none of the volumes submitted in their present form are indecent or obscene and they would not breach the prohibition on importation of indecent or obscene material established by S42 of the Customs Consolidation Act 1876. With your permission I would like to retain all of the magazines for future reference. Yours etc."*

Having already put in so much work on it, we felt it only right that Knockabout become publisher of the UK edition of the collected *FROM HELL* in 2000.

The panels on these two pages are from one of the scenes singled out as problematical, pages 9 and 10 of Chapter 7. Annie Chapman has a regular weekly job of bathing 'the pensioner' (an invalided soldier rather than an 'old aged' pensioner in the modern understanding, a concept first introduced in Germany in 1885). He spends several panels being concerned about her welfare, she bathes him, and manually gives him an orgasm. He sees her out, tying her hat ribbon for her. I can't recall if the two children walking past, holding hands, were in the script or my own addition. I think I saw the pair among my assorted period reference photos and felt they belonged here.

Chapter 9, page 13.

The movie adaptation of *FROM HELL* was pitched to us by producer Don Murphy in February 1994, before the book was complete. For the benefit of Murphy's Angry Films, Alan wrote a 5,000-word synopsis of the work still to be done. That's from Chapter 9 (not published till December '94) to the end. Describing this part of the book, Alan wrote, ***"This chapter details the increasingly chaotic period of thirty-nine days from the double murder of Catherine Eddowes and Elizabeth Stride to the eve of Marie Kelly's murder on November 9th. All the characters are gradually driven to points of extremity in their approach to the final apocalyptic slaughter."*** (I'll refer to this document as the "1994 synopsis'"). Chapter 9 is the longest chapter in the book at 58 pages.

The script for this page and the next stands out, perhaps because so much of it is beyond illustrating. The concentration of phrases to be relished is denser here than in any other two pages of the scripts.

PAGE 13. (987 words) PANEL 1.
THIS IS A SEVEN-PANEL PAGE, WITH THE FIRST PANEL BEING A BIG WIDE ONE AND THEN THREE PANELS ON EACH OF THE TIERS BELOW THAT. IN THE FIRST BIG PANEL WE HAVE AN INTERIOR SHOT OF THE EGYPTIAN ROOMS AT THE BRITISH MUSEUM, FOR WHICH I'M STILL TRYING TO FIND REFERENCE. I IMAGINE IT AS QUITE BIG AND SPACIOUS AND ECHOING, ITS TILED FLOORS POLISHED TO A DEEP AND LUSTROUS REFLECTIVE SHEEN. IF IT SHOULD TURN OUT TO BE AT ALL POSSIBLE WITHOUT STRAYING TOO FAR FROM REALITY, I'D LIKE SOME BIG AND SIZEABLE EGYPTIAN STATUES ARRANGED IN THE BACKGROUND OF THIS SCENE FOR REFERENCE. AS I SEE THE IMAGES HERE, WE ARE LOOKING AT ONE OF THE EXPANSIVE GALLERY WALLS OF THE EGYPTIAN ROOMS, ALONG WHICH THE TENTATIVE GIANT STATUES ARE ARRANGED, SEATED OR STANDING IN THEIR HIEROGLYPHIC POSES. WALKING ALONG THE GALLERY FROM LEFT TO RIGHT, QUITE SMALL IN COMPARISON TO THE HUGE STATUARY, WE SEE WILLIAM GULL, HIS TOP HAT NOW IN ONE HAND AND A BAG OF GRAPES IN THE OTHER, HIS

REFLECTION SHIMMERING IN THE TILED FLOOR AT HIS FEET. SOMEWHERE OVER TO THE RIGHT WE
CAN PERHAPS SEE SOMEONE WITH THE UNIFORM OF A MUSEUM CUSTODIAN OR ATTENDANT. HE IS
DEALING WITH SOME MENIAL DUTY AND PAYS NO ATTENTION TO GULL'S APPROACH.
No dialogue.

PANEL 2.

HERE WE HAVE CHANGED ANGLES BY ABOUT NINETY DEGREES SO THAT HERE WE ARE BEHIND GULL
AS HE WALKS ALONG. WE SEE HIM AS HE PAUSES, SOME DISTANCE AWAY FROM US ACROSS THE
TILED AND GLEAMING FLOOR, TO SPEAK WITH THE MUSEUM ATTENDANT MENTIONED LAST PANEL.
THE ATTENDANT INCLINES HIS HEAD TOWARDS SIR WILLIAM, LISTENING INTENTLY AND
RESPECTFULLY TO WHAT GULL IS SAYING. THEY ARE TOO FAR AWAY FROM US TO HEAR AT THIS
JUNCTURE. ALL AROUND THEM, THE EGYPTIAN EXHIBITS LOOM, STRANGE, ANCIENT AND SILENT.
No dialogue.

PANEL 3.

SAME SHOT. GULL IS STILL STANDING IN THE SAME PLACE, BUT THE ATTENDANT IS STARTING
TO HURRY OFF PANEL TO THE RIGHT, PERHAPS LOOKING BACK AT GULL AS HE DEPARTS AND
TIPPING HIS HAT RESPECTFULLY SO THAT WE RECEIVE THE IMPRESSION THAT HE IS HURRYING
OFF TO DO GULL'S BIDDING. GULL JUST STANDS THERE IMPASSIVELY AND WATCHES HIM GO,
COLOSSAL SLEEPING KINGS AND JACKAL-HEADED DEITIES KEEPING THEIR ETERNAL SILENT VIGIL
ALL ABOUT HIM. HALF-HOUR OLD ECHOES STILL WHISPER AND CLATTER FAINTLY. A ZOMBIE
SIBILANCE IN THE FAR CORNERS OF THE ROOM. MAYBE GULL EATS A GRAPE.
No dialogue.

PANEL 4.

SAME SHOT. HERE THE ATTENDANT IS GONE FROM THE SHOT, SOMEWHERE OFF THE RIGHT-HAND
SIDE OF THE PANEL, AND GULL IS LEFT ON HIS OWN, STANDING THERE IN THE GIANT MUSEUM
ROOM WITH ITS SOARING PILLARS. HE GAZES ABOUT AT THE VAULTED ARCHITECTURE AS HE
WAITS, WHICH, ON BALANCE, IS PROBABLY MUCH BETTER FOR ONE THAN LISTENING TO A MUZAK
RENDITION OF "UP, UP AND AWAY IN MY BEAUTIFUL BALLOON" FOR FIVE MINUTES.
No dialogue.

PANEL 5.

SAME SHOT, WITH GULL IN THE SAME PLACE, ONLY HERE HE HAS STOPPED LOOKING AT THE
SURROUNDING ARCHITECTURE AND PLUNDERED ART TREASURES TO GAZE TOWARDS THE RIGHT-
HAND SIDE OF THE PANEL WHERE WE SEE THE ATTENDANT RETURNING, USHERING A SMARTLY
DRESSED, PLUMP AND BESPECTACLED GENTLEMAN IN A SUIT BEFORE HIM, THIS MAN EVIDENTLY
BEING SOME SORT OF MUSEUM OFFICIAL THAT GULL HAS SENT THE ATTENDANT TO FIND FOR HIM.
THE MAN IS BREATHLESS AND HURRYING, PERHAPS WRINGING HIS HANDS SOLICITOUSLY BEFORE
HIM AS HE WALKS. IT IS EVIDENT FROM HIS POSTURE THAT HE CONSIDERS GULL A VERY
IMPORTANT VISITOR AND IS ANXIOUS TO PLEASE HIM IN WHATEVER WAY HE CAN.

FAT OFFICIAL: Sir William. We are honoured, sir, deeply honoured by your
                   visit.

FAT OFFICIAL: I am at your disposal, sir. If there is anything I can
                   assist with ...

PANEL 6.

CHANGE ANGLE NOW SO THAT IN THE RIGHT OF THE FOREGROUND, HEAD AND SHOULDERS AND
FACING AWAY FROM US AT A SLIGHT ANGLE TOWARDS THE LEFT OF THE NEAR BACKGROUND, WE SEE
THE FAT MUSEUM OFFICIAL, OR AT LEAST A PART OF HIM. OUR MAIN FOCUS, HOWEVER, IS ON
GULL, WHOM THE OFFICIAL IS STARING AT HERE. GULL STANDS IN THE LEFT NEAR BACKGROUND,
FACING THE OFFICIAL ROUGHLY HALF FIGURE AND US, THE OPEN BAG OF GRAPES STILL HELD
IN HIS HAND ALONG WITH THE TOP HAT. HERE, PERHAPS, AS HE SPEAKS TO THE OFFICIAL, HE
PICKS ANOTHER GRAPE FROM THE BUNCH IN THE BAG. HE FIXES HIS UNBLINKING AND UNNERVING
STARE UPON THE CLEARLY DISCOMFITED AND NERVOUS OFFICIAL AND SMILES. THE SMILE MIGHT
BE MISTAKEN FOR A FRIENDLY ONE WERE IT NOT FOR THE COLD, SARDONIC AND UNWAVERING
SUPERIORITY ALWAYS EVIDENT IN GULL'S EYES. TO HIM, EVERYONE ELSE IS A PARTICULARLY
AMUSING STRAIN OF PARAMECIUM.

GULL :	Let us hope so.
GULL :	There is in England a mummy-case from Thebes, currently in private hands. Does the British Museum intend to purchase it?

PANEL 7.

CHANGE ANGLE TO ALMOST A REVERSE OF OUR LAST SHOT, SO THAT NOW GULL IS FACING
SLIGHTLY AWAY FROM US, LESS THAN HEAD AND SHOULDERS IN THE RIGHT OF THE FOREGROUND.
WE CAN ONLY SEE HIM FROM THE BRIDGE OF HIS NOSEDOWN TO HIS CHEST HERE, WITH HIS EYES
OFF PANEL ABOVE. VERY SLOWLY AND DELIBERATELY, HE POPS A GRAPE INTO HIS MOUTH HERE AS
HE LISTENS TO THE REPLY OF THE NERVOUS MUSEUM OFFICIAL, WHOM WE SEE OVER ON THE LEFT
OF THE NEAR BACKGROUND, ROUGHLY HALF FIGURE AS HE FACES TOWARDS GULL, HIS HANDS SPREAD
IN NERVOUS AND APOLOGETIC EXPLANATION. ALTHOUGH THE MAN LOOKS OBSCURELY AGITATED AS
HE SPEAKS, WHAT WE CAN SEE OF GULL'S FACE REMAINS IMPASSIVE AND EXPRESSIONLESS AS HE
THOUGHTFULLY MASTICATES THE GRAPE.

OFFICIAL :	Ah yes. Yes, I have heard of the, ah, of the item. Excellent piece. First class.
OFFICIAL :	Of course, there IS the matter of its, ah, reputation, so to speak...

King Tut. *I sometimes think there should be more Egyptian detail in the art. At the time, however, I judged that it would make things more prosaic, more "midnight in the museum" than the majesty of eternity. Just now I started sketching a stone head and felt my original prognosis was confirmed.*

Chapter 9, page 14.

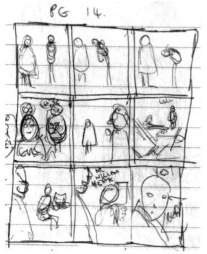

Another supreme page of script; Gull continues his tirade against the museum official, and Alan takes an opportunity to insert a cameo of the poet, W.B. Yeats. The business about Gary Groth and my using xeroxes refers to his *Comics Journal* interview with Alan, at which I took mild objection to the suggestion that my pages of static images were done using photocopies. I was just making the point that the interest lies in the subtle differences between the figures in a panel and the ones in the panels before and after it. Anyway, just to be contrary, I followed Alan's suggestion and photocopied Gull through the top tier.

PAGE 14. (1307 words) (panels 1-5) PANEL 1. NINE PANELS ON THIS PAGE, AND I WANT THE FIRST THREE TO BE ALL FROM THE SAME SHOT. WE SEE BOTH GULL AND THE FAT OFFICIAL FULL FIGURE HERE AS THEY STAND FACING EACH OTHER, WITH GULL ON THE LEFT. (THE ATTENDANT WE SAW EARLIER, NO LONGER NEEDED, HAS MELTED INTO THE BACKGROUND SOMEWHERE OVER THE LAST TWO OR THREE PANELS AND CONTINUES WITH HIS CHORES.) GULL, ON THE LEFT, STANDS IN PROFILE FACING THE OFFICIAL, WHO IS IN PROFILE ON THE RIGHT AND FACING LEFT, TOWARDS GULL. GULL STANDS IN A STOCKY AND SOLID-LOOKING MANNER, HIS LOW CENTRE OF GRAVITY IN PERFECT BALANCE, GIVING HIS BODY LANGUAGE A SUBTEXT OF IMMOVABILITY THAT HE WILL RETAIN THROUGHOUT THIS NEXT THREE PANELS (USE A XEROX IF YOU LIKE, JUST TO EXCITE GARY GROTH.) THE MUSEUM OFFICIAL, ON THE OTHER HAND, DOES CHANGE HIS POSTURE OVER THIS THREE-PANEL SEQUENCE, EVEN IF HE DOESN'T ACTUALLY MOVE ABOUT VERY MUCH. BY KEEPING GULL'S BODY POSTURE STATIC, I WANT TO FOCUS ATTENTION ON THE POSTURE OF THE OFFICIAL THAT HE IS TALKING TO, SO THAT OVER THIS THREE-PANEL SEQUENCE WE CAN WATCH THE MAN'S WILL SLOWLY CRUMBLING BEFORE GULL'S SUPERIOR RESOLUTION, AS REFLECTED IN HIS POSTURE. AS I SEE IT, THE OFFICIAL IS PERHAPS STILL STANDING UP FAIRLY STRAIGHT IN THIS FIRST PANEL, WITH HIS POSTURE GRADUALLY SLUMPING INTO COMPLETE SUBJUGATION OVER THE NEXT TWO FRAMES. AS THE TWO MEN STAND TALKING TO EACH OTHER, THEIR

REFLECTIONS WAVER INDISTINCTLY IN THE POLISHED TILES AT THEIR FEET, THEIR VOICES
RINGING AND ECHOING IN THE STONE EARS OF THE DEAD PHARAOHS.

GULL :   For shame! Do we approach the twentieth century beset yet by
                                such chimaera, that pagan curses daunt this noble institution?

OFFICIAL :   It-it's not that, sir, it's...

PANEL 2.

SAME SHOT, WITH GULL STILL IN EXACTLY THE SAME ROCK-LIKE POSTURE ON THE LEFT. THE
OFFICIAL IS STARTING TO SAG HERE, HIS SHOULDERS SLUMPING AS HE STARTS TO GO UNDER
BEFORE THE AVALANCHE FORCE OF GULL'S PERSONALITY. ABOUT THEM, THE DEAD LISTEN WITH
VARIOUS ATTITUDES OF CELESTIAL INDIFFERENCE.

GULL :   Think of it, man! What better place for such an artifact than
                                here in this museum, next to Hawksmoor's Bloomsbury church?

GULL :   Shall superstition weigh against good policy?

PANEL 3.

SAME SHOT, WITH GULL STILL UNMOVED ON THE LEFT. THE MUSEUM OFFICIAL HANGS HIS HEAD ON
THE RIGHT, COMPLETELY ABJECT AND COWED, TALKING TO THE POLISHED FLOOR RATHER THAN TO
SIR WILLIAM AS HE SPEAKS.

GULL :   Half London's mad for things Egyptian with the Royal
                                household held alike in thrall.

GULL :   It is, sir, an unconscionable oversight.

OFFICIAL :   I'll see to it, sir.

PANEL 4.

CHANGE ANGLE NOW AS GULL WALKS TOWARDS US OVER ON THE LEFT OF THE FOREGROUND, MAYBE
HALF FIGURE HERE. HE SMILES IN SATISFACTION, HIS BACK TURNED TO THE DEFEATED OFFICIAL
WHOM WE SEE STANDING TO THE RIGHT OF THE NEAR BACKGROUND, FULL FIGURE, TURNED TOWARDS
US AS HE WATCHES SIR WILLIAM WALK AWAY FROM HIM, HIS SHOULDERS STILL SLUMPED AND
DEFEATED. HE LOOKS AS IF HE IS ALMOST TREMBLING WITH NERVOUS EXHAUSTION FOLLOWING HIS
CONVERSATIONAL WORKING-OVER.

GULL :   Excellent. Then I shall not trouble you further. I take it
                                that your Blake exhibits are still in the same location?

OFFICIAL :   Yes, sir.

OFFICIAL :   Th-thank you, sir.

PANEL 5.

REVERSE ANGLE ON THE LAST SHOT, SO THAT HERE WE HAVE THE OFFICIAL STANDING HALF
FIGURE ON THE RIGHT OF THE FOREGROUND AND FACING AWAY FROM US TOWARDS THE LEFT OF
THE BACKGROUND WHERE WE SEE SIR WILLIAM WALKING AWAY, HIS FACE TURNED AWAY FROM US,
HIS DARK REFLECTION SHIMMERING, AN OMINOUS MIRAGE, IN THE TILES AT HIS FEET. IN THE
FOREGROUND, THE OFFICIAL WATCHES SIR WILLIAM WALKING AWAY AND EXHALES MEANINGFULLY,
PULLING A HANDKERCHIEF FROM HIS POCKET TO MOP AWAY THE SWEAT THAT HAS GATHERED ON HIS
BROW, SPRUNG THERE IN THE SUDDEN EGYPTIAN HEAT OF SIR WILLIAM'S INTERROGATION.

No dialogue. (end of script segment)

Chapter 9, page 6.

Abberline has just come from the crime scene at Mitre Square, where he watched a street pedlar selling mad monk walking canes and received unsolicited advice from a schoolboy named Aleister Crowley. Now he attends the inquest of Cathy Eddowes at the Golden Lane Mortuary.

Of the various comings and goings in this part of the narrative, we are particularly interested in the movements of two objects: Mary Kelly's doorkey and Cathy Eddowes kidney. That was supposed to be the latter on the cover of the Kitchen Sink Press edition of From Hell volume #5, dated June 1994. My grasp of internal anatomy is a bit vague, I'll be the first to admit, but this was just meant to be a big horrible piece of innard. I obtained a cow's liver, just to get the purple and texture of the object. It sat all day in the tropical heat here while I painted it, until my family demanded that it be removed

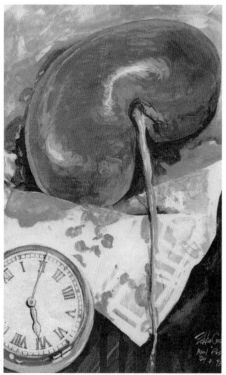

PAGE 6. (words) PANEL 1.
THERE ARE NINE PANELS ON THIS PAGE, IN THIS FIRST ONE WE SIMPLY REPRINT PANEL FOUR FROM PAGE THIRTY-EIGHT OF CHAPTER EIGHT, SHOWING GULL AS HE KNEELS ON EDDOWES RIGHT, RIPPING THE BLADE UP THROUGH HER ABDOMEN.
No dialogue

PANEL 2.
BACK IN THE POST MORTEM ROOM, WE ARE MAYBE LOOKING DOWN UPON THE SLAB FROM ABOVE, AND AT THE FOUR DOCTORS GATHERED AROUND IT. CATHY EDDOWES STARES BLANKLY UP AT US WHILE DR. SAUNDERS INDICATES THE STATE OF THE INTESTINES. THE ATMOSPHERE IS VERY COOL AND MEDICAL AND DETACHED, TO CONTRAST WITH THE SAVAGERY OF THE INTERCUTTING FLASHBACKS.

172

SAUNDERS: Note that the intestines are largely detached from the
                   mesentery, with about two feet of colon cut away

PANEL 3.

HERE WE REPRINT PANEL SEVEN FROM PAGE THIRTY-EIGHT OF CHAPTER EIGHT, SHOWING THE
CLOSE-UP OF GULL'S HANDS AS HE CUTS INTO EDDOWES INNARDS.

No dialogue

PANEL 4.

NOW PERHAPS A SHOT WITH ABBERLINE SITTING FACING MOSTLY AWAY FROM US IN THE
FOREGROUND, JUST TO REMIND US THAT HE'S STILL SITTING THERE. PERHAPS HE HAS A
NOTEPAD ON HIS KNEE NOW, NEXT TO THE BOWLER, AND IS JOTTING DOWN NOTES IN PENCIL
AS HE LISTENS TO THE DOCTORS. LOOKING BEYOND HIM, WE SEE THEM IN THE BACKGROUND
AS SAUNDERS NOW POINTS TO THE WOUNDS ON CATHY EDDOWES' FACE. THEY CONTINUE TO
IGNORE ABBERLINE.

SAUNDERS: The eyelids are both cut through, and there is a triangular
                   flap cut into either cheek.

SAUNDERS: Also, the tip of the nose has been detached by an oblique cut.

PANEL 5.

HERE WE REPRINT PANEL NINE FROM PAGE THIRTY-EIGHT, SHOWING GULL'S HANDS AND KNIFE
AS HE GOES TO WORK ON EDDOWES' FACE.

PANEL 6.

BACK IN THE POST MORTEM ROOM WE MAYBE HAVE A HEAD AND SHOPULDERS CLOSE-UP OF DR.
SAUNDERS IN THE FOREGROUND. HIS EYES ARE CAST DOWN, LOOKING DOWN AT SOEMTHING
WE CANNOT SEE OFF THE BOTTOM PANEL BORDER, THIS BEING THE BODY OF KATE EDDOWES.
BEHIND HIM TO ONE SIDE WE PERHAPS SEE DR. SEQUEIRA, WITH PERHAPS A LONG SHOT OF
ABBERLINE SEATED BY THE WALL TAKING NOTES IN THE FAR BACKGROUND.

SAUNDERS: The peritoneal lining is cut on the left side and the left
                   kidney carefully removed.

SAUNDERS: The lining over the uterus is also cut, and the womb partly
                   absent.

PANEL 7.

HERE WE REPRINT PANEL SIX FROM PAGE THIRTY-NONE OF CHAPTER EIGHT, BUT WE OMIT
GULL'S GUTTERAL WORD BALLOONS, SO THAT THE FLASHBACK IS SILENT.

No dialogue

PANEL 8.

BACK IN THE POST MORTEM ROOM WE HAVE A FULL FIGURE SHOT OF THE DOCTORTS GATHERED
AROUND THE BODY. DR. BROWN IS POIINTING TO THE AREA OF CATHY'S INNARDS FROM
WHICH THE KIDNEY HAS BEEN REMOVED. DR. SEQUIERA IS SHAKING HIS HEAD AND LOOKING
DISMISSIVE. DR. PHILLIPS NODS IN AGREEMENT.

DR BROWN: Surely the fact that he even found the kidney indicates
                   some surgical skill...

DR SEQUIERA: Not necessarily. more likely it was pure blind luck.
DR PHILLIPS: I agree.

PANEL 9.
NOW WE CUT ACROSS TO THE OTHER SIDE OF THE ROOM SO THAT IN THE FOREGROUND WE CAN
SEE ABBERLINE'S KNEES AT LEAST AS HE SITS FACING THE DOCTORS, WHO WE SEE STILL
ARGUING AROUND THE CORPSE IN THE FAR BACKGROUND HERE. ABBERLINE'S NOTEBOOK RESTS
OPEN ON HIS KNEE, AND WE CAN SEE IT CLEARLY ENOUGH TO BE AWARE THAT HE HAS WRITTEN
THE WORD "DOCTOR?" IN A QUERYING NOTE UPON THE MOSTLY OTHERWISE BLANK SHEET.
DR BROWN: Look, the kidney is completely hidden by a membrane.
                    To remove it in minutes under lightless conditions must
                    indicate surgical skill.
DR BROWN: CONSIDERABLE surgical skill.

Abberline leaves them to argue among themselves...

PAGE 7. (639 words) PANEL 1.
THERE ARE SEVEN PANELS ON THIS PAGE WITH THREE ON EACH OF THE TOP TWO TIERS WITH ONE
BIG PANEL TAKING UP THE BOTTOM TIER.IN THIS FIRST PANEL WE CAN PERHAPS SEE A LITTLE
OF THE QUAARTET OF DOCTORS IN THE FORGROUND, JUST HEAD AND SHOULDERS WITH THEIR EYES
DOWNCAST AS THEY GATHER AROUND THE BODY. BEHIND THEM, WE SEE THE REAR OF ABBERLINE
FULL FIGURE AS HE LEAVES THE ROOM BY THE DOOR WHICH IS VISIBLE IN THE BACKGROUND.
DR SAUNDERS: Well, frankly I'm not convinced either way...

And if the experts are at a loss, can you really expect much from Campbell?

anatomy lesson

My academic education didn't encompass biology or dissections of frogs. Internal body parts and their sources are no more readable to me than the steak on my dinner plate. My three or four art assistants over the years have invariably had a better grasp of the matter, as in the panel at right showing April Post, from The Dance of Lifey Death, *Aug. 1992, (in* Alec*) with the relevant* FROM HELL *panel from Chapter 7.*

The Rotton Kidney

There's one person who was witness to more of the *FROM HELL* pages' creation than any other, and that's wee Hayley Campbell. I was working at home in the sole company of my three year old daughter, when the gig came in, as depicted in this panel from *The Dance of the Gull Catchers* (right, top). The caption is Alan's. A few years later, in 1993, we see her setting up her own desk, an upended cardboard box, next to mine. The words spoken in the second panel at right were the subject's signing-off phrase before retiring to bed every night; indeed she tells me that she used it in London recently, resulting in the immediate bafflement of those present.

It's always been my habit to cut up books and rearrange their pages, keeping some, losing others. During this time wee Hayley Campbell was making her own compilations from the *Taboo* leftovers. For example, she was very fond of 'The Eyes of the Cat," drawn by Moebius. I must have known about that one, because I stapled it together for her and drew a cover on it. But surely I was unaware of the full extent of her interest in horror.

Let me acquaint you now with a document titled 'The Ripper File' in imitation of Melvin Harris' book, mentioned here on page 68. The pages of this artifact were drawn by wee Hayley Campbell shortly after her seventh birthday, a date retrospectively deduced from external evidence, the excuse for their fashioning being a birthday gift box of colour markers. Furthermore, one of the pages imitates the cover of the Kitchen Sink Press edition of From Hell volume #5, dated June 1994, which contained Chapter 8 (see page 100), and also Cathy Eddowes' kidney. Hayley, in a very rudimentary drawing shows us: "Rotton Kidney on a Hang kachef." (lower right). I can't recall if she sat beside me while I was working on my own version, but she has caught the flies that I missed.

Publicity around the Crimes'centennial, however, leads me to Knight's book. Ideas coalesce. Deciding on a serial in Steve Bissette's *Taboo*, I contact Eddie Campbell.

Twelve years ago I started drawing the book.

I finished Jackarippy. I go to bed now.

Rotton Kidney on a Hang kachef

175

Hayley's book consists of 35 A4 size loose pages in a binder. In it she catalogued, with one or two digressions, all the ways of dying that she could think of. The first page cited above is followed by "Witches cooking babies", "Being Shot," "Being buried Alive," "Being bitten on the neck by a vampire," "Being hit by Lightening," and "Being Basht to death," (right, top) in which I suddenly realized that the victim of these horrors looks a lot like their author. You can see how it has gone completely beyond the parameters of *FROM HELL*, and who it was that put these notions in her little wee head is anybody's guess. I hope you don't think it was I. Nor do we use matches on the soles of people's feet in our house.

"When your cut up while your sleeping" came from the movie *Gorillas in the Mist*, which she was probably encouraged to watch on account of it being a nature film. It is certainly one of he best pages in the series, for the clarity of its design, and the vibrancy of its execution, the kind of qualities we should try to steal from a seven year old. The "T-Rexs head", one of the thematic digressions I mentioned, is cartooning on a higher level altogether.

As to the long term effects of all this upon her mental health, note that she has lately taken up taxidermy as a hobby.

Previous page, from top, FROM HELL, *Appendix 2, page 16;* Alec: The Years Have Pants, *page 571; other images here and opposite are from* The Ripper File, *loose leaf, not paginated.*

177

Another pictorial interlude

The first thing I did when I signed up for FROM HELL was go out and buy a very old hat. It was made for a child or a very small person, or a large person with a very small cranium. Every time I needed to reference it on an actual head I had to call in one of the kids. In fact, that was Erin wearing it on the back cover of the first printing of my own 1999 complete edition. This was it on the front cover, being an oil-painted darker variation of the hat and grapes theme of the first Tundra volume (page 105). The colour has never reproduced true, because I tampered with it in Photoshop to make it darker. Let's see if it does better this time.

Cover of *Bacchus* no. 54, August 2000. Portrait of Alan Moore, I think in Acrylic.

Cover of *Bacchus* #53, June 2000, a self-portrait in gouache. Following three pages are all new watercolours.

A few favourite presentations of the complete edition. *1*. Spain, hardcover, using photo of real W. Gull (2000 and current). *2*. My own limited edition of 19 copies, bound in kangaroo leather (2002). *3*. I made a new cover for Top Shelf when they took over *From Hell* in 2003, but they were concerned about the bookstores being uncomfortable with all that blood on the front and only used it as a monochrome endpaper until their 2006 printing. *4*. Japan, second of two volumes (2009).

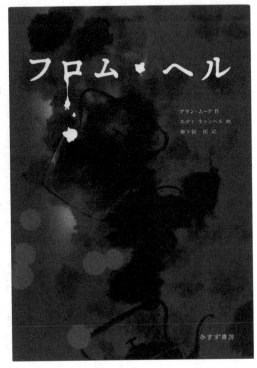

Photos
1999–2009

1999

2001
(in Hollywood)

2009
*(with Melinda
and Anne)*

About pen nibs. The degree of flexibility is the primary consideration. A fine little nib that suited my purposes was the Hunt 103 (first photo, left), used on the two portraits of Gull. That little florette-shaped cut hole enables the tines to spread wide for great flexibility. The more rigid Gillott 209 is next to it. I used that for back-up, when I needed to get in closer and manoeuvre in a tight space. The one on the far right is the quite different crowquill style. This has a cylinder in emulation of the bird feather from which it derives, as opposed to the flat reed in which the more flexible nibs originated. This style offered me a tighter control of the linework, but with less thick-and-thin dynamics (see lower two panels.) On occasion I would come across a box of rare nibs. The large Brandauers came as a present one Christmas many years ago. I mentioned them on my blog and was contacted by somebody making a short film about the Brandauer company. He wanted me to make an appearance until I told him I live on the other side of the planet.

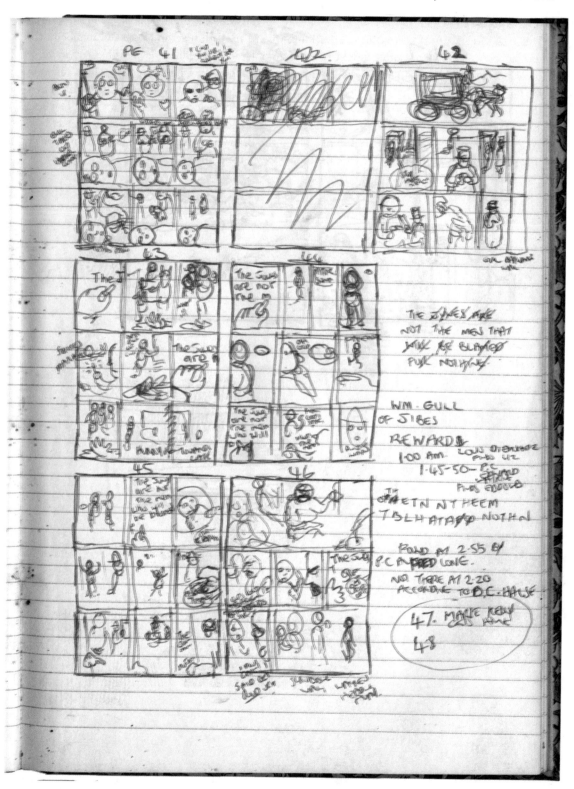

Chapter 9, pages 15-18. Alan uses a syncopation in which the long panels on the bottom tiers alternately conclude a scene or begin the next. This rhythm knits the chapter together.

Chapter 9, page 17.

The images are leap-frogging each other from page to page (see facing). Hogarth's *The Reward of Cruelty* (see here also pages 255/6), reflecting Marie's posture, appeared on the bottom tier of the page before this. The praying child was on the page that followed. I had no trouble finding a period piece.

PAGE 17 (811 words) PANEL 1.(3 edited out) ANOTHER SEVEN-PANEL PAGE, THIS TIME WITH THE BIG WIDE PANEL UP AT THE TOP, TAKING UP THE TOP TIER WITH THREE SMALLER PANELS ON THE TWO TIERS BENEATH. IN THIS FIRST PANEL WE CUT TO MARIE KELLY'S ROOM AT MILLER'S COURT FOR A SHOT OF MARIE SPRAWLED FACE UP ON THE BED. NAKED EXCEPT FOR A FILMY, DIRTY CHEMISE AND BLIND DRUNK. HER POSTURE IS EXACTLY THE SAME AS HER DEATH POSTURE, AS REVEALED IN THE TERRIBLE CRIME SCENE PHOTOGRAPH: THE EDGE OF THE BEDSIDE TABLE IS VISIBLE IN THE RIGHT BOTTOM CORNER. MARIE SPRAWLS ON THE GRUBBY BED WITH HER HEAD POINTING RIGHT AND HER HAIR DOWN. HER FACE IS TURNED TOWARDS US, HER EYES VAGUE AND BARELY FOCUSED. HER LEGS SPRAWL APART, REVEALING HER SEX, AND HER LEFT ARM IS DRAPED LIMPLY ACROSS HER BELLY. HER OTHER ARM IS PROBABLY INVISIBLE ON THE FAR SIDE OF HER BODY, BUT FOR FUTURE REFERENCE SHE IS CLUTCHING A HALF-EMPTY BOTTLE OF CHEAP BOOZE IN HER RIGHT HAND, WHICH MAY OR MAY NOT BE VISIBLE HERE. IT IS STILL LATE AFTERNOON. LOLLING IN THE EXACT POSTURE OF HER FUTURE DEATH, MARIE STARES OUT OF THE PANEL AT US, DULLY. No dialogue.

PANEL 2.
CHANGE ANGLE NOW. WE ARE NOW DOWN ON THE BED WITH MARIE, ON HER RIGHT-HAND SIDE AND LOOKING ACROSS HER INTO THE ROOM. IN THE BOTTOM FOREGROUND WE CAN SEE A LITTLE OF HER MIDDLE BODY, WITH THE HEAD OFF PANEL ON THE LEFT AND THE LEGS OFF PANEL ON THE RIGHT. WE SEE HER RIGHT HAND, LAZING BY HER SIDE AND CLUTCHING THE BOTTLE OF BOOZE. LOOKING ACROSS HER INTO THE ROOM WE CAN SEE JOE BARNETT SITTING IN THE ROOM'S OTHER CHAIR, FACING SLIGHTLY AWAY FROM US AS HE SITS READING THE PAPER, HIS BACK TURNED TO MARY. UP ON THE MURKY WALLS WE CAN SEE A LITTLE FRAMED PICTURE OF A CHILD KNEELING IN PRAYER WITH A LIGHT SHINING DOWN ON IT FROM ABOVE... JUST ONE OF THOSE HORRIBLE LITTLE SENTIMENTAL VICTORIAN CHEAP PRINTS. IF YOU CAN FIND A REAL ONE, SO MUCH THE BETTER. IF NOT, JUST FAKE ONE AND MAKE IT LOOK AS SENTIMENTAL AND KITSCH AS POSSIBLE. No dialogue.

PANEL 4.
SAME SHOT AS LAST PANEL, BUT HERE MARIE'S HAND FALLS BACK DOWN TO HER SIDE, STILL

CLUTCHING THE BOTTLE WHICH IS NOW EVEN MORE SORELY DEPLETED. LOOKING BEYOND HER WE SEE JOE BARNETT AS HE CONTINUES TO SIT WITH HIS BACK TO US READING THE PAPER BENEATH THE CHERUBIC GAZE OF THE LITTLE SAVED INFANT HUNG HIGH ON THE WALL.

MARIE (OFF, LEFT):   Joe?

PANEL 5.

REVERSE ANGLE HERE SO THAT WE HAVE JOE BARNETT SITTING FACING US IN THE FOREGROUND ROUGHLY HEAD AND SHOULDERS. HE DOESN'T LOOK HAPPY, AND IS TRYING TO CONCENTRATE ON THE PAPER AS IF TO BLOT OUT THE ROOM AND POSSIBLY THE REST OF HIS REDUCED LIFE AS WELL. HE LOOKS IRRITABLE. LOOKING BEYOND HIM AND MORE TO THE RIGHT OF THE NEAR BACKGROUND WE CAN SEE THE HALF-NAKED MARIE LOUNGING ON THE DIRTY BED WITH HER BOTTLE, LOOKING WITH GLAZED EYES TOWARDS JOE AS SHE SPEAKS. BY CONTRAST, JOE DOESN'T LOOK DRUNK,OR AT LEAST NOT ANYWHERE NEAR AS DRUNK AS MARIE. IN THE FOREGROUND WE CAN SEE JOE PRACTICALLY GRITTING HIS TEETH AT THE SOUND OF MARIE'S SLURRED VOICE. IT'S CLEAR THAT THEY'RE NOT GETTING ALONG TREMENDOUSLY AT THE MOMENT, EVEN IF MARIE IS TOO PISSED TO BE AWARE OF THE FACT.

MARIE: Joe, is th'r any more in the paper? About the murders, now?

MARIE: Joe, d'ye hear me? I said...

PANEL 6.

SAME SHOT AS LAST PANEL, WITH JOE STILL LOOKING IRRITABLE IN THE FOREGROUND AND GLARING DOGGEDLY AT HIS PAPER AS HE REPLIES TO THE INEBRIATED MARIE, WHO WE SEE SITTING UP NOW ON THE EDGE OF THE BED, BLEARILY. PERHAPS SHE SETS THE BOTTLE DOWN ON THE FLOOR AS SHE DOES SO.

JOE: I heard what ye said, and no there isn't, not since the last time ye asked. Dunno what yer so struck with 'em for.

MARIE: Why shouldn' I be?

PANEL 7.

SAME SHOT, WITH JOE LOOKING EVEN MORE IRRITABLE NOW AS HE TRIES TO READ HIS PAPER, EVEN THOUGH IN TRUTH HE'S BEEN SO ANGRY FOR THE LAST HALF-HOUR THAT HE'S JUST READ THE SAME LINE OVER AND OVER AGAIN WITHOUT UNDERSTANDING IT. TO THE RIGHT OF THE NEAR BACKGROUND BEHIND HIM, MARIE TEETERS UNSTEADILY ACROSS THE ROOM IN WHAT IS PROBABLY, IN HER MIND, AN ELEGANT AND SEDUCTIVE GLIDE. THERE ARE MAYBE OTHER BOTTLES VISIBLE, EMPTY ON THE FLOOR. MARIE HAS REALLY BEEN TYING ONE ON SINCE LAST ISSUE.

JOE: Because there's other things want doin'! You should pull yourself together and get dressed...

MARIE: I thought ye liked me this way best, I thought ye like me undressed.

First page of Eddy/Stephen scene, next.

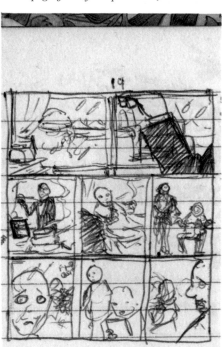

Chapter 9, page 20.

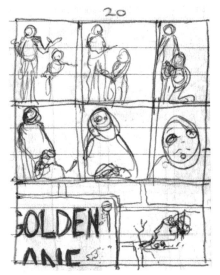

I have always suspected that here on page 20 Alan was having a dig at my tendency to skimp on the details. For once he was determined to sit me down and make me draw something insignificant in riveting close-up.

Remember also, in comparing how close Alan's thumbnail is to the finished arrangement, that I never got to see those sketches. Gary Millidge wrote: *"It's only once the pages are thumbnailed out that Moore takes his notebook to his surprisingly up-to-date computer (which he still calls 'the typewriter') in order to write up his scripts, using his 'virtually unintelligible scrawls' as the basis for his excessively detailed panel descriptions. The artist is never privy to Moore's original notebook thumbnails."*

(Alan Moore , Storyteller)

PAGE 20. (1006 words) PANEL 1.
SEVEN PANELS AGAIN, BUT THIS TIME WITH THE BIG WIDE ONE AS THE BOTTOM PANEL AND THREE SMALLER PANELS ON EACH OF THE TWO TIERS ABOVE. IN THIS FIRST PANEL, THE SHOT IS PRETTY MUCH THE SAME AS IN PANEL FOUR ON THE PREVIOUS PAGE: WE SEE EDDY AND STEPHEN FULL FIGURE, BOTH FACING US SIDE BY SIDE WITH STEPHEN SEATED ON THE RIGHT WITH THE TABLE JUST VISIBLE ON HIS LEFT (OUR RIGHT), AND PRINCE EDDY STANDING ON THE LEFT OF THE PANEL. EDDY'S HANDS ARE SPREAD HERE IN AN EXPLANATORY GESTURE AS HE TRIES TO CONVEY TO STEPHEN THE MISERY THAT HE IS FEELING. HE DOESN'T LOOK AT STEPHEN BUT GAZES HOPELESSLY INTO SPACE AS HE SPEAKS, HIS GIRLISH EYES TORMENTED. STEPHEN, WEARING A CALM EXPRESSION OF NO-NONSENSE RESOLUTION, TURNS BRIEFLY AWAY FROM EDDY AND PLACES THE BOOK OF POETRY FACE DOWN ON THE TABLE.

EDDY: I'd hoped I could shake off this beastly fit by visiting
                         you, but I can't.
EDDY: I-I return to London in a month. Perhaps I can do something then...

PANEL 2.

SAME SHOT AS LAST PANEL. EDDY IS STILL STANDING, IN THE FLOW OF DISCOURSE, BUT HE STOPS AND LOOKS DOWN AT JEM STEPHEN HERE WITH A LOOK OF SURPRISE. STEPHEN, HIS BOOK PUT ASIDE, IS STILL SEATED. HE TURNS BACK TOWARDS EDDY HERE AND TILTS HIS HEAD BACK TO LOOK UP AT THE PRINCE WITH A LEVEL-EYED AND OPEN EXPRESSION. AS HE DOES SO, HE REACHES OUT WITH HIS LEFT HAND AND GENTLY PLACES THE PALM FLAT AGAINST EDDY'S CROTCH, THUS OCCASIONING THE PRINCE'S EXPRESSION OF DULL SURPRISE HERE.

EDDY: ...although what can I do? Nobody tells me anything;
                                 they won't let me have a say, and...

EDDY: Jem?

PANEL 3.

SAME SHOT. STEPHEN NOW CLIMBS DOWN FROM HIS ARMCHAIR AND ONTO HIS KNEES IN FRONT OF EDDY, STILL WITH THE SAME CALM AND SERENE EXPRESSION AS IF NOTHING OUT OF THE ORDINARY WERE HAPPENING. KNEELING, HE BEGINS TO UNDO THE FRONT OF THE PRINCE'S TROUSERS. EDDY LOOKS SHAKEN, UNCERTAIN ABOUT WHETHER TO OR HOW TO PROTEST. MAYBE HE CLUTCHES THE BACK OF THE CHAIR FOR SUPPORT, STILL GAZING DOWN AT STEPHEN INCREDULOUSLY, TREMBLING SLIGHTLY FROM THE SUDDEN EROTIC STRESS OF THE MOMENT

EDDY: J-Jem? Jem, what are you...?

STEPHEN: Shhh. I want to gamahuche you, Eddy. Do say I might.

PANEL 4.

NOW WE START TO CLOSE IN SO THAT WE ONLY SEE EDDY ABOUT THREE-QUARTER FIGURE HERE, WITH STEPHEN ABOUT HALF FIGURE KNEELING THERE AT HIS FEET. THE TOP OF EDDY'S TROUSERS IS OPEN, AND STEPHEN HAS RELEASED THE PRINCE'S COCK, HALF AWAKE HERE; HALF ERECT. HOLDING THE SHAFT IN ONE HAND WHILE CUPPING EDDY'S BALLS WITH THE OTHER, HE CLOSES HIS EYES, DREAMILY. AND STARTS TO SUCK ON THE TIP. EDDY REELS, HOLDING ON TO THE BACK OF THE CHAIR FOR SUPPORT. HE STARES INTO SPACE WITH A HAUNTED, ALMOST FRIGHTENED LOOK AS WE SEE THE WILL POWER AND RESISTANCE SLOWLY LEAKING FROM HIM WITH EACH NEW WAVE OF PHYSICAL PLEASURE. PERHAPS HE PLACES HIS OTHER HAND GENTLY UPON STEPHEN'S HEAD AS IF TO PUSH IT AWAY. BUT THERE IS NO FORCE OR INTENTION BEHIND THE GESTURE. EDDY IS LOST.

EDDY: Jem, I... I don't think we should. It's not...

EDDY: I mean, I ... oh, God.

Abberline's comings and goings. *Chapter 9, pages 22-24. Cemetery, pub, passing Christ Church*

PANEL 5.

CONTINUE TO CLOSE IN SO THAT WE SEE EDDY ABOUT HALF FIGURE HERE, FACING US. ALL WE CAN SEE OF STEPHEN IS THE TOP OF HIS HEAD. EDDY'S HAND RESTS LOVINGLY IN HIS HAIR AS THE PRINCE GIVES UP ALL PRETENCE OF RESISTENCE AND GOES ALONG WITH THE ACT. HIS EYES ARE HALF-CLOSED AS HE GAZES OUT OF THE PANEL AT US HERE. AS THE STRESS MELTS FROM HIS FACE HE LOOKS LIKE A DRUGGED CHILD, EYES HEAVY-LIDDED AND MOUTH HANGING SLIGHTLY OPEN.

EDDY: Oh, god, Jem.

EDDY: Jem, I'm so weak. I-I'm not bad...

PANEL 6

A HEAD AND SHOULDERS SHOT OF EDDY NOW, WITH STEPHEN NO LONGER VISIBLE, OFF PANEL BELOW. EDDY TIPS HIS HEAD BACK SLIGHTLY AND CLOSES HIS EYES AS HE COMES, UTTERLY LOST IN A WARM AND INFANTILE PLEASURE THAT HE KNOWS WILL ALWAYS LEAD HIM, HOWEVER GRAVE THE CONSEQUENCES.

EDDY: Just weak.

PANEL 7.

CUT TO THE GOLDEN LANE MORTUARY WHERE THE INQUEST ON CATHERINE EDDOWES IS OPENING. I DUNNO HOW THIS WILL SOUND TO YOU, BUT WHAT IF WE CUT TO A TIGHT CLOSE-UP OF THE GOLDEN LANE STREET SIGN, BOLTED TO THE WALL, SO THAT THE WORDS ARE NOT COMPLETELY VISIBLE. PART OF THE G IN GOLDEN IS MISSING FOR EXAMPLE, AND THE L AND THE LOWER PART OF 'ANE' ARE MISSING IN THE SECOND WORD... WITH THIS EXTREME CLOSE-UP OF THE STREET SIGN FILLING THE WHOLE OF THIS COMPARATIVELY LARGE PANEL? I THOUGHT WE COULD MAYBE TAKE THE OPPORTUNITY TO SHOW SOMETHING ORDINARY AND MUNDANE IN SUPER-REAL AND HYPER CLOSE-UP DETAIL, SO THAT WE SEE THE CRUMBLING MORTAR IN BETWEEN THE BRICKS THAT MAKE THE WALL ON WHICH THE SIGN IS BOLTED, AND THE SKIDMARK SMEAR OF RUST THAT'S CREEPING DOWN THE METAL SIGN FROM WHERE THAT BOLT THAT HOLDS IT TO THE WALL HAS OXIDIZED. PERHAPS A SMALL BUT PERFECT WALLFLOWER ISSUES TENTATIVELY FROM THE CRUMBLING MORTAR IN BETWEEN THE BRICKS, A FRAGILE THING AGAINST THE SOOT-STREAKED WALL. I FIGURED IF WE ESTABLISH SOMETHING IN INTENSE DETAIL, JUST ONCE, THEN IN A WAY IT IMPLIES TO THE READER THAT THE WHOLE OF THE WORLD THAT WE'RE SHOWING IS THAT COMPLEX AND DETAILED, EVEN IF WE DON'T SHOW THE DETAILS ALL THE TIME. DOES THAT MAKE ANY SENSE AT ALL, OR HAVE THE MAGIC MUSHROOMS STARTED WORKING? ANYWAY, IF YOU DON'T LIKE IT AND HAVE SOME OTHER IDEA THAT WILL CONVEY THE CHANGE OF SCENE AS WELL, PLEASE FEEL FREE TO STICK IT IN (AS J.K.STEPHEN SAID TO THE DUKE OF CLARENCE AND AVONDALE).

No dialogue

pages 28-30. Abberline again: office, inquest. Above, a second sketch of the Golden Lane panel.

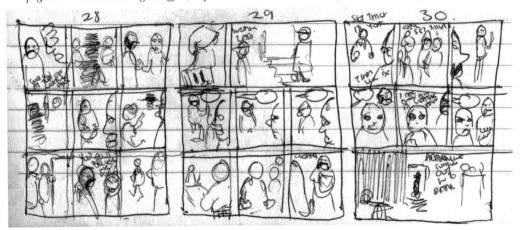

Chapter 9, pages 32, 33.

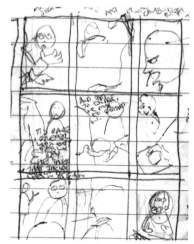

T his page explains the writing of the *FROM HELL* letter, sent to the police along with Cathy Eddowes' kidney, last seen in wee Hayley Campbell's Ripper File, and seen after this, if you have the book to hand, in a specimen jar on Abberline's desk.

PAGE 32, (864 words) PANEL 1.
THERE ARE NINE PANELS ON THIS PAGE. IN THIS FIRST ONE, WE ARE AGAIN ON THE EYE LEVEL OF THE SEATED NETLEY AS HE SITS FACING US FROM THE NEAR BACKGROUND, ROUGHLY HALF FIGURE. IN THE RIGHT OF THE FOREGROUND WE CAN SEE THE MIDDLE SECTION OF GULL, SO THAT WE CAN SEE HIS GESTURING ARMS EVEN THOUGH HIS HEAD AND SHOULDERS ARE OFF PANEL. ON THE LEFT OF THE FOREGROUND, HE IS FACING RIGHT, ACROSS NETLEY. FROM THE FOREGROUND, NETLEY SLOWLY RAISES HIS FEARFUL FACE AND GAZES UP AT WHERE GULL'S OFF-PANEL FACE MUST BE. NETLEY LOOKS BEWILDERED, UNABLE TO UNDERSTAND THE RELEVANCE OF WHAT HIS MASTER IS SAYING. GULL'S HANDS GESTURE DISMISSIVELY AS HE MAKES HIS POINT ABOUT THE PRESS COVERAGE OF THE MURDER.

GULL (OFF): Why, even I'm regarded by the press and public as a sexual murderer!

GULL (OFF): Had I killed artists and not whores, should I be an ARTISTIC murderer? Pah!

PANEL 2.
CHANGE ANGLE SO THAT WE'RE DOWN ON THE TABLETOP AMONGST THE PORNO AGAIN WITH A LITTLE OF NETLEY'S SIDE AND SHOULDER VISIBLE OVER ON THE RIGHT. LOOKING PAST THIS WE CAN SEE GULL AS HE TURNS AWAY FROM US AND NETLEY, PACING BACK TOWARDS THE WINDOW WITH FACE UNSEEN HERE, HANDS GESTICULATING ANGRILY.

GULL: It ANGERS me. And now, the wrong girl slain; the rightful victim still at large...

GULL: Ahh, this is Hell, make no mistake.

PANEL 3.
NOW WE CLOSE IN ON GULL FOR A HEAD-AND-SHOULDERS CLOSE UP AS HE STANDS IN PROFILE GAZING OUT OF THE WINDOW. HE STROKES HIS CHIN THOUGHTFULLY AND FROWNS A LITTLE, AS IF AT SOME UNPLEASANT THOUGHT THAT LATELY CROSSED HIS MIND. HIS OWN FACE CREASES,

SILVERED IN THE MOONLIGHT.

GULL: It is the hell of Faustus in a work I late admired but
                        recently have put aside.

GULL: It is the volume's end; of late, it troubles me.

PANEL 4.

CHANGE ANGLE AGAIN. GULL FACES US IN THE FOREGROUND NOW, BUT WE CAN ONLY SEE HIM FROM
THE UPPER CHEST DOWN TO THE BELLY HERE, HIS HEAD AND SHOULDERS OFF PANEL ABOVE SINCE
WE ARE ON THE EYE LEVEL OF THE SEATED NETLEY WHO WE SEE SITTING FACING US IN THE
BACKGROUND, LOOKING AT SIR WILLIAM'S TURNED BACK IN BLANK AND DISMAYED BEWILDERMENT.
GULL, WHOSE BALLOON ISSUES FROM OFF PANEL ABOVE, IS FUMBLING INSIDE THE INNER BREAST
POCKET OF HIS COAT AS IF TO RETRIEVE SOMETHING WHILE HE SPEAKS HERE.

GULL: 'tis Dante I prefer. In his inferno he suggests the
                        one true path from Hell lies at it's very heart...

PANEL 5.

SAME SHOT, WITH NETLEY STILL LOOKING ON FROM THE BACKGROUND. HERE, NETLEY'S JAW DROPS IN
SICK DISMAY AS HIS EYES FIX ON THE OBJECT THAT GULL HAS AT LAST RETRIEVED FROM HIS INNER
POCKET. WRAPPED LOOSELY IN A BLOOD-STAINED LINEN HANDKERCHIEF IT IS THE KIDNEY PLUCKED
FROM CATHY EDDOWES, RESTING THERE IN GULL'S RAISED PALM UP IN THE FOREGROUND.

GULL: ...and that in order to escape, we must instead go further in.

PANEL 6.

CLOSER IN ON NETLEY NOW WE STILL SEE GULL ONLY FROM THE SHOULDERS DOWN AS HE CALMLY
PLACES THE KIDNEY DOWN ON THE TABLE BESIDE NETLEY. (HE PLACES IT CARELESSLY ATOP THE
OPEN PORNOGRAPHIC LITERATURE, BUT WE NEEDN'T SEE THAT TOO CLEARLY HERE. NETLEY, SEATED
BY THE TABLE, JUST STARES DOWN AT THE EXCISED ORGAN IN MUTE INCOMPREHENSION, WIDE-EYED.

GULL (OFF):   With purpose thus renewed let us confront our persecutors.

GULL (OFF):   Newsmen mock us with their "Jack the Ripper" jibes; Let
                        us mock newsmen in return!

PANEL 7.

IN THE FOREGROUND NOW, WE HAVE A VIEW AT TABLE-LEVEL. THOUGH WE CANNOT SEE THE PORNO,
WE CAN SEE THE KIDNEY LOOMING BLACK AND STICKY UP INTO THE BOTTOM OF THE PANEL.
LOOKING UPWARDS PAST IT TO THE RIGHT OF THE NEAR BACKGROUND WE SEE NETLEY GAZING DOWN
IN HORROR AT THE ORGAN. IN THE FURTHER BACKGROUND WE SEE WILLIAM GULL AS HE PACES
RESTLESSLY AWAY FROM US TOWARDS THE WINDOW.

GULL: Let us reclaim from them the myth they sought to shape for profit.

GULL: Let us give them truer legends, grand enough to slake their
                        morbid thirsts.

PANEL 8.

WE CLOSE IN ON GULL AS HE STANDS FACING MOSTLY AWAY FROM US OUT OF THE WINDOW. HE
DOES NOT TURN AS HE SPEAKS, BUT WE CAN SEE A SLIVER OF HIS GRIM PROFILE OVER HIS
SHOULDER AS WE SEE HIM HEAD AND SHOULDERS HERE. HIS FACE IS AN EXPRESSIONLESS AND
UNFORGIVING MASK, COLD AND DISPASSIONATE.

GULL: Let us acquaint these fabricators with reality.

GULL: Tell me now, Netley; Can you write?

PANEL 9.

CHANGE ANGLE SO THAT WE CAN JUST SEE A LITTLE OF GULL'S SHOULDER IN THE BOTTOM LEFT
FOREGROUND AS HE STANDS FACING US JUST OFF PANEL ON THE LEFT. LOOKING OVER HIS
SHOULDER AND INTO THE ROOM WE SEE THE SEATED NETLEY AS HE LOOKS UP AT HIS MASTER'S
TURNED BACK WITH A TREMULOUS EXPRESSION, UNCERTAIN OF WHAT IS EXPECTED OF HIM.

NETLEY: W-well, it's the same as me readin', sir.

NETLEY: It's not much good, like.

*Following
the above,
page 33,
thunbnail
and finished
page.*

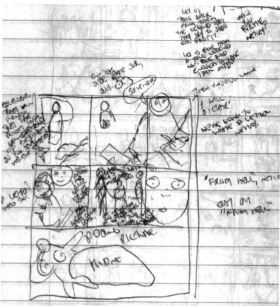

PAGE 33 (577 words), PANEL 3. (3, 6 and 7 only)

...WE SEE THE TRAPPED AND FIGHTENED NETLLEY LOOKING UP AT GULL'S OFF-PANEL FACE FOR
CLUES AS TO WHAT HE IS REQUIRED TO DO.

NETLEY: Uh, well, I suppose I'd put "Dear Mr. Lusk, sir."

GULL: Oh, come now! Are you not aware that one begins a letter with
                         one's own address?

PANEL 6.

NOW WE HAVE A TIGHT CLOSE UP OF GULL'S FACE, FILLING THE ENTIRE PANEL FROM BORDER TO
BORDER. HIS EYES ARE MAD AND FAR AWAY, BUT THERE IS ALMOST SOMETHING CHILDLIKE AT THE
CORNERS OF HIS FAINT AND WONDERING SMILE.

GULL: "From Hell", Netley. Write that down. "From Hell."

PANEL 7

NOW, IN THIS BIG PANEL, WE HAVE A CLOSE UP SHOT LOOKING DOWN AT THE BLOODY KIDNEY
LYING THERE UPON THE OPEN PORNOGRAPHY, STAINING THE PRINTED ORGIASTS WITH ITS RUST-
COLOURED SEEPAGES. THE PRINTED WOMEN POSE AND KNEEL. THE RENAL ARTERY PROTRUDES,
SEVERED TWO AND THREE QUARTER INCHES FROM ITS END.

No dialogue

Chapter 9, page 37.

Returning to "the graphics of theory and guesswork," specifically in relation to the Marie Kelly problem, now we meet a new character whose primary attribute will be that she is confusable with Marie Kelly. Thus, so far we have Marie Kelly, who may have been the subject of Sickert's *Blackmail or Mrs. Barrett*, secondly "Emma," who may have been Marie Kelly. Thirdly there is Julia, who kind of looks a bit like Marie Kelly, and needs to do so if an important plot twist is going to work. We'll come back to her.

In the meantime, all the humour has gone out of the sex in *FROM HELL*. Now it's "a reckless last bout of unbridled hedonism," with something sad about it.

PAGE 37. (1080 words) PANEL 1
THERE ARE NINE PANELS ON THIS PAGE. IN THIS FIRST ONE WE ARE IN MILLER'S COURT, WITH THE DOORWAY TO NUMBER 13 VISIBLE FACING US OVER TO THE LEFT IN THE NEAR FOREGROUND. BEYOND THAT AND MORE TO THE RIGHT WE ARE LOOKING DOWN THE LENGTH OF THE ALLEY THAT LEADS OUT INTO DORSET STREET. IT IS NIGHT TIME. COMING DOWN THE ALLEY FROM THE FAR END TOWARD US ARE TWO DRUNKEN WOMEN WHO ARE LEANING ON EACH OTHER FOR SUPPORT. ONE OF THEM IS A VERY PISSED MARIE KELLY. THE OTHER IS ANOTHER PROSTITUTE, ONE THAT WE HAVE NOT ENCOUNTERED BEFORE. HER NAME IS JULIA, AND SHE IS VERY SIMILAR IN BUILD AND COLOURING TO MARIE HERSELF, ALTHOUGH HER FACIAL CHARACTERISTICS ARE VERY DIFFERENT. SHE IS NEVERTHELESS A PRETTY GIRL, EVEN THOUGH WE CAN'T REALLY SEE MUCH OF EITHER HER OR MARIE HERE AS THEY COME DOWN THE ALLEY TOWARDS US IN THE DARK.

JULIA: Woops. Hahaha...

MARIE: Shhhh.

PANEL 2.
SAME SHOT, ONLY NOW THE TWO WOMEN HAVE REACHED THE FOREGROUND AND ARE STANDING JUST OUTSIDE THE CLOSED DOOR OF NUMBER THIRTEEN, ROUGHLY HALF FIGURE TO US HERE. JULIA IS MORE TO THE LEFT HERE, TURNING HER INEBRIATED FEATURES TOWARDS MARIE WITH A LOOK OF VAGUE AND BEFUDDLED WORRY. MARIE IS FROWNING IN CONCENTRATION AS SHE TRIES TO FIT HER KEY INTO THE LOCK OF THE DOOR. SHE LOOKS DETERMINED AND VERY PISSED.

JULIA: God, I'm pissed. We're real Lushingtons. Are you sure your
                Joe won't mind?

MARIE: 'Course he won't. He'll ... huc ...

MARIE: He'll love it, you see.

PANEL 3.

NOW WE ARE INSIDE THE SINGLE DOWNSTAIRS ROOM THAT IS NUMBER 13 MILLER'S COURT.
SEATED, AND VISIBLE HER ONLY IN HEAD AND SHOULDERS TO THE RIGHT OF THE PANEL WE HAVE
JOE BARNETT, MORE OR LESS IN PROFILE. HE LOOKS UP IN SURPRISE TOWARDS THE DOOR THAT
WE SEE IN THE LEFT OF THE BACKGROUND AS MARIE AND JULIA STUMBLE THROUGH IT. MARIE IS
SMILING BLISSFULLY AT JULIA, WHILE JULIA SMILES AT JOE A LITTLE MORE NERVOUSLY AND
TENTATIVELY. JOE JUST LOOKS BEWILDERED.

MARIE: Hello, Joe, me love. I'm back.

MARIE: There, now. Isn't he a lovely man?

JOE: Marie? I didn't know you'd be bringin' company...

PANEL 4.

HALF FIGURE TO HEAD AND SHOULDERS NOW WE HAVE THE TWO WOMEN FACING MOSTLY AWAY FROM
US TO EITHER SIDE OF THE FOREGROUND WITH MARIE ON THE LEFT AND JULIA ON THE RIGHT.
LOOKING BETWEEN THEM WE SEE JOE, STILL SEATED AND LOOKING UP AT THE TWO WOMEN IN
ASTONISHMENT. MARIE, ON THE LEFT, PUTS HER HAND ON JULIA'S ARM AS SHE INTRODUCES THE
WOMAN TO JOE. BOTH WOMEN ARE SMILING DRUNKENLY.

MARIE: Oh. Oh, yes. This is Julia. Isn't she a pretty girl, now?

JULIE: Hello, Joe. Marie's told me ever such a lot about you...

PANEL 5.

REVERSE ANGLES SO THAT NOW JOE IS IN THE FOREGROUND AND LOOKING SLIGHTLY AWAY FROM
US TOWARDS THE TWO WOMEN AS HE SITS MAYBE HEAD AND SHOULDERS TO THE RIGHT OF THE
FOREGROUND. THE WOMEN, IN THE BACKGROUND, ARE TAKING OFF THEIR COATS. MARIE IS ALSO
TAKING OFF HER JACKET. WE CAN SEE THE UNMADE BED IN THE BACKGROUND. JOE, IN THE
FOREGROUND, STILL LOOKS PRETTY DUMBFOUNDED. IN THE NEAR BACKGROUND, MARIE DOESN'T
LOOK AT JOE AS SHE LIES to HIM. SHE IS TRYING TO LOOK MATTER OF FACT.

JOE: Aye, well. Pleased to meet you, I'm sure.

MARIE: There. I said he'd be pleased.

MARIE: Y'see, Julia's got nowhere to stop. I knew ye wouldn't mind.

PANEL 6.

NOW WE ARE LOOKING AT JOE FROM THE FRONT. HIS EYES WIDEN AND HE LOOKS EVEN MORE
SURPRISED, PERHAPS STARTING TO RISE FROM HIS CHAIR. MARIE HAS CROSSED OVER TO HIM
AND SITS DOWN ON THE ARM OF THE CHAIR, STARTING TO STROKE HIS HEAD, SMILING PLACATINGLY
ALL THE TIME. HE IS LOOKING TOWARDS US AND THE OFF-PANEL JULIA HERE. WHEREAS THE
BOGGLE-EYED JOE JUST GAPES UP INCREDULOUSLY AT MARIE AS SHE TOYS WITH HIS HAIR.

JOE: Stop? Ay, look, you know we've only got the one bed...

MARIE: Oh Joe, that doesn't matter, me love.

MARIE: Does it, Julia?

PANEL 7.

PULL BACK SO THAT NOW JULIA IS FACING US IN THE LEFT OF THE FOREGROUND, HER BACK
TURNED TOWARDS MARIE AND JOE WHO WE SEE IN THE RIGHT OF THE NEAR BACKGROUND.

LOOKING UNCONCERNED, JULIA IS UNDRESSING FOR BED. SHE IS UNBUTTONING HER CHEMISE
HERE, REVEALING SMALL BUT NICELY SHAPED BREASTS. HER FACE IS PRETTY BLANK AND
DEVOID OF EXPRESSION. FROM THE BACKGROUND, JOE SITS IN HIS CHAIR AND JUST STARES
AT THE HALF-NAKED GIRL, EYES WIDE AND GLAZED WITH SHOCK. MARIE, SITTING ON THE
ARM OF HIS CHAIR, LEANS OVER AND KISSES HIS CHEEK IN A DRUNKEN, PATRONIZING WAY.
JOE, TRANSFIXED BY JULIA, DOESN'T APPEAR TO NOTICE.

JULIA: Oh no, not at all. That's how I like it, all cosy.

MARIE: There. Y'see, Joe? Julia doesn't mind.

MARIE: Mwuh.

PANEL 8.

NOW WE CHANGE ANGLES AGAIN SO THAT WE SEE JOE, HEAD AND SHOULDERS IN THE LEFT OF THE
FOREGROUND, FACING MOSTLY AWAY FROM US. HE LOOKS PALE AND SHAKEN. IN THE BACKGROUND
WE SEE JULIA, NOW NAKED, AS SHE CLIMBS INTO THE UNMADE BED, FACING MOSTLY AWAY FROM
US AS SHE DOES SO. MARIE, STANDING SOMEWHAT CLOSER AND MORE TO THE RIGHT, SMILES
CHIDINGLY AT JOE AS SHE STARTS TO TAKE OFF HER OWN CHEMISE AND SKIRTS.

JOE: But ... Marie, look, I don't know about this...

MARIE: Oh, Joe, c'mon. Don't be a spoilsport. We could... huc...

MARIE: We could all be dead tomorrow.

PANEL 9.

CHANGE ANGLE.   IN THE BOTTOM FOREGROUND IS THE BED. SITTING UP IN IT NAKED, ON THE
RIGHT OF THE FOREGROUND, WE CAN SEE SOME OF JULIA IN PROFILE. THE DIRTY BLANKET
IS PULLED UP TO HER WAIST. BEYOND HER AND MORE TO THE LEFT WE SEE MARIE. PERHAPS
DECAPITATED BY THE UPPER PANEL BORDER. SHE IS NAKED NOW APART FROM HER KNICKERS,
WHICH SHE IS JUST GUIDING DOWN AROUND HER KNEES HERE AS SHE PREPARES TO GET INTO BED
WITH JULIA. SHE HAS, AS JOE REMARKED LAST EPISODE, A LOVELY ARSE. JOE, TO THE RIGHT
OF THE NEAR BACKGROUND, SITS IN HIS CHAIR AS IF SUDDENLY TURNED TO STONE AND JUST
STARES SLACK-JAWED AT THE BED. HIS EYES ARE WIDE AND STARING. HE IS LOST.

JOE: Aye, b-but...

JOE: Oh God.

Marie's bed-pals

It wasn't something we discussed, but I always figured the narrative purpose of Marie's other bed-pal Maria Harvey (far right, from page 47 of Chapter 9) was to look quite unlike Marie Kelly, serving to emphasize the relative likeness of Marie and Julia (near right, page 41, see next) and show it to be not just an accident. I was pleased with my drawing of the seated figure.

Chapter 9, page 41.

I had already given the problem of the sunlight some consideration back in Chapter 8, Page 1, but I still couldn't figure out how it could get all the way across the room in these little hovels that were packed together so tightly. I asked Pete to work it out and tried not to look. At the end of this page a new problem arises, and that's the problem of the door key. Julia asks how she'll get in and on page 42, Marie leaves the key on the sill near the broken window. Keep an eye on it.

PAGE 41. (800 words) PANEL 1.
NINE PANELS. IN THIS FIRST ONE WE ARE INSIDE MARIE'S ROOM AND LOOKING AT THE BROKEN GLASS PANE OF THE WINDOW, (INCIDENTALLY, I THINK THE WINDOW BROKEN WAS A SMALL ONE RIGHT NEXT TO THE DOOR, SO THAT THE DOOR IS ON OUR LEFT OF IT HERE YOU MIGHT NEED TO FIX SOME OF THE EARLIER PICTURES. SEE WHAT YOU THINK. OUTSIDE THE BROKEN WINDOW THERE IS ONLY DARKNESS, AND THE INTERIOR OF THE ROOM IS SIMILARLY MURKY.
No dialogue. (for seven panels)

PANEL 2.
SAME SHOT, STILL LOOKING AT THE WINDOW WITH THE DOOR PARTLY VISIBLE TO OUR LEFT OF IT. AS WE SEE IT HERE, THE FIRST RAYS OF THE SUN ARE JUST STARTING TO RISE BEYOND THE BROKEN GLASS, WITH A SOLITARY SHAFT OF SUNLIGHT FALLING IN HERE THROUGH THE HOLE IN THE DUSTY, SMASHED WINDOW.

PANEL 3.
CHANGE ANGLE NOW. WE SEE THE OTHER END OF THE SUNBEAM AS IT FALLS UPON THE FLOOR OF MARIE'S ROOM, WHERE WE SEE EMPTY BOTTLES AND SCATTERED CLOTHING STREWN HAPHAZARDLY ABOUT. TOWARDS THE BACKGROUND WE CAN SEE THE BED WITH THE TWO SHADOWY AND INDISTINCT SHAPES OF MARIE AND JULIE AS THEY LIE THERE ASLEEP. THE SUNRAY IS BRIGHT ALMOST REDEMPTIVE, AS IT FALLS INTO THE DISMAL ROOM.

PANEL 4.
NOW WE MOVE CLOSER TO THE BED, AS IF WE WERE STANDING BESIDE IT AND LOOKING DOWN AT MARIE AND JULIA AS THEY LIE THERE ASLEEP IN EACH OTHERS ARMS. JULIA'S MOUTH HANGS OPEN, AS IF SHE MIGHT BE SNORING. THE PATCH OF LIGHT CAST BY THE SUNBEAM IS

CREEPING UP THE BED TOWARDS MARIE'S FACE, ALTHOUGH AS YET SHE IS STILL FAST ASLEEP.

PANEL 5.
SAME SHOT AS LAST PANEL, BUT NOW THE SUNLIGHT IS FALLING DIRECTLY ON MARIE'S FACE, AND WE SEE HER START TO SIT UP SLIGHTLY, SQUINTING AS SHE WAKES, MAYBE LIFTING ONE ARM TO SHIELD HERSELF FROM THE PAINFUL BRIGHTNESS. BESIDE HER JULIA SLEEPS ON.

PANEL 6.
CHANGE ANGLE FOR A LONG SHOT OF THE BED FROM THE OTHER SIDE OF THE ROOM. MARIE IS NOW SITTING NAKED ON THE EDGE OF THE BED, HER ELBOWS RESTING ON HER KNEES AND HER FACE SUNK IN HER HANDS. IT LOOKS AS IF SHE IS REMEMBERING THE NIGHT BEFORE WITH SOME REGRET. ALL OVER THE FLOOR THERE ARE SPILLED BOTTLES, ITEMS OF CLOTHING, BROKEN GLASS. IT'S A MESS. BEHIND THE SITTING MARIE, JULIA MAYBE STIRS SLIGHTLY, RUBBING A KNUCKLE INTO ONE EYE AS SHE STARES BLEARILY AND UNCERTAINLY AT MARIE WITH THE OTHER.

PANEL 7.
NOW WE CHANGE ANGLE AGAIN. IN THE FOREGROUND, MARIE IS STANDING AND FACING ROUGHLY TOWARDS US THREE-QUARTER FIGURE. SHE IS GETTING DRESSED HERE, HER BACK TURNED ON THE BED. IN THE BED, JULIA SORT OF HALF SITS UP AND GAZES UNCERTAINLY AT MARIE'S BACK, AS IF WONDERING HOW THINGS STAND BETWEEN THE TWO OF THEM AFTER LAST NIGHT. MARIE'S FACE IS UNREADABLE AS SHE BUTTONS HER DRESS; EXPRESSIONLESS AND MASK-LIKE, CONCEALING WHATEVER FEELINGS SHE MIGHT BE HAVING. THE MAIN VISUAL FOCUS OF THE PANEL IS THE QUESTIONING, UNCERTAIN LOOK THAT JULIA HAS ON HER FACE AS SHE GAZES TOWARDS MARIE'S TURNED BACK.

PANEL 8.
NOW WE CLOSE IN SLIGHTLY, SO THAT MARIE IS STILL VISIBLE OVER ON THE EXTREME LEFT OF THE FOREGROUND, STILL FACING US, BUT NOW SHE IS ONLY VISIBLE FROM THE TIP OF HER NOSE DOWN TO HER WAIST OR THEREABOUTS, WITH HER EYES NOT VISIBLE HERE, BEING OFF THE UPPER PANEL BORDER. SHE IS STILL FASTENING BUTTONS AND STRAIGHTENING HER CLOTHES, AND HER LIPS ARE STILL COMPOSED INTO AN UNREADABLE AND EXPRESSIONLESS LINE. LOOKING PAST HER AND MORE TO THE RIGHT OF THE PANEL WE CAN SEE JULIA SITTING UP NOW IN THE BED AND STILL LOOKING VERY WOEBEGONE, GUILTY AND UNCERTAIN AS SHE GAZES AT MARIE'S BACK, SPEAKING HESITANTLY AS SHE DOES SO. MAYBE SHE HAS THE SHEET PULLED UP DEFENSIVELY TO COVER HER BREASTS HERE.

JULIA: M-Marie? I-I'm sorry about what happened with you and Joe last night.

JULIA: I keep feelin' it's my fault, coming' 'ere. I'll go if you like.

PANEL 9.
REVERSE ANGLES SO THAT IN THE RIGHT OF THE FOREGROUND WE CAN SEE A LITTLE OF JULIA AS SHE SITS UP IN BED, FACING AWAY FROM US TOWARDS MARIE, WHO HAS TURNED TO FACE US FROM THE LEFT OF THE BACKGROUND, WHERE WE SEE HER STANDING ROUGHLY THREE-QUARTER FIGURE. SHE GAZES AT JULIA KINDLY AND SYMPATHETICALLY. BEYOND MARIE WE CAN SEE THE BROKEN WINDOW NEAR TO THE DOOR THAT LEADS OUT INTO MILLER'S COURT.

MARIE: Oh, don't be daft. Nothin's your fault, and ye're welcome to doss here whenever you want.

JULIA: Oh, that's lovely. But how'll I get in, if you're not here?

Talking buildings.

It was good to have Pete Mullins on hand for the architectural studies like Buckingham Palace in our top tier of page 43, (facing page and thumbnail right). It's an example of what is known in the trade as "the talking building."

One of the saddening tendencies of comic books of late is the habit of getting literal. There are some obvious outward signs of this. One such example is the decline of the thought balloon. We hear the speech of others, as seen in their speech balloons, but we are not privy to their thoughts and so, the theory goes, these should not be made visible. Thus in the more literal-minded comics of our days, thought balloons have been expunged and replaced by the cinematic technique of the voice-over. And as you know, I'm antagonistic to anything unthinkingly imported from cinema as though that were a more authentic medium. Another comics trick that has largely gone south is the talking building. This was a staple of the newspaper photorealist strips, used as a way of setting a scene while simultaneously jumping into the dialogue. It could also be a way of breaking up a static conversation, by inserting an exterior view. But buildings don't actually talk, so this too has been replaced by the caption. However, since we have done away with captions for the duration of *FROM HELL*, we get to do the talking building. There's another on page 31 of this chapter. (see below). I may have drawn that one myself, but it's one of those instances where I can't tell for sure.

Chapter 9, page 43.

The central panel of Eddy talking to his trousers is one of those images that works as well in both the thumbnail (facing) and the finished page.

PAGE 43. (732 words) PANEL 1.
THERE ARE SEVEN PANELS HERE, WITH ONE BIG ONE ON THE TOP TIER AND THEN THREE SMALLER ONES ON EACH OF THE TIERS BELOW THAT. IN THIS FIRST ONE WE JUST HAVE A WIDE-ANGLE ESTABLISHING SHOT OF BUCKINGHAM PALACE BENEATH A GREY AND OVERCAST LONDON SKY. WILLIAM GULL'S SPEECH BALLOONS ISSUE FROM SOMEWHERE IN ONE OF THE EXTENSIVE WINGS OF THE PALACE.

GULL (FROM PALACE):   I'm sorry I could not attend your Highness when you arrived from York yesterday. Sandringham next, isn't it?

GULL (FROM PALACE):   Ah well, I'm relieved to say that everything is in order...

PANEL 2.
NOW WE CUT TO AN INTERIOR PRIVATE CHAMBER OF THE PALACE, WHERE DR. GULL HAS JUST BEEN GIVING PRINCE EDDY A MEDICAL CHECKUP. GULL, HALF FIGURE TO THE LEFT OF THE FOREGROUND, STANDS IN PROFILE FACING LEFT AS HE PACKS AWAY HIS MEDICAL EQUIPMENT, NOT LOOKING ROUND TOWARDS PRINCE EDDY EVEN AS HE SPEAKS TO HIM. THE PRINCE IS STANDING THREE-QUARTER TO FULL FIGURE IN THE RIGHT OF THE NEAR BACKGROUND. HE HAS NO TROUSERS ON, AND IS JUST RE-BUTTONING HIS SHIRT HERE, LOOKING RATHER MOURNFULLY AT GULL AS HE LISTENS TO WHAT THE ROYAL PHYSICIAN IS SAYING TO HIM.

GULL: I thought I had detected a sarcocele but it was merely a blemish.

GULL: Still, I would respectfully suggest your Highness be discriminate in such liaisons.

PANEL 3.
NOW WE CLOSE IN SO THAT WE CAN JUST SEE PRINCE EDDY, DOWNCAST AND GAZING TOWARDS HIS FEET AS HE MOURNFULLY TAKES UP HIS NEATLY HUNG TROUSERS FROM THE BACK OF A CHAIR, GAZING AT THEM WITH A LOOK OF MISERY BEFORE HE PUTS THEM ON, SPEAKING MORE TO THE TROUSERS THAN THE OFF-PANEL SIR WILLIAM.

EDDY: Yes. Yes, I suppose I should. My affairs do rather tend to get people into trouble, don't they?

EDDY: Do you remember Annie Crook, Sir William?

PANEL 4.

CHANGE ANGLE. GULL FACES US IN THE FOREGROUND ON THE RIGHT. WE ARE SO CLOSE TO HIM THAT WE CAN ONLY SEE HIS FACE DOWN FROM THE BRIDGE OF HIS NOSE, WITH HIS EYES OFF PANEL ABOVE. HIS FACE, FROM WHAT WE CAN SEE OF IT, IS EXPRESSIONLESS AND DEVOID OF EMOTION AS HE SPEAKS ABOUT ANNIE. AS HE FACES US, HE IS STILL PACKING EVERYTHING AWAY TIDILY INTO HIS MEDICAL BAG, WHICH WE SEE IN THE BOTTOM FOREGROUND. LOOKING INTO THE LEFT OF THE NEAR BACKGROUND WE SEE EDDY AS HE STARTS TO STEP INTO HIS TROUSERS, GAZING MOURNFULLY AT SIR WILLIAM'S TURNED BACK AS HE DOES SO.

GULL: Hm? Ahh, yes. The Crook woman. What a hornet's nest she stirred up.

GULL: But no matter. That will all be concluded shortly.

PANEL 5.

CHANGE ANGLE AGAIN. EDDIE IS NOW HEAD AND SHOULDERS TO THE LEFT OF THE FOREGROUND, FACING AWAY FROM US TOWARDS GULL, WHO STANDS TO THE RIGHT OF THE NEAR BACKGROUND, STILL PACKING HIS MEDICAL BAG, NOT LOOKING ROUND AT THE PRINCE AS HE SPEAKS TO HIM. IN FACT, WE NEEDN'T SEE GULL'S FACE HERE. EDDIE LOOKS SICK AND ANXIOUS AS HE GAZES TOWARDS GULL'S TURNED BACK, STARTLED BY THIS SUDDEN OMINOUS NEWS.

EDDY: C-concluded? You mean, those women? The blackmail attempt...?

GULL: Please, your Highness, a little softer. There are footmen.

PANEL 6.

SAME SHOT, ONLY MAYBE WE ZOOM IN JUST A LITTLE SO THAT WE NOW HAVE JUST A SLIVER OF THE FRONT OF EDDY'S FACE VISIBLE IN THE EXTREME LEFT FOREGROUND, GAZING AWAY FROM US IN MUTE HORROR TOWARDS GULL, WHO IS NOW TURNING ROUND FROM HIS BAG TO FACE US. HE SMILES AT EDDY REASSURINGLY.

GULL: But to answer your question: yes. I have recently located the remaining woman in Dorset Street, Whitechapel.

GULL: So have no fear, your Highness...

PANEL 7.

CHANGE ANGLE. EDDY IS STARING AT US HALF TO THREE-QUARTER FIGURE FROM THE LEFT BACKGROUND, HIS EYES HAUNTED AS HE GAZES SILENTLY AT DR. GULL. WE SEE GULL IN THE RIGHT FOREGROUND, SO CLOSE THAT ONCE AGAIN WE CANNOT SEE HIS EYES, WHICH ARE INVISIBLE OFF THE UPPER PANEL BORDER AS HE STANDS THERE IN PROFILE, STILL WITH THE FAINT REASSURING SMILE UPON HIS LIPS AS HE SPEAKS TO THE MUTE AND HORRIFIED EDDY.

GULL: There are seven days remaining until the Lord Mayor's Parade. By then, this grave embarrassment shall be no more.

GULL: You have my oath.

Facing page: Alan's thumbnails for pages 41-47; (41 and 43 already discussed) 42 Netley steals key; 44 Abberline arrives at Ten Bells; Script for 45 is discussed next; 46 is Guy Fawkes night, when Julia reaches through the window to let herself in; 47 has another sex scene, sensitively drawn in the centre panel. **"We see Marie Kelly trying to lose herself in drink and promiscuous sex in the wake of learning that something much more terrible than a protection gang has been eliminating her friends on its way towards her."** *(1994 synopsis) For 49-54, see page 188 here.*

Chapter 9, pages 41-47. Commentary on facing page.

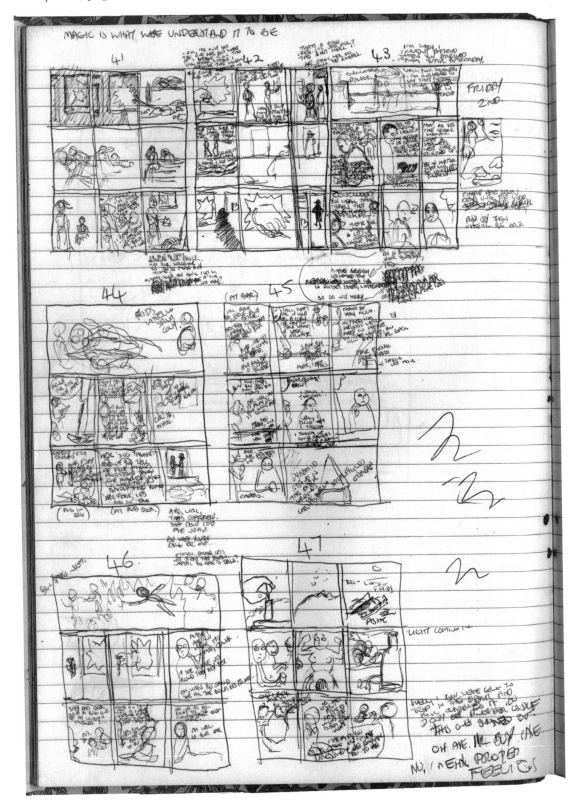

Chapter 9, page 45.

Alan described Abberline's part in this chapter: ***"He plods through the dismal workings of the case, attending post-mortem and inquiry with equal cheerlessness. meanwhile he pursues his chaste yet guilty relationship with the street-girl Emma"*** (1994 synopsis). Here Fred lends "Emma" five quid. I wracked my brain at the time to figure out if that was a huge amount or just a lot. He tentatively suggests getting a room and looks away. He is supposed to be looking at Emma in panel 6. I'm wondering why that came out otherwise. He has a guilty look about him, mixed with a thought that he might have stuck his neck out too far. Sometimes one draws a thing and redraws, and it ends up different from the original intention. Speaking of which, Alan planned nine panels at the top and then realized he'd miscounted and changed it to eight (as in the thumbnail overleaf). I can't remember if I made it nine because I'd already started in on a pre-lined page, or if I had an actual idea about it.

PAGE 45. (666 words) PANEL 1.
NINE PANELS. ABBERLINE STANDS AT THE BAR IN THE NEAR RIGHT BACKGROUND WHILE EMMA SEATS HERSELF AT THE TABLE IN THE LEFT OF THE FOREGROUND. HER FACE ARTFULLY CONCEALED OR TURNED AWAY. FRED IS NOT LOOKING AT HER, BUT AT THE BARMAN WHO HAS APPROACHED HIM FROM THE OTHER SIDE OF THE BAR.

EMMA: I'll have a half o' bitter. No. Y'know what I mean; I don't
                like takin' yer money.
FRED: You're not. It's just a loan. Pint'n 'alf o' bitter, please.

PANEL 2.
SIMILAR SHOT, WITH EMMA SITTING IN THE LEFT OF THE FOREGROUND WITH HER UPPER FACE INVISIBLE OFF THE TOP OF THE PANEL AND ONLY HER MOUTH VISIBLE HERE. SHE LOOKS RESOLVED. APPROACHING THE TABLE FROM THE NEAR BACKGROUND WE SEE FRED, CARRYING A PINT GLASS AND A HALF-PINT GLASS, WHICH HE HOLDS OUT FOR EMMA TO TAKE.

EMMA: Well, that's ALL it is. A loan. I'll pay you back next week, I promise.
FRED: I know you will. Let's 'ear no more of it. 'Ere, take this...

PANEL 3.
SAME SHOT AS LAST PANEL, WITH EMMA SEATED ON THE LEFT WITH HER EYES OFF PANEL ABOVE, WHILE FRED SEATS HIMSELF MORE TOWARDS THE RIGHT AND SLIGHTLY FURTHER AWAY FROM US,

GAZING TOWARDS US AND EMMA AS HE DOES SO, EMMA TAKES THE DRINK FROM FRED. AS HE SITS, HE IS MAYBE FISHING IN AN INSIDE POCKET FOR THE FIVE-POUND NOTE HE INTENDS TO LEND HER.

EMMA: Thank ye very much. No, I'm serious, Fred. We'll meet here on the ninth, an' I'll pay it back.

FRED: Fair enough. Here y'are...

PANEL 4.

SAME SHOT, WITH EMMA VISIBLE FROM THE NOSE DOWN ON THE NEAR LEFT AND FRED LOOKING FROM THE RIGHT OF THE NEAR BACKGROUND AS HE SITS FACING HER. EMMA TAKES THE FIVE-POUND NOTE FROM HIM, LOOKING DOWN AT IT IN GRATEFUL AWE AS SHE DOES SO. SIPPING FROM HIS BEER, FRED GLANCES AT HER A LITTLE NERVOUSLY AND ANXIOUSLY. HE'S TRYING TO PLUCK UP COURAGE TO SAY SOMETHING. EMMA IS OBLIVIOUS TO THIS.

EMMA: God, Fred, ye don't know what this means...

FRED: Aye, well, put it away or you won't 'ave it long.

FRED: Tell you what: on the ninth we'll celebrate, eh?

PAGE 5.

SAME SHOT. OBEDIENTLY TUCKING THE FOLDED FIVE-POUND NOTE AWAY IN SOME INNER POCKET OR RECESS OF HER DRESS, EMMA LOOKS UP AND GAZES AT FRED, SEEMING SLIGHTLY SURPRISED OR PUZZLED BY HIS SUGGESTION. FRED LOOKS DOWN INTO HIS DRINK AS HE REPLIES, TOO EMBARRASSED TO MEET HER EYES.

EMMA: Celebrate? How?

Fred: I dunno. I thought we could p'raps, y'know, find a room. Somewhere nice.

PANEL 6.

SAME SHOT. EMMA JUST GAZES AT FRED ACROSS THE TABLE AND DOESN'T SAY ANYTHING. ABBERLINE GLANCES AT HER OFF-PANEL EYES. THERE IS A TENSE SILENCE. No dialogue

PANEL 7.

SAME SHOT. IN THE LEFT OF THE FOREGROUND, EMMA LIFTS HER GLASS OF BEER TO HER LIPS AND SMILES, EVIDENTLY PLEASED BY THE IDEA. FRED JUST LOOKS AT HER FROM HIS SIDE OF THE TABLE, UNABLE TO BELIEVE HOW BEAUTIFUL SHE IS. AROUND THEM, THE BUSTLE OF THE BAR CONTINUES UNABATED, BUT THEY SIT THERE IN THEIR LITTLE POCKET OF CHARGED HUSH.

EMMA: Aye. Aye, perhaps we could. Cheers.

PANEL 8.

WHOOPS... I SAID THIS WAS A NINE-PANEL PAGE AT THE TOP, DIDN'T I? WELL, I'M SORRY, BUT I'D MISREAD MY OWN LAYOUTS AND IT'S ONLY AN EIGHT-PANEL PAGE AFTER ALL. THIS LAST PANEL IS A DOUBLE-SIZED PANEL COMPLETING THE BOTTOM TIER, AND WHAT WE SEE IS A VIEW OF SPITALFIELDS GARDENS, WITH THE STRANGE PYRAMID THAT WE SAW EARLIER PROMINENT IN THE FOREGROUND. LOOKING BEYOND IT AND INTO THE BACKGROUND WE CAN PERHAPS GLIMPSE THE TEN BELLS ACROSS THE STREET, IF THAT WORKS. IF NOT, LEAVE THE PUB OUT. THE MAIN FOCUS IS THE SINISTER AND SILENT PYRAMID OF WHITE PORTLAND STONE, REARING ENIGMATICALLY THERE IN THE SCRUFFY, TRAMP-HAUNTED GARDENS.

No dialogue

Chapter 9: a question.

The scenes at the flat here had me going back over and over the second half of chapter 9 for months after it was first published in December 1994, trying to figure out all the moves to be sure they made sense and to see if I'd done something wrong.

Following the key to the flat is a shell game. On page 42, Marie puts the key on the window ledge under the broken window, so that Julia can use it to get back in. On the same page, after they leave, Netley comes and reaches in and takes the key. On page 46, Julia lets herself in by reaching through the window all the way over to the door handle, and as she enters she makes a remark about the key still being missing, indicating that these characters have talked about it since we last saw them. I didn't set up the flat so that you can reach from the door to the window, and I'm hoping nobody makes an issue of the stretch. Marie is in bed with another woman (Maria Harvey), so Julia sleeps on the floor. Marie and her pal awake on page 47 and note that Julia is gone. Marie says Julia will be back tomorrow night (important). Another night passes. Gull is shown to now be in possession of the key.

Meanwhile, there is a parade of people being brought into the flat: Lizzie Albright, Barnett, a pick-up, then another pick-up. Note that Marie entered the flat in the same panel, the sixth, of pages 55 and 56, both times in company, so that we have established a presumption that the third time, page 57, is also Marie. Here is the relevant portion of the script:

Page 55, panels 5 and 6: Marie enters flat in 6. I gave the light a raggedness in these scenes to conceal the sleight of hand.

Page 56, panels 5 and 6: Marie enters the flat in 6.

Page 57, panels 5 and 6: Marie(?) enters the flat in 6.

PAGE 57 (363 words)   PANEL 5.
SAME SHOT. A SOLITARY WOMAN IS COMING DOWN THE ALLEYWAY TOWARDS US AND THE CLOSED DOOR. IT LOOKS LIKE MARIE KELLY, AND IN THE CONTEXT OF THE PREVIOUS COMINGS AND GOINGS, ONE WOULD PROBABLY ASSUME THAT'S WHO IT WAS. IT IS IN FACT JULIA, BUT IT IS IMPORTANT THAT NOBODY REALIZE THIS AT THIS STAGE, HENCE THE ABYSMAL LIGHT IN THE COURT. THE WOMAN HERE IS JUST COMING DOWN THE ALLEYWAY TOWARDS US AND HAS NOT YET REACHED THE FRONT DOOR.
PANEL 6.
SAME SHOT. WE SEE THE WOMAN AS SHE OPENS THE DOOR AND GOES INTO THE SOFTLY LIT ROOM. IT STILL LOOKS PRETTY MUCH LIKE MARIE KELLY.   No dialogue.

Alan works out the final comings and goings at 13 Miller's Court. Chapter 9, pages 55-58.

Note the drunken song at bottom of 55, shifted to top of 56 to make room for the advancing sequence of the coach arriving in the long lower-tier panels (see my note on 190)

(41-47 is on page 207
49-54 is on page 189.)

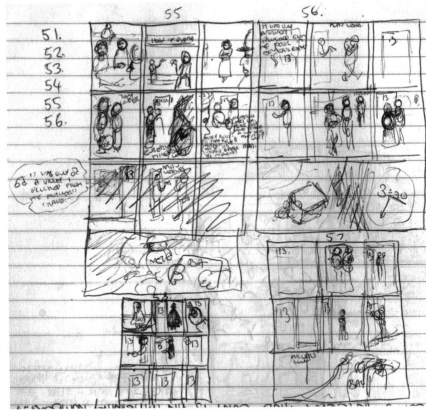

Page 58, panel 3, Gull uses the key

Page 58- panels 5 and 6: Gull enter flat in 5 (not 6), one panel ahead of "schedule."

Since Marie no longer has a key, I presumed that she was just leaving the door lightly pulled closed (she says there's nothing in here worth stealing), and once inside would bolt it. Note that Godley says in Chapter 11, page 5, that it is "spring-locked." Recall also that, when Marie was already inside, Julia had to reach through to the door handle the last time to let herself in, but doesn't do that here. The only person holding a key, Gull, turns up on 58 and lets himself in.

Here's a little trick that you may have missed: everybody else went through the door in panel 6 of a page. Gull enters in 5, creating a frisson of alarm in the reading by being one panel ahead of schedule.

However, the question is: have we tripped ourselves up? On leaving the final time, which we now know to be 56, did Marie know she wouldn't be back, and knowing that, did she still leave it unclosed?

Part 6
Pages 213 to 227.
The theme is
butchery.
How does one
show it with
honesty?

Chapter 10, pages 1, 2.

Alan's script for the first page of Chapter 10 is pretty much just stage direction, but I've shown a row of panels from it. A year before we started on this chapter, Alan wrote: *"While gathering data to aid in From Hell's reconstruction of the final murder, I was in receipt of a generous offer made by Martin Fido, noted Ripperologist and true-crime writer. Referring to details unearthed in his then still-to-be released Compendium and A-Z he suggested I might like to see newly published post-mortem details that related to Jack's final victim, the hideously mutilated Marie Jeanette Kelly, including some previously undisclosed facial wounds.*

"Now, I suppose that if you haven't been somebody who's spent the last four years engrossed in coroner's reports and mortuary photographs, the obvious appeal of such enticing information might be conceivably lost on you. 'Does it matter,' you ask, 'if the first cut was made in the face? He made hamburger out of the poor woman, for God's sake! Who wants to know the precise order he did it all in?'

"I do. I know it's a sickness, but I do. You see, that first facial incision can be matched exactly with cuts in the bed-sheet, which means that when she saw the man with the knife crossing over the dark, twelve-foot-square room to her bed, she pulled up the bed-covers instinctively, just like a small child afraid that the monsters will get her, to cover her face. It's so poignant, the image: how can I resist it?

"The surge of excitement I felt on receiving the offer of yet more details of the hideous things that were done to this woman was frankly as close as I've come to pure horror throughout this whole exercise. Not a revulsion at what had become of Marie Jeanette Kelly, her purely physical disfiguring, but a nausea predicated on myself, on all the Ripperati, fumbling elbow deep in pools of ancient blood, hoping to find some previously undiscovered talisman amongst the viscous, clotted bedsands: half a railway ticket, or a broken comb; a grape stem or ginny kidney." (Oct 1993, introduction to the "Compleat Scripts.")

PAGE 1. (847 words) (edited- only panels 2 and 5 complete) PANEL 1.
HELLO, EDDIE. WELL, THIS IS THE BIG NASTY ONE. NOT SO MUCH FROM HELL AS TO HELL IN
A HANDCART (OR "TO HELL IN A HANDBAG" AS MELINDA MALAPROPOSITIONED RECENTLY). THIS
FIRST PAGE HAS EIGHT PANELS INCLUDING THE OPENING TITLE FRAME...etc

PANEL 2.
DOUBLE-WIDTH PANEL, FINISHING OFF THIS OPENING TIER. WE ARE INSIDE NO.13 MILLER'S
COURT, FACING THE HOVEL'S DOOR, WHICH IS JUST OPENING TOWARDS US. FRAMED IN IT IS
WILLIAM GULL, ROUGHLY HALF FIGURE AS HE ENTERS THE DARK ROOM AND VERY WIDE AND
IMPRESSIVE. THE WEAK LIGHTING OF MILLER'S COURT GLIMMERS FAINTLY BEHIND HIM, ENOUGH
TO THROW HIS FEATURES INTO COMPLETE SMOTHERING SHADOW AS HE FACES US HERE,
A FEATURELESS AND NAMELESS CHTHONIC FORCE BLOWING INTO THE SMALL ROOM LIKE A WIND.

PANEL 5
CHANGE ANGLE SO THAT NOW WE ARE JUST BEHIND GULL AND CAN JUST SEE A LITTLE OF HIM...
PERHAPS HIS HAND HOLDING THE KNIFE OR MAYBE JUST THE EDGE OF HIS DARK ΓORM ENTERING
THE PANEL FROM THE LEFT OF THE FOREGROUND. LOOKING BEYOND THIS WE CAN SEE THE WOMAN
SITTING UP IN BED FACING US AND THE APPROACHING GULL. SHE HAS PULLED THE SHEET UP TO
THE BRIDGE OF HER NOSE IN TERROR, ONLY HER FRIGHTENED EYES STARING AT US FROM OVER
THE TOP OF THIS FUTILE, INFANTILE ATTEMPT AT CONCEALMENT AND PROTECTION. HER EYES ARE
AWFUL. SHE IS JUST THIS INSTANT UNDERSTANDING THAT SHE IS GOING TO DIE UNPLEASANTLY.
WOMAN: Oh no.
WOMAN: MURDER! HELP!

PAGE 2. (785 words) (edited to condense) PANEL 1.
NINE PANELS ON THIS SECOND PAGE, WITH THIS FIRST PANEL BEING MORE OR LESS THE SAME SHOT
AS THE LAST PANEL ON PAGE ONE, WITH GULL VISIBLE HALF FIGURE IN PROFILE, FACING TOWARDS
THE LEFT OF THE PANEL AND THE WOMAN OFF PANEL BENEATH HIM. IN THIS PANEL HE HAS SLASHED
THE KNIFE ACROSS IN A LONG AND WHISTLING ARC SO THAT HERE HIS RIGHT ARM IS CROSSED OVER
HIS BODY WITH THE KNIFE POINT LUNGING UP CLOSE TOWARDS US IN THE FOREGROUND, TRAILING A
TRAJECTORY LINE OF BLOOD. THE ARC OF THE KNIFE HAS SLICED THROUGH THE WOMAN'S OFF-PANEL
THROAT, AND THERE IS A SPRAY OF BLOOD UPWARDS INTO THE PANEL FROM BENEATH. GULL'S FACE
IS STILL EXPRESSIONLESS AS HE DELIVERS THE COUP DE GRACE.
No dialogue. (ditto all panels on this page)

PANEL 3.
NOW A HEAD-AND-SHOULDERS SHOT OF GULL FACING US, ANGLED SO THAT WE ARE PERHAPS
LOOKING UP AT HIM SLIGHTLY. HE WIPES A THIN FILM OF SWEAT FROM HIS BROW WITH THE BACK OF
ONE HAND, MAYBE WIPING SOME BLOOD ONTO HIS BROW IN THE PROCESS, UNLESS THAT LOOKS TOO
OVERDONE. HIS EXPRESSION IS EMOTIONLESS AND MASK-LIKE, STATUE-LIKE IN THE SHADOWY ROOM.
HE IS LOOKING DOWN AT HIS OFF-PANEL WORK WITHOUT A FLICKER OF REACTION.

PANEL 4.
WE ARE NOW CROUCHING JUST A FOOT ABOVE FLOOR LEVEL, UP AT THE HEAD OF THE BED,
SQUEEZED BETWEEN THE BEDSIDE TABLE ON THE LEFT AND THE BED ON THE RIGHT. THE EDGE

OF THE TABLE JUTS INTO THE LEFT OF THE FOREGROUND HERE, AND WE CAN SEE THE HANDLE OF GULL'S LISTON KNIFE, RESTING WHERE HE LEFT IT. FROM THE RIGHT, WHERE WE SEE THE EDGE OF THE BED, WE CAN SEE ONE OF THE WOMAN'S LIMP HANDS DANGLING DOWN OVER THE SIDE OF THE BED, LIFELESS AND INERT. LOOKING JUST BEYOND THE EDGE OF THE BEDSIDE TABLE IN THE LEFT FOREGROUND WE CAN SEE SOME OF GULL, ROUGHLY FROM HIS CALVES TO HIS MID-TORSO. HIS HANDS ARE REACHING DOWN INTO VIEW HERE AND WE CAN SEE THAT HE IS IN FACT BENDING HIS KNEES TO STOOP SLIGHTLY. AS HE REACHES DOWN AND GRASPS THE CREASES OF HIS TROUSERS AT THE KNEE, ONE CREASE IN EACH HAND. THIS IS A VERY SLIGHT BIT OF BUSINESS TO LAST THE NEXT THREE PANELS, BUT IT FEELS RIGHT, SO BEAR WITH ME.

PANEL 5.
SAME SHOT EXACTLY, THE ONLY MOVEMENT IS THAT GULL HAS HOISTED HIS TROUSER CREASES UP ABOUT THREE INCHES, TO ABOVE THE KNEE. NOTHING ELSE HAPPENS. THE HAND STILL DANGLES OFF THE EDGE OF THE BED OVER ON THE RIGHT.

PANEL 6.
SAME SHOT. HAVING HIKED UP HIS CREASES GULL NOW SQUATS DOWN ON HIS HAUNCHES, SO THAT WE CAN AT LEAST SEE HIS HEAD AND SHOULDERS AS HE CROUCHES BY THE BED. THESE LAST THREE PANELS ARE SOLELY CONCERNED WITH THE ACTION OF GULL HIKING HIS CREASES UP. I JUST THOUGHT IT A TELLING DETAIL IN THE WAKE OF SUCH A SAVAGE MURDER.

PANEL 7.
SAME SHOT. GULL NOW REACHES OUT AND TAKES THE WOMAN'S LIMP HAND. HOLDING IT BY THE WRIST. WITH HIS OTHER HAND HE FISHES INSIDE HIS WAISTCOAT POCKET TO RETRIEVE HIS FOB WATCH, WHICH WE PROBABLY CAN'T SEE YET.

PANEL 8.
SAME SHOT AS LAST PANEL, ONLY HERE GULL HAS TAKEN OUT THE FOB WATCH AND IS GAZING AT IT EXPRESSIONLESSLY AS HE HOLDS THE WOMAN'S LIMP WRIST IN THE FINGERS OF HIS OTHER HAND.

PANEL 9.
SAME SHOT EXACTLY. GULL CONTINUES TO GAZE AT THE WATCH WHILE HOLDING THE WOMAN'S WRIST. HE DOES NOT MOVE, NEITHER DOES HIS MASK-LIKE FACE SHOW ANY FLICKER OF EXPRESSION. No dialogue.

Alternative scene: *In the 1994 synopsis, Alan had the murder being committed on the last page of chapter 9, with a detail that doesn't appear in the book, but is only referred to.* **When she hears him enter and sees him walk toward the bed with the Liston knife in his hand she pulls the covers up over her face in a reflexive, child-like impulse and cries out "Murder." Calmly, Gull stabs her twice in the face through the raised bed sheet. In the lodging room upstairs from number 13, a small cat wakes Marie's sleeping neighbour by walking over the back of her neck (and imagine that, if you will). The neighbour hears a woman cry "Murder", but as this is a fairly common East End cry, she turns over and goes back to sleep. End of Chapter IX.** *The detail of the cat ("Diddles") got moved to the dialogue of the investigation in Chapter 11.*

Chapter 10, pages 5, 8.

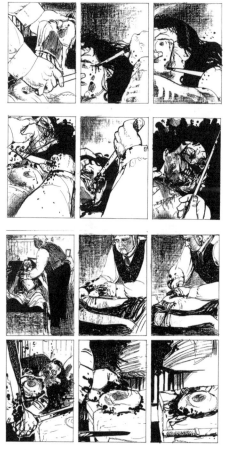

And so Alan set about reconstructing *"The precise order he did it all in."* He wrote, *"**Many serial murderers prefer to mutilate their victims' faces first, so as to, in effect, dehumanize their kill and rob it of identity, thus making it psychologically easier for them to carry out their further mutilations.**"* (FROM HELL appendix 1, page 33). This raises the problem that I have been leading up to here. Alan wanted to leave it as a possibility that the person killed here was not Marie but Julia. This, you may be surprised to hear, remained uncertain right up until he finished writing the final chapter.

The problem for me was what to show here before the face is destroyed. It wouldn't do to only half-show it, or have it happen off-panel, as that would be construed as squeamishness. Since I was already juggling with "the graphics of theory and guesswork," I was ready for it. It occurred to me that we had never seen either woman at close quarters, or at least not in the way that we had seen Gull and Abberline. Thus I could draw a face and the identity could remain deniable. Like one of those eyewitness situations: 'can you tell us exactly what you saw?' Or to put it another way, the reader must be as UNcertain that the person being murdered is Marie and not Julia, with a face visible, as they are elsewhere CERtain that "Emma" is Marie, with NO face visible. (excerpt from page 4, first tier at left)

Then there is the breast. He puts it on the bedside table. We are finished with neither the face or the breast.

PAGE 5. (384 words) PANEL 7 ONLY. (excerpt from page 5, second tier above))
BIG WIDE PANEL SHOWING A PANORAMIC VIEW OF THE WHOLE CANDLELIT ROOM. GULL STANDS
FULL FIGURE BY THE BEDSIDE TABLE. THE WOMAN IS VISIBLE LYING FULL LENGTH ON THE
BED. HER FACE LOOKS LIKE ONE OF THOSE MOSAIC AZTEC DEATH MASKS. HER BODY, UN-
TOUCHED AS YET, IS BEAUTIFUL BENEATH THE THIN CHEMISE. SHE LOOKS LIKE SOME KIND OF
ODD MYTHICAL CREATURE OR CHIMERA; THE BODY OF A BEAUTIFUL LIVE WOMAN, THE HEAD OF

A FLAYED CORPSE. THE SILENT, WITNESSING ROOM STRETCHES AROUND GULL AND THE BODY. WE CAN MAYBE USE THIS PANEL TO FIRMLY ESTABLISH ITS LAYOUT, SHOWING THE READER WHERE THE FIREPLACE IS AND EVERYTHING IN RELATION TO THE BED AND THE DOOR. EXPRESSIONLESS, GULL SETS THE KNIFE DOWN ON THE BEDSIDE TABLE. FACELESS, THE MOTIONLESS GIRL SEEMS TO GAZE IDLY TOWARDS HIM, LOLLING THERE LIKE A SATISFIED LOVER WATCHING HER PARTNER DRESS.

PAGE 8. (426 words) (7 of 9 panels) PANEL 1.
ANOTHER NINE-PANEL PAGE. WE CHANGE ANGLE SO THAT WE ARE LOOKING THROUGH GULL'S EYES, MORE OR LESS, AS HE LOOKS DOWN AT THE HEAD, SHOULDERS AND UPPER BODY OF THE MURDERED WOMAN. WITH ONE HAND HE REACHES OUT AND TAKES HOLD OF THE DEAD WOMAN'S HAIR. IN HIS OTHER HAND, VISIBLE IN THE BOTTOM FOREGROUND, HE HOLDS THE SEVERED BREAST. HER MUTILATED FACE STARES AT US DUMBLY.

PANEL 2.
SAME SHOT. PULLING THE DEAD WOMAN'S HEAD UP FROM THE PILLOW BY THE HAIR, GULL SLIDES HER BREAST UNDER HEAD LIKE AN FXTRA PILLOW.

PANEL 4.
CHANGE ANGLE. WE ARE NOW TOWARDS THE BOTTOM OF THE BED, LOOKING UP ITS LENGTH WITH GULL ON THE RIGHT OF THE BED AND THE WOMAN'S LEGS AND FEET POINTING TOWARDS US IN THE FOREGROUND. LOOKING DOWN WITHOUT EXPRESSION, GULL REACHES OUT AND TAKES THE WOMAN'S REMAINING BREAST IN HIS LEFT HAND. WITH HIS RIGHT HAND HE PICKS UP THE KNIFE.
GULL: Huh.

PANEL 5.
SAME SHOT. DISPASSIONATELY, GULL STARTS TO SAW OFF THE WOMAN'S OTHER BREAST, WORKING THE KNIFE AROUND THE EDGE OF ITS UNDERSIDE HERE.

PANEL 7.
CHANGE ANGLE. WE ARE NOW BEHIND GULL, WITH PART OF HIS BACK VISIBLE ON THE LEFT OF THE PANEL HERE. ON THE RIGHT WE SEE THE BEDSIDE TABLE, LOOMING IN THE FOREGROUND. AS WE SEE GULL HERE, BOTH HIS HANDS ARE VISIBLE. HIS RIGHT HAND HOLDS THE KNIFE. IN HIS LEFT HAND HE HOLDS THE NOW COMPLETELY SEVERED RIGHT BREAST OF THE DEAD WOMAN. HIS HEAD AND SHOULDERS ARE PROBABLY OFF PANEL HERE, ALTHOUGH WE CAN PROBABLY STILL SEE THE DEAD WOMAN'S MUTILATED FACE STARING AT US.
No dialogue.

PANEL 8.
SAME SHOT. TURNING SLIGHTLY, GULL SETS THE BREAST DOWN CAREFULLY ON THE BEDSIDE TABLE.
No dialogue.

PANEL 9.
SAME SHOT. GULL IS STANDING BY THE BEDSIDE TABLE WITH HIS HEAD AND SHOULDERS INVISIBLE OFF THE TOP PANEL BORDER, STANDING SO THAT HE IS ROUGHLY FACING TOWARDS US. HE SETS THE KNIFE DOWN ON THE TABLE BESIDE THE BREAST THAT IT HAS JUST REMOVED FROM THE WOMAN'S BODY.
No dialogue

Chapter 10, pages 12, 13.

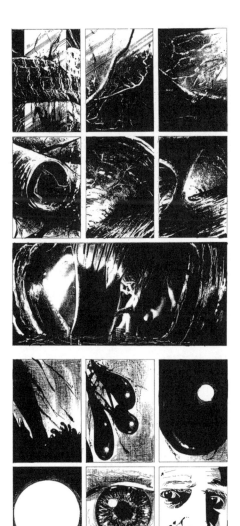

In *FROM HELL's* appendix notes, Alan reflected upon *"the view of life that doctors have, that they alone have been elected to that priesthood that may look upon the mysteries inside us... I hoped to create within the reader's mind... a brief glimpse through the alien eyes of something that's emotional response to mutilation might be very different from our own."* (From Hell appendix 1, page 35.)

As to the art, I would have selected and pasted on xeroxes of photos from a book on the human heart and then, since there were no characters to keep consistent, either regular or hypothetical, Pete Mullins would have done the inking over it all to bring it into *FROM HELL* stylistic territory. Taken out of its context the page looks almost abstract. One comics formalist critic called it "savagely avant-garde." The page that followed it, of which a part is shown at left, continues in the same manner. Note, by the way, that Alan refers to the victim as Marie Kelly in Page 13, panel 1.

PAGE 12.(432 words) (slight edit) PANEL 1.
ANOTHER SEVEN-PANEL PAGE, THIS TIME WITH THE BIG PANEL AT THE BOTTOM TIER AND THREE PANELS ON EACH OF THE TIERS ABOVE THAT. IN THIS FIRST PANEL WE HAVE CLOSED IN STILL FURTHER, ONTO THE VERY TIP OF THE BLADE AS IT ENTERS THE TISSUE. THE BLADE IS A GIANT WALL OF METAL DESCENDING INTO THE PICTURE FROM OFF, THE BODY CAVITY AROUND IT BECOMING A LANDSCAPE OF FLESH AS WE DESCEND FURTHER AND FURTHER.
No dialogue (all panels)

PANEL 2.
CLOSE IN SO THAT WE ARE RIGHT DOWN AT THE POINT WHERE THE GIANT EDGE OF THE METAL IS CUTTING THROUGH HUMAN MEAT. WE SEE THE LIPS OF THE WOUND PEEL BACK AWAY FROM THE SHARP BLADE AS IT SLICES THROUGH THE TISSUE. THE INSIDE OF THE CUT FLESH IS HONEYCOMBED WITH TINY CAPILLARY VEINS, HARDLY VISIBLE EVEN AT THIS MAGNIFICATION.

PANEL 3.
CLOSE IN FURTHER ONTO THE CUT SURFACE OF THE FLESH. THE PATTERNING OF SEVERED VEINS IS NOW MUCH MORE PROMINENT. THEY LOOK LIKE A SYSTEM OF TUNNELS SEEN FROM A DISTANCE.

PANEL 4.
CLOSE IN FURTHER, SO THAT WE ARE ZOOMING IN ON THE MOUTH OF ONE OF THE CAPILLARY VEIN TUNNELS. IT GAPES BEFORE US, HUGE AND DARK. A TRICKLE OF BLOOD RUNS SLUGGISHLY ALONG THE BOTTOM OF THIS HUGE WATER-PIPE.

PANEL 5.
WE ARE NOW MOVING DOWN THE TUNNEL OF THE VEIN, ITS RIBBED WALLS RISING AROUND US AND THE SPLASHING TRICKLE OF BLOOD SLAPPING AROUND BENEATH US IN THE BOTTOM OF THE VEIN.

PANEL 6.
WE CONTINUE ALONG THE VEIN AS IF WE WERE WHITEWATER RAFTING... OR RED PLASMA RAFTING IN THIS INSTANCE. WE CAN SEE THE PLATELETS AND THE WHITE CORPUSCLES IN THE SANGUINARY SOUP ALL AROUND US. UP AHEAD, DOWN THE TILTING BORE OF THE TUNNEL WE CAN SEE A COMPLEX JUNCTION APPROACHING, WHERE THE TUNNEL SEEMS TO WIDEN OUT INTO AN AS-YET UNGLIMPSED CHAMBER. WE SURGE FORWARD, THE WORLD ABOUT US GETTING BIGGER ALL THE TIME.

PANEL 7.
NOW THE BIG WIDE PANEL. ON A STREAM OF BLOOD WE POUR INTO THE GIANT CATHEDRAL-LIKE CHAMBERS OF THE DEAD HEART. THE INNER STRUCTURE OF THE HEART RISES UP ALL AROUND US, A BIZARRE AND GIGER-ESQUE LANDSCAPE, AWESOME AND WEIRD AND ODDLY BEAUTIFUL. WE SWIRL THROUGH IT ON THE BLOOD CURRENT, RAFTING THROUGH INCREDIBLE SUBTERRANEAN CAVERNS OF TRANSLUCENT FLESH AND TISSUE. THIS PANEL SHOULD LOOK REALLY STUNNING, ALMOST APOCALYPTIC IN ITS DEPICTION OF THE LANDSCAPES OF THE INNER BODY.

PAGE 13.(428 words) (edited- panels 1,2 and 4 only) PANEL 1.
... WE ARE MOVING THROUGH MARIE KELLY'S BLOODSTREAM, RAFTING ALONG THE BORE OF A VEIN WITH A BRANCHING OF TUNNELS AHEAD OF US. THE BLOOD TRICKLES LOW IN THE BED OF THE VEIN, SLOPPING VISCOUSLY AGAINST THE WALLS. BEADS OF BLOOD FLY UP FROM EACH SLASH, HANGING IN THE AIR LIKE BLACK PEARLS. THE LANDSCAPE IS STRANGE AND ALIEN AND BEAUTIFUL.

PANEL 2.
WE CLOSE IN UPON ONE OF THE SPLASHES OF BLOOD THAT WE SAW LAST PANEL, AS IF IT WERE A STILL AND FROZEN IMAGE. WE SEE THE ROUND AND PERFECTLY GLOBULAR BEAD OF BLOOD HANGING THERE IN FREEFALL AS IT SEPARATES FROM THE ARC OF BLOOD THAT WE SEE RISING UP FROM OFF PANEL BENEATH IT. IN THE BEAD OF BLOOD, A SINGLE HIGHLIGHT.

PANEL 4.
WE PULL BACK AGAIN. THE ROUND BLACK GLOBULE WITH THE SWIMMING WHITE HIGHLIGHT IS NOW PERCEIVED AS THE PUPIL OF AN EYE. WE CAN PERHAPS SEE A LITTLE OF THE IRIS WITH ITS STRIATED LINES FLOWERING AROUND THE BLACK PUPIL HERE. IT'S A BIT LIKE 2001: A SPACE ODYSSEY FOR SERIAL KILLERS REALLY.
No dialogue

Chapter 10, page 18.

Alan now found a problem with all these body parts he was trying to keep track of. Upon reexamining the forensic accounts of the situation he realized that the breast Gull put on the bedside table ten pages back was in the wrong place. At this stage of the project, the chapters were not being sent all in one package; there's a break after 12, and another after 28 (it would get even more fragmented before the end). So I had already drawn the page containing the problem and it would be difficult to try to go back and insert a new page when it was really only a panel that was wanting. His solution was to have Gull look at the breast, have a think, and then move it.

Incidentally, in addition to the one police photo of the corpse, a second one turned up in 1989 after we had started *FROM HELL*. I didn't see it till many years after we finished. It's from the same angle as our last three panels.

PAGE 18. (501 words) PANEL 1. (short edit)
A SEVEN-PANEL PAGE HERE, WITH THE BIG WIDE PANEL IN THE MIDDLE AND THREE SMALL ONES ON THE TOP AND BOTTOM TIERS. IN THIS FIRST PANEL WE HAVE CLOSED IN ON THE BEDSIDE TABLE. WE SEE GULL'S HAND ENTER FROM THE LEFT AND PICK UP THE SEVERED BREAST.

PANEL 3.
SAME SHOT, BUT NOW GULL HAS COME CLOSER. LEANING OVER TOWARDS US HE CAREFULLY PLACES THE SEVERED BREAST JUST TO THE RIGHT OF THE WOMAN'S RIGHT FOOT. HIS EXPRESSION IS VERY SERIOUS AND HIS ATTENTION TOTALLY CONCENTRATES ON WHAT HE IS DOING.

PANEL 4.
...THE MURDERED WOMAN'S HEAD POINTING TOWARDS THE RIGHT. SHE LIES THERE WITH HER LIVER BETWEEN HER FEET, ONE BREAST TO THE RIGHT OF HER RIGHT FOOT AND THE JUMBLE OF GLANDS AND ORGANS BENEATH HER HEAD. GULL'S BLADE LIES ON THE BED BY HER SIDE. WE SEE GULL HIMSELF FROM ABOVE AS HE STARES DOWN AT THE BODY. HE CUPS HIS CHIN AND REGARDS IT PENSIVELY. HE HAS THE EXACT AIR OF AN ARTIST STEPPING BACK FROM HIS CANVAS FOR A MOMENT TO JUDGE AS TO WHAT FURTHER STROKES ARE NECESSARY. HE REGARDS THE ARRANGEMENT OF THE BODY AND ITS ORGANS CRITICALLY: WHAT ELSE DOES THE COMPOSITION NEED?

Chapter 10, pages 21, 22.

This scene has an Alan Moore line that is much quoted: "It would seem we are to suffer an apocalypse of cockatoos." It goes on: "…Morose, barbaric children playing joylessly with your unfathomable toys. With all your shimmering numbers…" Regarding these numbers, on the cover of the original edition of this chapter I depicted a candle almost burned out beside a cell phone. Kitchen Sink Press were so perplexed by the image of a cell phone in a nineteenth century context that they nearly didn't notice it was their own number being called on the LCD. They printed it anyway. (vol 7, April 1995. see page 100 here).

We might find ourselves agreeing with Gull's profound soliloquy and then abruptly pull ourselves up and remember, as he in fact tells us, more or less, that it's a Grand Guignol theatre of horrors we're attending. Imagine what the movie might have made of it all if it had got past the whodunit cliché. This could have knocked the spots off Hannibal Lecter for grandiose villainy.

PAGE 21. (722 words) PANEL 1.
A SEVEN PANEL PAGE HERE, WITH THREE PANELS ON EACH OF THE UPPER TWO TIERS AND THEN ONE PANEL ON THE BOTTOM TIER. IN THIS FIRST PANEL, UP IN THE FOREGROUND, WE CAN SEE PART OF SOMEONE WORKING A PHOTOCOPY MACHINE, WITH MULTIPLE COPIES OF SOME IMAGE OR OTHER WHIRRING OUT OF THE SLOT. ALL AROUND THERE ARE TECHNOLOGIES, STYLES AND FASHIONS UNIMAGINABLE EVEN TO AN ENLIGHTENED AND FORWARD-THINKING VICTORIAN. SOMEWHERE IN THE NEAR BACKGROUND, GULL STANDS AMONGST THE ROWS OF DESKS, NEXT TO THE MURDERED WOMAN ON HER BED AND LOOKS ROUND AT THE OFFICE WONDERINGLY AS HE COMMENCES HIS SOLILOQUY.
GULL: Dear God, what is this Aethyr I am come upon?
GULL: What spirits are these, labouring in what heavenly light?

PANEL 2.
IN THE FOREGROUND A YOUNG POST-PUNK TEMP WORKER PASSES BY, WITH SEVERAL RINGS IN HER EAR AND A STUD IN HER NOSE, HER HAIR RAISED UP INTO A STILL PEAK, THICK WITH GEL. WE

SEE HER ROUGHLY HEAD AND SHOULDERS TO HALF FIGURE AS SHE PASSES. SHE IS WORKING OUT A SUM ON A HAND-HELD ELECTRONIC CALCULATOR. IN THE NEAR BACKGROUND, GULL WATCHES HER PASS, GAZING AT HER WITH AN AWED AND INCREDULOUS EXPRESSION. THE BUTCHERED CORPSE LIES ON THE STAINED BED IMMEDIATELY BEHIND HIM. ALL AROUND IN THE BACKGROUND BEHIND HIM WE CAN SEE OFFICE LIFE GOING ON AS NORMAL.

GULL: No...No, this is dazzle, but not yet divinity. Nor are these
                    heathen wraiths about me spirits, lacking even that vitality.

PANEL 3.

CHANGE ANGLE SO THAT THE MUTILATED FACE OF THE CORPSE IN RESTING ON THE BLOODY PILLOW DOWN IN THE BOTTOM FOREGROUND. LOOKING UP PAST THIS WE SEE GULL AS HE STANDS WITH HIS BACK TOWARDS US GAZING OUT OVER THE OFFICE FULL OF WORKERS AND GESTURING WITH HIS HANDS (ONE OF WHICH STILL HOLDS THE BLOODY KNIFE) AS HE SPEAKS.

GULL: What, then? Am I, like Saint John the Divine, vouchsafed a
                    glimpse of those last times?

GULL: Are these the days my death shall spare me?

PANEL 4.

SOMEWHERE IN THE FOREGROUND, A YOUNG MAN WITH A DIGITAL WATCH IS TYPING AT A COMPUTER KEYBOARD. HE DOES NOT BLINK OR PAY ANY ATTENTION AS THE PORTLY FORM OF GULL STARTS TO CLAMBER LABORIOUSLY UP PAST HIM AND ONTO AN OPEN SPACE ON THE DESK TOP, DECLAIMING WHILE HE DOES SO. ALL AROUND, OFFICE LIFE GOES ON AS NORMAL.

GULL: It would seem we are to suffer an apocalypse of cockatoos...
GULL: Morose, barbaric children playing joylessly with their
                    unfathomable toys.

PANEL 5.

MAYBE WE CHANGE ANGLE SLIGHTLY. THE MAN IS STILL TYPING, UNCONCERNED AND UNAWARE, AS GULL RISES UNSTEADILY TO HIS FEET ATOP THE SHINY DESKTOP, STILL DECLAIMING EARNESTLY TO THE UNHEEDING OFFICE.

GULL: Where comes this dullness in your eyes? How has your
                    century numbed you so?

GULL: Shall man be given marvels only when he is beyond all wonder?

PANEL 6.

NOW, SUDDENLY, WE ARE BACK IN MARY KELLY'S ROOM AT MILLER'S COURT. THE DEAD WOMAN'S BODY LIES IN THE FOREGROUND OF THE PICTURE, STILL SPRAWLED UPON THE BED. LOOKING PAST THIS, WE ARE LOOKING INTO THE CRAMPED CONFINES OF THE TINY SLUM ROOM. GULL, IN THE MIDDLE OF THE ROOM, IS STANDING PERCHED UPON THE CHAIR ON WHICH HE HUNG HIS JACKET EARLIER. HANDS SPREAD, HE SPEAKS WITH GREAT PASSION TO THE EMPTY ROOM.

GULL: Your days were born in blood and fires, whereof in you I may
                    not see the meanest spark!

GULL: Your past is pain and iron! Know yourselves!

PANEL 7.

IN THIS LAST WIDE PANEL, WE ARE BACK IN THE OFFICE. WE ARE LOOKING UP FROM A LOW ANGLE AT GULL AS HE STANDS THERE UPON THE DESKTOP, HANDS SPREAD AS HE ADDRESSES THE HORDE OF NINETIES OFFICE WORKERS WHO ALL CONTINUE WITH THEIR LABOURS, NOT PAYING HIM ANY

ATTENTION, HIS EYES ARE FILLED WITH ZEALOT FIRE AS HE SPEAKS.

GULL: With all your shimmering numbers and your lights, think not to be inured to history. Its black root succours you. It is INSIDE you!

GULL: Are you asleep to it, that cannot feel its breath upon your neck, nor see what soaks its cuffs?

GULL: See me! Wake and look upon me! I am come amongst you. I am with you always!

PAGE 22. (647 words) (edited, 4 panels out of 7) PANEL 3.

CLOSER IN ON GULL NOW AS HE STARTS TO CROUCH DOWN ON THE DESK TOP, PREPARING TO CLIMB BACK DOWN TO THE OFFICE FLOOR. HE LOOKS SUBDUED AND UPSET. THE TWENTIETH CENTURY BOYS AND GIRLS ABOUT HIM PAY HIM ABSOLUTELY NO ATTENTION WHATSOEVER. THE GUY SITTING AT THE DESK THAT GULL IS ON CONTINUES TO TYPE, EYES FIXED ON HIS MONITOR SCREEN.

GULL: How would I seem to you? Some antique fiend or penny dreadful horror, yet you frighten me!

GULL: You have not souls. With you I am alone.

PANEL 4

ON THE FOREGROUND NOW WE SEE A GLIMPSE OF THE BUTCHERED WOMAN LYING ON THE BED, IGNORED BY THE OFFICE STAFF. LOOKING BEYOND THIS WE SEE GULL AS HE CLIMBS BACK DOWN TO THE FLOOR. IN PASSING HE LOOKS AT THE SCREEN OF THE COMPUTER THAT THE YOUNG SEATED MAN BESIDE HIM IS TYPING AT.

GULL: Alone in an Olympus. Though accomplished in the sciences, your slightest mechanisms are beyond my grasp.

GULL: They HUMBLE me, yet they touch you not at all.

PANEL 5.

SAME SHOT. GULL IS NOW WALKING SLOWLY AND SADLY BACK ACROSS THE OFFICE TOWARDS THE BED AND THE MURDERED WOMAN IN THE FOREGROUND. HE GAZES AT THEM MELANCHOLICALLY AS HE APPROACHES, KNIFE IN HAND. THE OFFICE BUSTLES ALL ABOUT HIM, UNAWARE OF HIS PRESENCE.

GULL: This disaffection. THIS is Armageddon.

GULL: Ah, Mary, how time's levelled us. We are made equal, both mere curios of our vanished epoch in this lustless world.

PANEL 7.

IN THIS LAST WIDE PANEL, GULL CLOSES HIS EYES AND GATHERS THE UPPER PART OF THE DEAD WOMAN'S BODY UP IN HIS ARMS; HUGGING HER RAW CHEST TO HIM IN A TIGHT, INTENSE EMBRACE THAT IS ALMOST TEARFUL. HER ARMS DANGLE LIMPLY BY HER SIDES AS GULL HUGS HER, AND WE NOTE THAT THEY ARE COVERED WITH NUMEROUS CUTS AND SLASHES THAT SHE'S PRESUMABLY PICKED UP ALONG THE WAY. PROBABLY WE COULD SEE THEM EARLIER AS WELL. GULL CRUSHES HER TO HIS BOSOM AND BURIES HIS FACE IN HER BLOODY SHOULDER. BIG AND INTENSE IN THE FOREGROUND IT IS A MOMENT OF PURE AND AWFUL LOVE. IN THE BACKGROUND THE MODERN OFFICE SCENE CONTINUES UNABATED.

No dialogue

Chapter 10, pages 24-34. Working out the remainder of the chapter.

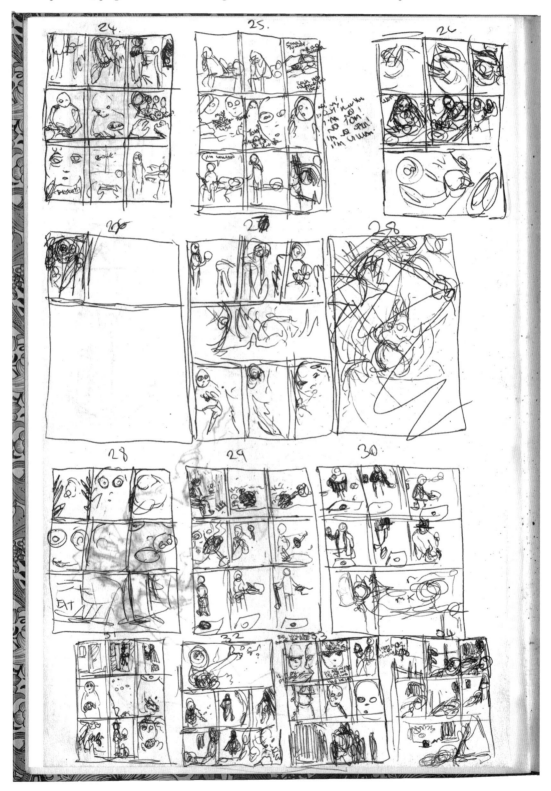

Chapter 10, page 32.

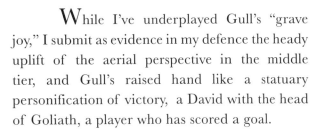While I've underplayed Gull's "grave joy," I submit as evidence in my defence the heady uplift of the aerial perspective in the middle tier, and Gull's raised hand like a statuary personification of victory, a David with the head of Goliath, a player who has scored a goal.

PAGE 32 (589 words) (4 panels only) PANEL 1. IN THIS FIRST CINEMASCOPE PANEL WE HAVE A SHOT OF GULL, PROBABLY HALF FIGURE. HOLDING HIS HAT CLASPED TO HIS BREAST WITH ONE HAND, WITH THE OTHER HE FLINGS THE ASHES OF THE DEAD WOMAN TO THE NIGHT, THE WIND AND THE STARS. HIS ARM IS OUTFLUNG AND FOR A MOMENT A KIND OF GRAVE JOY CROSSES HIS FACE; A KIND OF RAPTURE. THE ASHES WHIRL UP INTO THE NIGHT, INTO THE SCINTILLATING COGS OF THE ETERNAL STARRY DYNAMO. I WANT THIS PANEL TO LOOK AFFECTING AND LYRICAL AS YOU CAN MAKE IT.

PANEL 2.
WE ARE SLIGHTLY ABOVE GULL, LOOKING DOWN AT HIM, LOOKING UP AT US, HIS HAND STILL OUTFLUNG TOWARDS US. THE ASHES WHIRLING UP INTO THE FOREGROUND. TO GULL'S RIGHT (OUR LEFT) AS WE LOOK DOWN, WE CAN SEE A LITTLE OF THE ALLEY ENTRANCE THAT LEADS FROM MILLER'S COURT TO DORSET STREET. THE ASHES DANCE AND FLUTTER AS THEY RISE TOWARDS US.

PANEL 3.
MOVING STILL HIGHER...LOOKING DOWN AT ALL THIS FROM OUR SHEER PERSPECTIVE. THE ASHES OF THE DEAD WOMAN'S HEART SHIFT AND WHIRL IN A RIBBON OF TOOTHBRUSH FLECKS THROUGH THE FOREGROUND, DISPERSING, DISSOLVING INTO THE NIGHT.

PANEL 4.
SAME SHOT, BUT WE HAVE PULLED UP STILL, HIGHER ABOVE THE YARD. DOWN BELOW US WE SEE GULL HAS PICKED UP THE GLADSTONE BAG AND IS STARTING TO DISAPPEAR INTO THE ALLEY MOUTH THAT WILL LEAD HIM BACK TO DORSET STREET. ALL AROUND US THERE IS NIGHT AND DARKNESS AS THE TINY FIGURE BELOW PREPARES TO LEAVE THE SILENT COURTYARD. IN THE FOREGROUND, THE ASHES ARE DISPERSED AND GONE.

Chapter 10: an alternative ending

The 1994 synopsis (see page 171) contains passages which are quite different from the way they would turn out in the finished book. The summary of Chapter 10 demands to be shown here in full. One of its interesting features is the use of Ripperologist Colin Wilson's theory that the murderer worked naked. Alan tries it on here before rejecting it. A gain often involves a sacrifice. The soliloquy in the office, not in this early version, would have looked foolish if spoken by a man with his shirt off.

CHAPTER X: THE BEST OF ALL TAILORS

In contrast with our last chapter, this one is fairly simple to describe. It all takes place in the room at Miller's Court on the night of November 9th. Over thirty or forty pages, in excruciating real time, we watch Gull dissect Marie Kelly. This is the heart of his madness and his magic. This is the culmination of his blood alchemy. As he works upon the dismantling of the human body, we see through his eyes, zooming in along the coagulating tunnels of the arteries and orbiting around the cardiac cathedral chambers of the cooling heart. We see the heraldry of the rib cage laid bare, and we hear Gull describe the beautiful iridescent colours of the intestines as if they were a Cezanne painting. Every so often we are allowed to pull back briefly from our rapture to see the stark reality of the butchered woman on the bed beneath us, but then the hallucinatory glow enfolds us and we start once more to cut and to excise, muttering to ourself as we do so. The breasts are removed and placed upon the table. Reminded of the dome of St. Paul's cathedral, we laugh. After a while, we forget where we are and imagine that we're back in Guy's hospital, delivering an anatomical lecture to a bunch of eager students. The students sit behind us in their rows as we orate, all taking notes, their eyes bright and fixated. Amongst them there are recognizable faces: Peter Sutcliffe, the Yorkshire Ripper; Charles Manson; the Son of Man; and David Berkowitz, the Son of Sam. Gull's lecture drones on and the students' hands move across their notebook pages.

After a moment this delusion passes and we are back in the room, looking at the butchered body, which is now much worse than when we last saw it. Realizing that the heart will need to be burned to fulfill the ritual, Gull stokes up the fire in the room by burning some old clothing that he has found in one corner. The heat quickly becomes fierce, partially melting the kettle that stands in the hearth. Stripping to the waist, his pale and pendulous teats bearded with fine white hair, Gull picks up his knife and once more returns to his work. The hours crawl by, marked in gore and hallucination. He removes the woman's

heart and burns it in the raging fire, the sweat and blood trickling down across his naked belly. Angels are singing somewhere high above him. He licks his lips and tastes the holy blood of saints, which by now he is covered with. The heart, being muscle, does not burn easily, but eventually it is ash. Gull takes the pulverized remains of it to the front door and scatters them upon the night wind in accordance with the ritual. This is the perfect, sublime moment, frozen in the amber of Eternity.

The moment is followed by a sudden slump, a crash. The manic energy that has been firing Gull for so many chapters finally drains from him and an uneasy depression starts to slowly settle in. Returning to the room, he stares long and hard at the destroyed body of the woman, and knows it for what it is. Donning his clothing untidily he stumbles out into the dark pre-dawn streets and makes for where Netley and the coach have been waiting all this time, by the obelisk in Hanbury Street. As he passes in front of Christ Church Spitalfields he sees a figure in Seventeenth century dress and wearing a white periwig. The figure waves solemnly to him from between the giant Doric columns of the church, and then is gone. Sweating and trembling, Gull hurries on to where Netley waits. Explaining that he wishes to walk for a while in order to clear his head, Gull dismisses the coachman and walks through the dark streets of Whitechapel where he used to walk with Hinton in the old days, wandering further north towards the sordid slums of Hackney where Saxons once worshipped the murderer of the Moon in London Fields.

As he walks, Gull is seized by the horrifying conviction that his work is over now. His pinnacle has been reached and now is past. He feels that it would have been better if he had died there in that room, united with Mary Kelly in her death, their glorious moment together, sustained for all time. Depressed and lost, he wanders down Vallance Road. Passing a room of houses with cellar-rooms he hears a voice in the night, a rough male voice that calls out "Come back, Jack, and die like a man!" He looks round, startled. A bright and unearthly light is issuing from one of the basement rooms in the row (unearthly by Victorian standards, that is. Just plain electric lighting by ours). Gull sees a man struggling, trying to get out of the window, another man, the man whose voice Gull heard, hauls him roughly back in and glares out into the night. It is the 1960s gangster, Ronnie Kray. Gull turns away and covers his eyes, trembling. When he opens them again, the vision is gone. Shuddering against the November cold, Gull trudges off, a frightened old man, alone in the ancient London night. End of Chapter X

Part 7
Pages 229 to 247.
There were scenes of
the plotters at work, but
for some reason I've
picked pages where our
players are completely
in the dark.
Let that be our
stated theme.

Chapter 11, page 1.

A surreal cricket match. The surreal part about it is that it is taking place in winter. I did mention this to Alan at the time, but here we are anyway. Nobody else has ever said anything. Alan had worked out the entire chapter and cricket played a symbolic role in it (page 33, and page 46 with the lone batsman walking off the pitch), to the extent that it could not now be replaced by rugby football, the winter sport of English schools, or soccer, or tiddlywinks, or even hookey, which was my own sport of choice. You might recall however, that Druitt's chapter was originally set much earlier in the "program," just after Annie Chapman's murder on September 8 (see my notes on page 14 here) and cricket in Britain conventionally runs to mid-September.

But why am I complaining? To be able to draw several pages of cricket in an American-published comic book! Who'd have ever thought that could happen? Who else's Jack the Ripper has cricket in it?

PAGE 1. (670 words) PANEL 1.
THERE ARE SIX PANELS ON THIS FIRST PAGE WITH THIS FIRST PANEL BEING THE TITLE PANEL AND THEN A DOUBLE-WIDTH PANEL COMPLETING THE TOP TIER. THERE ARE THREE PANELS ON THE MIDDLE TIER AND THEN ONE BIG PANEL ON THE BOTTOM TIER. IN THIS FIRST PANEL, WE JUST HAVE THE TITLES.

TITLE: Chapter Eleven.
                       The Unfortunate Mr.Druitt.

PANEL 2.
WE ARE ON THE COMMON AT BLACKHEATH, AND IT IS EARLY TO MID-MORNING, FRIDAY NOVEMBER 9TH, 1988. THE BOYS FROM BLACKHEATH SCHOOL ARE PLAYING CRICKET ON THE COMMON, DRESSED IN THEIR OLD-FASHIONED WHITES. IN THE LEFT OF THE EXTREME FOREGROUND HERE WE CAN SEE THE WICKET, JUST AS IF WE WERE CROUCHED BEHIND IT WITH THE WICKET KEEPER. JUTTING INTO THE LEFT OF THE FOREGROUND WE CAN SEE THE HANDS OF THE BOY WHO IS UP TO BAT, HOLDING HIS CRICKET BAT WITH THE BLADE ENTERING THE LEFT OF THE FOREGROUND HERE. LOOKING PAST THIS WE ARE LOOKING ALONG THE LENGTH OF THE CRICKET PITCH TOWARDS THE FAR END, WHERE WE SEE THE BOWLER AS HE COMPLETES HIS RUN-UP AND LETS FLY WITH THE BALL. IT HURTLES TOWARDS US, SEEMING TO HANG FROZEN IN MIDAIR HERE. ALL AROUND THE FIELDERS ARE FANNED OUT, HOPPING NERVOUSLY BACK AND

FORTH LIKE GREAT ALBINO WATERFOWL BENEATH THE GREY AND OVERCAST SOUTH LONDON SKY.
No dialogue.

PANEL 3.

NOW WE CHANGE ANGLE, SWINGING AROUND TO THE SIDE OR FRONT OF THE WICKET FOR
A HALF-FIGURE CLOSE-UP OF THE YOUNG BATSMAN AS HE HITS THE BALL. LIKE ALL
OF THE BOYS PLAYING CRICKET ON THE COMMON HE IS ABOUT FIFTEEN OR SIXTEEN. HE
IS A SLIGHTLY BUILT BLOND BOY WITH GIRLISH GOOD LOOKS. HIS FEATURES SET IN
CONCENTRATION HERE AS HE SMACKS HIS BAT INTO THE HARD BALL WITH A CRACK THAT
SHOULD BE ALMOST AUDIBLE DESPITE THE LACK OF SOUND EFFECTS.
No dialogue.

PANEL 4.

PULL BACK FROM THE WICKET A LITTLE ALONG THE LENGTH OF THE PITCH. THE YOUNG
BATSMAN HAS STARTED TO RUN, AND ALL WE CAN SEE OF HIM HERE IS PERHAPS ONE OF HIS
PADDED LEGS AND ONE TRAILING HAND STILL CLUTCHING THE BAT, BOTH PROTRUDING
INTO THE PANEL FROM THE LEFT-HAND BORDER AS HE RUNS OFF PANEL IN THE FOREGROUND.
LOOKING BEYOND HIS WE CAN SEE THE WICKET HE HAS VACATED WITH THE YOUNG WICKET
KEEPER CROUCHED BEHIND IT. LOOKING FURTHER BACK STILL WE CAN SEE THE FIGURE OF
MONTAGUE DRUITT, THE SCHOOLTEACHER WHO HAPPENS TO BE SUPERVISING THE MATCH, AS HE
STANDS THERE AT THE EDGE OF THE PITCH CHEERING THE BOYS ON. HE IS DRESSED IN AN
OVERCOAT AND SCARF, HIS HANDS DEEP IN HIS POCKET. HE IS PROBABLY TOO FAR AWAY TO
SEE MUCH OF HERE, BUT HIS GENERAL BEARING SUGGESTS A KEEN SPORTING EXCITEMENT.
DRUITT: Oh, bravo, Glover! Well played!

PANEL 5.

CLOSE IN UPON DRUITT FOR A HALF-FIGURE SHOT HERE. HE STILL HAS ONE HAND IN
HIS COAT POCKET BUT HE HAS RAISED THE OTHER ONE TO HIS MOUTH AS IF IT WERE A
MEGAPHONE, TO AMPLIFY HIS VOICE AS HE CALLS OUT TO THE OFF-PANEL BOYS. HE LOOKS
HAPPY AND FLUSHED WITH THE EXCITEMENT OF THE GAME, THE NOVEMBER WIND RUFFLING HIS
NEAT HAIR. HIS DEEP, DARK EYES SPARKLE WITH ENTHUSIASM AND CONTENTMENT.
DRUITT: Come ON, you can get three OFF THAT!
DRUITT: Run for it, lad! RUN for it!

PANEL 6.

NOW WE HAVE THE BIG PANEL TAKING UP THE BOTTOM TIER, WE SEE THE PITCH FROM SIDE
ON, WITH THE TWO BATSMEN JUST CROSSING OVER IN THE MIDDLE AS THEY RUN FRANTICALLY
TOWARDS THEIR OPPOSING ENDS ALONG A PITCH STREWN WITH DEAD LEAVES UNDER A SKY
FULL OF RAGGED GREY CLOUDS. FROM THE BACKGROUND A FIELDER THROWS THE BALL BACK
TOWARDS THE BOWLER. THE OTHER FIELDERS SHUFFLE ANXIOUSLY. IN THE DISTANCE, FAR
BEHIND THEM, THE ASH-COLOURED CITY SMOKES AND SMOULDERS INDUSTRIOUSLY BENEATH THE
LEADEN SKY. AGAINST THE MIASMA, THE WHITE OF THE BOYS IS ALMOST LUMINOUS.
No dialogue.

Chapter 11, page 3.

In which Mr. Druitt is shown to have homosexual tendencies, the "difference" that will make him an ideal scapegoat. I notice that I haven't shown him placing his hand on the boy's shoulder. I can't remember if that was a decision or just an omission. Sometimes another panel lends its information to the ones around it, even if the relevant character is not in it. In this case, the panel at the bottom had it covered.

PAGE 3. (516 words) (highlights only) PANEL 1. ... IN THIS FIRST PANEL WE ARE ON BLACKHEATH COMMON. WE SEE THE HANDS OF ONE OF THE YOUNG FIELDERS ENTERING THE PANEL FROM OFF BELOW AND CATCHING THE CRICKET BALL THAT HAS DROPPED FROM ABOVE, OUT OF A SKY THE COLOUR OF TOOTHACHE...

PANEL 2.
NOW WE CAN SEE DRUITT IN THE F/G... HE IS WATCHING THE BLOND YOUNG BATSMAN, GLOVER, AS HE RETIRES FROM THE CREASE, WALKING DEJECTEDLY TOWARDS US AND DRUITT WITH HIS CRICKET BAT TRAILING IN ONE HAND WHILE THE GAME GOES ON BEHIND HIM. DRUITT GAZES AT THE BOY WITH CALF-LIKE EYES FULL OF SYMPATHY AND COMPASSION. HE LOOKS LOVESICK.

PANEL 3.
DRUITT STANDS ON THE LEFT, FACING RIGHT AS HE GAZES FONDLY DOWN AT GLOVER, THE BOY. HE REACHES OUT AND PLACES A CONSOLING HAND UPON THE BOY'S SHOULDER. GLOVER STARES UP AT HIM LEVELLY, HIS EYES FULL OF TRUST AND RESPECT.

DRUITT: Jolly bad luck that, Glover. Bit of trouble with the spin on
                     that last ball, eh?
DRUITT: Still, well done! How many did you notch up all told?

PANEL 6
DRUITT STANDS PARTLY VISIBLE, FACING MOSTLY AWAY FROM US IN THE FOREGROUND HEAD AND SHOULDERS, GAZING LONGINGLY AFTER THE DEPARTING FORM OF GLOVER, WHO WE SEE FROM THE REAR AS HE WALKS AWAY FROM US INTO THE BACKGROUND, BACK ACROSS THE COMMON TOWARDS THE ROAD AND THE SCHOOL BEYOND. NICE BUM.

PANEL 7
A WIDE-ANGLE SHOT OF THE SCHOOL CHANGING ROOMS, WITH ANTIQUATED SHOWERS PARTLY VIS-IBLE. VICTORIAN SCHOOLBOYS ARE SHOWERING, GETTING CHANGED, TORMENTING EACH OTHER PHYSICALLY AND VERBALLY. A FUG OF SWEAT AND STEAM AND TESTOSTERONE.
No dialogue

Chapter 11, page 5.

I changed a point-of-view here on account of my own personal pictorial logic. While it's commonplace technique in movies and comics to move the "camera" to any position where it will best show the situation, it's not commonplace with me. I would tend not to put it in a location where there is no living person to have such a "point-of-view," which is the case here with the murder room. It's the lens of cruel Fate anyway that has Abberline shifting in and out of view in that central tier of panels. In the movie, when he found the strand of hair in that room that was not golden-red, Johnny Depp/Fred understood the thing that he could never tell anybody and would take to his early opium-scrambled grave. Our Fred on the other hand, will be declining into disgruntled old age never knowing, which strikes me as more like real life. In fact this chapter is mainly alternating scenes between the detective and the scapegoat, neither of whom has a clue as to what's really going on.

PAGE 5. (882 words) PANEL 1.
A NINE-PANEL PAGE HERE. IN THIS FIRST PANEL WE ARE IN THE YARD OF MILLER'S COURT AND IT IS MAYBE AN HOUR LATER. WE ARE LOOKING FROM OUTSIDE NUMBER THIRTEEN DOWN THE LENGTH OF THE ALLEY LEADING TO THE STREET. GATHERED IN THE YARD, NOT ALL OF THEM VISIBLE HERE, ARE A COUPLE OF UNIFORMED POLICEMEN AND A COUPLE OF PLAINCLOTHESMEN INCLUDING DETECTIVE SERGEANT GODLEY. BOWYER AND McCARTHY ARE ALSO SOMEWHERE AROUND, ALTHOUGH LIKE I SAY, IT ISN'T NECESSARY TO SEE MORE THAN A GLIMPSE OF ANY OF THESE IN THE FIRST PANEL. OUR MAIN FOCUS OF ATTENTION IS ON INSPECTOR ABBERLINE AS HE COMES WALKING DOWN THE ALLEYWAY TOWARDS US FROM DORSET STREET, LOOKING SOMBRE.
HE IS DRESSED CONSPICUOUSLY DIFFERENTLY TO WHEN WE LAST SAW HIM; TONIGHT IS THE NIGHT THAT FRED HAS HIS DATE WITH 'EMMA' AND HE'S PUT ON HIS BEST CLOTHES FOR THE OCCASION AND PONCED HIMSELF UP A BIT. THE ATTEMPT AT SARTORIAL ELEGANCE LOOKS SADLY GAUCHE AND OUT OF PLACE IN THE SLAUGHTER-YARD ATMOSPHERE OF MILLER'S COURT.
No dialogue

PANEL 2.
STILL IN THE YARD. GODLEY STANDS FACING AWAY FROM US IN THE RIGHT OF THE FOREGROUND, HEAD AND SHOULDERS WITH ONLY A LITTLE OF HIS PROFILE VISIBLE AS

HE FACES TOWARDS THE RECENTLY ARRIVED ABBERLINE WHO WE SEE FACING GODLEY AND
US FROM THE NEAR LEFT BACKGROUND, HALF FIGURE TO HEAD AND SHOULDERS. GODLEY
LOOKS A BIT PALE AND DRAINED OF COLOUR. WHILE ABBERLINE JUST LOOKS GRUFF AND
BUSINESSLIKE AS EVER.

ABBERLINE: Alright, Godley? What's everybody doin' standin' about in
                       the yard?

GODLEY: Superintendent Arnold, Sir. He thought we should wait until
                       Sir Charles could bring 'is bloodhounds before we went in.

PANEL 3.

MAYBE A FULL-FIGURE SHOT OF BOTH MEN NOW AS THEY STAND THERE IN THE YARD, STILL
WITH ABBERLINE TOWARDS THE LEFT AND GODLEY TOWARDS THE RIGHT. HERE, BOTH MEN
ARE STANDING SO THAT THEY'RE ANGLED SLIGHTLY AWAY FROM US, STANDING GAZING
TOWARDS THE SIDE OF NUMBER THIRTEEN WITH THE BROKEN WINDOW, WHICH GODLEY IS
POINTING TO HERE. ABBERLINE FOLLOWS HIS GAZE, ALSO LOOKING IN THE WINDOW, ITS
BROKEN PANE AND ITS VEIL OF RAG.

ABBERLINE: Not them fuckin' dogs! How long 'ave you been waitin' 'ere,
                       then?

GODLEY: The rentman called us about eleven. He'd seen her through
                       the window there.

PANEL 4.

NOW WE ARE INSIDE NUMBER THIRTEEN, JUST INSIDE THE BROKEN WINDOW AND LOOKING
OUT. IN THIS FIRST PANEL ON THE TIER WE SEE ABBERLINE'S HAND REACHING THROUGH
THE WINDOW AND PULLING BACK THE DIRTY CURTAIN. BEYOND THAT WE CAN SEE HIS FACE
AS HE PEERS THROUGH INTO THE ROOM. HIS EXPRESSION IS SOBER AND NEUTRAL HERE.

No dialogue

PANEL 5.

SAME SHOT AS LAST PANEL. STILL WITH ABBERLINE PEERING IN AT US THROUGH THE
BROKEN WINDOW AS HE HOLDS BACK THE CURTAIN. HERE, HIS FACE REGISTERS WHAT HE
IS SEEING INSIDE THE ROOM; NOT BUG-EYED, JAW-DROPPING SURPRISE OR HORROR, BUT
SOMETHING SUBTLER. HE JUST ABOUT STARES, LEVELLY AND WITHOUT MUCH EXPRESSION,
BUT THERE'S SOMETHING AROUND HIS EYES. HE'S SEEING ONE OF THE ANTEROOMS OF HELL
AND HE'S NOT FLINCHING.

No dialogue

PANEL 6.

SAME SHOT, BUT HERE ABBERLINE HAS LET THE RAG FALL BACK ACROSS THE INSIDE OF
THE BROKEN WINDOW AS HE PULLS BACK HIS HANDS. HE DOESN'T WANT TO LOOK ANY MORE,
AND WE CAN NO LONGER SEE HIM. WE ARE LEFT STARING AT THE INSIDE OF THE BROKEN
WINDOW WITH ITS FILTHY CURTAIN HANGING LIMPLY.

No dialogue

PAGE 7.

WE ARE OUTSIDE IN THE YARD AGAIN. ABBERLINE, IN THE FOREGROUND HERE AND ROUGHLY

HEAD AND SHOULDERS IS TURNING AWAY FROM US (AND, PRESUMABLY, THE OFF-PANEL WINDOW) TO LOOK TOWARDS GODLEY WHO WE SEE LOUNGING MISERABLY IN THE NEAR BACKGROUND.

ABBERLINE: Hmm. What 'appens now, then?

GODLEY: Dunno. The door's spring-locked. I expect we wait for Tom Arnold to get back, then smash it in.

PAGE 8.

CHANGE ANGLE SO THAT WE'RE LOOKING TOWARDS THE WALL WITH THE BROKEN WINDOW, WHERE ABBERLINE STANDS WITH HIS BACK TO THE WINDOW, FULL FIGURE AND FACING US. A LITTLE OF GODLEY... HIS HANDS OR CHEST OR SOMETHING... IS JUST VISIBLE IN THE LEFT FOREGROUND AS HE SPEAKS TO ABBERLINE FROM OFF PANEL. FROM THE NEAR BACKGROUND, THE SMARTLY DRESSED ABBERLINE STANDS WITH HIS HANDS IN HIS COAT POCKETS, FACING US. HE GLOWERS AT GODLEY AND SAYS NOTHING.

GODLEY (OFF):   By the way, sir, you're lookin' very smart.

GODLEY (OFF):   Meetin' somebody?

PANEL 9.

NOW WE HAVE AN AERIAL SHOT, LOOKING DOWN FROM JUST ABOVE THE SPIRE OF CHRIST CHURCH SPITALFIELDS WITH THE FRIDAY BUSTLE OF WHITECHAPEL SPREAD BENEATH US. BY THE CLOCK ON CHTRIST CHURCH, THE TIME IS A COUPLE OF MINUTES BEFORE 1.00 PM.

Old pictures

A second Miller's Court crime scene photo, in addition to the well known one, turned up in 1989 while FROM HELL *was already underway (see page 220 herein). I was recently checking it at the Jack the Ripper Casebook (www.casebook.org). While there, under "Marie Kelly photo archive," I found one of my own drawings. There was no note as to its provenance. It was there among the old pictures, as though it were an actual period piece. April Post assisted me for a time circa 1991/92, and she inked this except for the face and hair. She also worked with me on some of the painted covers you can see in the colour section of this book and pops up again briefly as late as Chapter 8. At that time April would come in on Fridays, and I'd get her to put in textures and other details on pages that Pete and I had already worked on, such as the carpet and blanket on Chapter 8, page 1. The room was required to look* "SQUALID AND YET FAINTLY COSY...WITH SMALL AND POIGNANT FEMININE TOUCHES." *(see pages 135-137 here).*

Chapter 11, page 12.

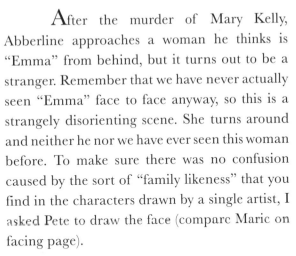

After the murder of Mary Kelly, Abberline approaches a woman he thinks is "Emma" from behind, but it turns out to be a stranger. Remember that we have never actually seen "Emma" face to face anyway, so this is a strangely disorienting scene. She turns around and neither he nor we have ever seen this woman before. To make sure there was no confusion caused by the sort of "family likeness" that you find in the characters drawn by a single artist, I asked Pete to draw the face (compare Maric on facing page).

PAGE 11. (540 words) PANEL 1.
ANOTHER SEVEN-PANEL PAGE, AGAIN WITH ONE BIG WIDE PANEL ON THE UPPERMOST TIER AND THEN THREE PANELS ON EACH OF THE TIERS BENEATH THAT. IN THIS FIRST PANEL WE ARE BEHIND ABBERLINE AS HE WALKS AWAY FROM US PAST THE FRONT OF CHRIST CHURCH, SPITALFIELDS, THE DORIC COLUMNS OF WHICH WE CAN SEE IN THE RIGHT MIDDLEGROUND. LOOKING BEYOND THIS WE CAN SEE THE CORNER OF THE STREET WHERE THE TEN BELLS IS SITUATED. THE PUB LOOKS RELATIVELY WELL LIT AND CHEERY AS ABBERLINE WALKS TOWARDS IT, HIS FACE TURNED AWAY FROM US HERE. MAYBE THERE ARE A COUPLE OF DRUNKEN COUPLES SPILLING OUT OF THE FRONT DOOR AS HE APPROACHES THE PUB, CLING TO EACH OTHER IN AMOROUS INEBRIATION. THERE'S ROMANCE IN THE AIR TONIGHT.
No dialogue

PANEL 2.
NOW WE ARE INSIDE THE TEN BELLS, LOOKING ACROSS THE CROWDED BARROOM TOWARDS THE FRONT DOOR AS ABBERLINE ENTERS IN THE BACKGROUND. LOOKING VERY OUT OF PLACE IN HIS BEST CLOTHES. HE IS ALREADY SCANNING THE PUB FOR SIGNS OF HIS DATE AS HE ENTERS. NOBODY PAYS HIM ANY ATTENTION.
No dialogue

PANEL 3.
NOW ABBERLINE IS IN THE RIGHT FOREGROUND, LOOKING AWAY FROM US INTO THE CROWD AS HE JOSTLES HIS WAY THROUGH THE BARROOM TOWARDS THE BAR, VISIBLE THERE IN THE

BACKGROUND. WE SEE HIM HEAD AND SHOULDERS IN THE RIGHT FOREGROUND HERE, LOOKING
AWAY FROM US TOWARDS THE LEFT MIDDLE GROUND. HIS EYES ARE FIXED UPON THE BACK OF A
WOMAN WHO STANDS FACING DIRECTLY AWAY FROM BOTH US AND FRED. SHE IS ALMOST CERTAINLY
EMMA. ABBERLINE SMILES IN RECOGNITION AS HIS EYES FALL UPON HER.
No dialogue

PANEL 4.

ROUGHLY THE SAME SHOT, BUT NOW WE AND FRED HAVE MOVED CLOSER TO THE WOMAN, WHO STILL
STANDS WITH HER FACE AWAY FROM US. STILL SMILING, FRED REACHES OUT AND CLASPS THE
WOMAN BY ONE SHOULDER AS HE SPEAKS TO HER.

ABBERLINE: Emma? I see you got here early too, then.

ABBERLINE: Will you 'ave a drink, or...

PANEL 5.

SAME SHOT. THE WOMAN TURNS HER HEAD AROUND TO GLARE AT ABBERLINE. IT CLEARLY ISN'T
EMMA. ABBERLINE LOOKS STARTLED, MAYBE HOLDING UP ONE HAND IN MUTE APOLOGY AS HE
BEGINS TO BACK OFF IN CONFUSED EMBARRASSMENT, TOWARDS THE RIGHT OF FOREGROUND HERE.

WOMAN: 'Ere, woss yor game? Bloomin' liberty!

ABBERLINE: Oh, Christ. Sorry, love. I'm sorry. Thought you were
                           somebody else.

ABBERLINE: Sorry.

PANEL 6.

NOW WE ARE BEHIND THE BAR, WHICH WE CAN SEE A BIT OF THE TOP OF, PUDDLED AND
GLISTENING, IN THE BOTTOM FOREGROUND. LOOKING ACROSS THIS WE SEE ABBERLINE AS HE
STANDS THREE-QUARTER FIGURE IN THE MIDDLE GROUND, LOOKING EMBARRASSED AS HE TURNS
HIS FACE SLIGHTLY AWAY FROM US TO WATCH THE OFFENDED EMMA LOOKALIKE WALK AWAY
FROM HIM INTO THE BACKGROUND OF THE PUB. HE RUNS HIS FINGER ROUND HIS COLLAR
NERVOUSLY AND UNCOMFORTABLY AS HE WATCHES HER GO.

PANEL 7.

SAME SHOT AS LAST PANEL, ONLY NOW FRED HAS TURNED ONCE MORE TOWARDS US AND STEPPED
UP TO THE BAR, STILL LOOKING A LITTLE UNCOMFORTABLE AFTER HIS FAUX PAS. HE LOOKS
STRAIGHT TOWARDS US AND PUTS SOME COPPER COINS ON THE BAR AS HE ORDERS HIS DRINK.

ABBERLINE: Pint and a half o' bitter, please.

Abberline. From the 1994 synopsis: *Abberline has agreed to meet his street-girl friend Emma so that she can pay him back the money that she owes him. He is maybe even contemplating going to bed with her this one time. At the pub where they have arranged to meet, the bar-man gives him a note left by Emma. She has taken the money to pay her fare to very far away, and won't be coming back. She says how sorry she is and asks Abberline to forgive her and believe she never meant to hurt him, and that she wouldn't have done it unless she had to. Love Emma. Abberline is crushed, starting to develop the hatred of prostitutes demonstrated in the prologue.*

Chapter 11, page 22.

It's the end of the party that had cameos of several interesting Victorians ("too many art-wallahs" in the dialogue below) including Wilde, Whistler and even Sickert, otherwise forgotten since Chapter 4 in the forward tilt of our narrative. I'm picking this one because it's the opposite of a "typical" page of Alan Moore script. There is very little detail, only 531 words. In fact, by the end of it, when he makes the crack about the bridge, we get the impression that Alan might have been feeling a bit irritable that day. If it was time for tax accounting I could usually detect a rumble of aggravation in the scripts. (For the record, I used the Old Putney Bridge loosely referenced, appropriately, from an 1879 etching by Whistler.)

PAGE 22. (531 words) PANEL 1.
NOW A SEVEN-PANEL PAGE, WITH THREE PANELS ON EACH OF THE UPPER TIERS AND ONE BIG WIDE ONE ON THE BOTTOM. IN THIS FIRST PANEL WE SEE DRUITT DRIFT AIMLESSLY PAST US IN THE FOREGROUND, EYES DARTING ABOUT HIM FOR A GLIMPSE OF SOMEONE HE KNOWS. HE LOOKS TERRIBLY OUT OF PLACE. BEHIND DRUITT AND UNOBSERVED BY HIM HERE WE SEE A MAN LEANING AGAINST THE WALL IN THE IMMEDIATE BACKGROUND AND SIPPING A DRINK. HE IS GAZING SPECULATIVELY AT THE UNAWARE DRUITT, AND WE CAN SEE THAT IT IS MELVILLE MACNAGHTEN, WHO WE MET EARLIER AT THE SUMMIT CONFERENCE WITH ANDERSON AND MONRO.

PANEL 2.
SAME SHOT, BUT HERE MACNAGHTEN SPEAKS TO DRUITT, CAUSING THE YOUNG BARRISTER/ TEACHER TO TURN AND LOOK AT THE SMART-LOOKING EX-MILITARY MAN. MACNAGHTEN SMILES ENGAGINGLY AS HE SPEAKS, MAYBE EXTENDING HIS HAND FOR DRUITT TO SHAKE.

MACNAGHTEN: Hello, there. You look as if you feel the way I always do at these affairs: Fish out of water, eh?

MACNAGHTEN: Name's MacNaghten. Live across the street at number nine.

PANEL 3.
LONG SHOT OF THE TWO AS THEY BOTH SHAKE HANDS. DRUITT STILL A LITTLE UNCERTAIN.

DRUITT: My name's Druitt. Do you like it? Chelsea, I mean.

DRUITT: Not my name.

MACNAGHTEN: Chelsea? It's alright, I suppose. Too many art-wallahs for my liking. What do YOU do?

PANEL 4.

CLOSE IN ON THE TWO OF THEM NOW, PERHAPS IN A SIMILAR SHOT TO PANELS ONE AND TWO. DRUITT IS STILL GLANCING ABOUT HIM NERVOUSLY EVEN AS HE SPEAKS TO MACNAGHTEN. MACNAGHTEN REGARDS DRUITT COOLLY AND SHREWDLY, WEIGHING THE MAN UP.

DRUITT: I'm uh, I'm a teacher. And a barrister.

DRUITT: I don't really socialize a lot, as a rule. O-Other than through cricket, I don't suppose I have that many friends.

MACNAGHTEN: Lone wolf, eh?

PANEL 5.

SAME SHOT, STILL LOOKING UNCOMFORTABLE, DRUITT MAKES HIS APOLOGIES WHILE MACNAGHTEN DOES HIS BEST TO LOOK UNDERSTANDING.

DRUITT: I suppose I am. I'm afraid I don't really feel at ease here. Perhaps I should be going.

DRUITT: Please don't think me rude. I'm very glad I met you.

MACNAGHTEN: Mutual, dear chap, I assure you.

PANEL 6.

SAME SHOT, BUT NOW DRUITT HAS GONE, LEAVING MACNAGHTEN STANDING THERE BY THE WALL. MACNAGHTEN TUGS HIS MOUSTACHE AND GAZES WITH A FROWN OF INTEREST AND CONSIDERATION IN THE DIRECTION THAT DRUITT HAS DEPARTED IN. HE LOOKS PENSIVE AS HE CONSIDERS WHETHER DRUITT ISN'T JUST THE MAN HE AND HIS COLLEAGUES ARE LOOKING FOR.

PANEL 7.

NOW, IN THIS FINAL WIDE PANEL, WE HAVE A SHOT OF DRUITT WALKING HOME, SOUTH ACROSS ONE OF THE BRIDGES. I'M NOT GOING TO SPECIFY WHICH ONE IN CASE YOU GET ALL SMART ON ME AGAIN AND DIG UP REFERENCE TO PROVE THAT IT WAS BEING PAINTED AND VARNISHED THAT PARTICULAR NIGHT OR SOMETHING. IT CAN BE ANY BLOODY BRIDGE YOU WANT. WE ARE DOWN AROUND THE LEVEL OF WATER, LOOKING UP TOWARDS THE BRIDGE AS DRUITT'S LONELY FIGURE WALKS ACROSS IT, ALL ALONE. HE GAZES DOWN MOURNFULLY INTO THE WATER, LITTLE DREAMING HE'LL BE BENEATH IT BEFORE THE YEAR IS OUT.

Druitt. From the 1994 synopsis: *Montague Druitt is not a happy man. A gentle homosexual, devoted to the noble game of cricket and to rights for women, Druitt is a sort of prototypical "New Man." He has just been fired from his job at the school after a disastrous relationship with one of the boys, and his family considers him a gross embarrassment and a perverted sexual monster to boot. He knows that his father has always hated him since he refused to follow the old man into the Freemasons like his brothers had. Often he thinks that the old man would rather he were dead. Druitt is a close neighbour of Oscar Wilde, and we see him mingling shyly with Whistler and Shaw at one of Wilde's parties, invited for his pretty good looks. Also invited, though for different reasons, is Sir Melville MacNaghten, who later became a high ranking police chief and principal commentator upon the Ripper case. He lived just across the street from Druitt. The reader starts to get the impression that Druitt is being singled out for something without his knowledge.*

Chapter 11, page 23

Sometimes favourite pages are ones where everything is just in its right place and the lettering is all legible and the quiet little actions are all just nicely timed. I also wanted to drop this one in here because of the desk diary. Alan started putting it at the beginning of Abberline's scenes in chapter 6. I gave the reader a reason to pay attention to it by making it one of those quote-of-the-day diaries. Then I'd save antique quotations to use on it, little things that might have a resonance if dropped into the *FROM HELL* environment. The one for 13th Nov said: *"It is too late to be ambitious; the mutations of the world are already acted."*
Sir Thomas Browne.

PAGE 23, (646 words) PANEL 1.
NINE PANEL PAGE HERE. HERE IN THIS FIRST SMALL PANEL WE ARE LOOKING AT THE DWINDLING CALENDAR ON ABBERLINE'S DESK AS HIS HAND ENTERS THE FRAME FROM OFF AND TEARS ANOTHER SHEET OFF TO REVEAL TODAY'S DATE, BEING TUESDAY THE 13th OF NOVEMBER. PLEASE FEEL FREE TO STICK IN ANOTHER ONE OF THOSE GREAT QUOTATIONS THAT YOU DIG UP, IF YOU HAVE ROOM. I QUITE LOOK FORWARD TO THEM.
No dialogue

PANEL 2.
WE ARE IN ABBERLINE'S WHITECHAPEL OFFICE, LOOKING IN FROM THE DOORWAY AS GODLEY ENTERS, LOOKING OVER HIS SHOULDER AND INTO THE ROOM AS HE FACES ROUGHLY AWAY FROM US ON THE LEFT OF THE FOREGROUND. ABBERLINE SITS IN THE NEAR BACKGROUND AT HIS DESK, BARELY LOOKING UP AS GODLEY ENTERS. HE IS HALF-READING FROM A NEWSPAPER HE HAS IN HIS HAND AS HE SPEAKS TO GODLEY.

GODLEY: Oh, you're in early. Good morning.

ABBERLINE: What's good about it? And what's all this rubbish in the papers about a "White Eyed man?"

PANEL 3.
REVERSE ANGLE SO THAT ABBERLINE, SEATED, IS LOOKING SLIGHTLY AWAY FROM US IN THE RIGHT FOREGROUND TOWARDS GODLEY, COMING INTO THE ROOM IN THE NEAR LEFT BACKGROUND. WE CAN SEE NOW THAT GODLEY IS CARRYING AN OPENED LETTER IN HIS HAND.

GODLEY: Oh, that. It was that barmy Dr. Holt who was trying to catch the murderer by hanging round Whitechapel in disguise.

GODLEY: His face was blacked up and he was wearing glasses.

PANEL 4,

CHANGE ANGLE AGAIN SO THAT GODLEY, THE OPENED LETTER DANGLING CASUALLY FROM HIS HAND, IS TOWARDS THE FOREGROUND. IN THE NEAR BACKGROUND, ABBERLINE GESTURES TOWARDS THE LETTER IN GODLEY'S HAND WITH IRRITATED CURIOSITY.

GODLEY: Sunday, it happened. The papers just reported his glasses as white-ringed eyes, that's all.

GODLEY: A mob nearly lynched him before we arrested him.

ABBERLINE: Hmph. What's that in yer 'and?

PANEL 5,

FULL-FIGURE LONG SHOT OF BOTH MEN NOW, WITH GODLEY STANDING AND PASSING THE OPENED LETTER TO ABBERLINE AS HE SPEAKS TO HIM. ABBERLINE TAKES THE LETTER FROM GODLEY, LOOKING AT IT WITH A BAD-TEMPERED AND DISMISSIVE EXPRESSION.

GODLEY: Oh, it's just another helpful theory we've had. Some chap reckons we should cover the murder scene with dust.

GODLEY: Says we'd find prints of the murderer's fingers.

ABBERLINE: Bloody amateur detectives.

PANEL 6.

CLOSE-UP OF ABBERLINE'S HAND ENTERING THE PANEL FROM OFF AS HE DISMISSIVELY DROPS THE NOW-CRUMPLED LETTER INTO A WICKER WASTE-PAPER BIN BESIDE HIS DESK. MAYBE GODLEY LOOKS ON AT THIS FROM THE NEAR BACKGROUND.

ABBERLINE: We've 'ad PSYCHICS, we've 'ad Mr. Conan DOYLE's friend, now somebody wants us makin' more of a mess at the murder scene than there is already.

PANEL 7.

CHANGE ANGLE AGAIN SO THAT ABBERLINE IS NOW SEATED LOOKING TOWARDS US FROM LEFT BACKGROUND WITH GODLEY PART VISIBLE IN THE RIGHT FOREGROUND, TALKING TO HIS SEATED SUPERIOR.

ABBERLINE: Dust! I ASK you.

ABBERLINE: Ah, well. Any REAL detective work to be done today, Godley?

GODLEY: Well, there's that woman you wanted to interview again. The wife of the lodging house deputy.

PANEL 8.

NOW ABBERLINE IS SITTING IN THE FOREGROUND AT HIS DESK, SORTING THROUGH SOME PAPERS AND NOT LOOKING UP AT GODLEY AS HE SPEAKS. GODLEY, IN THE BACKGROUND, STARTS TO OPEN THE OFFICE DOOR AND IS ABOUT TO STEP OUTSIDE AT HIS SUPERIOR'S REQUEST.

ABBERLINE: Oh, that's right. The Maxwell woman. I suppose I'd better see 'er, if she's 'ere. Send 'er in, lad, would you?

GODLEY: Right you are.

PANEL 9.

SAME SHOT AS LAST PANEL, BUT NOW GODLEY HAS GONE IN THE BACKGROUND, LEAVING THE DOOR SLIGHTLY AJAR BEHIND HIM. ABBERLINE, AT HIS DESK IN THE FOREGROUND, CONTINUES TO SORT THROUGH HIS PAPERS AS HE WAITS FOR GODLY TO BRING IN MRS. MAXWELL. HE LOOKS SURLY, AND NOT AS IF HE'S IN A VERY GOOD MOOD.

No dialogue

Chapter 11, page 35.

Somebody's always telling somebody else that it'll be alright when really it's all gone to fuck. Two very human little domestic scenes, one after the other. So they seem, and yet with so much going on in them both. First, Druitt arrives home by Hackney cab and is comforted by Bedford, his housemate. In fact, this is his Judas.

PAGE 35. (678 words) PANEL 1.
NINE-PANEL PAGE. IN THIS FIRST PANEL, WE'VE ARRIVED AT KING'S BENCH WALK. IN THE FOREGROUND WE CAN SEE THE COACHMAN'S HANDS AS HE DRIVES OFF, CLENCHED FAST UPON THE REINS. BEYOND THIS, WE SEE DRUITT AS HE WALKS DEJECTEDLY AWAY FROM US DOWN KING'S BENCH WALK.
No dialogue.

PANEL 2.
NOW WE ARE INSIDE NUMBER 9, KING'S BENCH WALK; IN THE HALLWAY WHICH WE LOOK ALONG TOWARDS THE FRONT DOOR. IN THE FOREGROUND WE CAN MAYBE SEE A LITTLE OF THE BANNISTER TO ADVERTISE THAT THERE ARE STAIRS THAT LEAD OFF FROM THE HALL. LOOKING BEYOND THIS TO THE BACKGROUND WE CAN SEE THE FRONT DOOR OF THE HOUSE IS OPEN, WITH MONTAGUE DRUITT STANDING FRAMED IN IT. HE GLANCES UP DEJECTEDLY TOWARDS THE STAIRS AS HE COMES IN.
No dialogue.

PANEL 3.
NOW WE ARE AT THE TOP OF THE STAIRS, ON THE FIRST FLOOR. IN THE FOREGROUND WE HAVE THE DOOR TO DRUITT'S ROOM WHILE LOOKING PAST THIS WE CAN SEE THE TOP OF THE STAIRS, WHERE THEY REACH THE LANDING. DRUITT IS WEARILY MOUNTING THE LAST STEP, GLANCING TOWARDS THE FOREGROUND AND HIS FRONT DOOR AS HE DOES SO, BRIEFCASE HEAVY IN HIS HAND.
No dialogue.

PANEL 4.
NOW WE ARE INSIDE DRUITT'S ROOM, WHICH IS SMALL, COMFORTABLE AND STUDENTISH, WITH PILES OF LAW BOOKS EVERYWHERE. A DESK PILED HIGH WITH BOOKS STANDS IN THE FORE-GROUND, AND WE LOOK UP PAST THIS AT THE DOOR AS DRUITT ENTERS, GLANCING MISERABLY TOWARDS THE DESK AS HE DOES SO.
No dialogue.

PANEL 5.

FULL-FIGURE SHOT OF DRUITT NOW. HE PUTS HIS BRIEFCASE DOWN BESIDE THE ROOM'S
ARMCHAIR, SITS DOWN IN IT WITH HEAD SUNK IN HIS HANDS AND STARTS TO WEEP. THE
SHADOWS LENGTHEN. DRUITT LOOKS ENTIRELY ABJECT AND ALONE.
No dialogue.

PANEL 6.

NOW IT IS SOME FEW MOMENTS LATER. WE ARE LOOKING AT THE SEATED DRUITT FROM THE
DOORWAY OF THE ROOM AS HE SITS WEEPING WITH HIS FACE SUNK IN HIS HANDS. STOOD IN
THE DOORWAY, ALSO LOOKING IN AT DRUITT, WE CAN SEE A LITTLE OF EDWARD HENSLOW
BEDFORD AS HE LOOKS IN ON DRUITT TO SEE IF HE'S ALRIGHT. MAYBE WE JUST SEE BEDFORD
FROM THE SHOULDERS DOWN TO THE WAIST, WITH THE REST CUT OFF BY THE PANEL BORDERS.
LOOKING PAST HIM WE SEE THE ABJECT, MISERABLE DRUITT.

BEDFORD: Monty?

PANEL 7.

NOW CHANGE ANGLES SO THAT WE HAVE DRUITT, HEAD AND SHOULDERS IN THE LEFT OF
FOREGROUND AS HE SITS IN PROFILE TO US, FACING RIGHT. HE HAS ONE HAND UP TO HIS
EYES TO WIPE HIS EYES, EMBARRASSED TO BE CAUGHT IN SUCH A STATE AS THIS. HIS
CHEEKS, BENEATH HIS HAND, ARE HOT AND WET WITH TEARS. WE LOOK UP PAST HIM NOW
AT EDWARD BEDFORD WHO STANDS LOOKING DOWN AT DRUITT WITH A GRAVE EXPRESSION OF
CONCERN ON HIS CHUBBY FACE.

BEDFORD: Alright, old chap? I heard you come in, then I heard you...
                        well, you seemed upset, that's all. Is something wrong?
DRUITT: Oh, Bedford, I'm in such a jam.

PANEL 8.

NOW, AS BEDFORD STANDS BY DRUITT'S CHAIR, DRUITT TURNS ROUND AND THROWS HIS ARMS
ROUND BEDFORD'S WAIST, BURYING HIS WEEPING FACE IN BEDFORD'S PLUSH WAIST-COATED
PAUNCH. BEDFORD LOOKS DOWN AT DRUITT'S HEAD, UNSURE OF WHETHER TO PAT IT
REASSURINGLY OR NOT. HIS HAND HOVERS AND HE LOOKS UNCOMFORTABLE WITH THE
SITUATION.

DRUITT: I don't know what's HAPPENING. I don't know what's (LETTERING
TAILS OFF HERE INTO UNREADABLE LITTLE SQUIGGLES THAT SUGGEST DRUITT'S INCREASINGLY
EMOTION-CHOKED VOICE AS IT BECOMES INAUDIBLE, LOST IN THE FOLDS OF BEDFORD'S
WAISTCOAT).

PANEL 9.

WE CLOSE ON BEDFORD HERE, HEAD AND SHOULDERS TO HALF FIGURE, SO THAT WE MAYBE
SEE A LITTLE OF THE TOP OF DRUITT'S HEAD DOWN AT THE BOTTOM OF THE PANEL AS HE
CLUTCHES ROUND HIS COMRADE'S MIDRIFF, BUT NO MORE THAN THAT. OUR MAIN ATTENTION
IS ON BEDFORD'S FACE AS HE STARES UNEASILY DOWN AT THE TOP OF DRUITT'S QUIVERING
HEAD. IT IS SUFFUSED WITH BADLY MASKED GUILT.

BEDFORD: There, there, old fellow. There, there. It's alright.
BEDFORD: Everything's alright.

Chapter 11, pages 36, 37.

Like Druitt, Abberline arrives home by cab to some domestic comforting. This is the real thing: the kind of subtleties I always wanted to see in comics. So much to get across in the pictures. ***"He does not notice her concern, or else he is affecting not to notice it."*** Abberline's wife, also named Emma: ***"She maybe understands more than Fred thinks she does."***

PAGE 36. (694 words) PANEL 1.
A SEVEN PANEL PAGE WITH ONE BIG PANEL AT THE TOP AND THREE SMALL PANELS ON EACH TIER BELOW THAT. IN THIS FIRST WIDE SHOT, IT IS THE SAME NIGHT, ELSEWHERE IN THE CITY. WE SEE ABBERLINE, JUST ARRIVED HOME FROM WORK, AS HE COMES THROUGH THE FRONT GATE OF HIS HOUSE, WHICH WE SEE OVER ON THE LEFT OF PANEL HERE. HE GENTLY SHUTS THE GATE AND LATCHES IT BEHIND HIM, GLANCING TO THE RIGHT OF THE PANEL WHERE WE SEE HIS WIFE, THE FORMER EMMA BEAUMONT, STANDING SWEETLY ON THE DOORSTEP WAITING FOR HIM, OVER ON THE RIGHT OF THIS WIDE PANEL HERE, IN PROFILE FACING LEFT WHILE ABBERLINE IS FACING RIGHT.
No dialogue.

PANEL 2.
NOW IT IS LATER IN THE EVENING AND WE'RE AT HOME WITH THE ABBERLINES. TOWARDS THE LEFT OF FOREGROUND WE SEE EMMA, HEAD AND SHOULDERS, AS SHE GLANCES MISERABLY TOWARDS THE BACKGROUND WHERE WE SEE FRED SITTING IN AN ARMCHAIR, SCOWLING FAINTLY IN MILD CONCENTRATION AS HE SCANS THE FILES OF DOCUMENTS THAT HE'S BROUGHT HOME TO WORK UPON. EMMA LOOKS WORRIED AS SHE GAZES AT HIM. ABBERLINE IS EITHER SO ENGROSSED HE DOES NOT NOTICE HER CONCERN, OR ELSE HE IS AFFECTING NOT TO NOTICE IT.
No dialogue.

PANEL 3.

CHANGE ANGLE NOW SO THAT WE HAVE ABBERLINE IN PROFILE HEAD AND SHOULDERS IN THE RIGHT OF FOREGROUND, FACING LEFT. BEYOND HIM WE SEE EMMA AS SHE SITS THERE IN THE BACKGROUND WITH HER KNITTING OR EMBROIDERY UPON HER LAP, LOOKING TOWARDS US WITH COMPASSION AND GREAT WORRY FOR HER HUSBAND AND HIS HAPPINESS.

EMMA: Frederick? I-is everything alright? I-I wouldn't ask, but it's just that you seem preoccupied of late...

FRED: Um? Oh, no. No, I'm fine. Everything's fine.

PANEL 4.

NOW EMMA RISES TO HER FEET IN THE FOREGROUND SO THAT WE ONLY SEE HER FROM HER TORSO DOWN TO HER KNEES AS SHE STANDS TO THE LEFT OF THE FOREGROUND, LOOKING TOWARDS FRED WHO SITS IN THE BACKGROUND WITH THE OPEN FILES SPREAD OUT ON HIS LAP. HE GESTURES TO THEM WITH A MILD EXPRESSION OF EXASPERATION.

FRED: It's just working on this case, that's all. There's nothing but loose ends.

FRED: You take this business about "Julia", for instance...

PANEL 5.

CHANGE ANGLE NOW SO THAT FRED ABBERLINE IS SEATED IN THE RIGHT OF FOREGROUND, FACING LEFT. WE SEE HIM JUST ABOUT FULL FIGURE HERE AS HE SITS WITH THE FILES UPON HIS LAP, GESTICULATING AS HE SPEAKS. EMMA IS STOOD BEHIND HIM, FACING US, SLOWLY APPROACHING HIM TO LAY HER HAND UPON HIS SHOULDER. HE DOES NOT LOOK AT HER AS HE SPEAKS, AND WE PERHAPS HAVE A SUGGESTION THAT THERE'S SOMETHING THAT'S ALMOST EVASIVE IN THE WAY HE BLANDLY RATTLES OFF A LOT OF TRIVIAL CASE DETAILS IN ORDER NOT TO TALK ABOUT WHAT'S REALLY ON HIS MIND. EMMA LOOKS DOWN ON HIM, WITH HER EXPRESSION CALM, WISE AND COMPASSIONATE. SHE MAYBE UNDERSTANDS MORE THAN FRED THINKS SHE DOES.

FRED: Now, Kelly had a woman lodge with her around the time that she was murdered, name of "Julia".

FRED: We've been assuming that was JULIA VENTURNEY...

PANEL 6.

SAME SHOT, BUT WE MOVE CLOSER IN UPON THE ABBERLINES, SO THAT WE SEE FRED AROUND HALF FIGURE AS HE SITS THERE NOW WITH FILES ON LAP, EXPLAINING DETAILS OF THE CASE TO EMMA, WHO STANDS QUIETLY THERE BEYOND HIM WITH HER HAND UPON HIS SHOULDER.

FRED: Now she's a laundress with a room in Miller's Court. Why would she NEED to stay with Kelly?

EMMA: I don't know, dear...

PANEL 7.

CONTINUE TO CLOSE IN SO THAT IN THIS PANEL WE HAVE A HEAD AND SHOULDERS SHOT OF ABBERLINE, WITH EMMA ONLY PARTLY VISIBLE BEHIND HIM, WITH HER DELICATE PALE HAND AT

REST UPON HIS SHOULDER. AS SHE SPEAKS, FRED SUDDENLY LOOKS TRAPPED AND FRIGHTENED. HAS HE BEEN FOUND OUT? HE STARES AHEAD OF HIM WITH HAUNTED EYES WHILE EMMA SPEAKS,

EMMA (OFF, ABOVE):   I only know you haven't been yourself since that last murder.

EMMA (OFF, ABOVE):   That's the morning that you went out all dressed up.

PAGE 37. (605 words) (edited) PANEL 1.

NOW ANOTHER SEVEN PANEL PAGE, THIS TIME WITH THE BIG WIDE PANEL ON THE BOTTOM TIER AND THEN THREE SMALLER PANELS ON EACH OF THE TWO TIERS ABOVE THAT. IN THIS FIRST PANEL WE CHANGE ANGLE SO THAT NOW WE'RE ON THE OTHER SIDE OF FRED'S CHAIR AND HAVE EMMA MORE TOWARDS THE FOREGROUND WITH FRED SAT IMMEDIATELY BEYOND HER, BOTH OF THEM IN LONG SHOT AND FULL FIGURE HERE, SURROUNDED BY THE COSY DOMESTICITY OF THEIR WARM, FIRELIT LIVING ROOM. EMMA STILL HAS HER HANDS UPON FRED'S SHOULDER. HE STILL GAZES STRAIGHT AHEAD WITH TRAPPED AND HAUNTED EYES.

FRED: It... it's just WHITECHAPEL. You don't know what it's LIKE.

FRED: I never WANTED to go back there.

PANEL 5.

PULL BACK A LITTLE NOW SO THAT WE SEE BOTH FRED AND EMMA. LOOKING OLD AND WEARY, FRED CLOSES HIS EYES. HE TAKES THE HAND OF EMMA'S THAT WAS PREVIOUSLY UPON HIS SHOULDER AND HE HOLDS IT TO HIS CHEEK, SOOTHED BY THE COOLNESS OF HER FINGERS. EMMA GAZES DOWN AT HIM, AND MAYBE STROKES HIS BRYLCREEMED HAIR.

FRED: You feel as if you're drowning in it, and you want to 'ang
                        ON; just 'ang on to someone.

FRED: I'm not strong. I thought I was once, but I'm not.

PANEL 6.

CLOSE IN NOW ON THE LOWER HALF OF FRED'S FACE, PRESSED AGAINST THE BACK OF EMMA'S HAND, WHICH HE HOLDS FAST BETWEEN HIS OWN. WE MAYBE CANNOT SEE HIS EYES, BUT JUST HIS MOUTH NOW AS HE SPEAKS, TENDERLY HOLDING EMMA'S HAND IN HIS, CRUSHED TO HIS FACE AS IF IT WERE A FLOWER.

FRED: Just don't let go, that's all.

FRED: Just don't let go of me.

PANEL 7.

NOW A BIG WIDE PANEL TO FINISH. WE CUT TO KING'S BENCH WALK. IT IS THE LATE AFTERNOON OF THE FIRST OF DECEMBER, 1888. WALKING ACROSS THE PANEL FROM LEFT TO RIGHT WE SEE AT LEAST PART OF THE DARK AND SINISTER FORMS OF TWO POLICEMEN (MAYBE WE SEE THEM FROM THEIR SHOULDERS TO THEIR KNEES, SO THAT THEIR HEADS ARE BOTH OFF PANEL, IF THAT WORKS). UP ON THE WALL BEHIND THEM THAT THEY'RE WALKING PAST WE SEE THE SIGN THAT BEARS THE LEGEND "KING'S BENCH WALK". THE TWO OF THEM WALK DOWN THE ROW, PRESUMABLY ON THEIR WAY TO NUMBER NINE. No dialogue.

Chapter 11, pages 45, 46.

Alan wraps up the final two pages of chapter 11 in just over 600 words between them, with hardly any of it dialogue. As one would expect, there's a natural tendency for the word rate to start large in the exposition and then diminish toward the resolution. Characters have been described and their motives analysed. All that remains is to put them through their physical paces. Druitt finishes in the dark, pretty much where he was all along.

PAGE 45. (201 words) (only 1 panel out of 7 transcribed) PANEL 1.
SEVEN PANELS, WITH THE BIG ONE ON THE BOTTOM TIER. IN THIS FIRST SMALL PANEL WE SEE THE TWO POLICEMEN STANDING BY THE WHARF'S EDGE, HOLDING DRUITT LIKE A HAMMOCK SLUNG BETWEEN THEM, WITH THE SERGEANT HOLDING DRUITT'S WRISTS WHILE THE CONSTABLE'S IN CHARGE OF DRUITT'S ANKLES.

PAGE 46. (419 words) PANEL 1. (edited)
NINE-PANEL PAGE. IN THIS FIRST SHOT WE SEE THE SURFACE OF THE THAMES AS DRUITT HITS WATER, WITH A GREAT SPLASH RISING UP INTO THE NIGHT.

PANEL 2.
A SUDDEN CUT NOW TO A LONELY CRICKET PITCH BENEATH AN OVERCAST AFTERNOON SKY (OR WOULD A NIGHT SKY BE MORE EERIE? YOU DECIDE). IN THE LEFT FOREGROUND WE SEE WICKETS WITH THE BAILS KNOCKED OFF, ONE WICKET AT AN ANGLE TO THE OTHERS. IMMEDIATELY BEYOND THE WICKET WE SEE DRUITT IN HIS CRICKET WHITES. HE IS TURNED TO FACE AWAY FROM US, DECLARED OUT AND RETIRING FROM THE CREASE. OFF IN THE BACKGROUND FAR ACROSS THE EMPTY CRICKET PITCH, WE SEE A DISTANT, LONE PAVILION. IT IS TOWARDS THIS THAT HE IS HEADED, BAT TRAILING BESIDE HIM. HE'S STILL CLOSE HERE, AND ABOUT HALF TO THREE-QUARTER FIGURE.

PANEL 3.
BACK TO THE RIVER. WE ARE UNDERWATER, WATCHING DRUITT AS HE TUMBLES DOWN UNCONSCIOUS THROUGH THE MURKY DEPTHS, THE BUBBLES RISING UP ABOUT HIM AS HE SINKS; THE BRICKS IN HIS POCKETS PULLING HIM INEXORABLY DOWN.

PANEL 4.

BACK ON THE CRICKET PITCH. THE WHITE-CLAD FORM OF DRUITT IS NOW FURTHER OFF FROM US AS HE WALKS SLOWLY OFF TOWARDS THE FARAWAY PAVILION, WITH HIS BAT DRAGGED BY HIS SIDE. THROUGHOUT ALL THIS HE LOOKS AWAY FROM US. WE CANNOT SEE HIS FACE.

PANEL 5.

BACK TO THE RIVER. VIEWED FROM UNDERWATER, WE SEE DRUITT'S FACE IN CLOSE-UP AS HE SINKS. THE BUBBLES ARE ESCAPING FROM HIS OPEN MOUTH. HIS WHITE EYES ARE JUST BARELY OPEN.

PANEL 6.

BACK ON THE CRICKET PITCH, THE STUMPS STILL STANDING SKEW-WIFF IN THE FOREGROUND, WE SEE DRUITT AS A TINY, DISTANT FIGURE NOW, THREE QUARTERS OF THE WAY BETWEEN OURSELVES AND THE PAVILION IN THE DISTANCE. HE DOES NOT LOOK BACK.

PANEL 7.

BACK IN THE RIVER. VIEWED FROM UNDERWATER, WE SEE DRUITT'S BODY IN FULL FIGURE LONG SHOT AS IT HITS THE RIVER BED AND SENDS UP CLOUDS OF LIQUID MUD. MAYBE UP IN THE FOREGROUND WE CAN SEE A RUSTED BED-STEAD JUTTING FROM THE BED-SANDS

PANEL 8.

THE STUMPS ARE IN THE FOREGROUND. THE PAVILION IS OFF IN THE BACKGROUND. DRUITT'S NOWHERE TO BE SEEN.

PANEL 9.

THIS FINAL PANEL IS AN UNRELIEVED AND ASPHYXIATED BLACK

alternative chapter ending

From Alan's synopsis for the movie company, a year before this chapter's release in July 1995. There are a couple of unexpected twists, and we don't yet have the cricket analogy.

Depressed about his circumstances, Druitt spills his troubles to another barrister at the rooms where he works in the Minories. As luck would have it, this barrister's brother is married to a doctor's daughter, one of the most eminent doctors in the Victorian world. Perhaps he could help cure Druitt's depression. So it is that Druitt is introduced to Dr. Gull. Gull listens sympathetically to Druitt's sad confessions, and then drugs him into unconsciousness with laudanum-painted grapes. At a prearranged signal, a brace of uniformed and presumably Masonic police officers enter. Escorting the drugged Druitt to the Thames they weigh his pockets with bricks according to Masonic custom and throw him in. The body tumbles down through the filthy green water. Sir Melville MacNaghten starts to prepare the first draft of his memoirs, mentioning an unnamed barrister found drowned in the Thames as the culprit behind the Ripper crimes. Druitt's body is tumbling amongst drowned bedsprings and the bones of minnows. Abberline has sex with his wife, thinking hot and loveless thoughts of the prostitute who used and betrayed him. Riverbed sands crawl slowly into Druitt's mouth and nostrils. Ears deaf with estuary mud, life bubbles out of him and he gives up his historical existence to fuse inextricably with the black lore of Whitechapel, the over-raked bone-fields of the Ripperologists. End of Chapter XI.

Chapter 12, page 1.

Alan hints at our previous lack of agreement about The Queen. But she is much more human in this scene, and I quite enjoyed drawing her. On the other hand, I've often looked back and felt that I haven't completely realized Mr. Lees as a character, or at least not as convincingly, let's say, as the just departed Mr. Druitt. I guess it's because I have no model for him in my personal experience, and I have shied from using someone else's. Donald Sutherland made him suitably foppish in *Murder by Decree*. If I had to sit through a Ripper movie it might be that one, but don't make me stay to the end.

Of Lees, Alan wrote: ***"Lees is an unfortunate class of psychic who, in his heart of hearts, believes himself to be a phoney. He thinks that he's inventing his 'psychic flashes'*** as a means of vengeance upon someone who has offended him. He doesn't for a moment believe that Gull is actually Jack the Ripper. As he stated ruefully in the prologue, 'I made it all up, and it all came true anyway.'"** (1994 synopsis)

PAGE 1. (893 words) PANEL 1.
AN EIGHT-PANEL PAGE HERE. AFTER THE TITLES PANEL THERE IS ONE DOUBLE SIZED PANEL
COMPLETING THE TIER, AND THEN THREE PANELS ON EACH OF THE TIERS BENEATH THAT.
TITLES: Chapter Twelve: The Apprehensions of Mr. Lees.

PANEL 2.
IN THIS DOUBLE WIDTH PANEL, I'M AFRAID THAT WE'RE BACK IN THE DARK ROOM FOR AN AUDIENCE
WITH QUEEN VICTORIA, EVEN THOUGH I PROMISED YOU FAITHFULLY THAT HER APPEARANCE IN
CHAPTER NINE WOULD BE THE LAST TIME THAT WE SAW HER. WE SEE BOTH THE SEATED VICTORIA,
OVER TO THE LEFT, AND THE STANDING FIGURE OF THE YOUNG ROBERT LEES OVER TOWARDS THE
RIGHT, BOTH FULL FIGURE. ABOVE VICTORIA'S SEATED FORM, UP IN THE DARKNESS OF THE VAULTED
CHAMBER'S UPPER REACHES, WE CAN SEE WHAT SEEMS TO BE THE HOVERING FIGURE OF THE LATE
PRINCE ALBERT. THE DECEASED ROYAL CONSORT HANGS THERE IN THE AIR ABOVE VICTORIA AT AN
ODDLY HORIZONTAL SLANT. HE LOOKS MUCH LIKE A CUT OUT PICTURE OF A STANDING PRINCE ALBERT
THAT HAS BEEN PASTED ON AT THE WRONG ANGLE. VICTORIA DOESN'T LOOK UP AT THE HOVERING
FORM ABOVE HER, BUT STARES WITH INSCRUTABLE HEAVY-LIDDED EYES AT THE STANDING FIGURE OF
THE YOUNG PSYCHIC BEFORE HER. LEES STANDS WITH HIS ARMS SPREAD SLIGHTLY AT HIS SIDES.
HIS HEAD IS TILTED BACK AS IF TO LOOK TOWARDS THE FIGURE HOVERING ABOVE THE SEATED QUEEN,
BUT HIS EYES ARE CLOSED. A PEACEFUL SMILE OF BLISSFUL RAPTURE IS UPON THE PSYCHIC'S FACE.
CAPTION: Buckingham Palace. November 29th, 1888.

PANEL 3.

NOW WE HAVE A SHOT LOOKING AT VICTORIA, SO THAT SHE SITS FACING US, AROUND HALF
FIGURE. SHE LOOKS UP AT US, AND THERE IS SOMETHING VAGUELY HUMAN IN HER EYES: A LOOK OF
APPREHENSION OR OF HOPE THAT SEEMS QUITE OUT OF PLACE IN THE EMOTIONLESS AND STATUE-LIKE
DEMEANOUR OF THE QUEEN AS WE'VE PORTRAYED HER.

VICTORIA: Can you see him, Mr. Lees? Is he present?

PANEL 4.

NOW A SHOT LOOKING AT LEES FROM VICTORIA'S POINT OF VIEW, SO THAT WE DON'T SEE VICTORIA
BUT ARE LOOKING SLIGHTLY UP AT LEES AS HE STANDS BEFORE US, HALF FIGURE AND FACING US WITH
HIS HANDS SPREAD SLIGHTLY LIKE ANGEL WINGS AT HIS SIDE AND HIS FACE TIPPED BACK AS IF TO
BASK IN OTHERWORLDLY RADIANCE THAT HE ALONE CAN SEE BEHIND HIS CLOSED EYES. I SHOULD PERHAPS
MENTION THAT AFTER PANEL TWO WE DON'T GET ANOTHER GLIMPSE OF THE SPECTRE OF PRINCE ALBERT.
HE WAS JUST MEANT TO REPRESENT THE IMAGE OF EVENTS THAT LEES IS ATTEMPTING TO CONVEY.

LEES: Oh yes. Yes, the Prince Consort is most definitely here.

LEES: I see him hovering above you now, Your Majesty. He seems so
                       peaceful. So contented.

PANEL 5.

NOW A FULL-FIGURE SHOT SHOWING THE TWO OF THEM IN PROFILE AS THEY FACE EACH OTHER. LEES RAISES
HIS HANDS ABOVE HIS HEAD, PALM OUTWARDS, AS IF TRYING TO ENCOMPASS THE MYSTICAL VISION THAT HE
ALLEGEDLY "SEES" ABOVE WHERE VICTORIA IS SEATED. THE QUEEN PERHAPS TILTS HER HEAD BACK SLIGHTLY
AND PEERS MYOPICALLY UP INTO THE EMPTY DARKNESS ABOVE HER THRONE WITH A SLIGHTLY QUIZZICAL
EXPRESSION, AS IF TRYING TO SEE WHAT LEES PROFESSES TO SEE. THE DARKNESS ABOVE HER IS EMPTY,
AND THE GHOST OF PRINCE ALBERT IS NOWHERE TO BE SEEN.

LEES: He says that he is very happy on the other side. He says...
                       What? What's that, Your Highness? Yes. Yes, I understand...

PANEL 6.

NOW ANOTHER SHOT OF VICTORIA HALF FIGURE FROM THE FRONT, MUCH LIKE PANEL THREE, EXCEPT THAT
HERE SHE HAS HER HEAD TIPPED SLIGHTLY BACK TO PEER INTO THE EMPTY DARK ABOVE HER WITH A
SOMEHOW WISTFUL LOOK. LEES' BALLOON ISSUES FROM OFF PANEL IN THE FOREGROUND,

LEES (OFF):   His Royal Highness says that one day he'll be reunited with your
                       Majesty. He says that Paradise is incomplete till you are there.

PANEL 7.

SAME SHOT, BUT HERE VICTORIA SAGS FORWARDS A LITTLE AND RAISES ONE HAND TO COVER HER EYES,
LETTING HER HAND SUPPORT THE WEIGHT OF HER HEAD. SHE LOOKS MOMENTARILY LIKE WHAT SHE IS: A
FRAIL AND LONELY WOMAN WHO HAS LIVED LONG PAST THE TIME WHEN SHE WAS TRULY HAPPY AND HAD
ALL THE ONES SHE LOVED ABOUT HER.

VICTORIA: How I like him. Dear, dear Albert...

PANEL 8.

NOW WE SEE A LITTLE BIT OF THE SEATED QUEEN IN THE LEFT OF FOREGROUND AS SHE SITS FACING
AWAY FROM US TOWARDS THE RIGHT, WHERE WE SEE LEES STANDING FACING US, FULL FIGURE. PERHAPS
WE JUST SEE ONE OF VICTORIA'S HANDS RESTING UPON THE ARM OF HER CHAIR, AND PERHAPS HER
SLIPPERY VELVET KNEES. LEES IS LOOKING TOWARDS HER WITH AN EXPRESSION OF HUMBLE CONCERN.

LEES: Y-Your Majesty? Are you unwell? I hope the messages that I relay
                       have not distressed you. Should I have the Royal Doctor summoned?

Chapter 12, page 8.

Having said what I said about Lees, I'm pleased with this one. Lees, the fictional one anyway, was a psychic who made it all up, but it came true anyway. In my depiction, he's not quite supported by the conviction of experience, but it kind of works anyway. This loony going down the street waving his arms about, like a signaller guiding a plane in, has presence enough for story purposes. Again, it's all in the body language, which has saved me when all else fails. Anyway, that's what I'm thinking, looking at it here. It was an example of successfully putting on the page what Alan had asked for. ***"Lees holds up one of his hands... as if introducing the main act of a variety show."***

PAGE 8. (595 words) PANEL 1.

A SEVEN-PANEL PAGE HERE, WITH ONE PANEL ON THE BOTTOM TIER. IN THIS FIRST PANEL WE ARE LOOKING DOWN THE STREET PAST CLARIDGE'S, WHICH IS OVER TO THE RIGHT OF FOREGROUND. LOOKING DOWN BEYOND THAT WE SEE ABBERLINE AND LEES AS THEY APPROACH US, WALKING UP THE STREET TOWARDS US, WITH ABBERLINE ON OUR LEFT AND LEES UPON OUR RIGHT.

ABBERLINE: Very unpleasant, I'm sure, sir. Are you CERTAIN it's up
        this way? I mean, that's CLARIDGE'S over there...

LEES: I'm positive, Inspector. The voices never lie.

PANEL 2.

NOW WE SEE THE TWO MEN AS THEY PASS BENEATH THE SIGN MOUNTED UP ON THE WALL THAT READS "BROOK STREET". LEES PAUSES AND GESTURES UP AT THIS AS IF IN AMAZEMENT. ABBERLINE HIMSELF LOOKS AT IT BLANKLY, SEEMING TO BE A LITTLE SURPRISED.

LEES: Oh my God.

LEES: There, Inspector. Do you SEE?

PANEL 3.

CLOSE IN UPON THE PAIR OF THEM FOR MAYBE A HALF-FIGURE TO HEAD-AND-SHOULDERS SHOT AS THEY CONTINUE UP BROOK STREET. ABBERLINE ISN'T LOOKING QUITE SO SURE OF HIS SKEPTICISM AS HE DID EARLIER. HE SEEMS A LITTLE PUZZLED. LEES, WHO STILL HAS HIS EYES CLOSED AS IF GUIDED BY INNER LIGHTS, FORGES AHEAD OF THE INSPECTOR WITH AN AIR OF IMPATIENCE.

ABBERLINE: Er, well... I mean, it's a coincidence, I'll grant you that ...

LEES: COINCIDENCE? Inspector, can't you HEAR it? Can't you smell the BLOOD? We're so CLOSE.

PANEL 4.

NOW WE ARE LOOKING DOWN BROOK STREET WITH THE DOORWAY OF NUMBER 74 VISIBLE AT A SLANT, UP CLOSE IN THE LEFT OF FOREGROUND. LOOKING BEYOND THIS, WAY DOWN THE STREET WE SEE ABBERLINE AND LEES AS THE PSYCHIC CONTINUES TO ACT LIKE HE'S BLINDFOLDED, LEADING THE INSPECTOR UP THE STREET TOWARDS US WITH HIS PSYCHIC ANTENNAE TWITCHING LIKE MAD. ABBERLINE TROTS ALONG BEHIND THE YOUNGER MAN, STARTING TO LOOK A LITTLE BIT LOST.

ABBERLINE: But... I mean, the class of people who live in 'ouses like this...

LEES: EVIL pays no need to RANK, Inspector. He is NEAR. I can FEEL him.

PANEL 5.

SAME SHOT, BUT ABBERLINE AND LEES ARE NOW CLOSER TO US. LEES SEEMS TO PAUSE IN FRONT OF ONE OF THE DOORS A FEW DOORS AWAY FROM US, AS IF PSYCHICALLY TESTING IT. ABBERLINE LOOKS ON, BEWILDERED.

LEES: But which HOUSE? Is it THIS one perhaps?

LEES: No. No, he isn't behind this door, or I would sense him.

PANEL 6.

SAME SHOT, BUT NOW ABBERLINE AND LEES ARE ALMOST UP TO THE FOREGROUND WITH LEES' EYES ALREADY FIXED UPON THE DOORWAY OF NUMBER SEVENTY-FOUR, OVER ON THE LEFT. ABBERLINE FOLLOWS BEHIND THE YOUNG PSYCHIC, PROTESTING AND LOOKING A TRIFLE ALARMED.

ABBERLINE: Ay, look, Mr. Lees, really, I think this 'as gone far enough...

LEES: NO! My GOD, man, we're almost on TOP of him! We're almost...

PANEL 7.

THIS FINAL FULL-TIER-WIDTH PANEL WE ARE STANDING FACING THE DOORWAY OF SEVENTY-FOUR BROOK STREET, SO THAT IT IS SOMEWHERE TOWARDS THE CENTRE OF THE IMMEDIATE BACKGROUND, WITH ITS BY-NOW-FAMILIAR FAÇADE BOLD AND PROMINENT. LEES AND ABBERLINE HAVE PAUSED OUTSIDE THE DOOR AND ARE FACING AWAY FROM US TOWARDS IT, WITH LEES ON THE LEFT. LEES HOLDS UP ONE OF HIS HANDS DRAMATICALLY, INDICATING THE DOORWAY AS IF INTRODUCING THE MAIN ACT OF A VARIETY SHOW. ABBERLINE TURNS AND LOOKS AT THE DOORWAY, WEARING A SLIGHTLY SLACK-JAWED AND VAGUELY STUPEFIED EXPRESSION. MAYBE HE TAKES A STEP BACK, CONFRONTED BY THE ENORMITY OF THE CLOSED BLACK FRONT DOOR.

LEES: There.

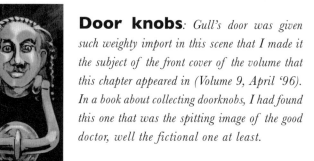

Door knobs: *Gull's door was given such weighty import in this scene that I made it the subject of the front cover of the volume that this chapter appeared in (Volume 9, April '96). In a book about collecting doorknobs, I had found this one that was the spitting image of the good doctor, well the fictional one at least.*

Chapter 12, page 11.

In the course of drawing *FROM HELL* I became rather fond of the real William Withey Gull and have no problem in separating him from our fictional character. The real Gull was the doctor who in 1873 established the medical term, *anorexia nervosa*. I like this summary of his career: ***"Gull died a very wealthy man, being especially able at handling neurotics. To one hypochondriac he said 'You are a healthy man out of health.' This satisfied the patient so much he wanted to know why the other doctors had not told him. Gull advocated the modern view that the object of the medical attention is the patient, not the disease housed in the patient."*** (Wikipedia entry for Gull)

Meanwhile, the script has the fictional Gull in his shirtsleeves and waistcoat. I wonder why the art doesn't. Perhaps I was thinking of Maggie and Jiggs in *Bringing Up Father* and how she would have a fainting spell if he came into the parlor, when guests were present, without having first put on his coat. Admittedly Jiggs was usually in his singlet, but it has always stuck with me that things were done differently then.

PAGE 11. (715 words) PANEL 1.
A SEVEN-PANEL PAGE, WITH THE BIG PANEL AT THE BOTTOM. PULL BACK SO THAT WE CAN SEE ALL THREE OF THEM. ABBERLINE, ON THE LEFT, SUDDENLY LOOKS A BIT SICK AND PALE. STARING AT LADY GULL WITH A STUNNED LOOK WHILE SHE GLARES BACK AT HIM ANGRILY. IN THE BACKGROUND, LEES TRIES VERY HARD TO CONCEAL A SMIRK. HE IS ENJOYING HIMSELF IMMENSELY.

ABBERLINE: S-Sir William GULL?

LADY GULL: Of COURSE Sir William Gull! Who did you THINK you were harassing?

LADY GULL: And over such SORDID little crimes! It's utterly OUTRAGEOUS!

PANEL 2.
CHANGE ANGLE. TO THE LEFT OF FOREGROUND WE SEE ROBERT LEES, HEAD AND SHOULDERS AS HE FACES SLIGHTLY AWAY FROM US TOWARDS ABBERLINE AND LADY GULL, WHO ARE IN THE RIGHT MIDDLE GROUND WITH THE OPEN DOOR OF THE DRAWING ROOM GAPING BEYOND THEM. LEES, IN THE FOREGROUND, HAS ONE HAND RAISED TO HIS MOUTH TO CONCEAL HIS SMIRK. NEITHER ABBERLINE NOR LADY GULL PAY HIM ANY ATTENTION AS THEY CONTINUE TO TALK TO EACH OTHER IN THE MIDDLE GROUND. ABBERLINE SPREADS HIS HANDS APOLOGETICALLY, DESPERATELY TRYING TO SMOOTH THINGS OVER, WEARING A VERY WORRIED LOOK ON HIS FACE. LADY GULL IS STILL IN

HIGH DUDGEON, TURNING A GORGON STARE UPON THE HAPLESS INSPECTOR.

ABBERLINE: Lady Gull, please, we simply wanted to...

LADY GULL: To know where my husband was on the night of the MURDERS?

                To implicate the finest surgeon in England with BUTCHERY?

PANEL 3.

CLOSE IN SO THAT WE JUST SEE ABBERLINE AND LADY GULL AS THEY FACE EACH OTHER. ABBERLINE STILL LOOKS MISERABLE AND APOLOGETIC WHILE LADY GULL LOOKS FURIOUS. THE OPEN DRAWING ROOM DOOR, LOOKING OUT ONTO THE HALLWAY, IS PROMINENT AS IT GAPES IN THE IMMEDIATE BACKGROUND BEYOND THEM.

ABBERLINE: Your Ladyship, please...

LADY GULL: What if he WASN'T home? My husband is a DOCTOR, Inspector.

                He's OFTEN called out in the evenings! Really, this is TOO bad!

PANEL 4.

CHANGE ANGLE. WE ARE NOW OUT IN THE HALLWAY, SOME DISTANCE FROM THE OPEN DRAWING ROOM DOOR WHICH WE CAN SEE IN THE BACKGROUND. THROUGH THE OPEN DOOR WE CAN SEE LADY GULL AS SHE SPEAKS CROSSLY TO ABBERLINE, AND MAYBE JUST A LITTLE OF THE ROOM THEY ARE IN, ALTHOUGH ALL THIS IS VERY SMALL AND FAR AWAY DOWN THE OTHER END OF THE HALL AS WE SEE IT HERE. LADY GULL'S ANGER IS SLOWLY FAILING HER TO BE GRADUALLY REPLACED BY A KIND OF ANXIOUS DISTRESS.

LADY GULL: A-as for his behaviour...

LADY GULL: Inspector, my husband isn't well. You must understand, he had

                a terrible heart-seizure almost a year ago. It affected him

                DREADFULLY.

PANEL 5.

SAME SHOT, BUT NOW WE START TO CLOSE IN ON THE DOOR IN THE BACKGROUND, AS IF WE WERE SOMEBODY WALKING DOWN THE HALLWAY TOWARDS THE DOOR, THROUGH WHICH WE CAN SEE ABBERLINE, LADY GULL, AND A LITTLE MORE OF THE BACKGROUND OF THE ROOM. NONE OF THEM ARE LOOKING TOWARDS US. ABBERLINE LOOKS AT LADY GULL WITH A KIND OF SYMPATHETIC BEWILDERMENT AS THE ARISTOCRATIC WOMAN RAISES HER HANDS TO HER FACE AND LOOKS UPSET.

ABBERLINE: Your Ladyship, there's no need...

LADY GULL: I mean, of COURSE I've been worried about him. Sometimes he

                seems so REMOTE. I-It's as if I hardly KNOW him...

PANEL 6.

SAME SHOT, BUT NOW WE ARE RIGHT UP CLOSE TO THE DOOR, LOOKING INTO THE ROOM. WE SEE ABBERLINE AND LADY GULL, MAYBE HALF FIGURE IN THE FOREGROUND, JUST INSIDE THE ROOM, BOTH OF THEM LOOKING STARTLED AS THEY HEAR THE SPEECH BALLOON ISSUING FROM THE FOREGROUND AND TURN TO FACE US. IN THE BACKGROUND WE SEE LEES, WHO LOOKS SURPRISED, ALSO FACING US.

WILLIAM GULL (OFF, FOREGROUND): Poor Susan, do not fret. All shall be well.

WILLIAM GULL (OFF, FOREGROUND): My GREETINGS, gentlemen...

PANEL 7.

NOW A WIDE PANEL FILLING THE BOTTOM TIER. DRESSED IN HIS WAISTCOAT AND SHIRT-SLEEVES, WILLIAM GULL STANDS IN THE OPEN DOORWAY, ROUGHLY HALF FIGURE, STARING AT US. HIS EYES ARE VERY FAR AWAY, AND THERE IS A VERY SPOOKY AND SPACED OUT QUALITY ABOUT HIM AS HE STANDS THERE CALMLY IN THE DOORWAY, RADIATING PRESENCE.

WILLIAM GULL: I am Sir William Withey Gull. How may I HELP YOU?

Chapter 12, page 17.

I'll lift another passage from Alan's synopsis as it succinctly bridges the gap between the previous selection and this one. ***"At this point Sir William comes downstairs. With an obviously feigned impersonation of bewilderment he confesses that why, yes, he has woken up with blood all over his shirt on the mornings after the murders with no memory of where he's been. In Gull's mind, he has reached an invulnerable place where it no longer matters if anyone knows what he did or not. It is more amusing to watch how the establishment will panic and attempt to cover his guilt than to remain silent. Why not confess? He is a god now. Nothing can hurt him... This leaves the establishment with the problem of what to do with Gull, who is clearly barking mad."*** (1994 synopsis)

And so we segue a few pages ahead to the scene where the men come for the doctor. The last line in this one appears very casual, but refers to a key object in the whole theory of Masonic involvement in the murders, the William Hogarth print, *The Reward of Cruelty* (the title of which is legible in panel 9). Hogarth's series, *The Four Stages of Cruelty,* is worth checking out for its own sake. Of all his work, it's the most easily readable to modern eyes. He portrayed the subject with little subtlety, intending it to be understood by "men of the lowest rank." In the first stage, his character, Tom Nero, is a child torturing a dog; in the second he is a man beating a horse; in the third he has seduced and murdered a woman; and in the fourth, the punchline, he has been executed and his body is being mutilated by surgeons in an anatomy lesson (see detail at end of this selection).

PAGE 17. (533 words) PANEL 1. (edited)
NINE PANELS. WE CUT TO BROOK STREET, AN UNSPECIFIED AMOUNT OF TIME LATER. IT IS DAYTIME. TO THE RIGHT OF THE FOREGROUND WE HAVE THE DOOR OF NUMBER 74, VERY PROMINENT. WE ARE LOOKING PAST THIS UP BROOK STREET. A VERY SERENE AND IMPORTANT-LOOKING BLACK COACH DRAWN BY TWO BLACK HORSES IS APPROACHING FROM THE FAR BACKGROUND, WAY OFF DOWN THE STREET HERE.
No dialogue

PANEL 5.

NOW WE ARE BEHIND THE TWO MEN AS THEY STAND FACING THE DOOR, SO THAT WE CAN SEE A LITTLE OF THE BACKS OF THEIR SHOULDERS, ENTERING FROM THE LEFT AND RIGHT OF THE FOREGROUND. LOOKING PAST THEM WE SEE GULL'S MAID, CHARLOTTE, AS SHE OPENS THE DOOR, LOOKING OUT TOWARDS US WITH A SPECULATIVE EXPRESSION.

MAID: Yes?

PANEL 6.

REVERSE ANGLE NOW SO THAT WE ARE LOOKING THROUGH THE MAID'S EYES AT THE TWO MEN AS THEY STAND THERE ON THE DOORSTEP FACING US, THEIR FACES COLD AND EXPRESSIONLESS, MAYBE BOTH OF THEM ABOUT HALF FIGURE HERE.

1ˢᵀ. MAN: We have come for Brother Gull.

PANEL 7.

NOW WE PULL BACK INTO THE HALL, SO THAT WE SEE THE MAID FROM BEHIND AND SLIGHTLY TO ONE SIDE AS SHE STANDS IN THE DOORWAY TALKING TO THE TWO MEN WHO LOOM JUST ON THE OTHER SIDE OF IT. GULL'S BALLOON ISSUES INTO VIEW FROM OFF PANEL TO THE RIGHT, BEHIND THE MAID.

MAID: H-Her Ladyship said that her and the master weren't to be
                        disturbed.

GULL (OFF, RIGHT):   It's alright, Charlotte...

PANEL 8.

CHANGE ANGLE SO THAT ONCE MORE WE ARE OUTSIDE THE FRONT DOOR, LOOKING IN OVER THE SHOULDERS OF THE TWO MEN, WHICH ARE VISIBLE ENTERING TO EITHER SIDE OF THE FOREGROUND HERE. BEYOND THEM WE SEE THE MAID, DRAWING BACK TO ONE SIDE AND TURNING TO LOOK ROUND AWAY FROM US AT WILLIAM GULL, DRESSED IN SHIRT AND WAISTCOAT AS HE STANDS THERE CALMLY IN THE BACKGROUND, HIS FACE EXPRESSIONLESS AS HE SPEAKS. HE DOESN'T LOOK AT THE MAID AS HE SPEAKS, BUT STARES DIRECTLY AT US AND THE TWO LARGELY OFF-PANEL MEN.

GULL: I've been expecting them.

GULL: Allow me, gentlemen, a moment to put on my coat. I shall be
                        with you presently.

PANEL 9.

NOW IT IS A FEW INSTANTS LATER. WE SEE GULL STANDING BY HIS HAT-AND-COAT STAND, GRAVELY PUTTING ON HIS COAT. ON THE HALLWAY WALL BEHIND HIM HANGS THE HOGARTH ILLUSTRATION, THE REWARD OF CRUELTY. PERHAPS HE GLANCES AT IT EXPRESSIONLESSLY AS HE SHUCKS THE COAT ON OVER HIS BROAD SHOULDERS.

No dialogue.

*Hogarth
detail.*

Chapter 12, page 19.

I found this page to be a lot of fun as it reminded me of spy shows in which HQ is always secreted behind an innocent shopfront. In *The Man From U.N.C.L.E.*, it was a tailor shop; in *Nick Fury, Agent of S.H.I.E.L.D.*, it was a barbershop. The agent would sit in the big barber's chair and it would disappear down a hole in the floor to a high-tech basement underneath. When I was a kid, no shop was ever just a boring shop. I always wondered what kind of skulduggery was going on in the backroom.

I omitted the statue of Eros only because evidence pointed to the probability that it wasn't there at the time. We have different ways of checking these things now, but I won't in case I get a different result.

PAGE 19. (759 words) PANEL 1.
NOW ANOTHER NINE PANEL PAGE. IN THIS FIRST PANEL WE ARE INSIDE THE COACH AS IT MOVES THROUGH LONDON, WITH GULL HEAD AND SHOULDERS UP IN THE RIGHT FOREGROUND, IN PROFILE WITH THE OPEN CARRIAGE WINDOW BEYOND HIM. HE IS TURNING HIS HEAD SLIGHTLY TO LOOK OUT OF THE WINDOW, WHERE WE SEE THE STATUE OF EROS GOING PAST. GULL SITS WITH ONE OF THE SILENT DARK-SUITED HEAVIES ON HIS LEFT AND THE OTHER ONE SITTING OPPOSITE HIM, NEITHER OF WHICH NEED TO BE ESPECIALLY VISIBLE HERE.
No dialogue

PANEL 2.
NOW WE ARE OUTSIDE THE COACH, IN A SIDE STREET THAT RUNS DIRECTLY OFF PICCADILLY CIRCUS, WITH THE CIRCUS AND THE STATUE VISIBLE AS WE LOOK DOWN IT TO THE FAR END IN THE BACKGROUND HERE. THE COACH HAS PULLED UP TO THE KERB ON THE RIGHT HERE, COMING TOWARDS US. IT IS STOPPING OUTSIDE A COMMERCIAL COFFEE HOUSE.
No dialogue

PANEL 3.
MORE OR LESS THE SAME SHOT. THE COACH IS NOW STILL, AND WE SEE THE TWO MEN AS THEY'RE SILENTLY SHEPHERDING GULL OUT OF THE CARRIAGE AND IN THROUGH THE DOOR OF THE COFFEE HOUSE.
No dialogue

PANEL 4.
NOW WE ARE INSIDE THE COFFEE HOUSE. A PLUMP, WORRIED-LOOKING MAN WHO IS OBVIOUSLY THE PROPRIETOR STANDS TO THE RIGHT OF THE FOREGROUND, WIPING HIS HANDS

ON A DISHCLOTH AS HE TURNS TO GAZE SLIGHTLY AWAY FROM US TOWARDS THE DOOR OF HIS SHOP, WHERE WE SEE GULL BEING SHOWN IN, BETWEEN THE TWO GRIM AND SILENT MASONIC HEAVIES THAT FLANK HIM. THEY GAZE AT THE NERVOUS PROPRIETOR IN THE FOREGROUND WITHOUT BLINKING AS THEY ENTER.
No dialogue

PANEL 5.
NOW WE SEE GULL BEING LED PAST IN THE FOREGROUND. ALTHOUGH MAYBE WE ONLY SEE A LITTLE OF THE BACK OF HIS HEAD IN PROFILE HERE. THE MASONIC HEAVY STANDING BEHIND HIM IS MOSTLY OFF PANEL, BUT PERHAPS HAS ONE HAND RESTING LIGHTLY ON GULL'S SHOULDER, STEERING HIM FORWARDS AND TOWARDS OUR RIGHT. WE CAN SEE THE WORRIED-LOOKING PROPRIETOR FACE ON, ABOUT HALF FIGURE. LOOKING AT US, GULL AND THE MEN, HE NERVOUSLY GESTURES EXPANSIVELY WITH ONE HAND, DIRECTING HIS VISITORS TOWARDS THE BACK OF THE SHOP, OFF PANEL LEFT. BEHIND THE NERVOUS MAN WITH HIS DISHCLOTH CLUTCHED IN ONE HAND WE SEE THE CUSTOMERS OF THE COFFEE SHOP SEATED AT TABLES, CALMLY SIPPING THEIR BEVERAGES AND TAKING NO NOTICE AS GULL IS LED THROUGH THE SHOP TOWARDS THE BACK. THE PROPRIETOR LOOKS VERY TENSE.
No dialogue

PANEL 6.
NOW WE ARE OUT THE BACK OF THE SHOP, LOOKING BACK ALONG A PASSAGEWAY OVER ON THE LEFT OF THE PANEL THAT LEADS BACK TOWARDS THE SHOP'S FRONT DOOR IN THE FAR BACKGROUND. AROUND THE CORNER FROM THIS PASSAGE AT OUR END WE CAN SEE A CELLAR DOOR THAT IS OPEN HERE, WITH STEPS LEADING DOWN INTO DARKNESS BEYOND. ONE OF THE MEN HAS ALREADY REACHED THIS DOOR AND IS OPENING IT AND HIS COMRADE STEERS AN EXPRESSIONLESS AND COMPLIANT WILLIAM GULL ALONG THE PASSAGEWAY TOWARDS US. IT'S ALL GETTING A BIT MYSTERIOUS AND SHADOWY.

PANEL 7.
NOW WE ARE ON THE CELLAR STAIRS IN THE DARK, WITH GULL AND THE TWO MEN THAT FLANK HIM COMING DOWN TOWARDS US IN THE DARK WITH THE LIGHTED RECTANGLE OF THE OPEN CELLAR DOOR HIGH IN THE BACKGROUND BEHIND THEM.

PANEL 8.
NOW WE ARE SLIGHTLY BEHIND GULL AND ONE OF THE MEN AS THEY WALK THROUGH THE SURPRISINGLY LARGE CELLARS OF THE COFFEE HOUSE TOWARDS A DOOR OF SOME KIND AT THE FAR END THAT ONE OF THE HEAVIES HAS ALREADY REACHED AND IS STARTING TO OPEN WHILE HIS PARTNER AND GULL FOLLOW HIM TOWARDS IT, HEADING AWAY FROM US IN THE FOREGROUND. GULL GAZES AROUND AT THE VARIOUS CRATES AND BOXES OF COFFEE BEANS AND SUCHLIKE THAT STOCK THE CELLAR. IT'S AN ALIEN AND SUBTERRANEAN WORLD OF ITS OWN.

PANEL 9.
WE ARE IN A DARK PASSAGEWAY WITH A LONG CARPET ON THE STONE FLOOR AND OIL LAMPS OR MAYBE CANDELABRA MOUNTED ON THE WALLS TO EITHER SIDE. THESE ONLY SERVE TO REINFORCE THE DARKNESS RATHER THAN TO DISPEL IT. WE ARE LOOKING DOWN THE CARPETED CORRIDOR TOWARDS THE ENTRANCE AT ITS FAR END IN THE NEAR BACKGROUND, WHERE THE TWO MASONIC HEAVIES ARE STEERING WILLIAM GULL TOWARDS US, INTO AND DOWN THE CORRIDOR WITH ITS FLICKERING AND EERIE SHADOWS. GULL'S EYES ARE DARK AND INTELLIGENT, DARTING ABOUT HIM TO DRINK IN THE DETAILS OF HIS LOCATION. HIS TWO GUARDS STARE GRIMLY DEAD AHEAD THROUGHOUT.
No dialogue

Chapter 12, page 21.

The Masonic angle hasn't played much of a role in my selections for this book and is getting a token inclusion here at the end. Alan's scripts tended to be more vivid in describing Marie Kelly's world than that of Warren, Anderson, *et al.* Furthermore, I became, over the years of working on the book, highly suspicious of anything that too thoroughly "makes sense." Humankind lives in terror of the unfathomable, and so we invent gods and conspiracies. We would rather believe that that evil people are in charge of things than entertain the possibility that nobody is. In a way, this is why Gull comes across so chillingly in this page. He has us believing that he KNOWS something. Then, thankfully, on the page after this one, he starts to lose the plot.

PAGE 21. (628 WORDS) PANEL 1.
NINE-PANEL PAGE. IN THIS FIRST PANEL WE ARE JUST BEHIND ANDERSON. LOOKING OVER HIS RIGHT SHOULDER AS HE SITS TO THE LEFT OF THE PANEL FACING MORE OR LESS AWAY FROM US TOWARDS GULL, WHO STANDS IN THE NEAR RIGHT BACKGROUND, FACING ANDERSON AND US THREE-QUARTER FIGURE, STILL AND MOTIONLESS AND GRAVE, HIS FACE EXPRESSIONLESS, UN-BLINKING AND UNREADABLE.

ANDERSON: Knight of the East, you stand accused of mayhems that have placed our brotherhood in jeopardy, before your peers, Masons and doctors both.

PANEL 2.
CLOSE IN UPON GULL FOR A HALF-FIGURE SHOT AS HE STANDS FACING US. HIS FACE RETAINS ITS UTTER LACK OF ANY EXPRESSION AND HIS EYES STARE AT US WITH UNBLINKING DISIN-TEREST. HE IS SOMEWHERE FAR ABOVE THE PETTY AFFAIRS OF THIS COURT, IN A COLD HIGH PLACE WHERE ONLY HE HAS ACCESS.

GULL: I have no peers here present.

PANEL 3.
NOW WE ARE BEHIND GULL, LOOKING OVER HIS RIGHT SHOULDER SO THAT WE HAVE A GLIMPSE OF THE SIDE OF HIS HEAD FACING AWAY FROM US OVER ON THE LEFT. LOOKING BEYOND THIS TO THE NEAR RIGHT BACKGROUND WE SEE ANDERSON AS HE SITS THERE IN JUDGEMENT. HE LIFTS UP HIS HEAD AND GAZES SHARPLY AT US, MAYBE LIFTING HIS SPECTACLES TO ADJUST THE FOCUS AS HE RAISES HIS HEAD TO GAZE AT GULL. HE LOOKS ANGRY AND INCREDULOUS.

ANDERSON: What?

PANEL 4.

SIDE-ON LONG SHOT OF THE COURT NOW WITH GULL OVER UPON THE LEFT FACING UP TOWARDS ANDERSON AND THE JURY AS THEY SIT IN JUDGEMENT OVER ON THE RIGHT. HE GAZES UP AT THEM GRAVELY AS HE SPEAKS.

GULL: I fancy that you understand me, sir.

GULL;   There is no man amongst you fit to judge the mighty art that
                        I have wrought.

PANEL 5.

NOW PERHAPS WE ARE BEHIND GULL, WITH HIS HEAD FACING AWAY FROM US IN THE FOREGROUND. LOOKING PAST THIS WE SEE ANDERSON AND JURY SITTING IN THE IMMEDIATE BACKGROUND, FACING US AND GULL AND LOOKING ON. ANDERSON GLOWERS AND GULL SPEAKS. THE OTHER JURY MEMBERS LOOK UNEASY AND SILENT.

GULL: Our rituals are empty oaths you neither understand nor live by.

GULL: You cite the Great Architect, yet would befoul yourselves
                        should he ADDRESS you.

PANEL 6.

CLOSE IN UPON A COUPLE OF THE ROW OF JURY MEMBERS. THESE INCLUDE DR. WOODFORD WESTCOTT IF I CAN FIND REFERENCE, AND DR. BENJAMIN HOWARD, A 52-YEAR-OLD DOCTOR OF WHOM NO PHOTOGRAPHS EXIST. FOR WHAT IT'S WORTH, IT'S BELIEVED THAT DR. HOWARD LIKED THE OCCASIONAL DRINK. GULL'S BALLOONS ISSUE FROM OFF.

GULL (OFF):   But he does NOT address you. Not Westcott there, nor
                        Woodford by his side, for all their mummery.

GULL (OFF):   Not Dr. Howard, ever in his cups.

PANEL 7.

NOW WE ARE BACK BEHIND ANDERSON, LOOKING THIS TIME OVER HIS LEFT SHOULDER AS HE SITS HEAD AND SHOULDERS FACING ROUGHLY AWAY FROM US TO THE RIGHT OF THE FOREGROUND. IN THE LEFT OF THE BACKGROUND WE SEE GULL, STANDING THERE MOTIONLESS AND GAZING AT ANDERSON DISPASSIONATELY.

GULL: And yet he speaks to ME. He is the balance where my deeds
                        are weighed and judged.

GULL: Not you.

ANDERSON: Sir William, this is insufferable.

PANEL 8.

NOW A CLOSE-UP OF ANDERSON'S FACE FROM THE FRONT. HE GLARES AT US, CLEARLY OFFENDED AND ANGRY.

ANDERSON: You do not seem to understand the seriousness of this charge.

ANDERSON: I fear that you are suffering from delusions.

PANEL 9.

NOW WE HAVE A VERY TIGHT CLOSE-UP OF GULL'S FACE, FILLING THE ENTIRE FRAME. HIS DARK EYES FIX US, LEVEL AND UNBLINKING. HIS FACE IS EXPRESSIONLESS. THERE IS SOMETHING POWERFUL AND TERRIFYING IN HIS ABSOLUTE CONVICTION.

GULL: Indeed?

GULL: Fear rather that I'm NOT.

Chapter 13, page 2.

This is one of those scenes in FROM HELL that show the world of 1888 to be really not much different from now. We have a Police stakeout. Nowadays, there might be electronic listening apparatus, but otherwise it's much the same. A bunch of guys looking bored to tears. On the subject of police methodology, Alan said: **"Fortean Times** *kept sending me Jack the Ripper books after I'd begged them to stop... one was someone writing a book about what would have happened to Jack the Ripper if we'd have had modern policing methods in the 1880s. It's a bit puzzling, because they'd got things like Fred Abberline picking up the phone to ask if the DNA report had come through yet and you think, 'Well, why bother to go through all that trouble, why not just say that they caught him on the security camera after the first murder and that was it?'"* (interview at Blather.net ('talking shite since 1997') from October 2000.)

PAGE 2. (724 words) PANEL 1.
SEVEN PANEL PAGE WITH THE BIG PANEL AT THE TOP AND THREE SMALL PANELS ON THE TWO TIERS BENEATH THAT. IN THIS FIRST BIG PANEL WE ARE IN A LARGE AND BARE ROOM THAT LOOKS RATHER LIKE AN UNLET FLAT, SOMEWHERE ON THE FIRST FLOOR OF A HOUSE IN CLEVELAND STREET ROUGHLY OPPOSITE NUMBER NINETEEN. THE ROOM IS FAIRLY DARK, WITH A WINDOW ON THE RIGHT LETTING IN THE LIGHT FROM OUTSIDE. SITTING AT A CHAIR BY THE WINDOW IS AN UNNAMED DETECTIVE SERGEANT WITH A PAIR OF BINOCULARS, THROUGH WHICH HE IS GAZING AVIDLY INTO THE STREET OUTSIDE. STANDING NEARBY IS FRED ABBERLINE, WEARING HIS SUMMER COAT HERE BUT NO BOWLER HAT. THE BOWLER HAT IS RESTING ON A CHAIR OVER IN THE BACKGROUND WHICH NEEDN'T BE VISIBLE HERE, ALONG WITH ABBERLINE'S FANCY WALKING STICK WHICH IS RESTING BESIDE THE CHAIR. THE OFFICER LOOKING THROUGH THE BINOCULARS SEEMS KEEN ENOUGH, BUT ABBERLINE LOOKS GLOOMY AND PESSIMISTIC. THERE IS ALSO A UNIFORMED CONSTABLE IN THE ROOM, PERHAPS TAKING NOTES. THIS IS P.C.SLADDEN. WE ARE LOOKING AT AN OBVIOUS POLICE STAKEOUT OF THE BROTHEL AT NUMBER NINETEEN CLEVELAND STREET.
DETECTIVE WITH BINOCULARS: They're inside. Somebody's closing the upstairs curtains.

I tell yer, Fred, they'll 'ave t'do summat about these filthy buggers, famous names or not. We've been watchin''em for weeks now.

ABBERLINE: Yes, and my bet is we'll be watchin''em a few weeks more. There's Royalty involved in this, lad. Everybody's treadin' careful.

PANEL 2.

CHANGE ANGLE. IN THE RIGHT FOREGROUND NOW WE SEE A WOODEN STRAIGHT-BACK CHAIR, WITH ABBERLINE'S BOWLER RESTING ON IT. LEANING AGAINST THE CHAIR IS ONE OF THE MITRE SQUARE "MAD MONK" WALKING STICKS, THE METAL FACE GAZING AT US IMPASSIVELY. LOOKING BEYOND THIS TOWARDS THE WINDOW WE CAN SEE THE THREE POLICEMEN. THE DETECTIVE WITH THE BINOCULARS HAS LOWERED THEM, AND IS LOOKING UP AT ABBERLINE AS ABBERLINE SPEAKS. P.C.SLADDEN LOOKS ON DUTIFULLY.

DETECTIVE: What, you reckon they'll spirit "P.A.V." away before arrestin' Hammond?

ABBERLINE: I doubt they WILL arrest Hammond, even if he DOES own the brothel.

PANEL 3.

SAME SHOT. ABBERLINE, ALTHOUGH STILL SPEAKING TO THE OTHER POLICEMEN, HAS TURNED AND IS LOOKING TOWARDS THE CHAIR IN THE FOREGROUND, WHERE HIS HAT AND CANE ARE RESTING. HE MAYBE STARTS TO MOVE SLOWLY TOWARDS THEM WHILE KEEPING UP HIS CONVERSATION WITH THE OTHER DETECTIVE AND THE POLICEMAN, WHO INTERJECTS HELPFULLY.

ABBERLINE: 'E knows too much. 'E could name Prince Albert Victor, Lord
                     Somerset or any of the other pansies.

P.C.SLADDEN: There was furniture bein' moved out the other day, sir.

PANEL 4.

SAME SHOT. NOW ABBERLINE HAS REACHED THE CHAIR IN THE FOREGROUND AND IS PICKING UP THE BOWLER HAT, HIS BACK TURNED TO THE DETECTIVE AND THE CONSTABLE AS HE SPEAKS. THE SILVER-TOPPED CANE GAZES OUT AT US FROM THE RIGHT FOREGROUND, ITS FACE UNREADABLE.

ABBERLINE: Frankly, Sladden, I'm not at all surprised. They'll probably
                     let him leave the country, and we'll keep quiet about it.

ABBERLINE: That's how it is with cases like this.

PANEL 5.

CHANGE ANGLE SO THAT NOW WE HAVE THE DETECTIVE AND THE CONSTABLE UP IN THE FOREGROUND, FACING SLIGHTLY AWAY FROM US TO EITHER SIDE OF THE PANEL AS THEY GAZE TOWARDS ABBERLINE, SETTLING HIS HAT ON HIS HEAD WITH ONE HAND AND STARTING TO REACH FOR HIS CANE.

DETECTIVE: Yeah, well, perhaps you're right.

DETECTIVE: You off out somewhere, then?

ABBERLINE: Thought I'd visit that sweetshop next door, see what they know.
                     I shan't be long.

PANEL 6.

MORE OR LESS THE SAME SHOT AS LAST PANEL. IN THE BACKGROUND, ABBERLINE PICKS UP THE METAL-TOPPED WALKING CANE. LOOKING AT IT BLANKLY AS THE DETECTIVE ASKS HIM ABOUT IT.

DETECTIVE: Fair enough.

DETECTIVE: Nice walkin' stick, by the way. Where's it from?

ABBERLINE: This? Godley and the lads got it for me after the Whitechapel case.

PANEL 7.

NOW WITH HAT ON AND CANE IN HAND, FRED MAKES HIS WAY OUT THROUGH A DOOR IN THE BACKGROUND. P.C.SLADDEN AND THE DETECTIVE WATCH HIM GO.

ABBERLINE: Only got me one wi' the Mad Monk o' Mitre Square on the 'andle
                     didn't they? Piss-takin' bunch o'cunts. I'll see you later, chaps.

Chapter 13, pages 9, 10.

Abberline, while on the stakeout in Cleveland Street, inadvertently discovers the secret of the sweetshop. There follows his confrontation with Anderson, in which the coverup is laid bare and the inspector is offered a nice pension to keep his mouth shut. It runs over five pages and ends with Fred throwing up in the toilet. With a handful of silent panels to work with, I overrode the panel descriptions and composed a vertiginous sequence using oblique angles.

PAGE 9. (649 words) (excerpt) PANEL 1.
NOW A NINE-PANEL PAGE. IN THIS FIRST PANEL WE SEE A LITTLE OF ANDERSON'S SIDE AS HE STANDS IN THE RIGHT FOREGROUND, MAYBE WITH ONE HAND HANGING DOWN AS HE STANDS MOSTLY OFF PANEL FACING ABBERLINE. ABBERLINE FACES US AND ANDERSON FROM THE NEAR LEFT BACKGROUND, HALF TO THREE-QUARTER FIGURE. HE LOOKS FURIOUS AS HE SHOUTS AT ANDERSON.

ABBERLINE: Oh dear? Oh DEAR? You told me Gull was MAD. That 'e'd just murdered those women on a WHIM.

ABBERLINE: You never told me 'e 'ad REASONS

PANEL 2.
SAME SHOT. ABBERLINE GETS MORE HEATED IN THE LEFT BACKGROUND, MAYBE WAGGING ONE FINGER AT THE LARGELY OFF-PANEL ANDERSON, WHO REMAINS STILL AND MOTIONLESS IN THE FOREGROUND. MAYBE WE CAN SEE THE MASONIC RING ON THE HAND THAT'S HANGING DOWN INTO VIEW.

ABBERLINE: I mean, what was it? Threaten to talk, did she?
ABBERLINE: You KNEW. From the first murder you knew and you let us carry on INVESTIGATIN'!

PANEL 3.
NOW ABBERLINE TURNS HIS BACK ON US AND ANDERSON, STARTING TO PACE DISTRACTEDLY. HE SPREADS HIS HANDS AS IF IMPLORING AN ANSWER AND LOOKS UP AWAY FROM ANDERSON TOWARDS THE CEILING. THE LITTLE WE CAN SEE OF ANDERSON REMAINS MOTIONLESS IN THE RIGHT FOREGROUND.

ABBERLINE: I suppose that's why I got this CLEVELAND STREET job. You thought if I'd been cunt enough to keep me trap shut once, I'd do it AGAIN.

ANDERSON (OFF): Abberline...

263

PANEL 5.

WE START TO CLOSE IN PAST ABBERLINE, SO THAT WE ONLY SEE A LITTLE OF HIM OVER ON THE LEFT SIDE OF THE PANEL. AND EVEN THEN NOT HIS FACE OR HEAD. WE ARE LOOKING AT THE GRIM-FACED ANDERSON AS HE STARES COLDLY AND MENACINGLY AT US.

ANDERSON: Gull WAS insane. We're considering locking him away. NOBODY expected him to do what he did. All the same, we have to live with it.

PANEL 6.

NOW WE CLOSE IN FOR A HEAD-AND-SHOULDERS SHOT OF ANDERSON FROM THE FRONT. HE GLARES OUT OF THE PANEL AT US AND THE OFF PANEL ABBERLINE, HIS EYES LIKE ICICLES; COLD AND PENETRATING.

ANDERSON: We live with it, and we say nothing. Not you. Not your silly little clairvoyant friend Mr. Lees.

ANDERSON: If asked, we make somethin' up.

PANEL 7.

CHANGE ANGLES SO THAT WE HAVE A LITTLE OF ABBERLINE'S SIDE VISIBLE AS HE STANDS FACING AWAY FROM US IN THE LEFT BACKGROUND. BEYOND THAT WE ARE LOOKING AT ANDERSON AS HE STANDS NEAR HIS DESK WITH THE WINDOW BEHIND HIM. HE IS STILL LOOKING AT US AND THE LARGELY OFF-PANEL ABBERLINE HERE, BUT HE IS STARTING TO TURN AWAY FROM US TOWARDS THE WINDOW.

ANDERSON: A barrister called Druitt was pulled out of the Thames around New Year. Perhaps HE was yer Ripper, now?

ANDERSON: Tell 'em any name ye want, save Gull's.

PAGE 10. (370 words) (excerpt) PANEL 5.

NOW WE ARE OUTSIDE THE OFFICE ON THE BROAD LANDING, WITH ANDERSON'S DOOR OVER ON OUR LEFT NOW AS ABBERLINE STEPS OUT INTO THE CORRIDOR AND PULLS IT SHUT BEHIND HIM. HE STILL LOOKS STUNNED. WE SEE HIM FULL FIGURE HERE.

No dialogue

PANEL 6.

SAME. ABBERLINE WALKS AWAY FROM US ALONG THE LANDING, LEAVING THE CLOSED DOOR BEHIND HIM.

PANEL 7.

CHANGE ANGLE. ABBERLINE IS NOW WALKING TOWARDS US. SET INTO THE WALL IN THE RIGHT FOREGROUND WE SEE A DOOR WITH THE LEGEND 'W.C. OFFICERS ONLY' ON THE DOOR. ABBERLINE IS WALKING TOWARDS THIS SOMEWHAT HURRIEDLY FROM THE NEAR BACKGROUND, FULL FIGURE AS HE APPROACHES US AND THE DOOR OF THE EXECUTIVE TOILET. HE LOOKS PALE AND SHAKEN. No dialogue

PANEL 8.

WE ARE NOW INSIDE THE TOILET FOR A LOW ANGLE SHOT FROM BESIDE THE BOWL. LOOKING UP PAST IT IN THE RIGHT FOREGROUND AT ABBERLINE AS HE LURCHES THROUGH THE TOILET DOOR IN THE NEAR BACKGROUND, STARING DESPERATELY AT THE TOILET, PERHAPS WITH ONE HAND RISEN TO HIS MOUTH.

PANEL 9.

FULL TO THREE-QUARTER-FIGURE SHOT OF ABBERLINE FROM THE SIDE. WITH ONE HAND HE LEANS AGAINST THE WALL BEHIND THE TOILET AND LOWERS HIS HEAD. THE VOMIT FALLS FROM HIS MOUTH TOWARDS THE WAITING TOILET BOWL.

ABBERLINE: hhuch

Chapter 14, page 5.

In his 1994 synopsis for this one, which wasn't published until August 1996, Alan wrote, *"This is the climactic chapter of **From Hell** and yet also the most difficult to describe. The episode will be reasonably lengthy, and yet will detail a single event, this being the lonely and ignominious death of William Gull as he lies there dying of a heart attack on the straw and vomit-strewn floor of his madhouse cell while uncaring attendants watch him die. They know him only as Thomas Mason, or, in their more light hearted moments, 'Old Tommy.' We cut between brief glimpses of the external reality of the cell with Gull twitching and convulsing on the floor and much longer sections in* which we show what is going on inside Gull's extraordinary mind as he dies. Basically, what we witness is Gull's apotheosis. He becomes a god. At the point of death and liberation from mortal laws and perceptions, Gull becomes a kind of black ripple pulsing out through the time stream, both backwards and forwards in time. The episode is a collage of Gull's impressions of the past and future assembled into a frighteningly suggestive pattern."* (1994 synopsis)

Alan invites me to get "strange and experimental." In not going all out I must have been clinging to my classical sense of form. In a given work, the parameters are laid out at the onset and that essentially is what you have to work with. Formal logic dictates that new material must not be introduced at the denouement. Thus, this page is a replay of a page in Chapter 2, except instead of a flock of ducks rising up as we exit the tunnel, it's gulls and we're high over the Aegean Sea.

PAGE 5. (715 words) PANEL 1. (edited)
A NINE PANEL PAGE HERE. JUST TO WARN YOU AHEAD OF TIME, FROM THIS POINT ON THE
IMAGES AND THE STORYTELLING GET INCREASINGLY STRANGE AND ABSTRACT. THIS IS DR.GULL
EXPERIENCING SOMETHING THAT IS LIKE A NEAR DEATH EXPERIENCE, ONLY CONSIDERABLY
CLOSER THAN NEAR THIS IS A DEATH EXPERIENCE FULL STOP. AS THE IMAGERY GETS WILDER
LATER ON, PLEASE FEEL FREE TO USE WHATEVER MEDIA YOU FEEL ARE APPROPRIATE. YOU
CAN AFFORD TO BE STRANGE AND EXPERIMENTAL HERE, AND AREN'T EVEN NECESSARILY BOUND
BY TECHNIQUES THAT SEEM APPROPRIATE TO THE VICTORIAN TIME PERIOD: GULL IS TO ALL
INTENTS AND PURPOSES OUTSIDE TIME HERE, IN A PLACE WHERE PAST, PRESENT AND FUTURE
CO-EXIST. ANYWAY, JUST FOLLOW WHAT COURSE FEELS RIGHT FOR YOU, BUT REMEMBER THAT YOU

HAVE FULL PERMISSION TO GET AS ABSTRACT AND PECULIAR AS YOU CARE TO. I SUPPOSE IN SOME SENSES, THIS FINAL EPISODE IS LIKE A DARK NIGHTMARE VERSION OF THE "STARGATE" SEQUENCE FROM KUBRICK'S 2001, CALLING AT SOME ODD STOPS ALONG THE WAY. THIS FIRST PANEL IS SOLID BLACK AGAIN, AS AT THE END OF THE PAGE FOUR. THIS PANEL IS IN FACT AN EXACT REPRODUCITON OF PANEL ONE ON PAGE TWO OF CHAPTER TWO, ONLY HERE THE BALLOON BELONGING TO WILLIAM'S FATHER JOHN GULL IS TAILLESS, AND JUST HANGING IN THE EMPTY DARKNESS.

TAILLESS BALLOON: William?

TAILLESS BALLOON: Did you speak, lad? I thought I heard your voice...

TAILLESS BALLOON: Uwp.

PANEL 2.

NOW ANOTHER BLACK PANEL, EXCEPT THAT HERE WE HAVE A TINY POINT OF LIGHT BECOME VISIBLE IN THE CENTRE OF THE BLACKNESS. THE CAPTION BOXES HERE ARE FREE-FLOATING, TREATED LIKE TAILLESS BALLOONS, AND CONTAINING GULL'S THOUGHTS; HIS VOICE, IF YOU LIKE. THE POINT OF LIGHT IS MORE OR LESS THE SAME AS IN PANEL THREE ON PAGE TWO OF EPISODE TWO, ALTHOUGH THE DIALOGUE IS DIFFERENT HERE, HANGING IN BOXES IN THE BLACKNESS.

CAPTION: No. I just made a little sound. I was listening to the echoes in...in the...

CAPTION: H-Has this happened before? Father?

CAPTION: Father, where am I?

PANEL 6.

THIS PANEL IS A REPRODUCTION OF PANEL ONE ON PAGE THREE OF CHAPTER TWO. WE CAN SEE THE LEFT HAND SIDE OF YOUNG WILLIAM GULL'S TURNED BACK ENTERING INTO THE RADIANCE OF THE TUNNEL MOUTH OVER ON THE RIGHT. THE ONLY DIFFERENCE IS THAT THE DIALOGUE BALLOONS ARE BLACKED OUT HERE AND REPLACED BY THE FREE-FLOATING CAPTION BOXES.

CAPTION: That was true, wasn't it? I was dying.

CAPTION: In a madhouse, I remember. "Mason, Thomas, 124?" "Here, sir!"

CAPTION: Yes. Yes, I remember now...

PANEL 7.

A REPRODUCTION OF PANEL THREE ON PAGE THREE OF CHAPTER TWO, BUT WITH BALLOONS BLACKED OUT AND CAPTIONS SUBSTITUTED.

CAPTION: My name is William Withey Gull and I'm dying.

CAPTION: I am Catch-Me-If-You-Can, and I am Leather Apron.

CAPTION: I am Jack the Ripper, on my way to Heaven.

PANEL 8.

NOW A REPRODUCTION OF PANEL FIVE ON PAGE THREE OF CHAPTER TWO, AGAIN WITH CAPTIONS SUBSTITUTED FOR THE BLACKED-OUT BALLOONS.

CAPTION: There's a tunnel.

CAPTION: There's a movement, out of dark and into brilliance...

PANEL 9.

NOW A REPRODUCTION OF PANEL SEVEN FROM PAGE THREE OF CHAPTER TWO, AGAIN WITH THE BALLOONS GONE AND SINGLE CAPTION IN THEIR PLACE.

CAPTION: Father?

Chapter 14, page 6.

On articulating pictorial space: An artist plots his way through pictorial space by putting one thing partially behind another. However, what if there's no 'nother thing to put a thing behind? Or any receding straight lines with which to lead the eye through a readable perspective? The script for this page caused a murmur between me and Pete when we first read it. It required a 3-dimensional hole in the middle of the air some distance away, in the sky high over the sea, with blood issuing from it both toward and away from "us." I had the help of the upper and lower panels in establishing an exaggerated dramatic depth of field as well as locating "up" and "down." To an extent you can depend on the white sky at the top of the second tier being read as a continuation of the white sky in the first, even though firstly we have now apparently moved some distance higher than where seagulls might be seen, and secondly the three horizons in the second tier are more or less continuous even though the altitude introduces curvature. Pictorial space on a multi-paneled page embraces simultaneous contradictions.

Were I to do this over, the fishermen would look more Greek. And like fishermen.

PAGE 6. (673 words) PANEL 1.
NOW A FIVE PANEL PAGE. THERE IS ONE BIG PANEL ON THE TOP TIER, THREE SMALLER PANELS ON THE MIDDLE TIER AND THEN ONE BIG PANEL ON THE BOTTOM TIER. IN THIS FIRST PANEL WE ARE LOOKING UPWARDS INTO THE BLINDING LIGHT OF THE BRIGHT MEDITERRANEAN SUN THAT HANGS ABOVE US IN A CLEAR SKY, WITH NO MORE THAN A FEW RAGGED AND RAPIDLY EVAPORATING WISPS OF CLOUD AROUND THE EDGES. THE LIGHT IS BLINDING. FLAPPING IN THE FOREGROUND AND BEYOND WE SEE A NUMBER OF SEAGULLS, REMINISCENT OF THE DUCKS WE SAW ERUPTING IN A FLAPPING CLOUD IN THE LAST PANEL OF PAGE THREE IN CHAPTER TWO. HERE, HOWEVER, WE CAN NO LONGER SEE ANY SIGN OF THE BARGE, OR OF THE YOUNG WILLIAM GULL. WE ARE HIGH IN THE HOT SKY ABOVE THE AEGEAN SEA. IT IS 1888. THE GULLS FLAP AND WHEEL AGAINST THE BLINDING DISC OF THE SUN, UP ABOVE US.

CAPTION: Light. Ecstasy. The sun.
CAPTION: Where am I now?

PANEL 2.
IN THIS FIRST SMALL PANEL ON THE SECOND TIER IT IS AS IF WE HAVE SHIFTED OUR GAZE

AWAY FROM THE SUN TO LOOK DOWN BENEATH US. FAR BELOW, WE CAN SEE THE GLITTERING AEGEAN, WITH ONLY GULLS AND A FEW WISPS OF CLOUD BETWEEN US AND THE SHINING WATERS FAR BELOW. UP TO ONE CORNER WE CAN MAYBE SEE PART OF THE COASTLINE OF ONE OF THE ISLANDS ENTERING THE PANEL, WITH A LINE OF SURF BOILING AND RIPPLING AROUND IT. FAR BELOW US, WE CAN SEE A COUPLE OF SMALL GREEK FISHING BOATS MAKING THEIR WAY ACROSS THE STILL AND SHIMMERING WATERS, LEAVING V-SHAPED WAKES BEHIND.

CAPTION: A knowledge comes to me that I am high above the glittering
                     Aegean, and it is no longer 1896.

CAPTION: It is instead the year of my achievement. It is 1888.

PANEL 3

SAME SHOT AS LAST PANEL, LOOKING DOWN ON THE AEGEAN WITH THE FISHING BOATS MOVED ON ONLY A LITTLE SINCE OUR LAST IMAGE, AND THE GULLS LIKEWISE WHIRLING INTO NEW POSITIONS. UP IN THE FOREGROUND, HANGING IN EMPTY SPACE IN FRONT OF US, SOMETHING QUITE SMALL IS STARTING TO ERUPT OUT OF EMPTY AIR, AS IF FROM A POINT. IT'S SORT OF LIKE A SMALL AND SYMMETRICAL SQUIRTING OR SPLATTERING OF A DARK AND VISCOUS LIQUID, JUST ERUPTING FROM A POINT OUT OF NOWHERE, THE THICK LIQUID GOBBETS ALMOST LIKE THE RADIATING PETALS OF A TERRIBLE FLOWER.

CAPTION: I hover on the brink of form, inchoate and ethereal, filled
                     with a fierce, exultant joy I must make manifest.

CAPTION: I concentrate my being to a single, bloody point.

PANEL 4.

SAME SHOT, WITH THE BOATS BELOW AND THE GULLS MOVED ON ONLY A LITTLE. UP IN THE FOREGROUND, THE SPLATTERING POINT OF BLOOD HAS NOW GROWN MUCH BIGGER, BLOSSOMING INTO A HUGE AND EXTRAORDINARILY LIQUID ALIEN FLOWER OF MOVING, FLOWING BLOOD. WEIRDLY BEAUTIFUL AND SYMMETRICAL, LIKE A THREE-DIMENSIONAL RORSCHACH BLOT, IT HANGS SUSPENDED IN THE SKY ABOVE THE AEGEAN, A VISIONARY MIRACLE HANGING THERE IN DEFIANCE OF GRAVITY AND PHYSICS. ITS SHAPE, THOUGH SYMMETRICAL, IS MONSTROUS AND IRREGULAR, GOBBETS AND BEADS OF THE THICK AND GLEAMING PLASMA HANG SUSPENDED IN THIN AIR ABOUT THE EDGES OF THE CENTRAL BLOSSOMING FORM, WHICH IS BOTH GORGEOUS AND APPALLING.

CAPTION: In rapture I explode, a scarlet cloudburst.

CAPTION: Fluids from Buck's row and Mitre square and Miller's Court,
                     rich and sublime they flower against the blue Aegean sky.

PANEL 5.

NOW, IN THIS FINAL WIDE PANEL, WE ARE DOWN ON THE DECK OF ONE OF THE NINETEENTH-CENTURY GREEK FISHING BOATS BELOW. IT'S RAINING BLOOD. THE SAILORS GAPE UP AT IT IN FEAR AND ALARM, IN STARK BEWILDERMENT. THE HEAVY CRIMSON DOWNPOUR SPATTERS OFF THE DECK AND TRICKLES DOWN THE ARMS AND FACES OF THE HORROR-STRICKEN SAILORS. IT STAINS THEIR SHIRTS AND RUNS INTO THEIR FRIGHTENED STARING EYES. IT PUDDLES THERE IN THE UNEVEN TIMBERS OF THE DECK.

CAPTION: A pelting thunderhead of murder, here I sign my year of
                     panics with appalling miracle.

Chapter 14, page 8.

Regarding what Alan refers to here as "ley lines," the pattern of connections that made up the London pentacle in Chapter 4, he said: ***"All the points in the past, whether they're so-called history or so-called myths, are points of information like the stars are points of information. We cannot reach out and touch them but we can see them, perceive them. We look at the stars and we say, 'Oh, well that group of stars looks like a hunter.' Now, they only look like that from here. In fact, the three stars that are so neatly lined up in Orion's belt are light years away from each other. From here they seem to be in a neat little line. Just as we might say that the pentacle does not exist apart from 'here,' from Alan Moore, and from bits of Iain Sinclair that I've borrowed, so these constellations aren't real. We've created them with imposed patterns, but we can use those patterns to navigate, and it is that which has changed the entire history of humanity."*** (interviewed by Roger Sabin for *The Edge* (#5 1997) quoted in Sabin's own *Below Critical Radar* (2001)

PAGE 8, (923 words) PANEL 1.
A SEVEN-PANEL PAGE HERE WITH A BIG WIDE PANEL ON THIS FIRST TIER AND THEN THREE SMALL PANELS ON EACH OF THE TIERS BENEATH IT. IN THIS FIRST PANEL, WE ARE STILL LOOKING THROUGH GULL'S EYES BUT IT IS AS IF HE HAS LOWERED HIS GAZE AND IS LOOKING OUT AT THE BROAD NIGHT STREET OF THE EMBANKMENT, PAST THE CROUCHING SPHINXES WITH THE OBELISK NOW SOMEWHERE OFF PANEL BEHIND US. MOVING BACK AND FORTH THROUGH THE STREETS IN FRONT OF US WE SEE A PECULIAR AND GHOSTLY PROCESSION. IT IS AS IF WE CAN SEE THREE OR FOUR DIFFERENT PERIODS ALL COEXISTING AT ONCE, AS FLIMSY OVERLAYS STACKED ONE ON TOP OF EACH OTHER. TRANSLUCENT IMAGES OF VICTORIAN HORSE DRAWN CARRIAGES INTERSECT AND OVERLAP WITH CARS OF THE TWENTIES OR MODERN VEHICLES FROM THE 1990s. STROLLING, GHOSTLY PEOPLE FROM THE EIGHTEEN HUNDREDS WALK OBLIVIOUSLY THROUGH YUPPIES, PUNKS AND AIR RAID WARDENS. NONE OF THEM SEEM TO NOTICE EACH OTHER AS THEY WALK THROUGH THEIR SEPARATE AND DIFFERENT NIGHTS, DISTANT FROM EACH OTHER BY DECADES. IT'S VERY EERIE. ONLY THE BASE OF THE MONUMENT AND THE ATTENDANT SPHINXES SEEM SHARP AND DEFINED, HAVING EXISTED THERE UNCHANGED THROUGHOUT THE PASSING YEARS.

HALF-FORMED PEOPLE WALK PAST, LIKE THE GHOSTS OF MOVEMENT THAT YOU GET ON LONG-EXPOSURE PHOTOGRAPHS.

CAPTION: The obelisk itself is solid, fixed and permanent in time.

CAPTION: About the stone pudenda of its base parade the oblivious phantoms that I know to be the living, although not of any single night, or century.

PANEL 2.

NOW IT IS AS IF GULL HAS TURNED TO LOOK OUT ONCE MORE OVER THE EMBANKMENT WALL, SOME YARDS AWAY, AT THE DARK AND MOONLIT THAMES BEYOND. ONCE MORE HE RAISES AT LEAST ONE OF HIS NAKED AND UNNATURALLY WHITE AND LUMINESCENT HANDS INTO VIEW IN THE FOREGROUND. BETWEEN US AND THE RIVER WE CAN SEE A COUPLE OF THE STROLLING, ANACHRONISTIC SPECTRES, INCLUDING A MAN AND WOMAN IN THIRTIES OR FORTIES DRESS, GHOSTLY AND SEMI-TRANSPARENT. THEY CHAT WITH EACH OTHER AS THEY STROLL AND DO NOT SEEM TO NOTICE US OR GULL.

CAPTION: Come from the Dionysiac heavens over Crete to these Egyptian shadows, I am following a current of transmission in Masonic mysteries.

CAPTION: I laugh amongst the apparitions; for delight.

PANEL 3.

SAME POINT OF VIEW, STILL LOOKING THROUGH GULL'S EYES, BUT NOW IT IS AS IF HE WERE RUSHING FORWARD TOWARDS THE EMBANKMENT WALL, NOW NOT SO FAR IN FRONT OF US, AND THE GLINTING WATERS BEYOND. WE SEE HIS THICK, SQUARE HANDS, RAISED INTO THE FOREGROUND, NAKED AND WHITE, AS HE RUNS TOWARDS THE WATER'S EDGE. TO THE LEFT OF THE FOREGROUND WE SEE THE GHOSTLY FORTIES MAN AND WOMAN PAUSING IN THEIR TRACKS AND BOTH STARTING TO GAPE AT US IN SURPRISE AND ALARM, AS IF THEY'VE SUDDENLY SEEN US, OR ALMOST SEEN US.

CAPTION: Naked, triumphant, I run laughing for the edge of the embankment and the ancient tide it binds.

CAPTION: Some of the idling spectres start, and seem almost to see me.

PANEL 4.

NOW WE ARE STILL LOOKING THROUGH GULL'S EYES, BUT IT IS AS IF HE HAS JUST LEAPED OVER THE EMBANKMENT AND IS DROPPING DOWN TOWARDS THE DARK, DIRTY WATERS BELOW. AGAIN WE SEE HIS NAKED HANDS, AND MAYBE A GLIMPSE OF HIS WHITE AND NAKED LOWER REACHES IF HE IS LOOKING DOWN THE LENGTH OF HIS BODY TOWARDS THE WATER BELOW AS HE PLUMMETS FEET FIRST.

CAPTION: "It is a haunt for suicides and ghosts; a naked man is seen, who leaps into the Thames."

PANEL 5.

STILL LOOKING THROUGH GULL'S EYES, AND STILL MAYBE LOOKING DOWN THE LENGTH OF HIS BODY WITH SOME OF HIS NAKED ARMS AND LOWER BODY VISIBLE. INSTEAD OF FALLING INTO THE THAMES, HE NOW SEEMS TO BE FLOATING UPWARDS ABOVE IT. BENEATH US WE CAN

SEE THE RIVER, PART OF THE EMBANKMENT AND PART OF CLEOPATRA'S NEEDLE AS GULL'S
SPIRIT IS PULLED UPWARDS BY AN IRRESISTIBLE FORCE.

CAPTION: "No splash is ever heard."

CAPTION: The filthy river falls away beneath me. I begin to rise.

PANEL 6.

WE CONTINUE TO FLOAT UPWARDS, STILL LOOKING THROUGH GULL'S EYES, WITH PARTS OF
HIS LOWER SPIRIT-BODY VISIBLE, WHITE AND LUMINOUS AND NAKED. WE ARE NOW SOME
DISTANCE ABOVE CLEOPATRA'S NEEDLE AND CAN SEE THE WHOLE OF THE MONUMENT ALONG
WITH PART OF THE CURVE OF THE THAMES THAT IT STANDS BESIDE. BENEATH US, THE
MONUMENT SEEMS TO GLOW IN THE DARK WITH A STRONG WHITE AURA. MAYBE THIS SHOT
LOOKS LIKE A PHOTO NEGATIVE OR SOMETHING. UP TO YOU.

CAPTION: Something is pulling me. Below, the needle's black stone
                    glows unearthly white.

CAPTION;   About its ageless beacon is the vaporous swirl of human life
                    and time continued.

PANEL 7.

WE ARE NOW HIGH ABOVE THE TIMELESS NIGHT CITY, WITH THE RIVER A SILVER RIBBON
FAR BENEATH US, ALMOST AS IF WE WERE LOOKING DOWN ON A MAP OF LONDON. WE CAN
STILL SEE THE LUMINOUS AND PHOSPHORESCENT BEACON THAT IS CLEOPATRA'S NEEDLE FAR
BELOW US, AND IT SEEMS A THIN LINE OF FLICKERING WHITE FIRE PASSING THROUGH IT,
A WHITE AND GLITTERING LINE DRAWN ON THIS NIGHTTIME MAP. THIS IS THE "LEY LINE"
THAT RUNS FROM BATTLE BRIDGE TO HERNE HILL, THROUGH HERCULES ROAD AND CLEOPATRA'S
OBELISK, VISIBLE TO GULL'S SPIRIT-VISION AS A LINE RULED IN WHITE FIRE.

CAPTION: High into the night, and higher still. Viewed from this
                    elevated station, lines and traceries are visible.

CAPTION: Luminous filaments connect the City's stones into a circuit.

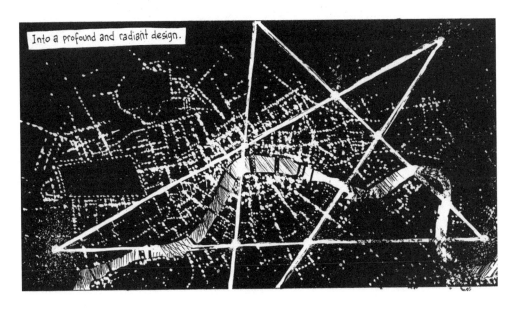

Into a profound and radiant design.

Chapter 14, page 18.

I've sat in too many English 1970s living rooms just like that one in the last panel. And I always felt ill at ease. Now I know it was because of the big fat naked bastard on the sofa. Alan said: *"Ten years wading through the material, the literature, not just Jack the Ripper but all of these fuckers. All these miserable little apologies for human beings. They're not supermen. They're not supermen at all. They're not Hannibal Lecter. You know, they're Peter Sutcliffe, they're a bloke with a dodgy perm. And some horrible screw-up in his relationship with his mother. They're little blokes."* (interview at Blather.net Oct 2000)

PAGE 18 (719 words) (edited-2 panels) PANEL 1.
...WE HAVE MOVED AROUND NINETY DEGREES SO THAT WE NOW SEE THE SCENE FROM THE SIDE AND CAN NOW SEE THE SOURCE OF THE LIGHT. TO THE SIDE OF THE PANEL HERE, WE SEE THE DISEMBODIED HEAD OF WILLIAM GULL. IT IS SUSPENDED AT AROUND NORMAL HEAD-HEIGHT ABOVE THE COBBLES OF THE DARK AND DESERTED STREET, AND IT IS GLOWING WITH WHAT BRADY DESCRIBED AS AN EERIE GREEN RADIANCE, SO JUST DO YOUR BEST. THE HEAD IS SMILING ALMOST PATERNALLY AT THE YOUNG BOY, WHO IS MORE OVER TO THE RIGHT. THE BICYCLE HAS NOW FALLEN OVER INTO THE GUTTER, SPILLING THE BOY ONTO THE PAVEMENT. HE MAYBE CRAWLS UP TOWARDS THE WALL OF A CLOSED SWEETSHOP OR SOME SUCH ESTABLISHMENT, CLUTCHING AT THE PEELING WOODEN LEDGE BENEATH ITS PICTURE WINDOW AS HE DRAGS HIMSELF FRANTIC AND WHIMPERING AWAY FROM THIS TERRIBLE APPARITION THAT SIMPLY HANGS THERE IN THE DARK AND DESERTED SLUM STREET, SMILING DOWN AT THE BOY. I FIGURE THIS IMAGE SHOULD HAVE ALMOST A TAROT-CARD-LIKE POWER TO IT; AN ALMOST ARCHETYPAL SCENE OF PARALYZING SUPERNATURAL DREAD.   No dialogue

PANEL 6.
WE CUT TO THE FRONT ROOM OF A WELL-KEPT WORKING CLASS HOME IN BRADFORD IN THE LATE 1970s. WE SEE A SOFA, AND ARMCHAIR AND TELEVISION, WHICH IS ON AND PERHAPS SHOWING SATURDAY NIGHT FOOTBALL. IN FRONT OF THE SOFA IS A LAMINATED COFFEE TABLE, ON WHICH RESTS A LARGE AND ATTRACTIVE CUT-CRYSTAL ASHTRAY, ALONG WITH OTHER ODDS AND ENDS INCLUDING A COPY OF THE RADIO TIMES OR WOMEN'S WEEKLY. A MAN IN HIS MID-THIRTIES SITS WATCHING THE TELEVISION INTENTLY ON ONE END OF THE SOFA, THE FURTHEST END FROM US. WE SEE THE MAN'S WIFE SITTING ON THE ARMCHAIR; AN UNPREPOSSESSING WOMAN OF A SIMILAR AGE. SHE IS PROBABLY KNITTING OR DOING THE WOMAN'S WEEKLY CROSSWORD OR SOMETHING. ON THE END OF THE SOFA NEAREST TO US, WILLIAM GULL IS SITTING, LOOKING ROUND THE ROOM WITH MILD PUZZLEMENT. IT IS CLEAR THAT NEITHER OF THE OTHER TWO PEOPLE IN THE ROOM CAN SEE HIM.
No dialogue

During the time we had been working on *FROM HELL*, new information on the case had been coming to light. ***"The 1980s saw a tide of books published to cash in on the centennial of the Murders in Whitechapel, and lost evidence was returned anonymously to the police."*** (Casebook.org)

In our long appendix, footnote to Chapter 1, page 2, Alan said that he wasn't even sure that John Netley was an actual person. By the time we got to this page we now had a photograph of him to take into account and it would take some accounting to make him to look like both the photo and the way I'd been drawing him previously. Another one to file under "the graphics of theory and guesswork." It turned out that at different times he drove hackney cabs and goods wagons; he was employed by Messrs. Thompson, McKay & co., who described him as "very steady." But then, employers have said the same about me.

PAGE 20, (589 words) PANEL 1.

NINE PANELS. IN THIS FIRST ONE, TO THE LEFT WE SEE THE RAILED GATE OF REGENT'S PARK WITH A SIGN SAYING "CLARENCE GATE" SOMEWHERE UP TO THE LEFT OF THE FOREGROUND. LOOKING ALONG PARK ROAD, WHICH RUNS BESIDE THE PARK DOWN INTO MARYLEBONE, AND INTO THE BACKGROUND, WE SEE A COACH APPROACHING FROM FAR OFF WITH THE DRIVER SAT ON TOP OF IT, ALTHOUGH HE IS TINY AND UNRECOGNIZABLE AT THIS DISTANCE.

CAPTION: I am at Regent's park, by Clarence Gate.

CAPTION: The sound of leaves, and birds. The smell of horse's shit. The perfect world.

PANEL 2.

SAME SHOT, ONLY NOW THE COACH DRAWS CLOSER. THE DRIVER SITTING ON TOP OF IT HAS A BEARD. THIS IS JOHN NETLEY, AGED FORTY-THREE YEARS OLD. HE DOES NOT LOOK UP TOWARDS US AS THE COACH TRUNDLES CLOSER, BOTH HE AND HIS HORSE WITH THEIR EYES DOWNCAST, LOOKING TOWARDS THE ROAD THEY DRIVE ALONG.

CAPTION: He's older, with a beard, yet I would know that hunched and feral posture anywhere.

PANEL 3.

SAME SHOT. THE COACH AND HORSE ARE RIGHT UP IN THE FOREGROUND NOW. BOTH THE HORSE AND THE DRIVER LOOK UP TOWARDS THE FOREGROUND SIMULTANEOUSLY, WITH ALMOST IDENTICAL EXPRESSIONS OF SHOCK. THE EYES OF THE HORSE ARE WHITE AND FRIGHTENED.

CAPTION: Hello, Netley.

PANEL 4.

CUT TO A SHOT FROM UP ON TOP OF THE COACH BEHIND NETLEY, SO THAT HE SITS FACING AWAY FROM US IN THE FOREGROUND, WITH HIS HORSE FACING AWAY FROM US BEYOND HIM. HANGING IN THE AIR ABOVE THE STREET IN FRONT OF THE HORSE AND SHINING WITH A BRIGHT LIGHT IS THE SMILING AND MALEVOLENT FLOATING HEAD OF SIR WILLIAM GULL. THE HORSE IS STARTING TO SHY FROM THE APPARITION.

No dialogue

PANEL 5.

NOW A TIGHT CLOSE-UP OF NETLEY'S FACE, STARING OUT OF THE PANEL AT US IN ABSOLUTE HOLY DREAD AND TERROR, HIS EYES WIDE AND BULGING.

NETLEY: No, you're dead.

NETLEY: You're dead.

PANEL 6.

REVERSE ANGLES. THE HEAD FLOATS, FACING AWAY FROM US, IN THE FOREGROUND. IMMEDIATELY BEYOND IT WE ARE LOOKING UP AT NETLEY'S HORSE AS IT REARS UP IN BLIND FOAMING PANIC. NETLEY TILTS ON HIS SEAT AND LOOKS TERRIFIED AS HE GRABS AT THE REINS TO STOP FROM FALLING.

NETLEY: You're...

NETLEY: AAAH!

PANEL 7.

NOW WE PULL BACK FOR A LONG SHOT OF THE HORSE AS IT BOLTS, DRAGGING THE COACH BEHIND IT. FALLING INTO THE PANEL FROM THE PICTURE IN THE FOREGROUND IS THE SHADOW OF AN OFF-PANEL OBELISK. IT POINTS INTO THE PANEL TOWARDS THE CAREENING HORSE AS NETLEY VAINLY TRIES TO REGAIN CONTROL OF HIS RUNAWAY CARRIAGE, HIS FACE A MASK OF STUNNED AND UNCOMPREHENDING HORROR. GULL'S HEAD NEEDN'T BE VISIBLE HERE. THE HORSE IS STARTING TO DRAG NETLEY TOWARDS THE FOREGROUND HERE.

NETLEY: Oh god. Whoaah.

NETLEY: WHOAAH!

PANEL 8.

SAME SHOT, BUT NOW THE HORSE HAS DRAGGED THE COACH MUCH CLOSER TO THE FOREGROUND, SO THAT THE SHADOW OF THE OFF-PANEL OBELISK FALLS ACROSS IT NOW. TOO LATE, NETLEY LOOKS UP FROM THE REINS, HIS HORRIFIED EYES GAZING DUMBSTRUCK AT WHATEVER HE CAN SEE OFF PANEL.

NETLEY: Come on, girl, don't...

NETLEY: Oh, my god.

PANEL 9.

CHANGE ANGLE. WE ARE ATOP THE COACH BEHIND NETLEY AS HE THROWS UP HIS HANDS IN USELESS TERROR. REARING UP ABOVE THE COACH WE SEE THE GRANITE OBELISK THAT NETLEY AND HIS COACH ARE ABOUT TO CRASH INTO. DIRECTLY BEHIND AND ABOVE THE OBELISK WE SEE THE CRUEL AND BLINDING DISC OF THE SEPTEMBER SUN.

No dialogue

Chapter 14, page 23.

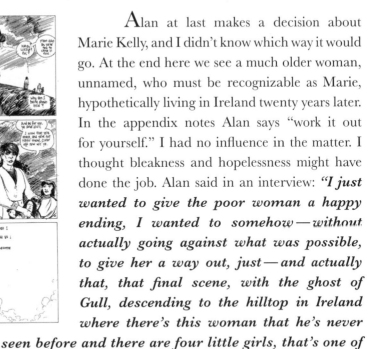

Alan at last makes a decision about Marie Kelly, and I didn't know which way it would go. At the end here we see a much older woman, unnamed, who must be recognizable as Marie, hypothetically living in Ireland twenty years later. In the appendix notes Alan says "work it out for yourself." I had no influence in the matter. I thought bleakness and hopelessness might have done the job. Alan said in an interview: *"I just wanted to give the poor woman a happy ending, I wanted to somehow — without actually going against what was possible, to give her a way out, just — and actually that, that final scene, with the ghost of Gull, descending to the hilltop in Ireland where there's this woman that he's never seen before and there are four little girls, that's one of the most powerful scenes in the book to me. There's something spine-tingling in the bit where she tells him to get back to Hell where he comes from. There's just something in that which I — I find really moving."* (blather.net, Oct 2000) They used a residue of this scene in the movie, with Kelly still alive in Ireland. Most of the people I spoke to at the premiere thought it was an invention of the screenwriter.

PAGE 23. (964 words) PANEL 1.
NINE-PANEL PAGE HERE. WE ARE NOW STANDING ON THE HILL, SOME SHORT WAY DOWN FROM ITS CREST, WHERE THE COTTAGE STANDS. THE FRONT DOOR IS OPEN AND A WOMAN STANDS ON THE STEP, EMERGING THROUGH IT TOWARDS US. SHE TURNS AND LOOKS TOWARDS THE RIGHT FORE-GROUND, WHERE A CHUBBY LITTLE GIRL OF MAYBE TEN OR TWELVE IS RUNNING INTO VIEW FROM OFF PANEL RIGHT, RUNNING UP HILL AWAY FROM US TOWARDS THE COTTAGE WHERE HER MOTHER STANDS. THE WOMAN IS A PRETTY IRISH WOMAN OF NEAR FORTY, NOT THAT TALL AND WITH HER DARK BUT GREY-FLECKED HAIR TIED BACK. HER FACE IS STRONG AND STERN, BUT NOT UNKIND. IT'S MORE "NOT TO BE MESSED WITH" THAN UNFRIENDLY OR UNLOVING. THIS IS A NICE, TOUGH, STILL ATTRACTIVE WOMAN, WORN BY LIFE AND CHILDBIRTH BUT STILL FAIR AND PROUD.

WOMAN: Anne? Come in, now, child.

CHILD: I'm comin', Mammy.

CAPTION: Ireland. Ireland somewhere, in 1904? 1905?

PANEL 2.

MOVE IN CLOSER ON THE WOMAN NOW AS HER PLUMP DAUGHTER RUNS UP TO HER. SHE BENDS IN ABOVE THE GRAVE-FACED, DARK-HAIRED CHILD AND GIVES INSTRUCTIONS WITH A SIMILARLY GRAVE YET KINDLY FACE. THERE'S SOMETHING VAGUELY FAMILIAR ABOUT THIS MOTHERLY WOMAN, BUT WE CANNOT PLACE IT YET.

WOMAN: Fetch your sisters in now, will ye? There's a cold wind
          getting' up tonight. I wan yez by me.

CHILD: Alright, then. I'll call 'em.

PANEL 3.

CHANGE ANGLE NOW FOR A SHOT FROM SOME DISTANCE BEHIND AND TO ONE SIDE OF THE WOMAN, SO THAT SHE STANDS OUTSIDE HER COTTAGE LOOKING AWAY FROM US AT A SLIGHT ANGLE, AWAY DOWN THE GENTLE HILL WHERE WE SEE THE CHUBBY GIRL STANDING CALLING OUT DOWN THE HILL, WHERE THREE YOUNGER GIRLS PAUSE IN THEIR PLAY TO LOOK UPHILL TOWARDS HER, SHE CUPS HER MOUTH AS SHE SHOUTS TO THEM. THEIR MOTHER STANDS, ARMS FOLDED UNDERNEATH HER BOSOM, LOOKING ON. THERE'S SOMETHING STILL FAMILIAR, EVEN IN THE QUARTER PROFILE WE SEE HERE. ABOVE THEM ALL, DARKENING CLOUDS MOVE ACROSS THE OVERCAST IRISH SKY, HANGING LIKE A WILD AND RAGGED-EDGED DEPRESSION OVER THE GREY FIELDS BELOW.

CHILD: Katey? Lizzie? Pol?

CHILD: Mam says as ye've got to come in now.

CAPTION: Why am I being shown this?

PANEL 4.

CLOSE IN NOW ON THE WOMAN, SO THAT WE'RE ALMOST JUST BEHIND HER SHOULDER AS SHE STANDS THERE ROUGHLY HEAD AND SHOULDERS ON THE LEFT OF PANEL. BEYOND HER, WE SEE THE THREE OTHER LITTLE GIRLS RUNNING UP THE HILL TO JOIN THEIR SISTER. THE YOUNGEST IS ABOUT FIVE AND THE OTHER TWO ARE AROUND SEVEN AND NINE. IN THE FOREGROUND, THE WOMAN TURNS HER HEAD TOWARDS US SLIGHTLY AS IF SENSING A PRESENCE BEHIND HER SHOULDER AS SHE STANDS THERE WITH HER ARMS FOLDED. SHE FROWNS, ONE GREYING STRAND ESCAPING FROM HER TIED-BACK HAIR TO FLUTTER IN THE RISING WIND. IT'S MARY KELLY, ON THE BRINK OF FORTY YEARS OLD BUT STILL RECOGNIZABLE.

CAPTION: I don't know these people. I have never seen this woman
          in my life, and yet...

CAPTION: And yet within her yes, that terrible ferocity.
          I am afraid of her.

PANEL 5.

CHANGE ANGLE SO THAT WE ARE LOOKING AT THE WOMAN FULL FIGURE FROM THE FRONT AT EYE-LEVEL AS HER FOUR DAUGHTERS GATHER ROUND HER, CLINGING TO HER SKIRTS AS SHE SMILES DOWN AT THEM AND EMBRACES THEM ALL IN A GENERALIZED HUG AS THEY GAZE UP AT HER. SHE LOOKS DOWN AT THE CHILDREN HERE, HER EYELIDS LOWERED, RATHER THAN AT

US. ONE OF THE GIRLS IS RATHER TALL AND THIN, ABOUT NINE OR TEN YEARS OF AGE. SHE LOOKS UP AT HER MOTHER EARNESTLY.

TALL THIN GIRL: We're here, mammy. Polly caught a frog, then let it go.

WOMAN: That's good. Ye ought t'let 'em go. That's good.

PANEL 6.

SAME SHOT AS LAST PANEL, ONLY HERE, WITH ELECTRIFYING EFFECT, THE WOMAN RAISES HER EYES AND STARES DIRECTLY AT US. HER EYES ARE FULL OF ANGER AND A FIERCE DEFIANCE. CLINGING TO HER SKIRTS, THE CHILDREN ALSO GLANCE TOWARDS US, WITH SULKY EXPRESSIONS AND THEIR FACES ALL BUT HIDDEN IN THEIR MOTHERS APRON FOLDS AS THEY STAND GATHERED THERE ABOUT HER. THEY LOOK REPROACHFUL AS THEY STARE TOWARDS US, WHILE THEIR MOTHER JUST LOOKS COLDLY ANGRY AS SHE STARES STRAIGHT AT US, EYES FILLED WITH A FRIGHTENING MATERNAL STRENGTH AND WILL.

WOMAN: And as for you, ye auld divil...

WOMAN: I know that ye're there, and ye're not havin' these. Clear off now wit' ye.

PANEL 7.

WE NOW START TO RISE AND DRAW BACKWARDS, AS IF WE ARE BEING BLOWN BACKWARDS AND INTO THE SKY BY A STRONG WIND. THE WOMAN RAISES ONE HAND AND POINTS STRAIGHT AT US, HER EYES FIERCE AND UNBLINKING, THE CHILDREN STILL CLINGING AROUND HER SKIRTS AS THEY ALL START TO FALL AWAY BELOW US.

WOMAN: Clear off back to Hell and leave us BE!

PANEL 8.

WE CONTINUE TO RISE, WITH THE COTTAGE FALLING AWAY BENEATH US AND THE WHITE CLOUDS STARTING TO CLOSE IN AROUND US AS WE RISE UP THROUGH THEM. WE CAN STILL SEE THE LITTLE FAMILY STOOD OUTSIDE THEIR COTTAGE BELOW, THOUGH THEY ARE VERY TINY, AND WE CAN PERHAPS MAKE OUT THAT THE WOMAN STILL STANDS WITH ONE ARM RAISED TOWARDS US, AND HER BANISHING FINGER POINTING COMMANDINGLY. THE OBLITERATING WHITENESS ROLLS IN AT THE EDGES OF OUR VISION AS WE RISE.

CAPTION: And this perplexing vision.

CAPTION: is the last thing

PANEL 9.

HIGHER AND HIGHER INTO THE OBSCURING WHITENESS. THIS PANEL IS ALMOST TOTALLY WHITE SAVE FOR A LITTLE GREY BIT IN THE MIDDLE WHERE THE CLOUDS ARE CLOSING OVER THE LAST OF THE TINY LANDSCAPE NOW FAR BELOW US. WE ARE VERY HIGH UP NOW.

CAPTION: that I

CAPTION: see as I

CAPTION: become

Image from the film From Hell © *20th Century Fox.*

Chapter 14, page 24.

It's not a completely blank page, as it's got four words on it. But the blank page, in this age of self-consciousness, is to be seen as an offering to Lawrence Sterne, historical breaker of moulds. Over two hundred years back he put a blank page in his novel and invited the reader to draw his own portrait of the Widow Wadman *"...as unlike your wife as your conscience will let you."* In the January 2004 issue of *Playboy*, Jonathan Safran Foer wrote about his collection of blank pages: *"I started collecting empty paper soon after I finished my first novel, about two years ago. A family friend had been helping to archive Isaac Bashevis Singer's belongings for the university where his papers and artifacts were to be kept. Among the many items to be disposed of was a stack of Singer's unused typewriter paper..."* He kept the topmost of these blank pages, and it became a spiritual talisman, launching an obsessive quest that led Foer to many blank pages, and ultimately to Freud and Anne Frank.

We who get paid by the page (as I did in the original serialisation of the present subject) don't mind being asked to leave one blank; it's like being told to take the day off. Part of the "graphic novel" phenomenon is that we started getting chances to do comics for traditional "book" publishers, and one of the aspects of the comics world they have trouble getting a handle on is the idea of "page rate." In the book world you negotiate an advance and then write your book. When it's finished it gets edited and made to fit into a format. Nobody talks about pages. Maybe a "novel of 70,000 words" approximately, but they don't then go and count them unless the manuscript is obviously a gyp. And another thing they do that amuses me is they refer to a big pile of comics artwork as "the manuscript." But then I'm one of those pedants who still chooses to differentiate between a typescript and a manuscript.

PAGE 24. (35 words) PANEL 1.
THERE IS ONE PANEL ON THIS PAGE. IT HAS NO BORDER AND NO IMAGE. WE TURN OVER TO A
PERFECT BLANK WHITE PAGE, WITH ONLY THE TWO LITTLE CAPTION BOXES SUSPENDED IN ITS
TERRIFYING EMPTINESS.
CAPTION: God.
CAPTION: and then I

Appendix II, Dance of the Gull-Catchers, page 1.

In one of the notebooks, Alan makes several attempts at a start on the *Gull-Catchers* appendix. It was 1998, two years since we had wrapped up the tenth volume of the work. This addition was to be an account and debunking of all the various Ripper theories including our own. It was tricky because it involved taking in the whole picture of Ripperology, so that we must appear in it ourselves.

That is, we are simply the next in a long line of fools who have claimed to have solved the century-old mystery. And we weren't the last either; there have been a number of new attempts in the fifteen years since we downed tools, a couple of which I've referred to in these pages.

The problem to be solved was how to avoid overt self-consciousness, as seen in the swiftly rejected first effort which starts with Alan, on-panel typing a letter, and follows with Campbell receiving it. He switches in the second excerpt to showing us having a fictional meeting in a pub. For a few rounds of the track the Sickert dinner scene is in the lead position. This will eventually be top of page 2. Finally he fastens on the metaphor of the men with the butterfly nets, trying in vain to catch their "gull" (old slang for a fool, or a hoax, to cheat or mislead).

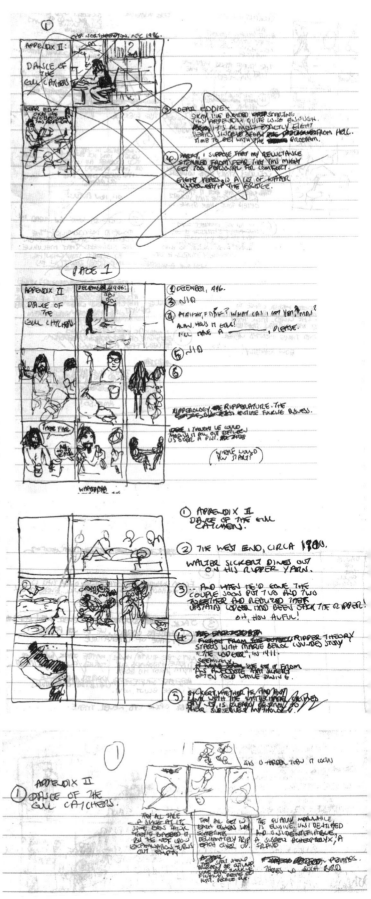

In the two-year interim since the last segment of script, Alan had acquired a new "typewriter"... as evidenced by effects such as bold and oblique lettering, which I've mildly hinted at below.

PAGE 1. (579 words) PANEL 1.

AN EIGHT-PANEL PAGE HERE, INCLUDING THE OPENING TITLE PANEL, WITH A DOUBLE PANEL COMPLETING THE OPENING TIER AND THEN THREE PANELS EACH ON THE TWO TIERS BELOW THAT. IN THIS FIRST PANEL WE JUST HAVE THE TITLES.

TITLES: ***APPENDIX II***

Dance of the Gull-Catchers

Panel 2.

DOUBLE-WIDTH PANEL IN WHICH WE SHOW A NUMBER OF MEN IN VARYING STYLES OF DRESS RANGING FROM THE TURN OF THE CENTURY TO THE PRESENT DAY. EACH OF THEM IS EQUIPPED WITH A LARGE BUTTERFLY NET. THEY ARE RUNNING AROUND IN FUTILE CIRCLES ON A PATCH OF GRASS IN A FIELD SOMEWHERE, HOPEFULLY WAVING THEIR NETS OVER THEIR HEADS, ALL TAKING WILD SWINGS AT A BIRD THAT IS FLYING IN CIRCLES IMMEDIATELY ABOVE THEM, JUST OUT OF REACH.

CAPTION: This is harder than it looks.

PANEL 3.

IN THIS FIRST SMALL PANEL ON THE SECOND TIER WE HAVE CLOSED IN ON THE GROUP'S EMPTY NETS, WAVING, SWINGING AND SWIPING USELESSLY AT THE BIRD ABOVE THEIR HEADS, WITH THE ACTUAL RUNNING MEN OFF PANEL BELOW HERE.

CAPTION: They all take a swing at it.

CAPTION: Some even think they've bagged it, but the net, upon examination, turns out empty.

PANEL 4.

NOW A SHOT OF THE FEET OF THE MEN AS THEY RUN AROUND ON THE TURF IN CIRCLES. THEY TRIP AND STUMBLE, ONE OF THE MEN, HIS FACE OFF PANEL ABOVE AS WITH ALL THE MEN, IS HOLDING HIS BUTTERFLY NET LOW, ABOUT TO TRIP UP ONE OF THE OTHER MEN WITH IT.

CAPTION: They all get in each other's way; sometimes deliberately trip each other up.

CAPTION: This sport should probably be outlawed, like bare-knuckles fighting. People are hurt, reputations slaughtered.

PANEL 5.

NOW PERHAPS A SHOT OF A SINGLE DISLODGED FEATHER OR TWO THAT HAS FALLEN FROM THE BIRD FLYING OUT OF SHOT OFF PANEL ABOVE. IF THAT IS TOO MINIMAL ON ITS OWN THEN HAVE A COUPLE OF THE NETS OR PERHAPS A REACHING HAND EXTENDING INTO THE PANEL FROM BELOW, TRYING TO CATCH THE FEATHER AS IT FALLS.

CAPTION: The quarry, meanwhile, is elusive. Unidentified and unidentifiable, a suspect archaeopteryx. A fraud.

CAPTION: Perhaps there's no such bird.

PANEL 6.

NOW WE HAVE A SHOT FROM OVERHEAD, LOOKING DOWN ON THE MEN AS THEY RUN ROUND IN CIRCLES BENEATH US, SWIPING UP AT US WITH THEIR NETS. THE PATCH OF GRASS THAT THEY'RE RUNNING IN CIRCLES ON IS ALMOST OBLITERATED, TURNED TO A QUAGMIRE BY THEIR CIRCLING FOOTSTEPS.

CAPTION: Its call, the colour of its plumage, these things are unknown. Its tracks are never found.

CAPTION: The tracks of its pursuers, to the contrary, are everywhere.

PANEL 7.

CLOSE IN EVEN FURTHER, LOOKING DOWN UPON THE CIRCLING FEET AND THE MUDDY TURF THEY ARE RUNNING AROUND ON, CHEWED UP AS A FOOTBALL PITCH.

CAPTION: In studded football boots they endlessly cross-track and over-print the field of their enquiry. They reduce its turf to mud.

CAPTION: Only their choreography remains readable.

PANEL 8.

NOW WE CLOSE ON ONE OF THE MEN WITH NETS FOR MAYBE A HALF FIGURE CLOSE UP OF HIM, SO THAT WE SEE HIM CLEARLY. IT IS WALTER SICKERT, DRESSED IN THE CHECQUERED CLOTHING THAT HE WORE IN THE EARLY EPISODES OF FROM HELL. HE WAVES HIS NET OFF PANEL ABOVE HIS HEAD, HIS EYES CAST UPWARDS WITH CHILDISH HOPEFULNESS AS HE TAKES ANOTHER FUTILE SWING AT THE OFF PANEL BIRD UP ABOVE.

CAPTION: The dance begins with Walter Sickert.

On finishing: a final thought.

Back in the day, Kitchen Sink Press asked the question, innocently, as to whether the appendices, which had appeared in the serialisation, were to be included in the collected edition when they came to do it (which didn't happen). Alan was adamant that they weren't just optional attachments, but an integral part of the structure of the work. The radical notion of a comic with 45 pages of footnotes, plus an illustrated appendix, appealed to his sense of novelty. It was another literary affectation to be adopted to expand the scope of the "graphic novel!" Which is not to say that these appendices were some vacuous pose. They were in fact the perfect means to achieve the desired artistic ends. Having executed the grand corpus of the work under severe formal restraints, a so-called "appendix" could blithely dispense with all austerics for the sake of a grander overview. It could adopt a completely different authorial voice.

Autobiography: Alan Moore gets out of a taxi in Whitechapel.

In retrospect I wish I'd left the spot illustrations out of the first, the annotations appendix. A big 43,000-word wedge of text so goes against the verbal-visual balance beloved of comics theorists, and they're always worth upsetting. *The Dance of the Gull Catchers* is a different matter, being a riot of captions, timelines only slightly less complicated than the telephone exchange, autobiography, cartoon metaphors, willful caricature, diagrammed chaos theory (a frustrated theme that sank with Big Numbers) and general high-minded sarcasm. Pete Mullins was no longer working with me at the time, but I thought it only right that he should be in on the finale as it was right up his alley. He came back for a month and we had a lot of fun with this one.

Chaos Theory: Koch's Snowflake.

Sarcasm: The Druitt theory is "floated."

Caricature: Mad versions of people I've been drawing seriously for ten years.

Pete gets to draw and ink more fore-ground stuff, such as this loony pair.

A Gull catcher.

Spiegelman in *MetaMaus* quotes a writer, whose name he can no longer remember, who said that the last chapter must be equal in weight to all the chapters that went before it. And the second paragraph in the last chapter must be twice the weight of the first, and so on until the last paragraph, when each sentence must double the weight of its predecessor. I have my own theory, not dissimilar, about finishing, which concerns an increase in the rate at which information is conveyed. This is not to be confused with a quickening of the action, which is the way a James Bond movie would always end. In the early stages, it's all mystery, more mystery, cross, double-cross, this country, that country, and somebody turns out to be who they're not supposed to be. The information constantly multiplies. Then we get into the finale and it's just people running around killing each other inside the villain's lair. There is no weight to any of it, least of all to human life. In fact, that's a value that tends to decline in the modern film/novel. An upset at a murder may set the action in motion, but in no time we're in a video game shooting gallery. Meanwhile back in the lair, the villain is putting the torpedo in its bay, Bond is knocking it out, now it's rolling around on the floor, now he's being hit on the head with it. The information is stuck in a loop.

The attentive reader will now say, but wait, on page 265 you say that narrative formal logic demands that no new material be introduced at the dénouement. That still applies; the challenge of storytelling is to form new compounds out of the elements already in play. Alan's *FROM HELL* sets out with a full tank, enough fuel for the long haul. That's the raw narrative material, the parameters of which are drawn in the prologue and opening chapters. Then in its last mile it is fast and refreshed, as though it has distilled a new kind of fuel out of the stuff that was on board at the start.

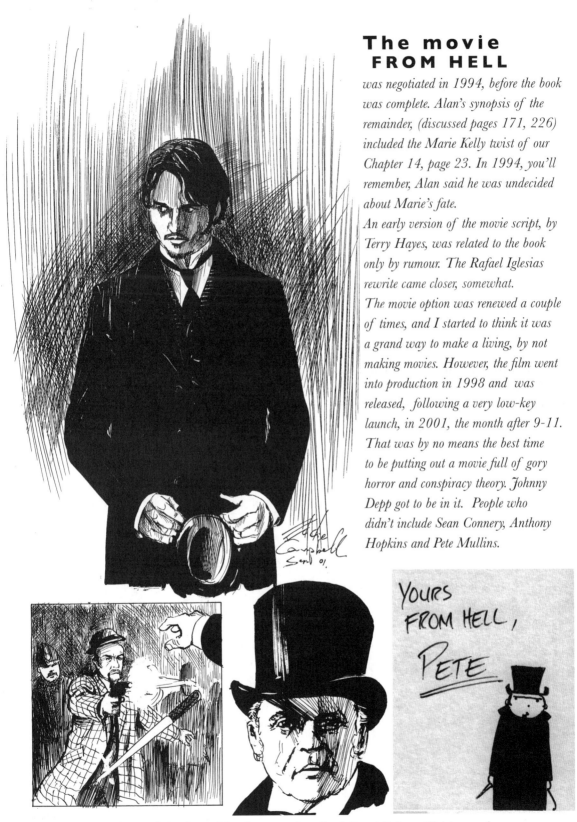

The movie FROM HELL

was negotiated in 1994, before the book was complete. Alan's synopsis of the remainder, (discussed pages 171, 226) included the Marie Kelly twist of our Chapter 14, page 23. In 1994, you'll remember, Alan said he was undecided about Marie's fate.

An early version of the movie script, by Terry Hayes, was related to the book only by rumour. The Rafael Iglesias rewrite came closer, somewhat.

The movie option was renewed a couple of times, and I started to think it was a grand way to make a living, by not making movies. However, the film went into production in 1998 and was released, following a very low-key launch, in 2001, the month after 9-11. That was by no means the best time to be putting out a movie full of gory horror and conspiracy theory. Johnny Depp got to be in it. People who didn't include Sean Connery, Anthony Hopkins and Pete Mullins.

YOURS FROM HELL,

PETE

Top was a magazine commission, bottom left and centre are from Alec, bottom right from a Christmas card.

284

Where does it leave us?

Art Spiegelman lately laments that with comics' conversion into a serious literature, and their embrace by academia, they risk losing, or have lost, their raffish nature. His comics world begins with Kurtzman's *Mad* that primed a generation to laugh at holy cows and question everything and, by extension he argued, protest against war. Now we're taken seriously. A medium that used to be kids stuff is analysed in universities and we receive honorariums to speak at symposiums.

We arrived at that by a complicated route. Art spent many years working for Woody Gelman at Topps bubblegum novelties. Gelman made a sideline for himself publishing, under his Nostalgia Press imprint, the great classics of comics such as *Little Nemo in Slumberland,* in beautiful hardcover volumes. Many of us looked at those and asked ourselves if we might ever create a comic worthy to be dressed so handsomely, so respectably even. Gelman's imprint appears, deleted but not removed, in the indicia of Spiegelman's first big take-me-seriously comics-as-art book, *Breakdowns.* Gelman may have been going to fund it or something. But my point here is that I have for a long time felt that this was the real origin of the idea of the "graphic novel." It left some of us with a longing to get out from among the toys and other embarrassing baloney of the comics market. Or as Alan put it when *Watchmen* was hailed as a serious novel, "We were caught on the Main Street of culture wearing our underpants on the outside."

FROM HELL was complete and in December 1999 appeared as one big book, published by myself, printed in Canada and distributed through U.S. comics channels. To my horror, I soon found it banned from importation to Australia. We had once again been censored! Australian Customs had sent a copy of Volume 7, nabbed from a shipment from Diamond Distribution to Quality Comics of Perth, Aus., to the Office of Film and Literature Classification, who advised that that it should not be imported. Customs expanded the ruling to include my big collected edition. Two weeks in, I talked them into submitting the big book to the OFLC on the principle that **context** made it very different from the slim part-volume. The OFLC made a positive decision in two days. Question: How many of the 12-person committee read the 576-page book in that time?

However, before that point, and with the movie release impending, I reasoned that the solution to the problem was to get an edition published locally. I got on the phone to book publisher Random House Australia and sold them on the idea. And so at last there we were, for a season, standing proudly on the "main street of culture," arm-in-arm with *The Natural Guide to Better Breast Feeding* and *The Dog Owner's Manual.*

from the publisher's catalogue 2001

Epilogue, page 2, or The Invisible Fred Abberline.

All the things you never get around to.

All the things that never get sorted out!

The action of the prologue continued straight into the epilogue, but there were eight whole years between the former and the latter. "There's no hurry," Abberline says in one panel (coincidentally reproduced here on page 102).

I no longer have the script for the epilogue. By the end of the project, it was arriving one page at a time by fax, which you may remember used to be printed on light-sensitive paper that caused it to fade to nothing within weeks and be lost if you didn't xerox it immediately. Script or not, I want to conclude with this page. What happened is that Anne, my wife, used to help out by erasing the pencil work off the pages after they were inked, and when I missed inking Abberline's small head in one panel, it was cleaned up and erased. The omission went unnoticed, and it was originally published that way. Thus the famous Invisible Fred Abberline. Dave Sim and Alan Moore seized upon it, mocking it mercilessly in a fax-to-fax chat Dave set up, to celebrate the conclusion of *FROM HELL*. This interview was serialized in the back of Sim's monthly comic book, *Cerebus* (A Correspondence From Hell, extract from part 1 in #217, April 1997). Dave, who had visited me and taken note of how I do things, tried to get Alan's goat by telling him that I don't actually read his scripts, but have an assistant who does that for me and goes through underlining the minimum number of phrases that I need to know to make each picture. Alan responded:

> *On the matter of what has been viewed in some quarters as an untoward wordiness in my panel descriptions, might I draw your attention to the final volume of* **From Hell**, *specifically to page 2, panel 5 of our epilogue. In the script description for this panel I unfortunately allowed myself a moment of laxity and omitted the words*

INSPECTOR ABBERLINE'S HEAD IS STILL ON HIS SHOULDERS DURING THIS PANEL. IT HAS NOT RETREATED TORTOISE-LIKE INTO HIS NECK, NOR HAS IT IN SOME FASHION MANAGED TO REFRACT LIGHT AROUND IT LIKE A KLINGON SPACESHIP SO THAT THE INSPECTOR RESEMBLES SOMETHING OUT OF MAGRITTE WITH HIS BOWLER FLOATING THERE SUSPENDED ABOVE THE EMPTY COLLAR OF HIS COAT.

> *Last time I'll make that mistake, obviously.*

The visit of Dave Sim was the one in 1994 during which he taught me how to publish my own comic books, just as he had already shown Alan and Steve Bissette how to do it. I had put out fifty issues of *Bacchus*, more or less monthly, when in 1999, after the demise of Kitchen Sink Press, *FROM HELL* was suddenly without a publisher. At first

I felt that the scale of the project put it out of my league (576-page book with a movie tie-in). However, inspired by the enthusiasm of my U.S. arm, Chris Staros of Top Shelf Productions, I decided to take it on. There was some legal messing about to get the rights clear, which involved writing off $15k in amounts owing.

Inked sketch for the painting for a Bacchus *comic book cover shown on page 179.*

      The collected edition was a runaway hit. Then a problem arose. The shape of the business was changing fast. It was no longer just a matter of getting comics into comic shops. The comics distributors had been going bankrupt one by one until out of the original fifteen or so, only Diamond was left standing. Now we also had to deal with the book trade to have any chance of surviving, and that's a completely different world. We found a book trade distributor (LPC) , but in 2002 they filed for bankruptcy (owing us about $50k at the time). I threw up my arms in despair, and with the sixth printing Top Shelf became *FROM HELL*'s fifth U.S. publisher. They've been doing a grand job of it ever since.

      Composing this *Companion* was almost like doing *FROM HELL* over, but at high speed, not just the fictional story but the planning and publishing ones too. In coming to the end, there's a sense of closing all the files in turn that have been left open, before switching off. Everything that has gone before is shown to have a formal and narrative purpose; the architecture of time, Alan Moore's London, the natural urges of little people, Cleveland Street, the two old codgers on the beach. It was just a hat that was missing the first time. I see it as I rush back through the way stations of our colossal construction. All the people that I worried I could never quite bring to life now sadden me with their last glimpse. I'd start over but it would break my heart.

E. C.

     The epilogue ends as the prologue began, with the two old men walking away from us down the beach. Breaking the silence, Lees blurts out that although he's never had a genuine psychic experience in his life, he has been having these funny dreams and feelings lately that are something to do with Whitechapel, something to do with Jews and old churches and blood. Abberline, puzzled and disturbed, asks him what he means. Lees frowns and gazes out at the grey sea. "I think we're going to have another War." The dialogue growing fainter and more inaudible, the two men walk away from us down the beach beneath an overcast sky. On the tideline in the foreground lies the fragile skeleton of a seagull, half buried in the fine white sand.

        THE END   (1994 synopsis)

Finding stuff.

FROM HELL is currently published in English by Top Shelf Productions in the USA and Knockabout in the UK, details in the indicia. It is in most other languages besides.

The single volume of *From Hell: The Compleat Scripts*, containing all the script material up to the end of chapter three, was published by Borderlands Press and Spiderbaby Graphics in 1994.

Rich Kreiner's review of it was in *The Comics Journal* #173, December 1994.

Clive Bloom's essay, "Jack the Ripper, a Legacy in Pictures," appeared in *Jack the Ripper and the East End*, edited by Alex Werner, 2008, published by Chatto and Windus.

Jamie Delano's memento was in a Semana Negra publication to accompany a *FROM HELL* exhibition in Gijon, Spain in 1999, later published in English in my own *Bacchus* # 60, May 20.

Alan Moore: Storyteller by Gary Spencer Millidge was published by Ilex Press, Brighton UK, in 2011.

Casebook.org is a recommended repository of information about the Whitechapel murders.

Other passing quotes and references I identified in their places. The small reproductions of the *FROM HELL* pages will help the reader relocate descriptions of characters and places. For returning to anything else in among my own blather this brief guide will have to suffice:

Alan Moore Interviews, quotes from. *4, 16, 79, 193, 213, 261, 269, 272, 275, 286.*

Alan's 1994 synopsis: *167, 206, 208, 215, 226, 227, 236, 238, 247, 255, 265, 284, 287.*

Alan's notebooks, scans from: *1, 13, 15, 71, 95, 97, 109, 110, 111, 113, 135, 138, 140, 141, 143, 144, 147, 152, 154, 167, 170, 187, 188, 189, 190, 192, 193, 194, 195, 196, 198, 202, 204, 207, 211, 220, 224, 225, 279.*

Art, new or unseen: *13, 37, 38, 46, 55, 62, 68, 72, 75, 81, 93, 169, 178, 182, 183, 184, 192, 223, 226, 227, 238, 245, 287, 288.*

Art, other, all out of *FROM HELL*; *Alec: 3, 4, 22, 84, 126, Bacchus: 179, 180;* misc, promo: *16/7, 90, 103, 107, 121, 156, 281, 284.*

Anecdotes: *9, 22, 32, 39, 47, 89, 127, 138, 153, 159, 167, 172, 174, 175, 220, 221, 229, 239, 252, 253, 255, 257, 278, 285, 286.*

Censorship: *32, 138, 164/5, 285.*

Comics, technique: *18, 23, 51, 66, 82, 92/3, 114, 116, 124, 150, 153, 157, 186, 204, 218, 231, 235, 246, 251, 263.*

Formal logic: *42, 55, 59, 63, 69, 85, 116, 118, 121, 132, 141, 144, 148, 161, 167, 201, 267, 282/3, 285, 287.*

Logistical problems: *27, 87, 90, 112, 135, 155, 199, 202, 210, 211, 216, 229, 273, 275.*

Movie: *15, 22, 110, 112, 121, 124, 128, 132, 167, 275, 277, 284.*

People who assisted: *23. 73, 76, 92/3, 95, 118, 126, 131, 150, 152, 153, 159, 218, 234, 235, 282/3, 284, 286.*

Publishing history: *11, 12, 32, 78, 79, 95, 98-101, 130, 133, 156, 169, 171, 178, 184, 247, 252, 265, 279, 285, 286/7.*

Ripperologists: *Knight and the Masonic cover-up 17, 32, 35, 50, 62, 68, 256, 259; Stowell 31; Fuller, Cornwell 62; Harris 68; Fido 213; Wilson 226; MacNaghten 247; Morrison 38; us 279.*